A Practical Guide to
Building Professional Competencies in School Psychology

Timothy M. Lionetti · Edward P. Snyder
Ray W. Christner

Editors

A Practical Guide to
Building Professional Competencies
in School Psychology

 Springer

Editors
Timothy M. Lionetti
Walden University
College of Social
and Behavioral Science
Minneapolis, MN 55401
USA
timothy.lionetti@waldenu.edu

Ray W. Christner
Cognitive Health Solutions, LLC
1201 West Elm Avenue, Unit 2
Hanover, PA 17331
USA
rwc@cognitivehealthsolutions.com

Edward P. Snyder
Edinboro University of Pennsylvania
Department of Professional Studies
Butterfield Hall 114
Edinboro, PA 16444
USA
esnyder@edinboro.edu

ISBN 978-1-4419-6255-3   e-ISBN 978-1-4419-6257-7
DOI 10.1007/978-1-4419-6257-7
Springer New York Dordrecht Heidelberg London

Library of Congress Control Number: 2010937770

Printed on acid-free paper

Springer is part of Springer Science+Business Media (www.springer.com)

Acknowledgments

Throughout the long journey of making this book come to fruition was the consistent and sustaining encouragement of my wife Juliann along with the understanding, patience and joy of my three children Spenser, Sondra and Anthony, for which I am most appreciative. I also wish to thank my parents, Mario and Lois, for their support that has been unwavering for decades. Finally, a special appreciation must be afforded to the authors who contributed to this text.

Timothy M. Lionetti

This book is dedicated to my wife, Nancy, and sons, Adam and Daniel. Thank you for the joy you provide on a daily basis. To my parents, Clarence and Virginia, thank you for your faith and support.

Edward P. Snyder

I want to thank my wife, Andrea, and my two girls, Alyssa and Sydney, who are the motivation behind all I do. Thank you for being so patient and understanding of my hectic schedule. Also, I am grateful for the support of my parents, Ray and Theresa, and my brother, Rich, who have always encouraged me to strive to reach my goals. Finally, I dedicate this book to a dear friend, Mia S., who helped me from a young age to understand the differences and strengths in others.

Ray W. Christner

Contents

About the Editors

Timothy M. Lionetti, Ph.D., is a full time faculty and the Coordinator of the School Psychology program at Walden University. Dr. Lionetti currently holds school psychology certification in Pennsylvania, and is a Licensed Psychologist in the same state. Dr. Lionetti earned his Doctorate degree in School Psychology from Lehigh University. He has contributed to the fields of psychology and education through multiple presentations and writings. Dr. Lionetti has presented at the national and state levels on a variety of topics, including improving student reading fluency, promoting physical activity in the schools and health promotion, and on recruiting school psychologists. Similarly, he has been published in scholarly journals on the same topics. His clinical and research interests include improving student reading, health promotion, effects of age on academic success, behavioral disorders, and the linking of the mental health and school systems. Lastly, Dr. Lionetti continues to work with children, schools, and families within the school and mental health systems and private practice using both direct and consultative services.

Edward P. Snyder, Ph.D., is Associate Professor and Coordinator of the Educational Psychology Program at Edinboro University of Pennsylvania and a certified school psychologist. Dr. Snyder earned his master's degree and school psychology certification from Bucknell University and his Ph.D. in School Psychology from Lehigh University. He has experience as a school psychologist in rural and urban settings. In addition, Dr. Snyder has worked as a school psychologist in residential programs for children and adolescents with dual diagnoses, and he worked in an approved private school for children with emotional and behavioral disorders. He has published research articles related to involving students, who receive special education services, in leading their own Individualized Education Program (IEP) meetings. Dr. Snyder has presented at national and state conferences. His research interests include assessment and treatment of students with behavior disorders, self-advocacy for student receiving special education services, and school violence prevention programs.

Ray W. Christner, Psy.D., NCSP, is Director of Cognitive Health Solutions, LLC in Hanover, Pennsylvania, where he provides psychological services to children, adolescents, families, and schools. He is also the consulting psychologist for the South Middleton School District, and he is a core faculty member at Walden University. Dr. Christner holds school psychology certifications from the Pennsylvania Department of Education and the National School Psychology Certification Board. He further maintains licensure in Pennsylvania as a Licensed Psychologist and a Licensed Professional Counselor. Dr. Christner earned his Masters and Doctorate degrees in Clinical Psychology from PCOM, as well as a Masters of Science degree and certification in School Psychology from California University of Pennsylvania. He has contributed to the fields of psychology and education through multiple presentations and writings. Dr. Christner has presented in the USA and England on cognitive-behavior therapy, school-based crisis intervention, and school-based mental health. He is a coeditor of three books entitled, *Cognitive-Behavioral Interventions for Educational Settings: A Handbook for Practice* (with Drs. Rosemary Mennuti and Arthur Freeman), *Handbook of Cognitive-Behavior Therapy Groups with Children and Adolescents: Specific Settings and Presenting Problems* (with Drs. Jessica Stewart and Arthur Freeman), and *School-Based Mental Health: A Practitioner's Guide to Comparative Practice* (with Dr. Rosemary Mennuti). He was the founding editor of *School Psychology Forum: Research in Practice*, a peer-reviewed journal published by the National Association of School Psychologists (NASP). Dr. Christner's clinical and research interests include cognitive-behavioral interventions and treatments for various disorders and issues, process-oriented assessment, crisis intervention, school-based mental health services, and the training of psychologists and mental health professionals.

Contributors

Leigh D. Armistead
Winthrop University, Rock Hill, SC 29733, USA

Jessica B. Bolton
Philadelphia College of Osteopathic Medicine, Philadelphia, PA 19131, USA

Stephen E. Brock
California State University, 6000 J Street, Sacramento, CA 95819, USA

Ray W. Christner
Cognitive Health Solutions, LLC, Unit 2, 1201 West Elm Avenue, Hanover, PA 17331, USA

Susan Clements
Philadelphia College of Osteopathic Medicine, Philadelphia, PA 19131, USA

Frank DeMatteo
Marywood University, 2300 Adams Avenue, Scranton, PA 18509, USA

Babara A. Fischetti
Westport Public Schools, Pupil Services Administration, 72 North Avenue, Westport, CT 06880, USA

Dan Florell
Eastern Kentucky University, Richmond, KY 40475, USA

Kathrine Gipe
Philadelphia College of Osteopathic Medicine, Philadelphia, PA, USA

Mary Heim
Philadelphia College of Osteopathic Medicine, Philadelphia, PA, USA

Jennifer L. Jeffrey-Pearsall
Devereux Center for Effective Schools, 2012 Renaissance Boulevard, King of Prussia, PA 19406, USA

Amanda L. Lannie
Devereux Center for Effective Schools, 2012 Renaissance Boulevard, King of Prussia, PA 19406, USA

Timothy M. Lionetti
College of Social and Behavioral Sciences, Walden University, Minneapolis, MN 55401, USA

Elizabeth McCallum
Duquesne University, 600 Forbes Avenue, Pittsburgh, PA 15282, USA

Barry L. McCurdy
Devereux Center for Effective Schools, 2012 Renaissance Boulevard, King of Prussia, PA 19406, USA

Amy L. McLaughlin
Philadelphia College of Osteopathic Medicine, Philadelphia, PA 19131, USA

Courtney L. McLaughlin
Titusville Area School District, Titusville, PA, USA

Rosemary B. Mennuti
Philadelphia College of Osteopathic Medicine, Philadelphia, PA, USA

David N. Miller
University of Albany, Albany, NY, USA

Christine E. Neddenriep
The University of Wisconsin-Whitewater, Whitewater, WI, USA

Amanda B. Nickerson
University Of Albany, 1400 Washington Avenue, ED 232, Albany, NY 12222, USA

Susan Perlis
Medical College of Pennsylvania, Philadelphia, PA, USA

Brian C. Poncy
Oklahoma State University, 420 Willard Hall, Stillwater, OK 74078, USA

Kim Quirk
Millcreek Township School District, 5300 Henderson Road, Erie, PA 16509, USA

Melissa A. Reeves
Winthrop University, 135 Kinard Hall, Oakland Avenue, Rock Hill, SC 29733, USA

Justin S. Rubenstein
Philadelphia College of Osteopathic Medicine, Philadelphia, PA, USA

Kristin D. Sawka-Miller
Siena College, Loudonville, NY, USA

Christopher H. Skinner
University of Tennessee-Knoxville, Claxton Complex A-518, Knoxville, TN, USA

Diane Smallwood
Philadelphia College of Osteopathic Medicine, Philadelphia, PA 19131, USA

Edward P. Snyder
Department of Professional Studies, Edinboro University of Pennsylvania, Butterfield Hall 114, Edinboro, PA 16444, USA

Yuma I. Tomes
Philadelphia College of Osteopathic Medicine, Philadelphia, PA, USA

Barbara Bole Williams
College of Education, Rowan University, Education Hall, 201 Mullica Hill Road, Glassboro, NJ 08028, USA

Chapter 1
Developing and Enhancing Competencies in the Practice of School Psychology

Timothy M. Lionetti, Edward P. Snyder, Ray W. Christner, and Courtney L. McLaughlin

Introduction

When we conceptualize our role as a school psychologist, we often think of practicing or striving to utilize "best practices." Unfortunately, the ideal of best practices may not be attainable as it is an ever moving and improving target. The desire to work in this manner defines our role and helps us create goals as we improve our practice as school psychologists. Certainly, best practices is a helpful concept in forming this role and helps us strive toward that goal, though its true purpose and major contributions become lost when we limit our use of this tool in this way.

The concept of best practices afforded the field with ideals for practice and training, but this concept lies on a continuum that represents our professional progress toward that ideal. With that concept in mind, we developed the idea for this book to serve as a "how to guide" and to chart our progress as we develop our school psychological practice toward a best practices model. As such, this book is not intended to teach the best practices ideals, but instead, it is meant to guide you along the continuum as you begin or continue to plan your professional career. One of the goals of this book is to illustrate how you can begin thinking about and planning for your career in school psychology. This striving toward ideals is similar to the tact promoted in Blueprint III (Ysseldyke et al., 2006). Blueprint III differs from its predecessors in that it begins to shape the fields thinking that school psychologists do not enter the work force as experts, yet they will continue to develop expertise as careers progress. Our goal for this book is intended to help you explore different areas of school psychology and to aid you in determining where you are along the career development path along the continuum of novice to expert. Each chapter should be read in the manner of examining your skills and knowledge of current trends to help map out areas in which you may benefit from further professional development or desire to develop greater expertise.

Often, individual competencies are developed through experiences, circumstances, environments, and, to an extent, chance. Individuals also gain competencies by targeting specific areas of interest in professional books and journal articles and at professional conferences, workshops, and professional development opportunities. To understand how we develop individual competence, we have to understand how our field has evolved. Although our individual competencies and expertise vary greatly, they can still be tied back to the development of the field of school psychology. For example, expertise in positive behavior support (PBS) and response-to-intervention (RtI) evolved

T.M. Lionetti (✉)
College of Social and Behavioral Sciences, Walden University, Minneapolis, MN 55401, USA
e-mail: timothy.lionetti@waldenu.edu

T.M. Lionetti et al. (eds.), *A Practical Guide to Building Professional Competencies in School Psychology*,
DOI 10.1007/978-1-4419-6257-7_1, © Springer Science+Business Media, LLC 2011

from the empirical research conducted by a united group of individuals. This growth has led future school psychologists and new practitioners to study the topic and gain practical experience about it in the schools, and in turn, it has led to changes in law, which subsequently changes the face of professional practice. It has also contributed to school psychology programs as they have included training in these areas as a core part of their curriculum. It is this recursive nature of the field that contributes to the ideal of best practices being so elusive. At this point on your journey, you may be asking yourself, "how do I gain competence in PBS and/or RtI or any of the practice standards?" As you read each chapter, you will obtain an understanding of a variety of topics that are driven by empirical research through the evolution of our field. Reading this book alone will not result in you gaining competence in a specific area, yet it will offer information that you can use to become more self-aware of your knowledge, strengths, and needs, and ultimately, it can be used to help form a professional development plan.

Embracing Change and Inspiring Growth

The field of school psychology has evolved significantly since the term "school psychologist" first appeared in the English language in 1911. Individual school psychologists have mirrored the field's development in their work in the schools and have continued to develop their competencies around the field's development. A new practitioner's development toward specific expertise areas in the field of school psychology will in large part be guided by changes in the fields of psychology, education, special education, neuroscience, law, school psychology, and numerous field affecting education and work with children. However, individual school psychologists ultimately select their goals for enhancing their competences and building their expertise based on their experiences, circumstances, environments, education, and areas of interest.

It is important to understand the history of our field and the changes in the role and function of school psychology. Although we have seen many significant changes, there are also historical themes that continue to guide our practice today. Fagan and Wise (2007) divided the history of school psychology into two distinct phases that they termed the "hybrid" (1890–1969) and "thoroughbred" years (1969 to present). During the hybrid years, Fagan and Wise indicated that psychoeducational assessment was the primary focus of the field. However, with the onset of the thoroughbred years, a surge in the growth of the role of the school psychologist occurred, and this surge is even present today. Although we believe that all school psychologists should have a good understanding of the history, it is not the purpose of this book to provide such detailed information. Instead, we refer readers to two comprehensive resources on the history of school psychology: *School Psychology Past, Present, and Future* (Fagan & Wise, 2007) and *School Psychology for the 21st Century: Foundations and Practices* (Merrell, Ervin, & Gimpel, 2006).

Recent changes in the field of school psychology continue to drive an individual's path toward expertise and have promoted major shifts in the functioning of school psychologists. For example, No Child Left Behind (2001) and recent revisions to the Individuals with Disabilities Education Improvement Act (2004) have spurred exciting changes and debates on fundamental aspects of how we practice. Similarly, service delivery models, such as a three-tiered approach (Sugai, Horner, & Gresham, 2002; Dwyer, 2002), help move school psychologists beyond our traditional roles. These changes hold the promise of many years toward a new direction. We may finally live the promise of educating all children, promoting mental health, and developing new programs. Yet, the changes of the field do not mean we abandon our traditions and our expertise in assessment and our roles within special education, though our functions will need to expand within other domain areas.

The chapters in this text are designed to continue to inspire by making evident an array of functions and a diversity of thinking of the school psychologist in a practical and an empirical manner. Certainly, there are many individual differences among practitioners and many different styles and/or theoretical perspectives. Universally, practitioners must continue to drive their practices by empirical evidence despite some of the theoretical riffs that may exist within the field. This connection between research and practice has been described as the "basis by which school psychology as a discipline and a science will remain vital" (Power, 2006; Sheridan, 2001, p. 1; Ysseldyke et al., 2006).

Using this Text

Although the book is organized in chapters, it is also organized around an essential tool for school psychologists, Blueprint III (Ysseldyke et al., 2006), is intended to be a "stimulus for discussion and change by school psychologists and those who educate them" (Ysseldyke et al. 2006, p. 5). Upon its release, practitioners in the field were encouraged to debate its contents, and it has certainly sparked that debate. Therefore, the chapters in this book aim to continue to promote discussions and thinking to further enhance our field, as well as your individual practice. The field of school psychology is guided by the NASP Standards for Training and Practice (NASP, 2000) and Blueprint III (Ysseldyke et al. 2006), so each of the chapters has a link to both the documents. Table 1.1 delineates our conceptualization of the relationship between the two aforementioned documents. As you can see in Table 1.1, there is not a one-to-one correspondence to the domains, as some have been collapsed into one domain and others appear to have been eliminated. The domains are presented as distinct skill sets, yet in reality, they are not designed to be viewed as distinct and separate. The model in Blueprint III attempted to insure that there is cohesion between competencies by including the three-tiered model of service delivery and professional outcomes.

Blueprint III (Ysseldyke et al., 2006) breaks down competencies into functional and foundational domains for practice. Prior to Blueprint III, training programs were expected to produce competent

Table 1.1 A comparison of NASP and Blueprint III domains

NASP domains	Blueprint III domains	
Data based decision making and accountability	Data based decision making and accountability	Functional domains
Interpersonal communication, collaboration and consultation	Systems-based service delivery	
Effective instruction and development of cognitive/academic skills	Enhancing the development of cognitive and academic skills	
Socialization and development of life competencies	Enhancing the development of wellness, social skills, mental health, and life competencies	
Student diversity in development and learning	Interpersonal and collaborative skills	Foundational domains
School culture, organization and climate	Diversity awareness and sensitive delivery	
Prevention, wellness promotion, and crisis intervention	Technological applications	
Home/school/community collaboration	Professional, legal, ethical, and social responsibility	
Research and program evaluation		
Legal, ethical practice and professional development		

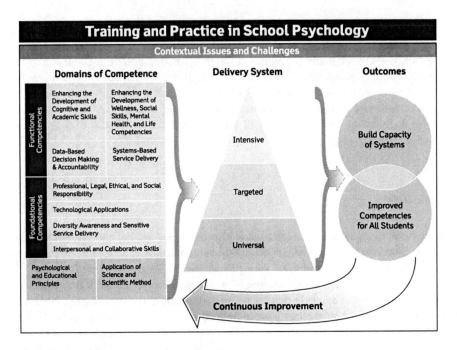

Fig. 1.1 Training and practice in school psychology. © 2006, National Association of School Psychologists, Bethesda, MD. Reprinted by permission of the publisher

practitioners in all domains, which many programs found to be a daunting task. However, over the course of the past decade and with the ongoing changes, we do not believe that training programs can adequately train all individuals to be competent in all domain areas to an expert level, and thus, it is imperative that practicing school psychologists continue to develop their skills. The authors of Blueprint III offer a new expectation that views the development of practitioners along a continuum, with the goal of students reaching the "novice" level of competence by the end of course training.. As students complete internship, the expectation is to be competent in one area and finally reaching "expertise" in one or two areas after 5–10 years of practice. Thus, professional growth and expertise are developed not in training alone but throughout one's career. Another change in Blueprint III from its predecessors is the tie in to the three levels of prevention and the explicit use of the problem-solving model similar to the public health model (see Fig. 1.1). In keeping with the developmental perspective taken in Blueprint III (Ysseldyke et al., 2006), the remainder of this text will allow new school psychologists and those in training, the opportunity to gain exposure to the wide variety of competencies that are needed to effectively perform their roles within the field and to expand their knowledge. For those seasoned school psychologists reading this text, the chapters can be used as a "check" for competence and development in a number of professional areas, which we hope you use to carry out the expansion of a professional development plan. To provide guidance on how each chapter aligns to NASP Training and Practice Standards and Blueprint III, we refer you to Table 1.2. As can be seen in this table, many of the chapters relate to multiple standards or competencies. Finally, Table 1.3 provides alignment between NASP Standards, Blueprint III, and the chapters of this text.

In addition to a historical understanding of the field, it is important to understand that competence in school psychology starts with a foundation of well-rounded academic skills. Initial training toward being a competent school psychologist began in undergraduate training that helped develop skills to write well, speak clearly, and think critically. These were prerequisite skills for becoming a competent school psychologist, and in turn, graduate training in school psychology builds on these academic skills as candidates develop "foundational and functional competencies."

Table 1.2 Chapters and NASP standards and Blueprint III domains

NASP standards	Chapter	Blueprint III domains
Data based decision making and accountability	5, 6, 11	Data based decision making and accountability
Interpersonal communication, collaboration and consultation	9, 11	Systems-based service delivery
Effective instruction and development of cognitive/ academic skills	5, 6, 7	Enhancing the development of cognitive and academic skills
Socialization and development of life competencies	8, 10	Enhancing the development of wellness, social skills, mental health, and life competencies
Student diversity in development and learning	4	Interpersonal and collaborative skills
School culture, organization and climate	15	Diversity awareness and sensitive delivery
Prevention, wellness promotion, and crisis intervention	14	Technological applications
Home/school/community collaboration	2, 3, 13, 15	Professional, legal, ethical, and social responsibility
Research and program evaluation	11	
Legal, ethical practice and professional development	2	

Table 1.3 List of competencies by domain and chapter

Foundational competence domains

1. Diversity awareness and sensitive service delivery domain

Chapter 15   Multicultural diversity and school psychology

Foundational

Understand cultural difference
Understand own culture
Understand values of majority culture

Functional

Gain informal experience with different populations
Professional experience with different populations

2. Technological applications domain

Chapter 14   Using advancing technologies in the practice of school psychology

Foundational

Understand software for psych tests
Understand assistive technology
Relate job requirements with technology tools

Functional

Gain experience/training with PC/MAC software and hardware

Exposure to different devices (cell phone, PDA)
Training with psych specific software (BASC-II)

3. Interpersonal and collaborative skills domain

Chapter 4   Consulting with families, schools, and communities

Foundational

Literature on different models
Efficacy studies

Functional

Observe consultation provide consultation with supervision vary experiences across populations

4. Professional, legal ethical and social responsibility domain

Chapter 2   Applying law and ethics in professional practice

Foundational

IDEA 2004, RtI, discipline, language and assessment, medication, student rights, ADA, Schaffer vs. West, NCLB, Ethics

Functional

Following legal guidelines in practice
Ethical guideline in context

Table 1.3 (continued)

Chapter 3	Managing your professional practice as a school psychologist

Foundational	Functional
Ethical guidelines	Understand system dynamics
System requirements (job description)	Supervision, goals
Legal regulations	Attend conferences

Chapter 13	Report writing and oral communication of results

Foundational	Functional
Understand technical aspects of psych assess	Review reports
Understand purpose of reports	Practice writing results
Understand ethics	Write different types of reports (intervention, diagnosis)
	Write/communicate with varying populations

Chapter 15	Making a career of school psychology

Foundational	Functional
Understand career development	Plan for competencies
Understand expectations and laws	Plan for job search
Understand ethical guidelines	Goal setting

Functional competencies

1. Enhancing the development of cognitive and academic skills domain

Chapter 7	Advocating for effective instruction: school psychologists as an instructional leader

Foundational	Functional
Intervention literature	Consultation
Reading literature	System-wide intervention packages (DIBELS)
Math literature	Data collection
Writing literature	Data based decision making
State curriculum	

Chapter 5	Assessing student skills using a nontraditional approach

Foundational	Functional
Technical aspects of assessment	Practice administering CBM
Efficacy/limits of CBM	Administer CBM with supervision
Ethics	CBM with different populations

Chapter 6	Assessing student skills using process-oriented approaches

Foundational	Functional
Technical aspects of psych testing	Practice administering different tests
Biological basis of learning (brain)	Administer tests with various populations with supervision and feedback
Definitions of intelligence	Administer tests independently write/communicate results
Test administration	
Cultural bias and testing literature	
Ethics	

2. Enhancing the development of wellness, social skills, mental health, and life competencies domain

Chapter 8	Evaluating candidates with emotional and behavioral concerns

Foundational	Functional
Ethics	Observe range of children with normal and abnormal functioning

(continued)

Table 1.3 (continued)

Mental health Disorders	Complete structured observations
How to diagnose (problem solving)	Administer rating scales
Technical aspects of psych testing	Write/communicate results
Technical aspects of interviewing	Consult of teachers and parents
Intervention literature	Interview teachers, parents, students
How to observe and FBA	Complete FBA
Family theory systems interventions	Implement interventions and evaluate
Rating scales	

Chapter 10   Preventing and intervening in crisis situations

Foundational	Functional
Crisis intervention literature	Crisis training
Prevention literature	Observe
Child development	Implement with supervision

3. Data-based decision making and accountability domain

Chapter 11   Beyond unproven trends: critically evaluating school-wide programs

Foundational	Functional
Intervention literature	Understand system needs
Program evaluation process	Survey
	Data based decision making
	Communicating result

Chapter 5   Assessing student skills using a nontraditional approach

Foundational	Functional
Technical aspects of assessment	Practice administering CBM
Efficacy/limits of CBM	Administer CBM with supervision
Ethics	CBM with different populations

Chapter 6   Assessing student skills using process-oriented approaches

Foundational	Functional
Technical aspects of psych testing	Practice administering different tests
Biological basis of learning (brain)	Administer tests with various populations with supervision and feedback
Definitions of intelligence	Administer tests independently write/communicate results

Test administration
Cultural bias and testing literature
Ethics

4. Systems-based service delivery domain

Chapter 9   Facilitating mental health services in schools: universal, selected, and targeted interventions

Foundational	Functional
Prevention literature	
Intervention literature	
Community/family theory	
Child development	

Chapter 11   Beyond unproven trends: critically evaluating school-wide programs

Foundational	Functional
Intervention literature	Understand system needs
Program evaluation process	Survey
	Data based decision making
	Communicating result

The challenge for school psychology trainers is that the skills candidates bring with them may vary considerably. For example, candidates who are education majors have a different skill set than candidates who graduate from college as psychology majors. Both candidates will have the potential to become good school psychologists, but each may require different levels of training for different skills. Likewise, the cultural experiences of candidates may vary considerably from one candidate to the next. These differences highlight the importance for candidates to learn to monitor their own professional development, so that they can meet their individual needs. As candidates progress and become school psychologists, they must continually monitor and enhance their professional development throughout their careers. Because there is a need for self-monitoring our progress toward competency in both foundational and functional competencies, the Development and Enhancement of Competencies Assessment Form (DECAF, see Fig. 1.2) has been included at the end of this chapter. This form is an assessment tool for school psychologists, both new and seasoned, to determine where they are along the continuum of competence on each of the BP III domains. In addition, the DECAF can be used to choose three priority areas in need of enhancement and to develop a plan of action to improve one's competency in those priority areas. It is suggested that readers use the DECAF at the beginning and at the end of the text and as they progress along in their careers.

To help determine priority areas on the DECAF, at the end of each chapter, a checklist is provided. These tools were created to allow school psychologists to monitor a range of professional competencies across the eight competency domains articulated in Blueprint III and are designed to work in tandem. The competency checklist, at the end of each chapter, lists functional and foundational competencies from the Blueprint III domains that are addressed in that chapter. Its intended purpose is to aid school psychologists in the assessment and creation of priority areas in need of professional development as they strive toward expertise in each of the foundational and/ or functional domains. On each checklist, mark the box next to each competency you have completed. Competencies with unmarked boxes may then be used to establish professional development goals on the DECAF. As professional development goals are attained, the competency checklist may be updated to monitor your competency development progress.

The reader is encouraged to use these tools to chart their progress as they move from novice to expert. By using these tools, we envision two general outcomes for the service delivery of school psychologists: building the capacity of school systems and increasing the competence for all students.

Broadening Perspectives

US News and World Report has twice cited school psychology as one of the best careers to pursue, and in part, this is due to the shortage of school psychologists. It has been estimated that there are between 25,000 (Fagan & Wise, 2000) and 30,000 (Reschly, 2000) school psychologists. Curtis, Grier, and Hunley (2004), however, have noted that the number may more likely be 34,000. Coupled with predicted retirements (e.g. two out of three by 2020) and attrition rates of 5% (Reschly, 2000), Curtis et al. (2004) predict that there will be a shortage of approximately 9,000 school psychologists as of this year (2010). They do not foresee the trend changing through 2020 and predict a shortage of nearly 15,000 school psychologists by 2020. The need for school psychologists is clearly vast and will continue to be so for the future.

With the need for personnel also comes a greater need for competent school psychologists. Although there are competencies and standards for school psychologists, not all school psychologists are trained in the same way or from the same perspective. As a result, this text includes perspectives that are not always in agreement with each other, yet are competency and standards based. For

Self Evaluation						
Blueprint III Domains of Competence for the Training and Practice of School Psychology	Chapter Title	Current Level of Competence			Current Priority	
		Low	Medium	High	Yes	No
Professional, Legal, Ethical, and Social Responsibility (Foundational Competence)	Applying Law and Ethics in Professional Practice					
Diversity Awareness and Sensitive Service Delivery (Foundational Competence)	Enhancing Competency in Cross-Cultural School Psychology					
Enhancing the Development of Wellness, Social Skills, Mental Health, and Life Competences (Functional Competences)	Managing Your Professional Practice as a School Psychologist					
Interpersonal and Collaborative Skills (Foundational Competences)	Consulting with Families, Schools, and Communities					
Systems-Based Service Delivery (Functional Competences)	Assessing Student Skills Using a Nontraditional Approach					
Data-Based Decision Making and Accountability (Functional Competences)	Assessing Student Skills Using a Process-Oriented Approach					
Enhancing the Development of Cognitive and Academic Skills (Functional Competences)	Evaluating Students with Emotional and Behavioral Concerns					
Data-Based Decision Making and Accountability AND Systems-Based Service Delivery (Functional Competences)	Beyond Unproven Trends: Critically Evaluating School-wide Programs					
Systems-Based Service Delivery (Functional Competences)	Advocating for Effective Instruction: School Psychologists as Instructional Leaders					
Systems-Based Service Delivery (Functional Competences)	Facilitating Mental Health Services in Schools: Universal, Selected, and Targeted Interventions					
Systems-Based Service Delivery (Functional Competences)	Preventing and Intervening in Crisis Situations					
Interpersonal and Collaborative Skills (Foundational Competencies)	Report Writing and Oral Communication of Results					
Technological Applications (Foundational Competencies)	Using Advancing Technologies in the Practice of School Psychology					

Planning and Self Contracting		
Priority Areas of Low or Medium Competency (write Blueprint Standard or Chapter name)	Plan for Enhancing Competency	Date for Achieving your Goal
	1. 2. 3. 4. 5.	
	1. 2. 3. 4. 5.	
	1. 2. 3. 4. 5.	

Fig. 1.2 Development and enhancement of competencies assessment form (DECAF)

example, the behavioral and cognitive processing views of assessment are not in full agreement on how to assess students. We welcome differences of opinion and hope we create and encourage a discussion about different topics from varying perspectives. Through discussion and debate, we believe progress and growth occur within our field. It is our belief that there is no one "right" way to practice or no one "right" perspective within the field of school psychology. Instead, this text attempts to provide multiple views. The important aspect to keep in mind is that no matter which view is taken, school psychologists base their practice and develop competencies using evidence-based practices. This diversity of thought based on empirical knowledge makes the field of school psychology so exciting. Similar to the developmental perspective taken in Blueprint III, we view that School Psychology is still in its early stages of development. Looking back on our history, we only began approximately 100 years ago, and according to Fagan and Wise (2007), we are still "thoroughbreds" in a fast-paced and ever-changing race to help schools help children. As we advance as a field, we are getting closer to improving our practices, so that we may better help schools and the missions they serve.

There are several themes and/or topics that reoccur throughout this text, which mirror the reality of the field. For instance, a problem-solving model will be discussed in several chapters along with the obligatory triangle depicting the three tiers of intervention. In fact, you have already seen a version of the model in this chapter. The problem-solving model has taken a strong hold on the field and we believe that it is worth repeating, as it is that important. The repetition is also helpful as one can see how the model is applied to a variety of topics and competencies.

We applaud you and your efforts to take a look at your current level of competence in each of the domains described above. As you read the chapters, we hope you use the DECAF and the checklists to develop your plan to gain in competence. It is also hoped that you will return to the DECAF as you progress along your journey toward competence from a novice to an expert. Use of this book, the DECAF, and checklists will serve as guides for you to develop and maintain a plan as you become increasingly competent school psychologists. We hope you enjoy your journey as much as we do!

References

Curtis, M. J., Grier, J. E., & Hunley, S. A. (2004). The changing face of school psychology:Trends in data and projections for the future. *School Psychology Review, 31,* 30–42.

Dwyer, K. P. (2002). Tools for building safe schools. In M. R. Shinn, H. M. Walker, & G. Stoner (Eds.), *Interventions for academic and behavior problems II: Preventive and remedial approaches* (pp. 315–350). Washington DC: National Association of School Psychologists.

Fagan, T. K., & Wise, P. S. (2000). *School psychology past, present and future.* Bethesda: National Association of School Psychologists.

Fagan, T. K., & Wise, P. S. (2007). *School psychology past, present and future.* Bethesda: National Association of School Psychologists.

Individuals with Disabilities Education Improvement Act of 2004, Pub.L. 108–446, 118 Stat. 2647 (2006).

Merrell, K. W., Ervin, R. A., & Gimpel, G. A. (2006). *School psychology for the 21st century: Foundations and practices.* New York: The Guilford Press.

National Association of School Psychologists (2000). *Standards for training and field placement programs in school psychology. Standards for credentialing of school psychologists.* Retrieved May 21, 2007 from http://www. nasponline.org.

No Child Left Behind Act of 2001 (Pub. L. No. 107–110).

Power, T. J. (2006). School psychology review 2006–2010. *School Psychology Review, 35,* 3–10.

Reschly, D. J. (2000). The present and future status of school psychology in the United States. *School Psychology Review, 29,* 507–522.

Sheridan, S. (2001). Approach to the task of editor of school psychology review: Conceptual and practical frameworks. *School Psychology Review, 30,* 1–8.

Sugai, G., Horner, R. H., & Gresham, F. M. (2002). Behaviorally effective school environments. In M. R. Shinn, H. M. Walker, & G. Stoner (Eds.), *Interventions for academic and behavior problems II: Preventive and remedial approaches* (pp. 315–350). Washington, DC: National Association of School Psychologists.

Ysseldyke, J. E., Burns, M., Dawson, P., Kelly, B., Morrison, D., Ortiz, S., et al. (2006). *School psychology: A blueprint for training and practice III*. Bethesda: National Association of School Psychologists.

Chapter 2
Applying Law and Ethics in Professional Practice

Barbara Bole Williams and Leigh Armistead

This chapter will provide an explanation of how educational law, professional ethics, and professional standards are the principles that regulate and guide the practice of school psychology. As either a novice or experienced school psychologist, it is important to be aware of how contemporary legal and ethical guidelines form the basis for the practice of school psychology. This applies to the multiple roles school psychologists assume each day as they assess and counsel students, consult with teachers and parents, plan and develop educational programs, and respond to a myriad of questions regarding best practice decisions impacting the students. Moreover, this chapter will focus on the use of educational law and professional ethics as the *scaffolding* that school psychologists should rely upon to guide their professional practice.

The authors will first discuss the importance of law and ethics in school psychology providing the context and rationale for including this topic in a text on developing competencies in school psychology. Second, the school psychologists' basic "rules to live by" will be examined including review of special education law with emphasis on recent revisions to Individuals with Disabilities Improvement Education Act, 2004 (IDEA, 2004), other federal legislation, court cases, National Association of School Psychologists (NASP) and American Psychological Association (APA) ethical codes, and professional literature, particularly in the area of cultural competence. Third, the authors will recommend the use of a legal and ethical decision-making model to link these areas to the practice of school psychology and provide explicated examples of legal and ethical dilemmas that school psychologists experience in their professional lives. The chapter will conclude with suggestions for developing professional competence in these areas and becoming prepared to handle future work-related challenges in the practice of school psychology.

Law and Ethical Standards as the Scaffolding for the Practice of School Psychology

In educational terms, *scaffolding* is any supporting framework used to organize and sustain investigation or inquiry. The use of scaffolding in educational research has been suggested as a means to propel researchers along the path to the "truth" about an issue, problem, or question

B.B. Williams (✉)
College of Education, Rowan University, Education Hall, 201 Mullica Hill Road, Glassboro, NJ 08028, USA
e-mail: williamsb@rowan.edu

T.M. Lionetti et al. (eds.), *A Practical Guide to Building Professional Competencies in School Psychology*, DOI 10.1007/978-1-4419-6257-7_2, © Springer Science+Business Media, LLC 2011

(McKenzie, 1999). When used as a supporting framework, scaffolding can help to provide clear directions and clarify purpose in research.

In a similar manner, law and ethical standards are the *scaffolding* or supporting framework that guide the practice of school psychology. In graduate school, school psychology candidates study the legal and ethical basis of their profession. According to *A Blueprint for Training and Practice III*, the domain of professional legal, ethical, and social responsibility is one of the four areas of school psychological training and practice that is foundational and permeates all types of work performed by school psychologists. *Blueprint III* describes professional, legal, ethical, and social responsibility as follows:

> The issues addressed by this foundational domain are relatively straightforward but absolutely central to the efficacy of a school psychologist's work. School psychologists should be prepared to practice in ways that meet all appropriate professional (practice and ethical) and legal standards, in order to enhance the quality of services and protect the rights of all parties. This includes adhering to due process guidelines in all decisions affecting students, maintaining accepted professional and ethical standards in assessment, consultation, and general professional practice, and fulfilling all legal requirements, including those in response to legislative and judicial decisions (p. 17).

University and college graduate courses within school psychology programs often are designed to cover the content of NASP (2010) *Standards for Graduate Preparation of School Psychologists. Legal, Ethical, and Professional Practice* is one of these domains encompassing legal, ethical, and professional principles in school psychology. The curriculum of these courses typically includes topics such as federal laws and regulations governing both general and special education, Supreme Court decisions and federal case laws, state laws and regulations, local school district policies and procedures adopted by Boards of Education, NASP credentialing standards, NASP and APA ethical codes, professional association position statements, consensus "best practice" publications, literature on evidence-based practice, and benefits of professional supervision and collaboration with colleagues. Each of these topics plays a role in providing the *scaffolding* that will support, guide, and assist the decisions that school psychologists will be making throughout their professional practice.

Literature Review

In order for school psychologists to be proficient in the *Blueprint III's* domain of competence of Professional, Legal, Ethical, and Social Responsibility, they must be aware of the "basic rules" by which they must practice. While the objective of this chapter is not to provide a review of US Civics or Ethics 101, there are basic legal, ethical, and professional guidelines that are important to this discussion.

Federal Legislation Impacting the Practice of School Psychology

Within the United States government's federalist structure, the US Constitution is known as the "supreme law of the land" and outlines the federal government's role as the protector of the rights and liberties of the people. The US Constitution does not guarantee the provision of education to US citizens, but through the 10th Amendment to the Constitution, gives that responsibility to the individual states. However, the US Constitution and the 14th Amendment provide the basis or origins for contemporary special education law through the *equal protection clause* and *due process rights* (Jacob & Hartshorne, 2007). The Supreme Court of the United States has become involved in the states' jurisdiction over public education when individuals' rights guaranteed under the Constitution have been violated (refer to Jacob & Hartshorne, 2007 for a comprehensive discussion of this topic.)

In 1977, the United States Congress implemented the Education for All Handicapped Children Act, originally enacted in 1975 as Public Law 94–142, which mandated the education of children with disabilities be within the *least restrictive environment* (LRE). Later, Public Law 94–142 was reauthorized under the IDEA (1990, 1997) and its most recent revision and reauthorization under IDEA (2004). These statutes form the basis for federal education law that govern special education and have direct impact on the professional practice of school psychology. Murdick, Gartin and Crabtree (2007) outline six basic principles of special education legislation. These require children with a disability to have: (1) the provision of a free appropriate public education (or *FAPE*) for all children regardless of disability; (2) the guarantee of a nondiscriminatory assessment to identify any potentially disabling conditions; (3) development of an individualized educational program or IEP to insure that the entitled instruction and services are provided to the student with a disability; (4) the right to be educated within the *LRE*, including opportunities to be in general education classes for as much of the time as is deemed appropriate; (5) the right to procedural due process should there be a disagreement between parties; and (6) the assurance of parental rights and procedural safeguards to insure parental participation in their child's education.

The long-awaited final regulations for Part B of the IDEA 2004 law were released on August 3, 2006. The US Department of Education touts these regulations as designed to raise the achievement of students with disabilities. Similar to earlier legislation (e.g., No Child Left Behind), the revisions to IDEA 2004 "put the needs of students with disabilities front and center" (press release, August 3, 2006) by focusing on instruction, high standards for learning, and academic outcomes. US Secretary of Education, Margaret Spellings explained that among the issues that received the greatest revisions by the US Department of Education was Response to Intervention (RtI). This and other significant changes (i.e., redefinition of native language, use of medication and discipline) that impact the practice of school psychology will be discussed in this chapter. For additional information on IDEA 2004, the reader is referred to the US Department of Education's interactive web` at http://idea.ed.gov.

Identification of Learning Disabilities and Response to Intervention

Students with specific learning disabilities (SLD) make up approximately half of the students who are determined to be eligible for special education (Zirkel, 2006). Prior to IDEA 2004, eligibility under SLD was usually determined by documenting that a significant discrepancy existed between the student's intellectual abilities and his or her academic achievement. However, a great deal of research and best practice literature in the school psychology community recommends an alternative method of identifying a student with a SLD by determining how well he/she did or did not respond to increasingly intensive academic interventions.

The final IDEA 2004 regulations allowed for both these models to remain. The regulations specify that the State must not *require* the use a severe discrepancy between individual ability and achievement for determining whether a student demonstrates a SLD. Added to the federal regulations was the provision that a State "must permit the use of a process based on the child's response to scientific, research-based intervention" (IDEA 2004, §300.307 [2]), and may also "permit the use of other alternative research-based procedures" (§300.307 [3]) to determine if a student is eligible for special education under the category of SLD. Following the release of IDEA 2004 regulations, state departments of education, in each individual state, have revised their "rules and regulations" to comply with IDEA 2004.

Under most RtI models, academic instruction is delivered using a three-tiered model of service delivery (i.e., universal, targeted, and intensive) (see *Blueprint III*, pp. 13, 14). The emphasis is on providing good academic instruction at the universal level, with ongoing progress monitoring using a timely, informative, and systematic approach. At the targeted level, instruction takes on a small-group focus and finally at the intensive level, the focus is on the individual student's achievement. Determining eligibility for special education under the category of SLD using the RtI model would necessitate looking at the preponderance of the evidence collected throughout the systematic progress monitoring. Posny (2007), Director of the Office of Special Education Program (OSEP), and others indicate that, in the final analysis, the RtI data collection and progress-monitoring processes do not necessarily take the place of a comprehensive evaluation in order to determine eligibility.

The implications for the practice of school psychology point to an increased role for school psychologists to play at the universal, targeted, and intensive levels of academic instruction and in creating learning environments that promote mentally healthy youngsters. According to *Blueprint III* (p. 13), school psychologists should be "instructional consultants who assist parents and teachers to understand how students learn and what effective instruction looks like." In addition, school psychologists should be "mental health practitioners who can guide parents and teachers in learning how to create environments where children and youth feel protected and cared for as well as suffi-ciently self-confident to take risks and expand their competence" (p. 13).

Native Language

IDEA 2004 redefined the term *native language* within the context of assessing or evaluating children. Evaluations now are to be conducted in the language, "most likely to yield accurate information on what the child knows and can do academically, developmentally and functionally ..." (300 CFR § 300.304[c] [1] [ii]). School psychologists need to consider how long the child has been educated in an English-speaking learning environment or classroom. On the one hand, the implication is that a child's native language not being English does not in all cases mandate that the assessment should be conducted in the child's native language. On the other hand, it also does not assume that if a child has completed the English as a Second Language (ESL) program that he or she gives up the right to an interpreter or to be assessed in his or her native language. The school psychologist must consider on a case-by-case basis which language would most likely yield accurate information. Choices may include English, other language, use of a nonverbal assessment, or other mode of communication.

Medication

Essentially, IDEA 2004 stipulates that a child cannot be barred from attending school because he or she is not taking his or her prescribed medication to address behavioral or emotional issues. Much of this controversy has centered on students' prescribed medications to treat attention-deficit-hyperactivity disorder (ADHD) and school personnel *overstepping their boundaries* between medical and educational practice by attempting to insist a child's school placement be contingent upon his or her taking prescribed medication. For school psychologists, this is clearly a call to utilize our skills and expertise in behavioral intervention planning. We need to comply with IDEA 2004 and *program for the student as he or she presents* by working with teachers, parents, and students to develop effective behavioral intervention plans.

Discipline

Federal regulations governing discipline of students with disabilities historically have been both controversial and complicated. Because students with behavioral disabilities are those youngsters who often display challenging behaviors, inherent in the disciplinary provisions of IDEA from its inception was protection from the overuse of suspension and expulsion that would exclude students with disabilities from attending public schools, and thereby deprive a student with disabilities of FAPE. While a thorough discussion of IDEA 2004 disciplinary procedures for students with disabilities is beyond the scope of this chapter, some important changes in how disciplinary cases must be handled will be highlighted. For a more complete discussion, the reader is referred to Jacob and Hartshorne (2007).

Changes in the disciplinary procedures for students with disabilities under IDEA 2004 involve two important points: The *10-day rule* and *unique circumstances*. According to Jacob and Hartshorne citing 34 CFR § 300.530[b] [1]:

> IDEA 2004 allows school officials to remove a child with a disability who violates a student conduct code from his or her current placement to an appropriate interim alternative educational setting, another setting, or suspension for not more than ten consecutive school days to the extent that those alternatives are applied to children without disabilities (pp. 260–261).

This 10-day removal can occur without a manifestation determination (MD) meeting being held. (IDEA 2004 also addresses the issue of *cumulative* days referring to those cumulative days of removal from school throughout the school year and whether it would be considered to be a change of placement.) Some confusion has occurred around the 10-day rule. It is important for school psychologists to be aware that the *10-day rule* (IDEA, 20 USC 1415[k] [4] does not permit a change in placement for a student with disabilities without a MD meeting. This MD meeting must be held within ten school days of a disciplinary decision that results in a change of placement. Furthermore, schools now are allowed to consider any *unique circumstances* on a case-by-case basis when determining whether a change in placement for a student with a disability who violates a code of student conduct should occur (34 CFR § 300.530[a]). It suffices to say it would be beneficial for school psychologists to be thoroughly conversant in the portion of their state rules and regulations governing special education that deal with disciplining of students with disabilities. The authors would recommend that every school psychologist attends a professional development workshop or seminar on this topic, preferably conducted by the US Department of Education, your state department of education, or through NASP.

Family Educational Rights and Privacy Act of 1974

In addition to IDEA 2004, other federal legislation has influenced provision of educational services to students in the public schools. The Family Educational Rights and Privacy Act of 1974 (FERPA), also known as the Buckley Amendment, protects and safeguards the rights of parents by guaranteeing privacy and confidentiality of student records. Under FERPA, an educational agency that receives federal funds is required to develop policies and procedures that mandate written consent of the parent for releasing educational records. The exceptions to this requirement apply if the party with whom the records are shared has legitimate interest in the student, are officials of the school system in which the student is enrolled, are authorized officers of state or federal agencies, or are from certain judicial and law enforcement agencies (FERPA, 20 U.S.C. § 1232 g; 34 CFR Part 99). "Education records" are defined under FERPA as records, files, documents and other materials that contain information directly related to a student or are maintained by an educational agency (34 C.F.R. § 99.3). Jacob and Hartshorne have clarified that school districts must develop policies that adhere to FERPA rather than to Health Insurance Portability and Accountability Act (HIPAA).

Section 504 of the Rehabilitation Act of 1973 (PL 93–112)

Any discussion of federal regulations that are important for the practice of school psychology must include the Rehabilitation Act of 1973 (PL 93–112). Perhaps the most familiar part of this Act is its

Section 504, which specifically addresses the intent of this federal antidiscrimination regulation by prohibiting discrimination of the basis of a disability. Section 504 states that:

> No otherwise qualified individual with a disability ... shall solely by reason of her or his disability, be excluded from participation in, be denied the benefits of, or be subjected to discrimination under any program or activity receiving federal financial assistance (29 USC § 794).

As civil rights legislation, all students within a school receiving federal financial assistance have protection against antidiscriminatory practices in the areas of programming and physical accessibility.

A disability (referred to as handicap) under Section 504 is defined more broadly than a disability under IDEA 2004. According to Section 504, a handicap is defined as a *physical or mental impairment* that interferes with a major life activity including, among other areas, caring for one's self, walking, seeing, hearing, speaking, breathing, or learning (34 CFR § 104.3). Thus any student who has a physical or mental impairment that interferes with learning (or other areas) would be considered to be handicapped under Section 504. If so, these students are entitled to reasonable accommodations, which are typically stipulated in a 504 Accommodation Plan. For school psychologists working in public schools, best practice would suggest that a 504 Accommodation Plan is the first line of defense for accommodating youngster facing learning and behavioral challenges (e.g., ADHD).

The Americans with Disabilities Act of 1990

The Americans with Disabilities Act of 1990 (ADA) is a far-reaching legislation that sets a national agenda for elimination of discrimination against individuals with disabilities. While it impacts schools, it also guarantees equal opportunity to individuals with disabilities in employment, public services, transportation, state and local government services, and telecommunications (PL 101–336). According to Jacob and Hartshorne, Title II, Subtitle A of the ADA applies directly to public schools. It defines a *qualified individual with a disability* who may require "reasonable modifications of rules, policies, or practices" including the "removal of architectural, communication, or transportation barriers, or the provision of auxiliary aids and services" to participate in programs and activities in public schools (28 C.F.R. § 35.104).

The No Child Left Behind Act of 2001

President George W. Bush enacted the No Child Left Behind Act of 2001 (NCLB) in response to his administration's concern that too many of our nation's neediest children are being "left behind." The NCLB Act reauthorized the Elementary and Secondary Education Act of 1965 (ESEA) and called for improvement in the performance of America's elementary and secondary schools through increased accountability for States, school districts and schools, greater parental choice, and a stronger emphasis on reading, especially for children in kindergarten through third grade.

For school psychologists, practitioners working in the public school since 2001, NCLB translated into increased emphasis on school-wide annual testing, academic progress measured by "adequate yearly progress," annual state report cards, highly qualified teachers, the Reading First program, and some funding changes. The ultimate goal is that by the 2013–2014 school year, states must bring all students up to the "proficient" level on state tests.

Schaffer v. Weast

Some would argue that the US Supreme Court decision *Schaffer v. Weast 546 US (2005)* is the most significant case in the last 10 years in terms of impacting special education litigation. *Schaffer v. Weast* deals with the issue of which party (parent or school district) in a due process special education hearing must bear the *burden of persuasion*. Jacob and Hartshorne state that in the *Schaffer v. Weast* case, "the court held that the burden of persuasion in an administrative hearing challenging a child's IEP falls on the party seeking relief, whether it be the child with a disability or the school." Comegno (2006) suggests that this decision addresses the issue of *fairness* in special education due process litigation, i.e., that prior to this decision, the burden of proof was assigned to the school district to defend their actions, and school districts because of their natural advantages of resources were considered guilty until proven innocent. In this decision, Justice O'Connor wrote that the natural advantage of resources is addressed elsewhere … and out of fairness, the party bringing the claim has the responsibility to show the burden of proof.

Ethical Guidelines

The NASP' (2010) *Principles for Professional Ethics* (NASP-PPE) are ethical guidelines that specifically address the practice of school psychology. By joining NASP, each member agrees to abide by these guidelines in their professional interaction with students, parents, families, teachers, other school personnel, fellow school psychologists, and other consumers of school psychological services. The APA's (2002) *Ethical Principles of Psychologists and Code of Conduct* have been developed for psychologists trained in diverse specialty areas and whose work settings including private practice, industry, hospitals and clinics, schools, university teaching, and research. By virtue of its specificity to the practice of school psychology, the NASP-PPE are typically those ethical guidelines most school psychologists refer to and use as a resource to guide their practice of school psychology.

There are advantages in being familiar with both NASP's *Principles for Professional Ethics* and APA's *Ethical Principles of Psychologists and Code of Conduct*. According to Jacob (2005), a school psychologist practitioner with a broad knowledge base in ethical principles and standards is more likely to anticipate and prevent ethical problems from arising. Moreover, this school psychologist is more likely to make ethically and legally sound choices when challenging situations occur.

A brief review of the NASP-PPE finds that its underlying principles are twofold: (a) school psychologists act as advocates for their students/clients; and (b) at the very least, school psychologist do no harm (NASP-PPE, Introduction). The NASP-PPE were developed to provide guidelines for school psychologist practitioners employed in schools and focus on protecting the well-being of students, parents, teachers, and other constituent groups. Among those people listed, children are the top priority for protection. School psychologists are obligated ethically to address concerns for the rights and welfare of children. The NASP-PPE addresses four broad areas: (a) professional competence; (b) professional relationships; (c) professional practices; and (d) professional practice setting. Each of these areas will be discussed below.

Professional Competence

This section of the NASP-PPE stipulates that school psychologists engage only in those practices for which they are qualified by virtue of their training. In order to update their skills and remain current in their profession, school psychologists engage in continuing professional development. Furthermore, school psychologists refrain from any activity in which their personal problems might interfere with the professional effectiveness. Finally, school psychologists assume the responsibility to be knowledgeable about the *Principles* and to apply them; ignorance of the ethical code is no excuse.

Professional Relationships

The NASP-PPE states that school psychologists are committed to promoting improvement in the quality of life of children, their families and the school community. School psychologists respect diversity in all persons without regard to their disabilities, race, ethnicity, gender, sexual orientation or religion. Dual relationships are to be avoided because engaging in both a personal and business relationship concurrently could cloud one's judgment. School psychologists try to informally resolve any concerns about their colleagues' professional conduct but, if necessary, consult state and national ethics committees for assistance. An extremely important area for school psychologists is that they are knowledgeable about, and honor confidentiality; they understand the limits of confidentiality, e.g., *informed consent* and *need to know* principles. School psychologists maintain the dignity and integrity of children and other clients and understand their responsibilities when interacting with parents, legal guardian, and surrogates. The area of professional relationships also extends to principles involving the community, other professionals, trainees and interns, and school psychology faculty.

Professional Practice – General Principles

NASP-PPE requires school psychologists to serve as advocates for children, always remembering that their primary client is the child. When delivering services, school psychologists are knowledgeable about the school or other organization and attempt to become integral members of their school. In instances when conflicted loyalties might occur, school psychologists clearly communicate their roles in advance. In the role of performing assessment and developing interventions, school psychologists remain knowledgeable regarding current practices in the areas of assessment, direct and indirect intervention, and counseling. NASP-PPE provides guidelines in the areas of reporting data and conference results in terms of using understandable language, and avoiding the use of unedited computerized reports as their own. Alterations of previously released reports should be done only by the author of that report. School psychologists use materials and technology responsibly respecting test security and assume responsibility for electronically transmitted information. Finally, school psychologists engage in ethical behavior with regard to research, publications, and presentations; they do not plagiarize or fabricate data and accurately reflect contributions of authors in publications and presentations.

Professional Practice Settings – Independent Practice

Among the areas addressed in this section of NASP-PPE are ethical guidelines regarding school psychologists dually employed in independent practice and school districts. School psychologists act responsibly and ethically in these situations, e.g., they do not accept remuneration from clients who are entitled to the same service provided by the school district employing the school psychologist. Further, they are obligated to inform the child's parent of the availability of services in the public schools. When school psychologists are dually employed, they do not use materials in their independent setting that belong to the district unless approved in advance by their employer.

The reader should be aware that the 2010 version of the NASP Principles for Professional Ethics has been extensively revised. It is organized around these four broad ethical themes:

- Respecting the Dignity and Rights of All Persons
- Professional Competence and Responsibility
- Honesty and Integrity in Professional Relationships
- Responsibility to Schools, Families, Communities, the Profession, and Society

The four ethical themes subsume 17 ethical principles each of which is further articulated by multiple specific standards of conduct.

Culturally Competent Practice

Both legal and ethical guidelines described for school psychologists in this chapter address the issue of diversity in a variety of ways. The importance of developing cultural competence as a school psychologist is crucial to developing ethically and legally sound practices. Williams (2007) defines culturally competent practices as behaviors and policies that enable school psychologists to work effectively to address the social, behavioral, mental health, and educational needs of diverse students from various cultures. According to the US Department of Education (2004), 5.5 million English language learners are attending US public schools and speak more than 400 different languages. By the year 2040, no one ethnic or racial group will make up a majority of the US school-age population (National Association of School Boards of Education, 2002). It is safe to say that students who are attending US schools are becoming increasingly diverse. It is important for school psychologists to develop and continually upgrade their skills by becoming *cross cultural helpers* in order to better assist students from diverse backgrounds who may be experiencing problems.

School psychologists can become more culturally competent by first doing a self-appraisal of their own cultural experiences, so as to understand themselves and the role that culture plays in their own lives. It is also helpful for school psychologists to assess their own multicultural competencies and, if necessary, increase them. Once the cultural groups represented in a school are identified, a school psychologist can become more knowledgeable about the customs and values of the representative groups. School psychologists should interact with students and families from diverse backgrounds to assist them in becoming more familiar with the school's culture. It is helpful to identify other school-based personnel and community-based resources that have expertise to serve as consultants or resources to various cultural groups. School psychologists benefit from expanding their knowledge of best practices in providing educational services to English Language Learners.

In areas of ethics and law, school psychologists should promote fairness and nondiscrimination in providing school-based services and should champion the laws that prohibit discrimination and harassment in schools.

Ethical and Legal Decision-Making Model

School psychologists who are knowledgeable about educational law and codes of ethics (e.g., NASP's *Principles of Professional Ethics* and APA's *Ethical Principles of Psychologists and Code of Conduct*) and use these principles to guide their practice are more likely to engage in sound professional practice. School psychologists who actively engage in professional development and upgrade their skills by becoming more knowledgeable about evidence-based practices will become more effective in their service delivery. School psychologists who read *NASP's Best Practices in School Psychology–IV*, NASP's position papers, and other school psychology professional literature will become more knowledgeable and contemporary in their role as practitioners.

Consider again the analogy of educational law, professional ethics and standards as the *scaffolding* or supporting framework that guides the practice of school psychology. In order to implement the research-to-practice connection, the authors recommend the use of a legal and ethical decision-making model to link these areas to the practice of school psychology. If this ethical and legal problem-solving model is followed, the decision that results is more likely to be viewed as

Table 2.1 Ethical and legal decision-making model

1. *Describe the problem situation*
   The first step is to focus on available information and attempt to gather and objectively state the issues or controversies. Breaking down complex, sometimes emotionally-charged situations into clear, behavioral statements is helpful
2. *Define the potential ethical-legal issues involved*
   Enumerate the ethical and legal issues that are in question. Again, state these as clearly and accurately as possible, without bias or exaggeration
3. *Consult available ethical-legal guidelines*
   Research the issues in question using reference sources, e.g., NASP's *Principles for Professional Ethics*, IDEA 2004, state guidelines governing special education, textbooks in ethics and legal issues in school psychology, e.g., Jacob and Hartshorne's *Ethics and Law for School Psychologists*, 5th Edition, NASP's *Best Practices in School Psychology IV*, job descriptions, school board policies and other appropriate sources
4. *Consult with supervisors and colleagues*
   Talk with your supervisor and trusted colleagues who are familiar with the legal and ethical guidelines that apply to school psychology. On a need-to-know basis, share information specifically about the issues you have identified. Brainstorm possible alternatives and consequences and seek input from those whose opinions you value
5. *Evaluate the rights, responsibilities, and welfare of all affected parties*
   Look at the big picture, rather than focusing on the isolated details of the controversy. Consider the implications for students, families, teachers, administrators, other school personnel and yourself. How will the various alternative courses of action affect each party involved? Remember two basic assumptions underlying NASP's *Principles for Professional Ethics*: (1) school psychologists act as advocates for their students/clients, and (2) at the very least, school psychologists will do no harm
6. *Consider alternative solutions and consequences of making each decision*
   Carefully evaluate in a step-by-step manner how each alternative solution will impact the involved parties. Who and how will they be affected? What are the positive and negative outcomes of each alternative? Weigh the pros and cons. Step back and carefully consider the information you have gathered
7. *Make the decision and take responsibility for it*
   Once all the other steps are completed, make a decision that is consistent with ethical and legal guidelines and one that you feel confident is the best choice. Take responsibility for following through on that decision, attend to the details and attempt to bring closure to the scenario

Note: Adapted from Koocher and Keith-Spiegel (1998, In Williams, Armistead, and Jacob (in press))

ethically and legally appropriate. By applying the principles discussed in this chapter in a logical and reasoned manner, it is more likely that the reasoned outcome will be consistent with best practice. Refer to Table 2.1 for the steps in the ethical and legal decision-making model.

Explicated Cases to Illustrate Use of the Ethical and Legal Decision-Making Model

Below are four examples of ethical and legal dilemmas that illustrate the use of the decision-making model. In most cases, the analyzes followed the seven-step decision-making model because the authors believe that many ethical and legal dilemmas encountered by school psychologists are complex and require a degree of deliberation and consultation in order to arrive at an appropriate decision. However, some dilemmas may be handled with a streamlined approach to problem solving, because once legal and ethical principles are consulted, the decision is rather straightforward and arrived at more expeditiously. In either case, the ethical and legal decision-making model serves as the basic framework to approach the problem-solving process.

The first case depicts a dilemma for the school psychologist when Sam, a fifth grader diagnosed with ADHD, discontinues his medication at his father's insistence. Prior to this, Sam was functioning well with a combination of classroom modifications, a behavior management plan and medication prescribed by his physician.

Case 1: Sam Boswell

Samuel Boswell is a fifth grader at my school. Sam's parents are divorced and have joint custody. Until recently, he lived with his mother most of the time. Two years ago, our Student Support Team conducted a Section 504 evaluation for Samuel due to significant behavior problems and frequent suspensions from school. The results suggested that impulsive behaviors characteristic of ADHD were contributing to Samuel's problems. The Team, which included Sam's mother, developed a 504 Plan that recommended classroom accommodations, parent collaboration with the school psychologist, participation in an ADHD counseling/support group, an individual behavior management plan, and referral for a medical evaluation and possible treatment. All the interventions were implemented and proved helpful. Samuel's pediatrician reviewed the 504 evaluation report, interviewed him and his mother, and decided to try a stimulant medication. After a few days on medication, Sam's behavior improved dramatically with a real reduction in impulsivity. Sam also began working harder on his behavior plan and participated more effectively in the counseling group. Sam's mother began reading some materials I provided and took the lead in communicating with his teacher and monitoring his response to medication. I was very pleased with the resolution of this case and followed up periodically to see how Sam was doing.

Recently, Sam began living with his father because his mother was sent overseas on a military assignment. Mr. Boswell soon began protesting Sam's medical expenses and insisting that Sam did not need to be on a stimulant. About 3 weeks ago, Sam ran out of medication and his father decided not to refill the prescription. Almost immediately, Sam's teacher noticed a major change in his behavior. He began talking back and arguing with her about class work. His work completion and class participation deteriorated. Impulsive comments and actions resulted in escalating peer conflicts. Finally, a pushing incident led to his hitting another student, an office referral, and a 5-day out-of-school suspension.

After the suspension, Mr. Boswell accompanied him back to school and met with the principal, Mr. Johnson, and me. Mr. Johnson reviewed the recent changes in Sam's behavior and suggested that discontinuing his medication may have been a factor. Mr. Boswell went ballistic! He exclaimed that he had heard on talk radio that Federal law now prohibits schools from requiring stimulant drugs for a student to attend school. He stormed out of the meeting shouting something about, "over my dead body!" Mr. Johnson and I discussed the situation and both remembered reading that IDEA 2004 indeed has a provision pertaining to required medication. Mr. Johnson decided that we should not try to discuss medication again lest we get in some sort of legal trouble. I went back to my office and decided to think through this situation in a systematic fashion using the seven-step decision-making model advised in this chapter.

1. *Describe the Problem Situation.* As a psychologist, the most troublesome aspect of this situation for me was that medical treatment – along with other interventions – had proven very effective for Sam. However, Federal law, apparently, prevented me from advocating for Sam's continued treatment. I decided to explore this further.
2. & 3. *Define the Potential Ethical–Legal Issues. Consult Available Ethical–Legal Guidelines.* It was immediately apparent that this was one of those ethical dilemmas in which my various clients – child, school, and parents – seem to have conflicting needs and interests. Sam's principal and teacher have an interest in managing his behavior to enhance his learning and minimize the effects of his disruptive behavior on the learning of his peers. They had previously seen the benefits of medication for Sam and would like to see it reinstated. However, Sam's parents have the right to determine medical treatment for their child.

A quick internet search at www.idea.ed.gov showed that indeed there is a provision in IDEA 2004 (citation) that states, " (A) In general – The State educational agency shall prohibit State and local educational agency personnel from requiring a child to obtain a prescription for a substance covered by the Controlled Substances Act (21 U.S.C. 801 et seq.) as a condition of attending school, receiving

an evaluation under subsection (a) or (c) of section 614, or receiving services under this title."
{Section 612 (a) (25)} However, I found that Section 612 (a) (25) goes further and states, "(B) Rule
of construction – Nothing in subparagraph (A) shall be construed to create a Federal prohibition
against teachers and other school personnel consulting or sharing classroom-based observations
with parents or guardians regarding a student's academic and functional performance, or behavior
in the classroom or school, or regarding the need for evaluation for special education or related
services under paragraph (3)."

On my state's Department of Public Education web site, I found a memo clarifying the state's
interpretation of the preceding Federal regulation. In part, it said:

> Personnel may not state or suggest that a student with a disability (or a suspected disability) must obtain a
> prescribed medication that is covered by the Controlled Substances Act before the student may attend school,
> return to school. However, IDEA 2004 explicitly allows personnel to consult with parents or guardians about
> their observations of a student's academic, functional, and behavioral performance in school, or regarding the
> need for an evaluation for special education services. However, these observations must be concrete and fact-
> based, and should not include opinions about how a particular medication may or could affect a student.

4. *Consult with Supervisors and Colleagues.* I was beginning to get some possible ideas about
   how to proceed but I decided to email the school district attorney for advice. I briefly
   described the situation and asked if IDEA 2004 prohibited a school psychologist from
   discussing possible medical treatments – including stimulant therapy – with a parent as
   long as I did not give the impression that the school was requiring stimulant medication.
   The attorney said that her opinion was that I could discuss medical treatment options with
   the parent. However, she pointed out that future court decisions and regulatory changes
   could influence her opinion.

5. & 6. *Evaluate the rights, responsibilities, and welfare of all affected parties. Consider alternative
   solutions, and the consequences of making each decision.* After my review of these legal and
   ethical guidelines, I concluded that I could advocate for a comprehensive intervention program for Sam without specifically recommending medication for him. I could even give Mr.
   Boswell a handout about the American Academic of Pediatrics-recommended protocol for
   treating ADHD, which includes a medication component (www.aap.org). However, I
   would have to respect Mr. Boswell's right to determine Sam's medical treatment. I would
   also need to help my colleagues at school to avoid any violation of IDEA 2004 and our state
   regulations about mandating medication. I also had some ideas about encouraging them that
   we could help Sam with more intensive behavioral interventions.

7. *Make the Decision and Take Responsibility for it.* I shared my thinking about Sam's situation
   with the Principal and he agreed to support my recommended actions. First, I contacted
   Mr. Boswell and asked to meet with him at his office. Briefly, the meeting went well. I assured
   Mr. Boswell that, as a professional school psychologist, I had Sam's well-being as my first
   priority but respected his rights as the parent. He reiterated his opposition to medication
   because of its expense. I acknowledged that medical care is expensive but shared with him
   some handouts about ADHD and encouraged him to consult with Sam's pediatrician about
   his options. I reassured him that school personnel would not pressure him about any particular medical treatment. Finally, I invited him to a meeting of the Student Support Team at
   which we planned to review the accommodations, interventions, and modifications specified
   in Sam's 504 plan.

At the Support Team meeting the following week, Mr. Boswell shared that he had an appointment
with Sam's doctor and would consider all his options but asserted that, "The school isn't going to
tell me what to do!" I quickly assured him we had no intention of doing so. However, I gave him a
pamphlet about our state Children's Health Insurance Program in case he wanted to look into it. The
rest of the meeting went well and we secured Mr. Boswell's support for our behavioral interventions
and counseling program.

Several months later, Mr. Boswell did reinstate Sam's medication regime but told me it was his wife's idea. He still didn't think Sam needed it.

The second case presents a situation whereby the special education director is expediting the change of placement for a student with disabilities who is considered a troublemaker. The director has neglected to follow the procedures under IDEA 2004.

Case 2: Expedited Special Education

The school psychologists in Udonia Public Schools began hearing about an increasing number of what were called "administrative" changes of placement. That is, a principal wanted to get a troublesome student – or one with low test scores – out of his or her school. In collusion with the special education director, the principal was able to arrange a quick change of placement to another program, usually a more restrictive one in another building. Then, the secretary in the special education office called a parent to get verbal consent and mailed all the forms for signatures. When the school psychologists in the district questioned these practices, the special education director explained the need to keep principals happy – to be "team players," as he put it. He also insisted that Udonia needed to streamline procedures and reduce meeting time and paperwork devoted to routine matters such as changes of placement. He encouraged the school psychologists that sometimes they should just, "go along to get along."

Analysis: Although the Director's goal of reducing the amount of paperwork and number of meetings is admirable, these streamlined changes of placement are problematic. They do not meet the legal requirements of IDEA 2004 (citation), which specify that special education placement decisions must be made by an Individualized Education Program (IEP) Team consisting of:

- The parents of a student with a disability
- When appropriate, at least one regular education teacher of the student
- At least one special education teacher of the student
- A representative of the local education agency (who must meet certain requirements)
- An individual who can interpret the instructional implications of evaluation results
- At the discretion of the parents or district, other individuals who have knowledge or expertise about the student
- When appropriate, the student with a disability.

In addition to the legal requirements of IDEA, school psychologists are compelled by their own ethical standards to attempt to influence this practice. NASP's *Principles for Professional Ethics* (NASP, 2000) require that, "school psychologists consider children and other clients to be their primary responsibility, acting as advocates for their rights and welfare. If conflicts of interest between clients are present, the school psychologist supports conclusions that are in the best interest of the child" (NASP-PPE, IV, A, #2). The *Principles* also require that school psychologists support parental participation in decision making about special education and psychological services and respect their right to object to those services (NASP-PPE, III, C, #s 3–5).

If the Udonia school psychologists carefully examine IDEA 2004, they will find provisions that they could use to help their district streamline procedures without violating student and parent rights. For example, Section 1414 (f) permits certain meetings, including IEP and placement meetings, to be held by conference call or videoconference. In addition, Section 1414 (d) (1) (C) permits parents and the district to agree that certain members of the IEP Team do not need to attend a meeting if the Team members' curriculum or service area will not be discussed or if the members submit written reports in advance. Finally, it is even possible to change an IEP without convening a meeting if the parents and school agree to do so by means of a written document. The Udonia school psychologists should offer to investigate these and other provisions of IDEA 2004 and consult with the district's attorney. This could enable the district to make their procedures more efficient as well as comply with relevant legal and ethical guidelines.

The third dilemma deals with a school psychologist attempting to resolve an ethical issue informally by discussing his concerns about a fellow school psychologist practice.

Case 3: Making an Ethical/Professional Practice Complaint

Paul has been practicing school psychology for about 4 years. While completing reevaluations, he began getting very different IQ scores from those obtained previously by one of his colleagues, Dr. Solkk. He began keeping some notes and found that about half the time, the full-scale scores were more than ten points apart, and his scores were almost always lower than his colleague's. In examining protocols, he found many errors in scoring in which Dr. Solkk did not query when necessary and was overly generous in scoring. When Paul reviewed the psychological reports from these evaluations, he found additional areas of concern. The reports often overreached in suggesting diagnoses and often misinterpreted scores. He even found several instances of students being categorized as learning disabled in the wrong academic areas. Then one day, Paul overheard Dr. Solkk administering an IQ test in the next office. On a digit memory subtest, he seemed to be "chunking" digits and using too much voice inflection. His presentation of digits was far from the usual one per second. Dr. Solkk even left the office during one subtest and left the student working alone while he took a brief call on his cell phone.

Paul spoke with his colleague after this incident and tried to make some suggestions about test administration. Dr. Solkk listened but dismissed his concerns as "picky." When Paul pointed out the problems he had found with some of Dr. Solkk's psychological reports, his colleague became upset and told Paul he had too much time on his hands and should find something else to do rather than critique old psych reports.

Paul continued to be concerned, so he met with the district Supervisor of Student Services (who was not a school psychologist). Paul mentioned his ethical obligation to address Dr. Solkk's assessment practices and tried to frame his actions as supportive of good practice rather than critical of his colleague. Nevertheless, the supervisor reproached Paul for criticizing Dr. Solkk, who was more experienced, and for Paul's not being a "team player." Paul is not sure whether he has fulfilled his ethical obligations and whether he should make any further complaints.

Analysis: Paul clearly understands his professional obligation to attempt to resolve unethical and unprofessional practices. He probably understands that one of the hallmarks of any profession is its efforts to enforce its own ethical codes. In fact, attempting to resolve suspected unethical behavior is actually required by the NASP *Ethical Principles* which make this obligation quite clear.

NASP 2000 Ethical Principle III.A.8: School psychologists attempt to resolve suspected detrimental or unethical practices on an informal level. If informal efforts are not productive, the appropriate professional organization is contacted for assistance, and procedures established for questioning ethical practice are followed:

1. The filing of an ethical complaint is a serious matter. It is intended to improve the behavior of a colleague that is harmful to the profession and/or the public. Therefore, school psychologists make every effort to discuss the ethical principles with other professionals who may be in violation.
2. School psychologists enter into the complaint process thoughtfully and with concern for the well-being of all parties involved. They do not file or encourage the filing of an ethics complaint that is frivolous or motivated by revenge.
3. Some situations may be particularly difficult to analyze from an ethical perspective. School psychologists consult ethical standards from knowledgeable, experienced school psychologists, and relevant state/national associations to ascertain an appropriate course of action.

Paul's actions thus far comprise reasonable efforts to informally resolve the apparent ethical and professional practice violations. Despite his being rebuffed by Dr. Solkk and his supervisor, it is possible that his providing feedback about careless assessment practices will result in improvements. An additional informal step that Paul could take would be offering to participate in peer "supervision" with Dr. Solkk. He could point out that all practitioners benefit from participating in supervision and his willingness to assist his colleague – and accept supervision himself – might be viewed more positively than his complaints were.

If Dr. Solkk's assessment practices do not improve, Paul will need to decide whether the problem is serious enough to take the next step and report the matter to a professional association ethics committee. Before doing so, Paul is advised to consult with a trusted colleague. Many state school psychology associations have an ethics and professional practices chairperson or committee. Some of them attempt to resolve problems through education and mediation without fixing blame. Paul could approach his state association first and then decide whether to make a complaint with the national APA or NASP ethics committees. Paul must decide how far he is willing to go in attempting to resolve the matter. Ultimately, his decision should be based on his appraisal of the effects of Dr. Solkk's practices on his clients.

The fourth and final case involves a parent's request to see copies of the school psychologist's counseling notes from his sessions with her son.

Confidentiality of Counseling Notes

1. *Description of the Problem Situation.* George Benson provided weekly individual and group counseling to a second grade student named Robby as specified in his IEP for special education services related to an emotional disturbance. His mother requested a meeting to discuss his progress. Because of prior conflicts between the mother and the school district, Dr. Benson asked the special education director to join his meeting with the mother. As the meeting began, he reminded the mother that she had previously signed a counseling consent form that explained the importance of confidentiality in a counseling relationship. The form stated that Dr. Benson would be sharing general information about the student's progress with the parents, but that the details of sessions would remain confidential. Dr. Benson noted that he had reached an agreement with Robby regarding this limit to confidentiality. Dr. Benson described Robby's current goals, the format of the counseling sessions, typical activities, and the student's responsiveness and progress. In addition, the psychologist showed the mother a worksheet from a recent session. Citing her rights, the mother demanded copies of the worksheet and all other counseling notes in Robby's file. Unsure of his ethical and legal standing, Dr. Benson asked for time to consider the situation before deciding what to do.

2. *Defining the Potential Ethical–Legal Issues.* Several ethical and professional practice issues are represented by this case. They involve confidentiality when providing direct services to students as well as parents' rights to inspect educational records and rights to determine intervention methods. George is to be commended for the manner in which he handled the confidentiality of his counseling sessions with Robby. He is probably aware that students who are minors actually have no legal right to confidentiality independent of their parents. Therefore it is quite important, prior to the start of counseling, to come to an agreement with parents, so that a limited assurance of confidentiality can be extended to students as part of establishing effective counseling relationships (Jacob & Hartshorne, 2007). Usually those limitations include situations in which, (1) a student requests disclosure of confidential information to others, (2) situations involving danger to the student or others, or (3) when the school psychologist is compelled to testify in court (Hummel, Talbutt, & Alexander, 1985). NASP's *Principles for Professional Ethics* (2000) recognizes these limitations to confidentiality and state that school psychologists, "secure continuing parental involvement by a frank and prompt reporting to the parent of findings and progress that conforms to the limits of previously determined confidentiality" (p. 21).

3. *Consulting Available Ethical-Legal Guidelines.* George was quite familiar with the ethical and legal guidelines regarding confidentiality. However, he was not so familiar with the legal issues related to student records. In an internet search at the U.S. Department of Education's web site (www.ed.gov), George learned that the FERPA (20 U.S.C. § 1232 g; 34 CFR Part 99) is a Federal law that protects the privacy of student educational records. It also gives parents certain rights regarding those records. Parents have the right to inspect and review their children's education records maintained by the school. Schools are not required to provide copies of records unless, for reasons such as having to travel great distance, it is not possible for them to review the records. Parents may also request that schools correct records, which they believe to be inaccurate or misleading. FERPA's definition of educational records is broad and includes any records maintained by a school that directly relate to a student. However, the definition does exclude private records, "that are kept in the sole possession of the maker, are only used as a personal memory aid, and are not accessible or revealed to any other person except a temporary substitute for the maker of the record" (34 C.F.R. § 99.3). These private notes are intended to jog a practitioner's memory regarding counseling sessions and can include material intended to be completely confidential. If such records are shared with anyone other than a substitute (as in the case of a substitute therapist filling in for the primary therapist), then they become part of a student's educational record and are subject to FERPA's provisions regarding disclosure.

4. *Consulting with Supervisors and Colleagues.* George decided to talk with his special education director before deciding what to do about the mother's request. George pointed out that he did not really maintain confidential notes about student's progress. But he did have a counseling folder for each student with whom he had worked in which he filed completed worksheets and made comments about completed and upcoming activities. The Director agreed with George that these notes and work samples could probably be considered sole possession records and were not part of Robby's educational record. However, she asked whether it might be possible that George was concerned that the parent's interest in his counseling materials reflected her desire to criticize and/or direct the type of counseling techniques he uses with Robby. She pointed out that if this occurred, George could diplomatically remind the mother that under IDEA, courts have generally determined that parents do not have the right to determine specific teaching or counseling methods. He only needed to provide the mother with general information about his methods and assure her that they are evidence based. Although she could withdraw consent for counseling, she would have no legal grounds to determine his counseling methods (Jacob, personal communication).

During the meeting, George recalled that there is a NASP ethical standard about collaborating with parents regarding treatment plans. Back in his office, he looked it up and found that Principle III.C.5 states that school psychologists, "discuss with parents the recommendations and plans for assisting their children. The discussion includes alternatives associated with each set of plans which show respect for the ethnic/cultural values of the family" (NASP, 2000, p. 21).

5. & 6. *Evaluating the rights, responsibilities and welfare of all affected parties. Considering alternative solutions, and the consequences of making each decision.* As George reflected on what he had learned, his first inclination was to reject the mother's request to review Robby's counseling records. He reasoned that his counseling records *were* private and the mother did not really have any right to see them. Then he started thinking about the tendency that school personnel often have to "circle the wagons" when parents complain and make demands and perhaps a little openness would reduce the existing alienation. He considered that counseling was benefiting Robby and he did not want his mother to withdraw consent. He also reasoned that if he could not explain and defend his counseling methods, then maybe he should reconsider why he was using them. The worse thing that could happen by being open with Robby's

mother would be that she would be critical of his therapeutic approaches. But if he was not open, he might not be able to help Robby in the future.

7. *Making the Decision and Taking Responsibility For It.* George decided to meet with Robby and discuss the situation with him. Robby seemed to understand and agree that there was nothing in his counseling folder that was embarrassing to him and he stated that it would be okay to share it with his mother. Several days later, George met with Robby's mother and went through the folder with her. He explained his cognitive-behavioral methods and how he was trying to help Robby make changes in his thinking patterns as well as in his behavior at school. To his surprise, Robby's mother made some positive comments and asked how she could help at home. She apologized for being so demanding at the previous meeting and promised to keep in touch (Scenario adapted from Williams, Armistead, & Jacob, 2008).

Next Steps

This chapter has shown how legal, ethical and professional practice guidelines and standards provide a "scaffold" for one's practice of school psychology. However, it is evident that with multiple clients – children, parents, teachers, administrators, etc. – professional judgments must be made. It is also common for school psychologists to encounter competing demands made by their ethical standards as compared to laws and regulations, and feel the "pull" of those demands (Jacob-Timm, 1999). So, the chapter has provided an ethical problem-solving model with examples of its use in resolving ethical dilemmas. It should be evident that practicing school psychology in an ethically, legally, and professionally responsible manner is a career-long challenge. To become competent at professional problem solving requires continual attention to professional development, networking, mentoring, and supervision. Because there are skills involved, it may get easier with experience, but it will be a career-long challenge. To relatively new practitioners, the authors offer the following ten suggestions for preventing problems in their practices and beginning to acquire expert ethical and professional practice problem-solving skills.

1. *Join a professional association.* If you have not already done so, join your state school psychology professional association and get involved in some way. This will provide an immediate source of professional development opportunities. It will also give you access to networking and informal supervision with your colleagues. Many state associations also have ethical and professional practices committees with whom members can consult when they encounter problems in their practice. These committees may also advocate for best practices within your state and present professional development programs for members.

2. *Know the rules.* As soon as possible, join a national association – the NASP, or the APA – whichever one that best meets your practice needs. These organizations also advocate for best practices, are a source of professional development, and have ethics committees to assist members. Additional information regarding professional association involvement is provided in Chap. 15.

    Most practitioners receive an introduction to legal, ethical, and professional practice guidelines during their graduate education programs. As a practitioner, a challenge is accessing that information when you have a need to know something. Finding and keeping up with "the law" can be challenging because the law is changing all the time. Many school psychologists find Jacob and Hartshorne (2007) to be an excellent resource. In addition, two web resources are helpful. To access information about specific cases, try www.findlaw.com. For specific information about special education law, try www.wrightslaw.com. It is also important to be able to quickly access core ethical and professional practice reference materials. You will want to have copies of NASP's *Principles for Professional Ethics* (2000) and *Guidelines for the*

Provision of School Psychological Services (2000). These are published as NASP's *Professional Conduct Manual* (2000). A free pdf version may be downloaded from www. nasponline.org. APA's *Ethical Principles for Psychologists and Code of Conduct* may be downloaded from www.apa.org.

All practitioners involved in special education will need ready access to federal and state guidelines for provision of special education services. A convenient way to review the current 2004 version of the federal Individuals with Disabilities Act is at www.idea.ed.gov/. Special education guidelines for most states are available online as well.

Finally, a new practitioner must learn school district rules – both written and unwritten. Be sure to get a thorough orientation to your new district and schools and get to know the key administrators. Get copies of employee handbooks, policy documents, and learn about procedures. And be observant for and ask your colleagues about unwritten rules.

3. *Get backup.* Professional supervisors are an excellent source of backup, and supervision has long been regarded as essential for school psychologists' professional development (Harvey & Struzziero, 2000). NASP and APA professional practice standards both emphasize the value of supervision and encourage employers to provide it. Unfortunately, few school psychologists actually receive professional supervision. In one survey, less than a third of the respondents who had less than 3 years experience reported at least an hour of supervision each month. Questions were also raised about the effectiveness of supervision that respondents did receive (Ross & Goh, 1993).

There is another way to think about supervision that deemphasizes the hierarchical qualities that may be associated with it. One such definition is: "an interpersonal interaction between two or more individuals for the purpose of sharing knowledge, assessing professional competencies, and providing objective feedback with the terminal goals of developing new competencies, facilitating effective delivery of psychological services, and maintaining professional competencies" (McIntosh & Phelps, 2000, pp. 33, 34). This type of supervision can occur within mentoring or other collegial relationships. If your district does not assign you to a mentor, the authors encourage you to develop a mentoring relationship with a more experienced colleague yourself.

Finally, we suggest you to join or develop a peer consultation or peer support group. (Zins & Murphy, 1996) found that about 64% of the school psychologists they surveyed had participated in a peer support group. Benefits reported by a majority included improved skills, expanded range of services offered, increased professional enthusiasm, more involvement in professional associations, and a better professional knowledge base. It seems apparent that such a group could also be an important source of social support for coping with the stress of what will be a challenging occupation.

4. *Keep confidences.* Get off to a good start in your new practice with regard to confidentiality. There are many nuances about confidentiality that your graduate education program may not have emphasized. One way to begin appreciating these nuances is to study cases that illustrate ethical dilemmas. Such cases are often part of district or professional association CPD programs. A collection of cases illustrating all of the NASP ethical standards is also available (Williams, Armistead, & Jacob, 2008).

Be sure you develop a standard approach to discussing confidentiality (and the limits thereof) with students. Develop a counseling permission form that discusses the need for confidentiality, what information will be shared with parents, and any limitations to confidentiality.

Many school psychologists have difficulty with limiting access to confidential information to those individuals who have authorized access or have a need to know. Be sure you understand ethical principles in this area and develop practices that are consistent with them as well as with district policies. Be sure to think about safeguarding both paper as well as digital records.

5. *Set high standards.* Setting high standards for professional behavior starting with your first day on the job is important. You can always loosen up if you need to, but it is very difficult to tighten up if you start too loosely. Be sure you dress and act in a professional manner. Set boundaries very early for the way you talk about students and parents and with whom you do so. Also be clear about what you can and cannot do – you must practice only within your areas of competence. However, you should quickly develop additional areas of competence to meet needs of your district.

6. *Go slow on school reform.* One of the most frequent complaints of novice school psychologists is about unreasonable supervisor expectations. Be sure you understand your supervisors' expectations and strive to meet them in an ethical and professional manner. Some new practitioners do not understand that the NASP ethical standards are enforceable, whereas practice guidelines are merely advisory. Insisting that your district must comply with national practice standards may be unrealistic. In fact, the NASP *Guidelines* state, "School psychologists adhere to federal, state, and local laws and ordinances governing their practice and advocacy efforts. If regulations conflict with ethical guidelines, school psychologists seek to resolve such conflict through positive, respected, and legal channels, including advocacy efforts involving public policy (Ethical Principle III.D.5). In other words, you may need to "go along" with your employer's expectations while professionally and strategically working toward changing those expectations. However, be sure you do not fall into the trap of just going along to get along. Change will never result from such a strategy.

7. *Develop your power bases.* When seeking change in your district's policies and practices, it is important to use your knowledge and skills as a psychologist. Change requires influencing people. It is important to remember that school psychologists usually have little real authority within a school district but instead function with a blend of both "expert power" and "referent power" (French & Raven, 1959). A psychologist may be able to quickly establish expert power by being knowledgeable, having good credentials and having skills needed by the school district. However, referent power has to be developed. It refers to the ability to influence others and requires charisma and interpersonal skills. It is only developed when clients perceive us as having values and goals that are similar to theirs.

8. *Implement a professional development plan.* There are numerous reasons to immediately develop and begin implementing a personal professional development plan. They include meeting your ethical and professional responsibility to do so, to maintain skills, to cope with changing roles, to develop a specialty, and to maintain your credentials. However, a most important reason is to increase your competence as part of life-long career development. In *School Psychology: A Blueprint for Training and Practice III* (Ysseldyke et al., 2006), the authors assert, "the job of training programs is to ensure that students are at a 'novice' level in all domains by the time they complete the coursework phase of their training, and are at a 'competent' level by the conclusion of internships, with the expectation that "expert" practice will be achieved only after some post-graduate experience and likely only in some domains" (p. 11). The authors suggest that such expertise could take 5–10 years of practice to achieve. (Harvey & Struzziero, 2000), in their book on professional supervision, discuss five stages of growth – novice, advanced beginner, competent, proficient, and expert – through which we progress. They point out that the level at which we function is really "context dependent." That is, we may be very proficient in a certain area of our practice but complete novices in another area. After several years of practice, most school psychologists function at the competent level, but moving beyond that level requires effective supervision of an on-going professional development activity. (For more on professional development, see (Armistead, 2008).)

9. *Develop your EPP problem-solving skills.* Another reason for continuing professional development is to keep up to date with changes in laws, legal opinions, as well as ethical and

professional standards. This chapter has presented a problem-solving model for use with difficult situations involving ethical and professional practices. Your skills with this model and your overall knowledge base about professional practices will continue to improve if you attend workshops on legal issues, talk about challenging situations with your supervisor, and consult with a professional support group.

10. *Take care of yourself.* Finally, take care of yourself. It is much more difficult to practice ethically and professionally if you are under stress and overwhelmed by too much work that you do not feel competent to perform. Use your professional skills to be a *resilient* school psychologist – one who is actively making a career out of school psychology, who is building skills, who is able to manage stress, who knows when to take time away, one who has a social support network, and one who avoids professional burnout.

Chapter Competency Checklist

DOMAIN 1 – Professional, legal ethical and social responsibility domain

Foundational	Functional
Understand and explain the following:	Gain practice:
□ IDEA 2004	□ Relating personal and professional experiences to key foundational concepts
□ FERPA	
□ Section 504 of the Rehabilitation Act of 1973	□ Articulating questions about law and ethics
□ Americans with Disabilities Act	
□ No Child Left Behind	□ Discussing questions with colleagues and supervisors
Least restrictive environment	□ Searching for solutions to unanswered questions
□ RtI	
□ Discipline	
□ Language and assessment	
□ Medication	
□ Student rights	
□ Schaffer v. West	
□ Ethics principles related to Professional competence; Professional relationships; General practice; and Independent practice	
□ Cultural competence	
□ Legal and ethical decision making model	

References

Armistead, L. D. (2008). Best practices in continuing professional development for school psychologists. In A. Thomas & J. Grimes (Eds.), *Best practices in school psychology-V*. Bethesda: National Association of School Psychologists.

Comegno, J. (2006). *Hot legal issues*. Presentation at the NASP 2006 Summer Conference. Atlantic City, NJ.

French, J., & Raven, B. (1959). The bases of social power. In D. Cartwright (Ed.), *Studies in social power*. Ann Arbor: University of Michigan Press.

Harvey, V. S., & Struzziero, J. A. (2000). *Effective supervision in school psychology*. Bethesda: National Association of School Psychologists.

Hummel, D. L., Talbutt, L. C., & Alexander, M. D. (1985). *Law and ethics in counseling*. New York: Van Nostrand-Reinhold.

IDEA (2004). Available from: http://idea.ed.gov.

Jacob-Timm, S. (1999). Ethical dilemmas encountered by members of the National Association of School Psychologists. *Psychology in the Schools, 36*, 205–217.

Jacob, S. (2005). *Ethics and law update for school psychologists*. Presentation at the NASP 2005 Summer Conference, Philadelphia, PA.

Jacob, S., & Hartshorne, T. S. (2007). *Ethics and law for school psychologists* (5th ed.). Hoboken, NJ: John Wiley & Sons.

Koocher, G. P., & Keith-Spiegel, P. (2008). *Ethics in psychology and the mental health professions: Standards and cases*. New York: Oxford University Press.

McIntosh, D. E., & Phelps, L. (2000). Supervision in school psychology: Where will the future take us? *Psychology in the Schools, 37*(1), 33–38.

McKenzie, J. (1999). *Scaffolding for success*. Bellingham, WA.: FNO Press. Available from: http://fno.org/dec99/scaffold.html.

Murdick, N.L., Gartin, B.C. & Crabtree, T.L. (2007). *Special education law* (2nd ed.). Columbus, Ohio: Merrill Publishing.

National Association of School Psychologists. (2000). *National Association of School Psychologists Principles for Professional Ethics*. Bethesda, MD: Author. Available from: http://www.nasponline.org.

National Association of State Boards of Education (2002). *A more perfect union: Building an education system that embraces all children*. Retrieved from www.nasbe.org/Educational_Issues/Reports/More_Perfect_Union.PDF.

National Association of School Psychologists. (2010a). *National Association of School Psychologists Principles for Professional Ethics*. Bethesda, MD: Author. Available from: http://www.nasponline.org.

National Association of School Psychologists. (2010d). *Standards for the graduate preparation of school psychologists*. Bethesda, MD: Author. Available from: http://www.nasponline.org.

Posny, A. (2007). *RTI alone is not sufficient for SLD identification*. Keynote presentation at the NASP 2007 Convention, NY, NY.

Ross, R. P., & Goh, D. S. (1993). Participating in supervision in school psychology: A national survey of practices and training. *School Psychology Review, 22*(1), 63–81.

U.S. Department of Education (2004). *Fact sheet: NCLB provisions ensure flexibility and accountability for limited English proficient students*. Retrieved from www.ed.gov/print/nclb/accountability/schools/factsheet-english.html.

Williams, B.B. (2007). Culturally competent mental health services in the schools in the schools: Tips for teachers. Retrieved from: www.nasponline.org/communications/spawareness/cultcompmhservices.doc.

Williams, B.B., Armistead, L. & Jacob, S. (2008). *Professional ethics for school psychologists: A problem-solving model casebook*. Bethesda, MD: NASP.

Ysseldyke, J., Burns, M., Dawson, P., Kelley, B., Morrison, D., Ortiz, S., Rosenfield, S., & Telzrow, C. (2006). School psychology: A blueprint for training and practice III. Bethesda: National Association of School Psychologists.

Zins, J. E., & Murphy, J. J. (1996). Consultation with professional peers: A national survey of the practices of school psychologists. *Journal of Educational and Psychological Consultation, 7*(1), 61–70.

Zirkel, P. (2006). *SLD eligibility: A users guide to the new regulations*. National Research Center on Learning Disabilities.

Chapter 3
Building Competency in Cross-Cultural School Psychology

Yuma I. Tomes

Culturally competent is the new mantra of today's professional society, especially as it relates to almost every human service field. But what exactly does it mean to be culturally competent? How does one measure cultural competence? Is everyone capable of *truly* being culturally competent? Is it quantitatively or qualitatively measured? Is there another term to use? These are just some questions surrounding the culturally competent movement; yet, they are critical in grasping the magnitude of meeting the needs of diverse individuals in the United States of America. The American school system is based upon a white, middle-class value system that supports uniqueness and individual characteristics over unity and interdependence (Oakland, 2005); therefore, in order to support all classes and races of students, it is important to delve further into understanding the dynamics of multiculturalism.

The recent 2003 US Census illustrated that over 78 million persons of color live in the United States, and approximately 53 million students of color are in the over 92,000 public school systems (US Department of Education, 2007). Recent projects suggest that students of color will become the majority in public education by the year 2020 (less than 10 years away) (Campbell, 1994). Moreover, Ponterotto and Casas (1991) project that one out of three children attending public schools in the US will represent a racially, ethnically, or culturally diverse group. "In response to the increasing cultural pluralism in elementary and secondary educational environments, it is urgent that psychologists and mental health professionals working in school systems demonstrate cultural responsiveness and sensitivity in their practice and service" (Kindaichi & Constantine, 2005, p. 180).

Multicultural Competence

Multicultural competence can be defined as a sincere understanding in various influences that reflect our culture of family beliefs, behaviors, but is not limited to the majority/common culture (NASP Resources). This is different from the traditional "melting pot" theory that has been supported in the American culture. Today, and rightfully so, multiculturalism is seen as a tossed salad. Individuals are able to preserve and present their uniqueness when combined with other groups while respecting the contribution of others. But there is also cross-cultural competence. Mestas and Peterson (2004) define cultural competency as "having the evolving knowledge and skills used for maintaining a process to increase one's respect, understanding and knowledge of the similarities and

Y.I. Tomes (✉)
Philadelphia College of Osteopathic Medicine, Philadelphia, PA, USA
e-mail: yumato@pcom.edu

T.M. Lionetti et al. (eds.), *A Practical Guide to Building Professional Competencies in School Psychology*, DOI 10.1007/978-1-4419-6257-7_3, © Springer Science+Business Media, LLC 2011

differences between one's self and others" (p. 43). Moreover, Lynch and Hanson (1993) view cross-cultural competence as a thinking, feeling, acting ability that acknowledge, respect, build on ethnic, cultural, and linguistic diversity. Finally, Rogers, Ponterotto, Conoley, and Wiese (1992) found that most training directors viewed cross-cultural competencies as "the psychologist's knowledge, awareness, and sensitivity to differences in culture" (p. 610). The commonality between these two terms is culture. Culture can be defined as "the attitudes, beliefs, behaviors and rites of a particular group regardless of racial and/or ethnic background" (Tomes, 2004, p. 23). Culture under girds every lifestyle, interaction, and decision made. Culture is life. It is the substrata upon which everyone lives. As culture changes, the population dynamics will also change. Hence, the culture shock school districts are experiencing throughout the country. As new students of varied background move into lower, middle, and upper class neighbors, the dynamics of neighborhood, magnet, and charter schools begin to change.

School Psychology and Culture

The profession of school psychology has grown significantly over the past couple of decades. The burgeoning roles and functions of a school psychologist have made the profession more appealing for many, yet there is still much work to be done. Currently, it is one of the hottest ten professions in the United States (NASP Resources). One of the reasons for the profession's popularity centers on working with children from various backgrounds. While this is an attraction to the profession, it is also a weakness of many current school psychologists and the training programs/graduate schools they graduated from over the last 15 years (Miranda & Gutter, 2002). As recently as 2002, the National Association of School Psychologists (NASP) requires a multicultural component to all training programs. Most school psychology programs have little in the way of multicultural "immersion" programs, thereby, limiting the actual contact graduate students have during their training. Moreover, there appear to be fewer and fewer persons of color choosing to pursue school psychology as a profession given the fact that minority representation within the profession has yet to significantly increase over the last 10 years. Membership for NASP during the 2004–2005 year yielded less than 7% minority representation, with Hispanic/Latino being the largest minority group with 2.99% (Curtis, Lopez, Batsche, & Smith, 2006). While Hispanic/Latino school psychologists have increased slightly, African American school psychologist numbers have declined slightly (NASP Resources).

In the evaluation of cultural competence, the American Psychological Association (APA) and the National Association of School Psychologists have adopted multicultural guidelines for assessments and diagnosis of psychological disorders. The APA Multicultural Guidelines are rooted in six principles that "articulate respect inclusiveness for the national heritage of all groups' lived experiences, and the role of external forces such as historical, economic, and socio-political events" (APA, 2003, p. 382). The six principles of APA follow. Additionally, a brief summary of what this means for the profession of school psychology along with provided information may illuminate opportunities for school psychologists to take the lead in many child advocacy areas that have been left unchallenged.

Principle 1 Ethical conduct of psychologists is enhanced by knowledge of differences in beliefs and practices that emerge from socialization through racial and ethnic group affiliation and membership and how those beliefs and practices will necessarily affect the education, training, and practice of psychology (APA, 2003).

Possibly, the most difficult classification is ascertaining the major belief theme of a people, and how this and other factors influence their attitudes toward themselves, others, and what happens in their world. Through active and continuous self-exploration, school psychologists' cultural self-awareness can guide their recognition of the ways that others might deal with cultural differences, and they can use that recognition to develop interpersonal and systemic interventions in the schools (Constantine & Sue, 2005). Moreover, Arnold (1993) suggests that psychologists participate in experiential exercises, wherein they work to develop cultural empathy, reflect on their experiences of difference, and identify their reactions to various cross-cultural issues. For a school psychologist, it is imperative to reflect on decisions that have been made "in the interest of the child." Some decisions, as it relates to culturally and linguistically diverse children, are not always in the best interest of the child, but appear more supportive of school districts and administrators, especially if *these* children cause tests result to plummet.

Principle 2 Understanding and recognizing the interface between individuals' socialization experiences based on ethnic and racial heritage can enhance the quality of education, training, practices, and research in the field of psychology (APA, 2003).

Cultural identity models are becoming increasingly important as students with varying backgrounds enter today's primary and secondary classrooms. Researchers such as Cross (1971) and Parham and Helms (1985) have been the leaders in racial identity models. In 1971, Cross presented the Racial Identity Development Model for Blacks. According to Cross, there are five developmental stages every African American progresses through during their lifetime. The stages are: (1) Pre-encounter, (2) Encounter, (3) Immersion/Emersion, (4) Internalization, (5) Internalization Commitment. Somewhat different, Helms believes that the majority of the population encounters stages, but through a slightly different process. There are six stages of development: (1) contact, (2) disintegration, (3) reintegration, (4) pseudo-independent, (5) immersion/emersion, and (6) autonomy. While few school psychologists have knowledge of these developmental models, they are still expected to help with transitional plans for children of all ages and backgrounds. The more school psychologists have an understanding of various racial and ethnic identity development models as applied to specific cultural populations, the more likely they are to understand and appreciate less homogeneity of racial and ethnic attitudes and experiences within cultural groups (Constantine & Sue, 2005). Moreover, these models may shed some light on how students of diverse backgrounds might develop their identities in the context of a dominant white, middle-class school system and society.

Nestled in identity models are aspects of cognitive style. Cognitive style refers to how an individual processes information. Historically speaking, African American, Latino, and American Indian children have learned better through Field Dependent/Global processes (Tomes, 2004). These methods encouraged students to learn by doing through novel activities, and students were expected to engage in dialogue and group processing in order to answer or overcome a problem. These students were also teacher motivated, which suggests that as teachers place high expectations on the students, the likelihood increases that the students will perform at or exceed the expectations. Yet, if teachers do not promote a student's creativity, the likelihood that student will not perform at his or her best is fairly high.

Principle 3 Recognition of the ways in which the intersection of racial and ethnic group membership with other dimensions of identity (e.g., gender, age, sexual orientation, disability, religion/spiritual orientation, educational attainment/experiences, and socioeconomic status) enhances the understanding and treatment of all people.

Consultation continues to surface as a critical component of school psychology. As this aspect of the profession continues to grow and develop creating interventions that are culturally sensitive is critical. In doing so, the school psychologist must understand how to collaborate with individuals outside of their training purview. Tarver Behring and Ingraham (1998) and Ingraham (2000) have conducted extensive research describing the consequences of providing consultation services without a cross-cultural approach. When a consultant (i.e., the school psychologist) is not competent in using a cross-cultural approach, critical resources are not engaged. Moreover, the teacher remains uninformed, changes that could benefit the instructional environment go untapped, and ultimately lead to the child's needs being unmet (Rogers & Lopez, 2002). Consultation should be conducted with strong consideration given to the hierarchy in the relationship, and the nature of the intervention should be influenced by the *current* cultural belief (Brown, Pryzwansky, & Schulte, 2006). For example, to determine the hierarchy in the relationship, the school psychologist can ask if someone prefers to be called by their first name or a more formal approach. It is through these hierarchical approaches of establishing the roles/responsibilities of the consultant and consultee that a consultant may be able to engage the consultee in high levels of moral reasoning and other ways to analyze problems from different perspectives, especially if it relates to culturally specific attitude.

Consultation is becoming an increasingly important area in which school psychologists will need to become even more competent in over the next few years. Understanding and acknowledging cultural-specific behaviors is necessary for educators and administrators. Part of the experiences in school for students of culturally and linguistically different backgrounds is that they are being asked to check their cultural normalcy at the front door of the school house and put on the school's value system. Research has shown that students of color, in particular, African Americans are active/tactile/kinesthetic learners (Tomes, 2004), but this may contrast aspects of the traditional methods of teaching and teacher expectations. Metaphorically, it is like asking a high school senior to wear a kindergarten's jacket; it just does not fit. The skill here is for school psychologists to discern how cultural background is contributing to the student's learning, then find ways to reconcile the differences to better assist the student.

Principle 4 Knowledge of historically derived approaches that have viewed cultural differences as deficits and have not valued certain social identities helps psychologists to understand the under-representation of ethnic minorities in the profession and affirms and values the role of ethnicity and race in developing personal identity.

"Historical knowledge of the institutional uses of psychology to promote oppressive systems, such as academic segregation … may lead psychologists to reflect on the systemic implications of research, treatment, conceptualization, and education models" (Constantine & Sue, 2005). With the influx of immigrants, to the country, meeting their needs can border on the perpetuation of a prejudicial system. English-as-a-Second-Language (ESL) students and English Language Learners (ELL) can be stereotyped into particular groups that receive less attention than other students (Thao, 2005). Moreover, as a result of their linguistic diversity, Latino(a) students are already segregated. Also, these students can be referred for countless number of referrals and are normally assessed in the English language, further clouding the social identities to understand the underrepresented by school psychologists. Just recently, a Superior Court Judge in San Francisco ruled that ten Hispanic children are required to take the state assessment test in English, "since we expect all citizens to speak English competently, these students should be tested in English" (The San Diego Union Tribune, 2007). While the expectation is that U.S. residents speak English, it requires time spent learning the language. Immigrant children to the United States of America need sufficient time and instruction to develop competent language skills in what has been termed the most challenging language to master (Belgrave & Allison, 2006). School psychologists must advocate for these children to be assessed with tests that support their true current academic/socio-emotional function.

Principle 5 Psychologists are uniquely able to promote racial equity and social justice. This is aided by their awareness of their impact on others and the influence of their personal and professional roles in society.

Given the history of the educational system, racial equity and social justice in the schools may be questioned by many, even those who are educators in the school system. The public school system is supported by White, middle-class American values (Kincheloe, 2007). A significant portion of what is considered appropriate academic achievement and desirable classroom behavior is inductively learned by teachers and students as they interact with one another (Clark, 1983). Primarily, White teachers have had lower expectations of students of color, as reported by Clark. These lower expectations have encouraged parents of children of color to feel that school districts are not invested in educating their children; thereby, creating racial distrust. Numerous books, such as Jonathan Kozol's (1975), Savage Inequalities, chronicle the racial disparities in the educational system when school districts spend minimally on children and educate children in deplorable physical environments. What role does a school psychologist have in creating social justice? The school psychologist should be a champion of equality for all students, but especially for those who are underserved or "tracked" unfairly.

Principle 6 Psychologists' knowledge about the roles of organizations, including employers and professional psychological associations, are potential sources of behavioral practices that encourage discourse, education and training, institutional change, and research and policy development that reflect rather than neglect cultural differences. Psychologists recognize that organizations can be gatekeepers or agents of the status quo, rather than leaders in a changing society with respect to multiculturalism.

During Individualized Educational Plan (IEP) meetings, school psychologists should not only present data results but also be a support system for the parents for all students. IEP meetings, however, may be especially intimidating if not overwhelming for parents of students of color. Having numerous *educated* persons sharing information about a student's emotional/intellectual ability may cause trepidation about asking or answering question for the parents of diverse students. Part of the cultural barriers may include language difficulties. Having someone in the "system" sit by the parent and explain what will and is taking place is pivotal to maximum understanding (language barriers will be discussed later in the chapter).

Cross-Cultural Competencies

Culturally competent practice as a school psychologist means to utilize culturally sensitive tests, multicultural consultations, appropriate individual/group counseling, and preventions/interventions. It is imperative for school psychologists to understand that culture provides the content for attitudes, thoughts, and actions; it determines the kinds of cognitive strategies and learning modes that individuals use for solving complex problems within their group.

Through using the Delphi procedure, Rogers and Lopez (2002) delineated the three areas of cross-cultural competencies critical to the school psychology profession (Fig. 3.1): (1) Assessment, (2) Report writing, and (3) Laws and regulations. Their study highlighted that these three areas received the lowest mean (1.00–1.49), thereby, suggesting that these are the areas school psychologist should be and/or receive significant training in order to be a competent, cross-cultural psychologist. The remaining areas were working with an interpreter, working with parents, theoretical paradigms, counseling, professional characteristics, consultation, culture, academic interventions, research methods, working with organizations, and language.

It is not surprising to understand why assessment is critical for cultural competence. The choice of tests to assess students may significantly impact decisions made about their future educational attainment. Yet, as viewed by Rogers and Casas (2002), report writing is also important. Incorporating elements of the child's background into reports as well as cultural knowledge of the child helps to accurately reflect child's character and ability level. While assessment procedures can be biased, reports can be equally biased by the lack of information about the child and his/her culture in the report.

Competency Category	Skill Area	Mean	S.D.
Assessment			
	Nonbiased assessment and the process of adapting available instruments to assess LCD students	1.04	0.20
	Alternative assessment methods	1.29	0.46
	Using instruments sensitive to cultural and linguistic differences	1.04	0.20
	Using assessment results to formulate recommendations that facilitate language acquisition	1.29	0.46
Report Writing			
	The importance of integrating cultural and language background of the family and child, language proficiency, and learning style information in the report	1.20	0.50
	Incorporating information about family origins, family composition, parental attitudes about education and handicapping conditions, and levels of acculturation into report	1.29	0.55
	Reporting the use of translations during assessment	1.20	0.65

Fig. 3.1 Culturally competent skill areas modified from Rogers and Lopez (2002)

Family Makeup

Dealing with families requires the school psychologist to deal with a diversity of family structures. There may be a traditional nuclear family with a father, mother, and possible siblings. However, with students coming from diverse families, it is highly likely for the school psychologist to meet with extended family members such as grandparents, aunts/uncles, and close family friends/neighbors. Moreover, American Indian families designate certain responsibilities to particular family members. For example, in some American Indian tribes, the uncle may be the disciplinarian of the family. Therefore, if a student is engaged in inappropriate behaviors while at school, the uncle may offer the disciplinary action instead of the parents addressing the issue.

Overcoming Language Barriers

The communication system—verbal and nonverbal—distinguishes one group from another. Apart from the multitude of "foreign" languages, some nations have 15 or more major spoken languages (within one language group there are dialects, accents, slang, jargon, and other such variations). Furthermore, the meanings given to gestures, for example, often differ by culture. While body language may be universal, its manifestation differs by locality.

In conducting evaluations of students who are apart of another culture or speak a different language, extreme sensitivity must be employed. Verbal and nonverbal communication can be difficult and frustrating for persons who are listening to another language or speaking another language other than their native tongue. Even if students and family members speak the majority language, the language of a school psychologist is often technical and filled with jargon. If family members have no understanding of the English language, they must rely on interpreters, which is questionable at best. They are words, which when translated, do not have equivalent explanations in another language. For example, it is difficult to define the nuances of behavior management to someone from a culture that children are expected to "act out" or if the culture does not have an "adolescent" transition time period. As students from these diverse backgrounds take residence in the classroom, traditional American values have to supplement native culture.

Systems Barriers

School systems think that children who are having difficulty should be "labeled" and then receive an intervention plan, although this is changing due to recent legislation. The understanding and knowledge of prevention and intervention programs of immigrants to the United States of America may be extremely limited, especially if they are arriving from an underdeveloped country (Hernandez, 2006). Moreover, this is further complicated when parents of children from less industrialized countries have a poor outlook on health diagnosis. This may cause some to think that parents are neglecting their children by not seeking services, when in actuality; these parents may not be aware of, or understand, the services. Traditionally, systems such as educational institutions have not been as responsive to cultural differences, but they are steadily improving (Walker, Saravanabhavan, Williams, Brown, & West, 1996). There are strategies school psychologists can employ such as gathering information from older adults (i.e., patriarchs and matriarchs) throughout the community, speaking with healers, engaging politicians to address immigration and cultural concerns on local, educational levels to help schools be more responsive to these students' needs.

Family Priorities

"Family priorities should guide all interventions with young children with disabilities, especially when the family's culture differs from that of the service provider" (Lynch & Hanson, 2004, p. 33). For example, by the time children begin kindergarten, most believe that the child should be ambulatory and in control of bodily functions. Aspects of toilet training and some personal hygiene should be fulfilled. Yet, there are some cultures that do not place emphasis on these milestones, and as a result, some children may require extra services when they enter the school system. This should not reflect negatively on the child and/or parents because the cultural norms may support this behavior. Additionally, this difference does not suggest that the child is suffering from emotional abuse or other psychopathologies.

Family's Belief System

Children from a different cultural background may begin school with different cultural assumptions; thereby, they may come to school lacking certain concepts. For instance, the Hopi Indians are illiterate as it relates to math skills. Being introduced to mathematical computations and math concepts would be foreign to them in a classroom environment. Parents have supported this belief in order to instill family values of trust and interdependence amongst their family, nuclear and extended. Moreover, math has no place in the daily living of the various tribes, so teaching it becomes unnecessary.

Mental Process and Learning

Some cultures emphasize one aspect of brain development over another, so that one may observe striking differences in the way people think and learn. Anthropologist Edward Hall (1981) maintains that the mind is internalized culture, and the process involves how people organize and processes information. Life in a particular locale defines the rewards and punishment for learning or not learning certain information or in a certain way, and this is confirmed and reinforced by the culture at that locale. For example, Germans tend to stress logic to their children, while Japanese and Navajo reject this Western system of thinking. Logic for a Hopi Indian is based on preserving the integrity of their social system and all the relationships connected with it. Therefore, a Hopi child would not likely adapt easily to independent learning or seatwork, which could be perceived as a problem in the American culture that values autonomous learning and individualistic achievement.

Cultural cognitive styles are also ways to assess learning. Tomes (2004, 2007) suggests that by understanding the manner in which children of different cultural backgrounds process information, academic and behavioral difficulties could be minimized. Moreover, there tends to be a mismatch between cultural expectations of the teachers and cultural capabilities of the students. Differences between African Americans and Whites in learning, cognitive patterns, and language should not be perceived as deficits for either group. However, school teachers and districts have denounced linguistic patterns associated with Ebonics as non-legitimate language, meaning it should not be taught or spoken in a standard American classroom. "Yet, the unique features of Ebonics have evolved from legitimate language structures used by speakers from both Africa and the United States" (Belgrave & Allison, 2006, pp. 162–163). As a result, cultural and cognitive dissonance may arise for the student as he/she speaks in a language reflective of their cultural norms and heritage, but not appreciated in the majority society.

Effective Steps of a Fair Psychoeducational Assessment

The steps to take when working with a student from a differing cultural group from your own are as follows.

Step 1: Do an Observation of the Student

Observations serve many purposes, especially as it relates to understanding cultural idiosyncrasies. The obvious reason for an observation is to uncover the problem behavior(s) and make a determination of how significant the behavior is from the *normal* mainstream population. After this comparison is made, the school psychologist should then view the problem intra-culturally and make a determination of deviance. If the behavior is not deemed deviant from their culture, then the school psychologist must re-examine aspects of the behavior. For example, children of Asian descent are less likely to make eye contact and appear withdrawn in traditional American setting. This is not an example of depression; yet, many school psychologists have inappropriately diagnosed depression without consideration of the student's culture. While it is important to observe the student in the environment considered problematic, it is also necessary to see how the student responds in environments where the behavior may be less likely manifested. Following with this example, first-generation Asian American students may be suffering from adjustments to a new city, state, and/or country. As a result, what kinds of relationships does the student have at home with siblings and other family members. This would require a school psychologist to conduct a home visit; however, when questioning parents, there are cultural issues to be aware of ahead of time. Asian Americans are less likely to discuss mental health issues publicly as it may bring shame to their family (Sue & Sue, 1990). The school psychologist must take a direct and active role because the parents will rely on the direction of the professional. This would require the school psychologist to ask succinct and direct questions regarding the child's emotional functioning at home. Then observations should be conducted of the child in community settings, if available.

Step 2: Seek Out Cultural Information Regarding the Student's Background

Sound assessments call for school psychologists to be knowledgeable about the child's language development. Additionally, acquire knowledge about the potential influence of culture on mental health. It is important to identify similarities within and between cultures. This is an important element, the school psychologist should not stereotype a student based on his/her racial/cultural background. The halo effect has followed countless number of students throughout school systems and it may unfairly bias teachers and administrators regarding a student's true capabilities. Moreover, by seeking additional information on a student's cultural background, everyone wins, even if it is determined that the student needs to be referred for additional assessment. The more school psychologists discover hidden aspects of children in the context of cultural control, the better equipped the school psychologist will be in the future to address similar cultural areas.

Step 3: Student Interview

(A) *Meet with the teacher regarding "cultural" nuances that are manifested in the classroom.* This would entail conducting a teacher interview (mentioned later in the chapter).
(B) *Conduct an interview with the student* (i.e., language spoken while at home, family language, familial relationships, etc.)

Suggested Questions for Diverse Students

1. Can you share with me who lives in your home? Does everyone at home speak English or other languages? Do you have brothers/sisters? What is your relationship with them?
2. What are some activities that you do at home? Do you know of other children your age doing the same activities? Who?
3. What makes you happy in attending this school? When do you feel sad in attending this school? What subjects do you like (dislike) at school? Do you feel comfortable at school?

4. When you are in class, do you feel students look and act like you or are different than you? How does this make you feel?
5. How often do you work with your classmates on assignments? How does this make you feel when you work with classmates? How do you feel when you have to do work by yourself?
6. Do you have friends at school? What kinds of things do you do with your friends? What do you do in your free time at school? At home?
7. If you can make 3 wishes for anything you can think of, what would you wish for?

Step 4: Referral Question

Determine the nature of the presenting difficulty. This would involve uncovering any living situations usually translating to a lack of familiarity with specific skills needed for success in dominant cultures.

Primary complaints—What is the extent to which the presenting problem influences competence, aptitude, and attitude. It is important to explore possible cultural influences that may have precipitated the referral.

Present functioning—Chronological details of the problem behavior from the onset. Understand the behavior in the context of family's social class, possible child rearing practices, gender roles with family and dissonance that may be found at school, deference and trust regarding school, etc.

Step 5: Teacher Interview with Records Review

Gather information from the teacher regarding the child's cognitive strengths and weaknesses, especially in particular subjects. Any assessment of the child's cognitive style or learning preferences can be used as targeted interventions with the promise of improving brain function and behavior (Tomes, in press). Moreover, Kimberly et al. (2005) further support brain-based cognitive functions. "Three neurocognitive systems—cognitive control, learning and memory, and reading—are essential for school success" (p. 71).

Possible questions to ask teacher during interview

1. How do you see the student's behavior different from others?
2. What type of verbal/nonverbal language does the student use with you?
3. What types of affect does the student demonstrate in class? Outside? With other students? (i.e., do they express themselves, sullen, reserve, etc.)
4. Does the student make eye contact when spoken to? When speaking?
5. Is the student more responsive or assertive with communication styles?
6. Does the student desire to perform activities with other students or do things by him/herself?

Step 6: Parent Interviews

Parent interviews should include the following areas:

1. Developmental history—Pregnancy and delivery difficulties, knowledge regarding the infancy, medical history (i.e., family history, hospitalization)
2. Family history

   (a) Child's behavior as it is influenced by the family sentence (what does this mean?).
   (b) The capacity of the family to change problem behavior.
   (c) Family's nonverbal communication.

(d) Assignment of roles, conflict resolution.
(e) Any structural imbalances in the family.
(f) The role of the extended family.
(g) Age and language fluency.
(h) Protective family factors (i.e., rules are consistently enforced, etc.).
(i) What are the culturally defined norms?

Choosing Culture-Fair Measurements

The above information should provide critical information about the student's development and possible difficulties that the student is experiencing. All this information should lead to determining what is the next step and possible assessment instruments for the student. The determination of the most appropriate assessment instruments is necessary for obtaining the most accurate information regarding the child's cognitive, socio-emotional, or academic functioning. For example, the choice of an intellectual assessment tool, as with other kinds of instruments, must be made on the technical and psychometric merits of the instrument and the utility with the particular population. While the Wechsler Intelligence Scale for Children IV (WISC-IV) is the most common intellectual measurement used by school psychologists, it is not always the most appropriate for populations of color. The WISC-IV is very much a language-based test with a normative sample stratified on age, sex, parent education level, geographic region, and race/ethnicity. The four index areas address verbal comprehension, perceptual reasoning, working memory, and processing speed. With a heavy emphasis on left brain activity, the WISC-IV may not be the best instrument for students with a multiracial/multicultural background. However, certain subtests on the measures of the WISC-IV and WAIS-III are relatively culture independent (Shuttleworth-Edwards, Donnelly, Reid, & Radloff, 2004). More empirical research is being conducted by neuropsychologists supporting the creativity of right brain functions in varied populations and how these functions are not being fairly assessed in testing situations or classrooms. Moreover, research is yielding results that right brain hemisphere is responsible for more language development than initially thought (Bryan & Hale, 2001). Moreover, Ortiz (2005) points out that while knowledge of language is important when assessing cultural and linguistic students, "questions regarding opportunity to learn, the level and manner of instruction, the curriculum's linguistic relevancy and appropriateness, expected level of functioning or performance relative to English language development" can impact how students are assessed and the responses they may give on standardized assessments.

However, the Kaufman Assessment Battery for Children – Second Edition (KABC-II), presents a slightly different perspective on assessing intellectual capabilities. The KABC-II combines the assessment approaches of Luria's neuropsychological model and Cattell/Horn/Carroll method of categorizing cognitive abilities. The battery has optional information that can be gathered through Knowledge/Crystallized Ability Scale, but as a whole, it continues to measure other broad abilities and processes with a minimum of verbalization. As a result, the training manual suggests that it is best suited for children with varied linguistic and cultural backgrounds.

The Comprehensive Test of Nonverbal Intelligence (CTONI), according to the training manual, is an unbiased test that measures nonverbal reasoning abilities of individuals for whom most other mental ability tests are either inappropriate or biased. Results of the CTONI tend to be most useful for estimating the intelligence of individuals who experience undue difficulty in language or fine motor skills, including individuals who are bilingual, who speak a language other than English, or who are socioeconomically disadvantaged, deaf, language disordered, motor disabled, or neurologically impaired (Cohen & Swerdlik, 2005). Other tests that are considered more culturally fair are: Differential Ability Scales, Second Edition (DAS-II), Test of Nonverbal Intelligence – Third Edition (TONI-3), Leiter International Performance Scale, Revised (Leiter-R), and Process Assessment of the Learner (PAL).

In order to get the most accurate and comprehensive snapshot of a student's capability, the school psychologist may need to "test the limits" (Canino & Spurlock, 2000). This would engage the school psychologist in using alternative assessment procedures after a standardized administration. For example, a school psychologist would allow the student to work beyond a time limit on a measure to see if the student can figure out the problem or sequence. This is especially beneficial for students who do not regard time within the same context as traditional American schools. If the child is able to complete the tasks within a few extra seconds, this provides critical information about the child's abilities minus time constraints. Also, while directions may instruct the child to perform a task as quickly as possible in order to receive extra points, the child may work more laboriously exploring multiple options before settling on a solution. This action may be a cultural phenomenon that has translated into a detailed work ethic. Moreover, when an individual's cultural background, experiences, and exposure are dissimilar or not consistent with the individuals comprising a norm group, tests will tend to measure a lower range of abilities (Ortiz, 2005). Therefore, nontraditional assessments offer an alternative approach to capitalize on a student's abilities that otherwise may have been considered a failure or overlooked based on majority population principles. Also, tests may more accurately characterize untapped areas of the students that would facilitate greater skill or ability.

Cultural Equivalence

Cultural Equivalence is a problem of whether or not inferences resulting in a common psychological dimension can be made in different groups of subjects on the basis of measurement and observation. For example, "children may not be familiar with concepts and vocabulary outside of their social sphere as a function of limited experience resulting from social classes and ethnic group membership" (Rodriguez, 2000, p. 94). The following areas are germane to cultural equivalence in that they represent how culture is not an isolated, individual experience (Rodriguez, 2000).

A. Functional—test scores have a consistent meaning for different racial groups
B. Conceptual—information contained in the test items is equally familiar to different groups
C. Linguistic—the language presented in the test has similar meaning to different groups
D. Psychometric—the instrument measures the same things at the same levels across cultural groups
E. Testing condition—testing procedures are familiar and "acceptable" to different groups
F. Contextual—environments in which the person functions
G. Sampling—samples on which the test is developed and validated

When administering various tests, children often base their answers to questions about life events on the norms within their community. The significance comes into play when the norms deviate from the mainstream responses (Canino & Spurlock, 2000).

The Link to Training and Practice

In the forthcoming NASP Blueprint III, programs are being asked to move toward an orientation that considers not only student performance but also the integration of data for intervening and monitoring outcomes at individual and systems level. To accomplish these principles, Blueprint III outlines foundational and functional competencies for training and practice of school psychology. Foundational competencies include: (1) Interpersonal and collaborative skills, (2) Diversity awareness and sensitive service delivery, (3) Technological applications, and (4) Professional, legal, ethical, and social responsibility. Functional competences are: (1) Data-based decision making and accountability, (2) Systems-based service delivery, (3) Enhancing the development of cognitive and academic skills, and (4) Enhancing the development of wellness, social skills, mental health, and life competencies. The extent to which these competencies are met is dependent on the level of training school psychologists receive during graduate coursework and professional practice. Moreover, "having a personal awareness and a knowledge base of cultures are essential prerequisites to practicing school psychology" (Miranda, 2002, p. 357).

While knowledge of culture permeates each competency, Blueprint III specifically targets diversity in Foundational Competence. For school psychologists, this means a significant commitment to becoming more of a consultant where the student is talked about less and becomes an active agent in the process. A central tenet of most consultation models is that the consultee is an active agent in the consultation process (Sandoval, 2003). A multi-informant process is necessary to fully understand aspects of diversity as it relates to every child. Particularly, in the case of linguistic and cultural concerns, diagnostic input from teachers, parents (or family members), and the students provides information that enhances the accuracy of interpretation of student's individual abilities. Moreover, it is through the role of being a consultant that school psychologists remain neutral, and advocates of the process in helping parents and teachers help their children and students, respectively. Also, consulting with teachers/administrators on diversity awareness issues may lead to changes on multiple levels. School psychologists possess some level of expertise in child development; however, when respect to diversity is included by understanding aspects of multicultural child development, the consultant role allows for school psychologists to have a voice in curriculum, social skills, behavior management, and other school areas. Moreover, this may be seen in devising effective instruction for English as a Second Language learner if the school psychologist is aware of cognitive development for bilingual individuals.

Diversity awareness is just one aspect, school psychologists also must be sensitive to how services are delivered to culturally diverse students/parents. It is not unusual for individuals associated with education to perceive infrequent or inconsistent parental involvement as reflecting a lack of interest in children's education. However, in the case of non-English–speaking families, a lack of involvement may be due to inability to communicate with the school. Yet, there may be situations where language is not problematic; in those cases, work responsibilities, transportation difficulties, or distrust of the school may lead to absent parents for meetings or other functions. Moreover, in some cultures, parents may feel uncomfortable discussing personal issues with their child's teacher in a formal setting (Barona, 2006). As a result, efforts should be made to identify safe environments for parents to feel less threatened and able to discuss personal issues. This aspect clearly demonstrates the need for Home and School Collaboration not only on the school psychologist's behalf but the entire school system as well.

Conclusion

"For those students who are at greatest risk due to accumulation of multiple risk factors, schools may represent one of the most potentially protective environments—encouraging the development of good problem-solving and academic skills, individual talents and other productive activities and social competence" (Doll & Lyon, 1998, p. 356). In order to work effectively with families of different cultural/racial backgrounds as a school psychologist, one must first understand their own value and belief system. Additionally, the school psychologist must recognize that their own language, culture, and ethnicity influence *all* interactions. We, as school psychologists, must always remember our responsibility as a student advocate. Vacating this premise is not an option and must be employed at all times, especially with children who are immigrating to our country or indigenous children who have been marginalized and ostracized based upon color and other cultural factors.

Chapter Competency Checklist

DOMAIN 3 – Diversity awareness and sensitive service delivery

Foundational	Functional
Understand and explain the following:	Gain practice:
☐ Multicultural competence	☐ Observing different groups of people
☐ Multicultural guidelines	☐ Interacting with various cultural groups
☐ Three areas of cross-cultural	☐ Delivering psychological services to students
☐ Understanding Families	and families from various cultural groups with
☐ Overcoming Language Barriers	supervision
☐ System barriers	☐ Developing questions about psychological
☐ Steps for fair psychoeducational assessments	services with specific cultural groups
☐ Cultural equivalence	
☐ Personal culture and values	
☐ Values of majority culture	

References

American Psychological Association. (2003). Guidelines on multicultural education, training, research, practice, and organizational change for psychologists. *American Psychologist, 58*, 377–402.

Arnold, M. S. (1993). Ethnicity and training marital and family therapist. *Counselor Education and Supervision, 33*, 139–147.

Barona, A. (2006). School counselors and school psychologists: Collaborating to ensure minority students receive appropriate consideration for special educational programs. *Professional School Counseling, 1*, 1–18.

Belgrave, F. Z., & Allison, K. W. (2006). *African American psychology: From Africa to America*. Thousand Oaks, CA: Sage.

Brown, D., Pryzwansky, W. B., & Schulte, A. C. (2006). *Psychological consultation and collaboration: Introduction to theory and practice* (6th ed.). Boston: Pearson.

Bryan, K. L., & Hale, J. B. (2001). Differential effects of left and right cerebral vascular accidents on language competency. *Journal of the International Neuropsychological Society, 7*, 655–664.

Campbell, P. R. (1994). *Population projections for states, by age, race, sex: 1993 to 2020*: Current population reports, P25–P1111. Washington, DC: U.S. Bureau of the Census.

Canino, I. A., & Spurlock, J. (2000). *Culturally diverse children and adolescents* (2nd ed.). New York: The Guilford Press.

Clark, R. M. (1983). *Family life and school achievement: Why poor black children succeed or fail*. Chicago: The University of Chicago Press.

Cohen, R. J., & Swerdlik, M. E. (2005). *Psychological testing and assessment* (6th ed.). Boston: McGraw Hill.

Cross, W. E. (1971). The Negro-to-Black conversion experience: Toward a psychology of black liberation. *Black World, 20*, 13–27.

Curtis, M. J., Lopez, A. D., Batsche, G. M., & Smith, J. C. (2006, March). *School psychology 2005: A national perspective*. Paper presented at the Annual Meeting of the National Association of School Psychologists, Anaheim, CA.

Doll, B., & Lyon, M. A. (1998). Risk and resilience: Implications for the delivery of educational and mental health services in schools. *School Psychology Review, 27*(3), 348–363.

Hall, E. (1981). Beyond culture. New York: Doubleday.

Hernandez, L. (2006). Becoming a cross-culturally intelligent evaluator. The Digest, 3, 24.

Ingraham, C. L. (2000). Consultation through a multicultural lens: Multicultural and cross-cultural consultation in schools. *School Psychology Review, 29*, 320–343.

Kimberly, E. and Kratochill, T. (2005). Evidence-based parents and family interventions of school psychologists: Conceptual and methodological considerations in advancing best practices. *School Psychology Quarterly, 20*, 504–511.

Kincheloe, J. L. (2007). City kids-not the kind of students you'd want to teach. In J. Kincheloe & K. Hayes (Eds.), *Teaching city kids: Understanding and appreciating them* (pp. 3–38). New York: Peter Lang Publishing.

Kindaichi, M. M., & Constantine, M. G. (2005). Application of the multicultural guidelines to psychologists working in elementary and secondary schools. In M. G. Constantine & D. W. Sue (Eds.), *Strategies for building multicultural competence in mental health and educational settings* (pp. 180–191). Hoboken, NJ: Wiley.

Kozol, J. (1975). *Savage inequalities: Children in America's schools*. New York: Harper Perennial.

Lynch, E. W., & Hanson, M. J. (1993). Changing demographics: Implications for training in early intervention. *Infants and Young Children, 6*(1), 50–55.

Lynch, E. W., & Hanson, M. J. (2004). *Developing cross-cultural competence: A guide for working with children and their families* (3rd ed.). Baltimore, MD: Paul H. Brookes Publishing.

Mestas, M. & Peterson, R. (2004). The goal behind performance goals. *Journal of Educational Psychology, 98*, 42–63.

Miranda, A. H. (2002). Best practices in increasing cross-cultural competence. In A. Thomas & J. Grimes (Eds.), *Best practices in school psychology IV*. Washington, DC: National Association of School Psychology.

Miranda, A. H., & Gutter, P. B. (2002). Diversity research literature in school psychology: 1990–1999. *Psychology in the Schools, 39*(5), 597–604.

NASP Resources. (n.d.). *The provision of culturally competent services in the school setting*. Retrieved May 5, 2007, from http://www.nasponline.org.

Oakland, T. (2005). Commentary #1: What is multicultural school psychology? In C. L. Frisby & C. R. Reynolds (Eds.), *Comprehensive handbook of multicultural school psychology* (pp. 3–13). Hoboken, NJ: Wiley.

Ortiz, S. (2005). Best practices in nondiscriminatory assessment. In A. Thomas & J. Grimes (Eds.), *Best practices in school psychology IV*. Washington, DC: National Association of School Psychologists.

Parham, T., & Helms, J. (1985). Attitudes of racial identity and self-esteem of black students: An exploratory investigation. *Journal of College Student Personnel, 26*(2), 143–147.

Ponterotto, J. G., & Casas, J. M. (1991). *Handbook of racial/ethnic minority counseling research*. Springfield, IL: Charles C. Thomas.

Rodriguez, C. (2000). Culturally sensitive psychological assessment. In I. A. Canino & J. Spurlock (Eds.), *Culturally diverse children and adolescents: Assessments, diagnosis, and treatment* (pp. 84–102). New York: The Guilford Press.

Rogers, M. R., & Lopez, C. (2002). Identifying critical cross-cultural school psychology competencies. *Journal of School Psychology, 40*(2), 115–141.

Rogers, M. R., Ponterotto, J. G., Conoley, J. C., & Wiese, M. J. (1992). Multicultural training in school psychology: A national survey. *School Psychology Review, 21*, 603–616.

Rogers, R. (2002). Psychoeducational assessment of culturally and linguistically diverse children and youth. In H.B. Vance (Ed.), *Psychological assessment of children : Best practices for school and clinical settings*. (2nd ed. pp. 355–384). New York: John Wiley & Sons.

The Truth About Educating Differences. (2007, June 3). *The San Diego Union Tribune*, p. C13.

Sandoval, J. (2003). Constructing conceptual change in consultee-centered consultation. *Journal of Educational and Psychological Consultation, 14*, 251–261.

Shuttleworth-Edwards, A. B., Donnelly, M., Reid, I., & Radloff, S. E. (2004). A cross cultural study with culture fair normative indications on WAIS-III digit symbol – incidental learning. *Journal of Clinical and Experimental Neuropsychology, 26*(7), 921–932.

Sue, D. W., & Sue, D. (1990). *Counseling the culturally different: Theory and practice* (2nd ed.). New York: Wiley.

Thao, P. (2005). Cultural variation within Southeast Asian American families. In C. L. Frisby & C. R. Reynolds (Eds.), *Comprehensive handbook of multicultural school psychology* (pp. 173–204). Hoboken, NJ: Wiley.

Tomes, Y. (2004). Cognitive style, achievement, and ethnicity: A study in higher education. *Dissertation Abstracts International, 66*(01). (UMI No. 3161498)

Tomes, Y. (2008). Ethnicity, cognitive style, and math achievement: Variability within post-secondary students. *Multicultural Perspectives, 10*(1), 17–23

Tarver Behring, S., & Ingraham, C. L. (1998). Culture as a central component of consultation: A call to the field. *Journal of Educational and Psychological Consultation, 9*, 57–72.

U.S. Census Bureau. (2003). Retrieved June 15, 2007, from http://www.census.gov/population.

United States Department of Education. (2007). Retrieved June 15, 2007, from http://www.ed.gov.

Walker, S., Saravanabhavan, R. C., Williams, V., Brown, O., & West, T. (1996). *An examination of the impact of federally supported community services and educational systems on underserved people with disabilities from diverse cultural populations*. Unpublished manuscript, Howard University Research and Training Center for Access to Rehabilitation and Economic Opportunity, Washington, DC.

Chapter 4
Managing Your Professional Practice as a School Psychologist

Barbara A. Fischetti

Introduction

The newly minted school psychologist enters the profession with a diverse array of skills and expectations. To get to this point in their career, they have succeeded in completing a difficult school psychology training program and a full year internship. The goal for many beginning school psychologists is to acquire fulfilling employment that will expect them to use their varied school psychology skills and to help children, adolescents, and families. Additionally, school psychologists look to school districts to provide them the opportunity to hone their professional skills as well as to update and acquire new skills as required for their individual development and as needed by the children and families in their place of employment. For many school psychologists, managing the expectations of their employment in concert with the ongoing skill development can be a challenge. This challenge has been noted to make new school psychologists most vulnerable to daily job-related stressors (Huebner & Mills, 1997).

The way school psychologists manage their professional practice on both individual and system levels may enhance services for children and families as well as lead to greater job satisfaction. Huebner, Gilligan, and Cobb (2002) noted four organizational approaches that encourage professional resiliency and job satisfaction. These included good supervision opportunities, formal peer support groups, minimal role conflict, clear delineation of roles and responsibilities, and avoidance of role overload. Additionally, they stressed the importance of the school psychologist's role in the prevention and management of their practice as a professional. School psychologists must consider managing their professional practice as part of their daily job requirements.

In general, a school psychologist faces three areas for maintaining professional practice on an individual and relatively regular basis. These include a professional portfolio, a school-based file, and professional development. On an individual level, the newly trained school psychologist needs to manage the following in their employment system: a job description, a job evaluation, and role and function expectations. Finally, the practicing school psychologist needs to address state and national trends that effect day-to-day management issues. The complexity of managing a school psychology career and employment can be overwhelming for the early career professional. It is

B.A. Fischetti (✉)
Westport Public Schools, Pupil Services Administration, 72 North Avenue, Westport, CT 06880, USA
e-mail: bfischetti@westport.k12.ct.us

clear that each of the management issues for the school psychologist overlaps and impacts each other. The present chapter will offer suggestions and recommendations that may assist the beginning school psychologist in having a productive, and satisfying career; one that may impact the field of school psychology, both directly and indirectly, and thus provide students and families effective state-of-the-art services.

Individual Management Practice

Professional Portfolio

During the course of a school psychology training program, a school psychologist develops a professional portfolio which generally includes a resume or curriculum vita, psychological report samples, recommendations, a professional philosophy statement, and other relevant information. Crespi, Fischetti, and Gill Lopez (1998) provided a guide for professional employment preparation. They noted that this area in school psychology training is generally lacking and can be critical for hiring and matching school district needs with a school psychologist's skills and development. Upon employment, the school psychologist should continue to add to the professional portfolio, since its maintenance is critical to managing future professional practice.

Living Resume/Curriculum Vita

A school psychologist develops a resume or curriculum vita during the school psychology training program. This document summarizes the psychologist's training and experiences and assists him/her in becoming gainfully employed by a school system. After hiring, it becomes critically important for a school psychologist to continue updating this document. The current accessibility of computers for school psychologists assists in maintaining a living resume. Presentations, publications, new training experiences, volunteer activities, awards, and other related information should be added to the resume. In this way, school psychologists maintain a personal history of their training and experiences.

School-Based File

During each employed school year, a school psychologist should keep a file that contains events of the school year. Letters from parents and administrators should be placed in this file. Additionally, observations and evaluations of school psychologist practice should be housed here. It is also helpful to keep presentation announcements, copies of articles, or any published materials in this file. Continuing professional development documents may also be placed in the school-based file. A record of supervision activities and session summaries should be kept in this file as well. At the end of the school year, this file should be reviewed and relevant material can be placed in the professional portfolio. School-based files are helpful to share with administrators to summarize accomplishments during the school year and for program planning for the upcoming school year.

Additionally, this information kept in the school-based file is critical if the school psychologist makes the decision to seek other employment.

Professional Development/Supervision

The need for ongoing professional development is a clear expectation for all school psychologists. The National Association of School Psychologists (NASP) as well as the American Psychological Association (APA) support and approve continuing education activities for professionals. The NASP Principles of Professional Ethics located in the Professional Conduct Manual (2000c) delineates the following:

> School Psychologists engage in continuing professional development. They remain current regarding developments in research, training, and professional practices that benefit children, families, and schools. (p.16)

Practicing school psychologists must, therefore, ensure that they plan useful and effective professional development opportunities. Both national associations do not quantify the continuing education requirement. Although for those nationally certified by NASP, 75 h of continuing professional development activities are required for a 3-year period (National Association of School Psychologist, 2003). Additionally, school psychologists should review both state and Department of Public Health requirements for continuing education activities.

Therefore, it is incumbent upon the practicing school psychologist to develop and plan for activities to continue their professional growth and development. School psychologists can attend local, state, and national workshops and in-service trainings to continue their professional development. School systems, at times, find it difficult to fund such activities and the practicing school psychologist may be faced with these expenditures. Additionally, school psychologists can join state and national associations for opportunities to remain current in the field by having access to other school psychologists, professional development activities and written materials such as books, newsletters, and journals. A recent workgroup of APA (Elman, Illfelder-Kaye, & Robiner, 2005) emphasized the outcome of professional development to be professionalism which includes interpersonal functioning and thinking like a psychologist.

Brown (2002) noted that professional development is a requisite for practicing school psychologists. According to Brown, best practice dictates that school psychologists need to engage in planned continuing professional development activities. Professional development activities should take into account the individual's previous training and needs as well as current position demands and future career aspirations. Professional development can be useful for addressing both individual practice issues and organizational changes.

School psychologists can also meet their need for professional development through an active supervision plan. The Guidelines for the Provision of School Psychological Services (National Association of School Psychologists, 2000b) outlines the importance of supervision for both an individual and a school psychology services unit. Unit Guideline 5: Supervision states the following:

> The school psychological services unit ensures that all personnel have levels and types of supervision adequate to ensure the provision of effective and accountable services. Supervision is provided through an ongoing, positive, systematic, collaborative process between the school psychologist and a school psychology supervisor. This process focuses on promoting professional growth and exemplary professional practice leading to improved performance by all concerned including a school psychologist, supervisor, students, and the entire school community. (p. 56)

The unit guidelines further delineate the role of the supervisor of psychological services and the amount of supervision required for school psychologists and school psychology interns. When required, NASP 2000b, 2000c indicates that a minimum of 2 h per week of supervision be made available for full-time employed school psychologists. NASP also emphasizes that supervision or peer review should be available throughout the career of a school psychologist. The American Psychological Association (1981) also requires the provision of appropriate supervision for school psychologists. The Specialty Guidelines for the Delivery of Services by School Psychologists (American Psychological Association) advocates that a professional school psychologist supervise a specialist in school psychology, and defines the supervision as:

> an appropriate number of hours per week are devoted to direct face-to-face supervision of each full-time school psychological service staff member. In no event is this supervision less than one hour per week for each staff member. The more comprehensive the psychological services are, the more supervision is needed. A plan for relating increased amounts of supervisory time to the complexity of professional responsibilities is to be developed. The amount and nature of supervision is specified in writing to all parties concerned. (p. 674)

Supervision literature (Hunley, Curtis, & Batsche, 2002; Crespi & Fischetti, 1997; Harvey & Struzziero, 2000) has noted the importance of this activity for school psychologists. Supervision studies (Fischetti & Crespi, 1999; Chafouleas, Clonan, & Vanuaken, 2002) have highlighted the critical lack of supervision available to practicing professionals. The importance of maturing as a professional school psychologist requires the development of a supervision plan with respective employers. It becomes critically important to think outside the box in this area. In the best situation and consistent with National Association of School Psychologists, 2000b, 2000c recommendations, a school psychologist would be supervised by a practicing school psychologist who can help him/her develop an individual and system supervision plan. In instances where this is unavailable, school psychologists need to consider viable alternatives (Fischetti & Lines, 2003), such as peer mentoring, state consultants, neighboring district supervisors, part-time supervisors, contracted supervisors, and cyber mentoring.

A supervision plan should include goals, session schedules, supervision format, supervision techniques, methods for assessing progress, and an evaluation process. Harvey and Struzziero (2000) noted that a written supervision plan is the most important supervision strategy. For doctoral level school psychologists interested in meeting post-doctoral supervision requirements for credentialing as a licensed psychologist, a written supervision plan with a licensed psychologist, the clinical supervisor in a school setting, can assist them in meeting the Department of Public Health requirements. Fischetti and Mortati (1998) shared a successful school-based option for meeting Department of Public Health licensing requirements. The school-based option included weekly individual face-to-face individual supervision, monthly group supervision, professional development training, and the development of an individual professional growth and skill enhancement plan. Activities of supervision included review of psychological reports, complex diagnostic cases, individual and group counseling cases; intervention strategies for students and families; and ethics and professional practice issues.

After a practicing school psychologist successfully navigates individual management practice issues, it is important to begin the process of managing school system practices. For the newly minted school psychologist, this process can be daunting. It is critically important to a school psychologist's career to manage school system practices actively. Additionally, school system practices can also impact local, state, and national school psychology practices. As noted by Fagan and Wise (2000), the strongest determinants of role and function for a school psychologist are local. Although treated as separate entities in this chapter, individual and system management issues may and often do occur simultaneously. The successful school psychologist navigates the interplay of these practice issues.

System Management Practices

School psychologists enter a system and often find themselves unsure of their position's role and function as well as system management practices. The school psychologist should first ask for a job description and a description of the position's evaluation process to clarify the employer's expectations. Questions such as these should be asked of the employer prior to accepting the position. Crespi et al. (1998) noted the importance of interviewing prospective employment opportunities to assist in establishing oneself as a professional school psychologist. In instances where a job description is not available, the school psychologist should work with the system to develop a description and evaluation process relevant to the system and professional standards for school psychologists.

If the employing system has an evaluation process for teachers, it is helpful to develop comparable job standards and an evaluation process for school psychologists. If not, the school psychologist should look to national associations, state education departments, and their state school psychology and psychology associations for assistance. In 1993, the Connecticut State Department of Education developed competencies and indicators for performance evaluation of pupil services specialists (Connecticut State Department of Education, 1993). A companion document, *Developing Quality Programs for Pupil Services: A Self-Evaluative Guide* (Connecticut State Department of Education, 1999), was designed to assist school districts with evaluating and enhancing pupil services programs. It is important to note that practicing school psychologists, state education staff, university trainers, and school district personnel developed these documents.

In the Connecticut documents, pupil services specialists include counseling, nursing, school psychology, school social work, and speech language pathology positions. Of considerable importance to the profession of school psychology was the task force recommendation that pupil services specialists should receive supervision and evaluation of their clinical practice by personnel of the same discipline. If this was not available, it was recommended that supervision and evaluation of school psychologists by non-school psychologists only occur on non-clinical indicators.

In order to begin the process of developing a job description and an evaluation process, it is important to review the Domains of School Psychology Training and Practice found in the Standards for Training and Field Placement Programs in School Psychology (National Association of School Psychologists, 2000a). School psychology graduates are expected to demonstrate at least entry-level competency in each of 11 domains of practice. These domains include data-based decision making and accountability; consultation and collaboration; effective instruction and development of cognitive/academic skills; socialization and development of life skills; student diversity in development and learning; school and systems organization, policy development, and climate; prevention, crisis intervention, and mental health; home/school/community collaboration; research and program evaluation; school psychology practice and development; and information technology. Further discussion of the domains of school psychology practice can be found in the NASP publication entitled: *School Psychology: A Blueprint for Training and Practice II* (Ysseldyke, Dawson, Lehr, Reschly, Reynolds, et al., 1997). This document was recently updated, *School Psychology: A Blueprint for Training and Practice III* (Ysseldyke, Burns, Dawson, Kelley, Morrison, et al., 2006), to add to the discussion of practice and training in school psychology. It is important for the professional school psychologist and school systems to revise and add to the domains based on the school system's and practicing school psychologist's expectations.

Harvey and Struzziero (2000) provided a Job Description-Based Individual Performance Evaluation Form which covered communication skills, consultation skills, assessment skills,

direct services, developing programs, maintaining professional skills, and demonstrating accountability. The importance of having a systemic model of evaluation that addresses individual
performance evaluation from vision to evaluation was emphasized. Harvey and Struzziero (2000)
noted:

> Performance evaluations serve three fundamental purposes. They assess and recognize quality of service,
> guide future professional development, and provide direction for future practice. (p. 94)

A local school district example of school psychology job standards can be located in Appendix 4.1.
The Westport Public Schools are located in Westport, Connecticut, and serve 5,500 students across
eight buildings. The standards were developed as part of a Professional Development and
Evaluation Plan for the Westport (CT) Public Schools' teachers and address an evaluation process
for the beginning to seasoned school psychologist. While they emphasized specific skills critical
to the functioning of school psychologists, they did so in a similar format similar to that of the
teacher standards documents. In this way, the differences between the teacher and school psychologist standards were in content and, more critically, included a clinical supervisor specifically
trained in school psychology in the formal evaluation process for school psychologists. Similar
standards were also developed for school counselors and school social workers. The evaluation
form for the non-tenured school psychologist utilized the content of the school psychologist standards and the same evaluation criteria for all school personnel. The school psychologists also
developed goal setting and observations forms consistent with school psychology standards and
mirroring the teacher forms.

The second example of an evaluation process with performance standards and criteria specific
for school psychologists is available at the Montgomery County Public Schools (2004–2005)
website. Montgomery County Public Schools located in Rockville, Maryland, serve 138,000 students and includes 199 schools. Although a much larger school system, Montgomery County has
developed school psychologist standards that are consistent with the Professional Growth System
for teachers. Similar to the Westport evaluation process, the standards of performance are linked
with the NASP domains of training and practice. The evaluation process also involves a supervisor
of psychological services specifically trained as a school psychologist.

It is helpful to the newly entering school psychologist to ask if mission, vision, and goal
statements exist for the school psychology department. If none are available, it gives the school
psychology department another opportunity to develop these for the system. The *NASP Strategic
Plan* (National Association of School Psychologists, 2002) identified the mission, values, and key
areas of work for school psychologists. The NASP mission statement noted:

> The National Association of School Psychologists represents and supports school psychology through leader-
> ship to enhance the mental health and educational competence of all children. (p. 1)

This mission statement may be too broad for a local educational system. It is important that the
local school psychologists develop a mission statement that best fits the needs of their children
and families and maximizes the role and function of school psychologists in their specific system.
A local school system's mission statement is located in Appendix 4.2. The pupil services department mission statement was consistent with the school system's mission. Additionally, role and
functions of a pupil services department are located in Appendix 4.3. A particular strength to these
documents is the diversity of services offered by school psychologists and their availability to all
children without the need for special education identification.

School psychologists need to deliver services as outlined by their role and function definitions
in concert with system expectations. These services are defined by the job standards and mission
of the department and school system. Critical to successful management practice is involvement
in district committees and staff trainings. Volunteering to conduct workshops (on suicide prevention, for example) for staff and becoming a member of the job standards development committee

are two ways to help the school district. High visibility is critical to a school psychology unit and may assist in generating support for the school psychology department, help with role expansion efforts, and provide support for professional development activities (Franklin & Duley, 2002). Helping others understand the role of the school psychologist not only helps the department but also generates support for school psychological services for all students and families.

State and National Management Practices

Effective school psychology practice management requires involvement in state and national school psychology venues. Newly minted school psychologists usually begin this process by joining state and national associations. On a national level for school psychologists, this includes NASP, www.nasponline.org, and APA, www.apa.org. In most states, there is an affiliate of NASP and APA. These organizations provide the beginning school psychologist with access to the latest school psychology and psychology practice information. Additionally, it is helpful for school psychologists to begin the process of becoming a part of the governing body of the state and national associations. This is especially effective for networking with other practicing school psychologists. More importantly, it provides the school psychologist the opportunity to impact the profession on a state and national level.

In the best of circumstances, school psychology associations should be connected to state departments of education. This link is crucial to help manage practice issues on a state and local level. For example, Connecticut has a viable link between the state association and the state education department. As a point of fact, the state continues to employ a state consultant for school psychology. This important relationship has resulted in school psychologists being invited to many state-level committees to represent the role and function of school psychologists. In a basic way, it has opened doors for practice issues.

An example of the collaborative relationship between the Connecticut Association of School Psychologists and the Connecticut State Department of Education is the annual New School Psychologists Orientation. This co-sponsored activity introduces new school psychologists to the field of school psychology in Connecticut. A recent publication, *Guidelines for the Practice of School Psychology* (2004), explained the many ways school psychologists can support students' academic learning and social–emotional development. The goal of this document was to help educators understand the full range of services provided by school psychologists. It was released by the Commissioner of Education and sent to the principal in every school building in the state. While an activity of this magnitude would be impossible for one school psychologist, the involvement of the state association with the state education department proved that state and local management practices are critical for the professional school psychologist.

On a state level, the Connecticut State Association of School Psychologists published a resource guide for school administrators. This document, *Effective Utilization of School Psychologists in Today's Educational Environment* (Desrochers & Fanelli, 2003), was designed as a reference tool for school administrators on how to maximize the service benefits that school psychologists provide in their districts. It was especially helpful to the practicing school psychologist since it addressed important topics on a state level. The content areas included the school psychologist shortage; contemporary roles and functions; supervision; Attention Deficit/Hyperactivity Disorder (ADHD); Lesbian, Gay & Bisexual students; high stakes testing; and fair and effective discipline. The articles within this publication were completed by state association members. This is another example of a project that could be daunting for any individual school psychologist, but the involvement of the state association made it a viable project for the field of school psychology.

While not all school psychologists have time available to run for state and national offices, there are many activities on both levels that require volunteer time. Writing articles for newsletters, stuffing envelopes for renewal applications, and visiting state and local legislators to share information about student needs and the role and function of school psychologists are necessary to assist with managing school psychology practice issues. It is critical for the profession to have its members available and willing to support its practice. A call or an e-mail to an association is often all it takes to become involved in state and national activities.

Evaluating Management Practices

The school psychologist enters the job market with many task masters and responsibilities for juggling individual, state, and national management issues. Each of these issues requires ongoing program accountability. Fagan and Wise (2000) cited five reasons for professional accountability: helping children more effectively, improving individual professional effectiveness and professional renewal, impacting district-wide practices, impacting the profession of school psychology as a whole, and, finally, ethical responsibility.

Zins (1990) noted that accountability data are an essential component of school psychological services and suggested that school psychologists focus their accountability data in two areas: consumers of psychological services and providers of psychological services. Additionally, he recommended that accountability data can be obtained from several different consumer groups and in relation to the many services offered by school psychologists. Fairchild (1980) noted that there were a range of evaluative methods from which to choose, but the choice was dependent upon the types of data being sought by the practitioner. According to Fairchild, school psychologists can utilize the following evaluation methods: tabulation, time analysis, case studies, interviews, observations, tests, expert opinions, grading scales, and questionnaires.

Many systems utilize tabulation and time analyses by having school psychologists keep a log of activities and time spent in each of the activities. Surveys of parents, teachers, administrators, and students about the effectiveness of school psychological services are another means to measure accountability of services. As Gibbons and Shinn (2002) noted, these types of accountability measures do not necessarily measure the effectiveness of the services. They recommended methods of measuring student outcome data to assist with the evaluation of school psychological services.

National Association of School Psychologists, 2000b, in the Guidelines for the Provision of School Psychological Services, noted the importance of evaluation for the individual school psychologist and for school psychological services unit. Unit Practice Guideline 1.5 states:

> School psychological service units conduct regular evaluations of the collective services provided by the unit as well as those services provided by individual practitioners. The evaluation process focuses on both the nature and extent of the services provided (process) and the student/family focused outcomes of those services (product). (p. 52)

Consistent with the individual and system practice management approach, school psychologists must make accountability an integral part of their ongoing practice.

The School Psychological Services Unit in conjunction with the individual school psychologist can proceed and begin the process of program evaluation. In the Guidelines for Evaluating School Psychological Services, Harvey (1996) provided a comprehensive approach to completing a program evaluation. These guidelines discussed the preparation for evaluation, components of a program evaluation, and shared questionnaires for use with consumers of school psychological services. Consumers of school psychological services included administrators, school psychologists, school personnel, and parents. These questionnaires were designed to answer the following evaluation questions: Are we providing quality services? How do our services compare with professional standards? Do procedures comply with local, state, and federal guidelines? How do we know if services are having an impact on students or staff? and How can school psychological services be improved? (Harvey, 1996).

Harvey and Struzziero (2000) updated the questionnaires to aid individuals and school systems in successfully completing a program evaluation. They noted that conducting a program evaluation guides professional development, documents effective practices, leads to improved performance, and provides the opportunity for professional recognition. A random sample of parents, school personnel, administrators, and other relevant consumers of school psychological services are asked to complete a questionnaire relative to school psychological services. The results of these questionnaires are tabulated, analyzed, and then shared with others. Recommendations for individual school psychology practice and for the school psychological services unit are developed and planned for the ensuing school year. Harvey (1996) also suggested additional types of data collection for program evaluation. These included interviews, file reviews, and collecting outcome and frequency data relative to activities performed by school psychologists. Finally, the author emphasized that not all evaluative questions should be included for a program evaluation.

D'Amato and Copeland (2006) utilized consumer satisfaction questionnaires to assess an alternative school psychological services model. Consistent with the recommendations of Harvey and Struzziero (2000), questionnaires were given to teachers, administrators, and support personnel. These were administered both before and after implementation of the new model. Results revealed support and positive perceptions of the new services model. Additional program evaluation components entailed time use survey and an analysis of emotional disturbance identification rates. The results of this program evaluation gave the district the information to evaluate and assist with the decision to continue the model.

Program evaluation is a critical and necessary component of school psychology practice. The practicing school psychologist and school psychology services unit must include program evaluation as an important accountability measure of services and consumer satisfaction. Innovative school psychology practice that leads to more effective services for students and families can also be measured through program evaluation. The need for program evaluation is also consistent with the recommendations of the National Association of School Psychologists, 2000b *Guidelines for the Provision of School Psychological Services* and the National Association of School Psychologists, 2000a *Standards for Training and Field Placement Programs in School Psychology.*

Future Directions

The practice of school psychology has moved from a test and place paradigm to a full service delivery model. Consumers of psychological services have demanded the shift and are asking for accountability for the full range of services. This has placed greater emphasis on the need for school psychologists to manage their practice on a local, state, and national level. Specifically, school psychologists now need to develop a service model and practice that meets the needs of children and families. This model must include accountability and evaluation measures. Likewise, the model must also lead the school psychologist and the school psychological services unit to develop and sustain professionalism. Children and their families deserve nothing less than the highest level of training and professionalism from their school psychologist and their school psychological services unit.

Appendix 1

Westport Public Schools: School Psychologist Standards

School Psychologists' knowledge, clinical skills and professional practices are primary factors that affect student achievement and social–emotional functioning. This document is intended to provide descriptive common language for school psychologists in Westport articulating the expectations for school psychologists' inputs which promote student social–emotional development and learning.

Description of Category

Data-Based Decision-Making and Accountability

- School psychologists define current problem areas, strengths, and needs (at the individual, group, and systems level) through assessment, and measure the effects of the decisions that result from the problem-solving process.

Sample Performance Indicators

The school psychologist:

- has knowledge of various models and methods of assessment that yield information useful in identifying strengths and needs, in understanding problems, and in measuring progress and accomplishments.
- uses varied models and methods as part of a systemic process to collect data and other information.
- uses varied models and methods to translate assessment results into empirically based decisions about service delivery.
- uses varied models to evaluate the outcomes of services.
- practices such that data-based decision-making permeates every aspect of professional practice.
- conducts comprehensive psychological evaluations.
- writes effective psychological reports.

Description of Category

Consultant and Collaboration

- School psychologists demonstrate the ability to listen well, participate in discussions, convey information and work together with others at an individual, group and systems level.

Sample Performance Indicators

The school psychologist:

- knows behavioral, mental health, collaborative, and/or other consultation models and methods.
- applies behavioral, mental health, collaborative, and/or consultation models and methods appropriately to particular situations.
- collaborates effectively with others in planning and decision-making processes at the individual, group, and system levels.

Description of Category

Effective Instruction and Development of Cognitive/Academic Skills

- School psychologists develop challenging but achievable cognitive and academic goals for all students, provide information about ways in which students can achieve these goals, and monitor student progress toward these goals.

Sample Performance Indicators

The school psychologist:

- understands human learning processes, techniques to assess them, and direct and indirect services applicable to the development of cognitive and academic skills.
- develops, in collaboration with others, appropriate cognitive and academic goals for children and adolescents with different abilities, disabilities, strengths, and needs.
- implements interventions, including instructional interventions and consultation, to achieve the above goals.
- evaluates the effectiveness of such interventions.

Description of Category

Socialization and Development of Life Skills

- School psychologists develop challenging but achievable behavioral, affective, counseling, or adaptive goals for all students, provide information about ways in which students can achieve these goals, and monitor student progress toward these goals.

(continued)

Sample Performance Indicators

The school psychologist:
- knows human development processes, techniques to assess these processes, and direct and indirect services applicable to the development of behavioral, affective, adaptive, and social skills.
- develops, in collaboration with others, appropriate behavioral, affective, adaptive, and social goals for children and adolescents of varying abilities, disabilities, strengths, and needs.
- implements interventions including consultation, behavioral assessment/intervention and individual, small group, and large group counseling to achieve these goals.
- evaluates the effectiveness of these interventions.

Description of Category

Diversity in Development and Learning
- School psychologists are aware of, appreciate, and work with individuals and groups with a variety of strengths and needs from a variety of racial, cultural, ethnic, experiential, and linguistic backgrounds.

Sample Performance Indicators

The school psychologist:
- knows individual differences, abilities, and disabilities and the potential influence of biological, social, cultural, ethnic, experiential, socioeconomic, gender-related, and linguistic factors in development and learning.
- demonstrates the sensitivity and skills needed to work with individuals of diverse characteristics.
- implements strategies selected and/or adapted based on individual characteristics, strengths, and needs.

Description of Category

School and System Organization, Policy Development, and Climate
- School psychologists understand the school as a system and work with individuals and groups to facilitate structure and policies that create and maintain schools as safe, caring and inviting places for members of the school community.

Sample Performance Indicators

The school psychologist:
- demonstrates knowledge of general education, special education, and other educational and related services.
- understands schools and other settings as systems.
- works with individuals and groups to facilitate policies and practices that create and maintain safe, supportive, and effective learning environments for children and adolescents.

Description of Category

Prevention, Crisis Intervention, and Mental Health
- School psychologists have knowledge of child development and psychopathology in order to develop and implement prevention and intervention programs for students with a wide range of needs and disorders.

Sample Performance Indicators

The school psychologist:
- understands human development, psychopathology, and the associated biological, cultural, and social influences on human behavior.
- provides or contributes to prevention programs that promote the mental health and physical well-being of children and adolescents.
- provides or contributes to intervention programs that promote the mental health and physical well-being of children and adolescents.

Description of Category

Home/School/Community Collaboration
- School psychologists have knowledge of family influences that affect students' wellness, learning, and achievement and form partnerships between parents, educators, and the community.

Sample Performance Indicators

The school psychologist:
- demonstrates knowledge of family systems, including family strengths and influences on child and adolescent development, learning, and behavior, and of methods to involve families in education and service delivery.
- works effectively with families, educators, and others in the community to promote and provide comprehensive services to children, adolescents, and families.

(continued)

Appendix 1 (continued)

Description of Category

Research and Program Evaluation
- School psychologists know current literature on various aspects of education and child development, translate research into practice, and understand research design and statistics in sufficient depth to conduct investigations relevant to their own work and for their district.

Sample Performance Indicators

The school psychologist:
- demonstrates knowledge of research, statistics, and evaluation methods.
- evaluates research studies and translates research into practice.
- understands research design and statistics in sufficient depth to plan and conduct investigations and program evaluations for improvement of services.

Description of Category

School Psychology Practice and Professional Development
- School psychologists take responsibility for developing as professionals and practice in ways which meet all appropriate ethical, professional, and legal standards to enhance the quality of services, and to protect the rights of all parties.

Sample Performance Indicators

The school psychologist:
- demonstrates knowledge of the history and foundations of the profession; of various service models and methods; of public policy development applicable to services to children, adolescents, and families; and of ethical, professional, and legal standards.
- practices in ways that are consistent with applicable ethical and professional standards.
- is involved in the profession.
- has the knowledge and skills needed to acquire career-long professional development.
- has knowledge of, access to, evaluates, and utilizes information sources and technology in ways that safeguard and enhance the quality of school psychological services.
- is committed to his or her professional growth and contributes to the continuous improvement of the school, district, and profession.
- participates in the Professional Development and Evaluation Plan goal-setting process – collaboratively working with his/her administrator(s) to select a goal which focuses on the improvement of student learning and social emotional development.
- implements strategies to support student achievement and social–emotional development associated with the Professional Development and Evaluation Plan goal.
- analyzes the success of efforts undertaken during the Professional Development and Evaluation Plan goal process in terms of the impact on student achievement and social–emotional development.
- continuously reflects upon his/her practice in relation to the impact on student learning and social–emotional development and utilizes feedback from sources including colleagues, administrators, and students to continuously improve professional practice.
- pursues opportunities to increase school psychology skills as well as contributing to the profession through ongoing professional development. Examples of professional growth activities include (but are not limited to):
  - reviewing current research and using it as a foundation for planning delivery of school psychological services.
  - interacting with colleagues to discuss and reflect upon a specific aspect of school psychology practice, including participating in a peer-reflective conversations.
  - participating in a study group on a topic that is central to the craft of school psychology and has the potential to improve the achievement and social–emotional development of students.
  - leading or facilitating a workshop or course.
  - participating in curriculum reviews.
  - engaging in school improvement dialogues.
  - participating in clinical supervision on an individual and group level.

Appendix 2

Westport Public Schools: Pupil Services Mission Statement

The Westport Public Schools' goal is to help students acquire the attributes necessary to be successful in the complex and rapidly changing world. To this end, the counseling, social work and psychological services provided by the Westport Pupil Services staff support children in the learning process and assist them in the development of their maximum potential as emotionally healthy, socially competent, productive members of society. All students in the Westport Public Schools, Pre-K-12, have access to comprehensive pupil services.

All children can learn. Every child has their own unique learning style which should be recognized and fostered. Pupil Services staff work collaboratively with students, parents, teachers and the community to understand learning and social–emotional processes in order to maximize each student's potential.

The Westport School System has made a commitment to provide programs and services that includes developmental counseling, consultation, staff development, early intervention, and prevention, crisis intervention, systemic consultation/intervention and referral to community agencies and services. This is a shared partnership amongst Pupil Services, parents, teachers and the community.

Appendix 3

Westport Public Schools: Pupil Services Roles and Functions

Definition of Terms

The following definitions describe the range of Pupil Services provided within the schools. They describe interrelated services, which include direct and indirect services to students and their families. These definitions specify a range of services, which implies significant collaboration amongst pupil services, administrative, instructional, and non-instructional staff.

Developmental Counseling

A systematic, ongoing, developmental program for all students, which provides an opportunity for counseling with students and parents dealing with:

a. Academic growth
b. Personal/Social growth
c. Self-awareness
d. Career planning
e. Problem resolution
f. Family counseling
g. Early identification and prevention
h. Consultation

Prevention

Individual or group programs to help students anticipate and/or avoid problems, which might interfere with their education. Activities which might be utilized as preventative include:

a. Educational programs directed toward the prevention of specific problems
b. Community and parent outreach
c. Parenting programs
d. Consultation
e. Staff development
f. Curriculum development
g. Peer group counseling
h. Individual/Group counseling
i. Developmental guidance
j. Social skills development

Early Intervention

Early identification and assessment of problems, which result in programs, or individual interventions, which are designed to eliminate or reduce the problem(s) at its inception. Examples of activities in this category are:

a. Early Intervention Process/Student Support Team/Student Assistance Team
b. Referral to other agencies or individuals
c. Periodic monitoring of student progress:

   – observation based assessment
   – report cards
   – interim report
   – attendance records
   – standardized test scores
   – disciplinary records
   – curriculum based assessment

d. Psychological assessment as necessary, which may include:

   – cognitive functioning
   – behavior assessment
   – executive function, attention
   – processing abilities
   – memory
   – academic screening
   – fine and gross motor skills
   – social/emotional status

e. Mentoring programs
f. Correct educational placements
g. Consultation for appropriate instruction and management
h. Development guidance on specific topics

Problem-Centered Counseling

a. Identification and assessment of problem
b. Goal setting
c. Development and implementation of strategies

  - behavior management
  - individual counseling
  - group counseling
  - family counseling
  - parent education
  - consultation
  - mobilization of appropriate resources

d. Evaluation of results
e. Reformulation of strategy, if indicated
f. Referral to other staff or community agency/practitioner

Consultation

A collaborative process in which teachers, administrators and parents work with pupil services consultants to identify and develop strategies to ameliorate problems by bridging the knowledge gap between the mental health field and the consultee. There are specific steps in consultation, which are as follows:

a. Establishment of a consultation agreement between consultant and consultee
b. Identification of problem
c. Gather data
d. Statement of problem
e. Intervention strategies
f. Measure progress
g. Evaluate and reformulate strategies as necessary

Professional Development

Pupil Services staff have a major role to present and participate in professional development for all staff where they have expertise. The use of professional development programs can serve to initiate, implement, or supplement programs for positive emotional health of students and staff.

Crisis Intervention

A planned strategic response to relieve immediate distress of students with the goal of short-term reduction of stress and follow-up planning and referral where necessary. Focus may be on the individual or a group of students. Activities, which are included in this process, are:

a. Catharsis
b. Problem identification
c. Conflict resolution

d. Parent involvement
e. Mediation
f. Advocacy
g. Monitoring and follow-up
h. Consultation
i. Referral to other resources
j. Staff involvement

Referral to Community Agencies and Services

Referrals to outside resources involves a planned process which utilizes the expertise of the pupil services staff to deal with complex issues of identification, awareness, motivation and follow-through. The necessary steps to effect a referral successfully are as follows:

a. Identification and assessment of problem
b. Develop acceptance of need for referral
c. Identify resources appropriate for referral
d. Insure necessary contact with referral resource
e. Provide follow-up to ensure referral has been accomplished

Provide liaison and consultation between school and referral resource.

Chapter Competency Checklist

DOMAIN 1 – Professional, legal ethical and social responsibility domain

Foundational	Functional
Understand and explain the following:	Gain practice:
□ Rationale for managing professional development	□ Developing a plan for supervision
□ Professional portfolio	□ Describing the system dynamics in which you work
□ School-based file	□ Articulating questions about the system in which you work
□ Professional development	□ Discussing system dynamics with your supervisor and colleagues
□ Supervision plan	□ Setting goals for professional development
□ Ethical guidelines	□ Monitoring professional goals
□ System management practices	□ Attending professional conferences
□ Job description	□ Joining professional organizations
□ Performance Evaluation	
□ State and national management practices	
□ Legal regulations	

References

American Psychological Association. (1981). Specialty guidelines for the delivery of services by school psychologists. *American Psychologist,* 670–681.

Brown, M. (2002). Best practices in professional development. In A. Thomas & J. Grimes (Eds.), *Best practices in school psychology IV* (pp. 183–194). Bethesda, MD: National Association of School Psychologists.

Chafouleas, S. M., Clonan, S. M., & Vanuaken, T. L. (2002). A national survey of current supervision and evaluation practices of school psychologists. *Psychology in the Schools, 39*(3), 317–325.

Connecticut State Department of Education. (1993). *Evaluating pupil services specialists: A report by the state committee for evaluation of pupil services specialists.* Hartford, CT: Author.

Connecticut State Department of Education. (1999). *Developing quality programs for pupil services: A self-evaluative guide*. Hartford, CT: Author.

Connecticut State Department of Education. (2004). *Guidelines for the practice of school psychology*. Hartford, CT: Author.

Crespi, T. D., & Fischetti, B. A. (1997). Clinical supervision of school psychologists: Bridging theory and practice. *School Psychology International, 18*(1), 41–48.

Crespi, T. D., Fischetti, B. A., & Gill Lopez, P. (1998). Supervision and mentoring for professional employment: Resumes and interviewing for prospective school psychologists. *School Psychology International, 19*, 239–250.

D'Amato, R. C., & Copeland, E. P. (2006). Integrated psychological services in the Greeley-Evans Public Schools. *School Psychology Quarterly, 21*(4), 445–467.

Desrochers, J. E., & Fanelli, R. (Eds.). (2003). *Effective utilization of school psychologists in today's educational environment*. Hartford, CT: Connecticut Association of School Psychologists.

Elman, N. S., Illfelder-Kaye, J., & Robiner, W. N. (2005). Professional development: Training for professionalism as a foundation for competent practice in psychology. *Professional Psychology: Research and Practice, 36*(4), 367–375.

Fagan, T. K., & Wise, P. S. (2000). *School psychology: Past, present, and future* (2nd ed.). Bethesda, MD: National Association of School Psychologists.

Fairchild, T. N. (1980). STEPPS: A model for the evaluation of school psychological services. *School Psychology Review, 9*(3), 252–258.

Fischetti, B. A., & Crespi, T. D. (1999). Clinical supervision for school psychologists: National practices, trends and future implications. *School Psychology International, 20*(3), 278–288.

Fischetti, B. A., & Lines, C. L. (2003). Views from the field: Models for school-based clinical supervision. *The Clinical Supervisor, 22*(1), 75–86.

Fischetti, B. A., & Mortati, A. L. (1998). Post-doctoral school-based clinical supervision:A training model for credentialing as a licensed psychologist. *The School Psychologist, 52*(4), 120–121.

Franklin, M., & Duley, S. M. (2002). Best practices in planning school psychology service delivery: An update. In A. Thomas & J. Grimes (Eds.), *Best practices in school psychology IV* (pp. 145–158). Bethesda, MD: National Association of School Psychologists.

Gibbons, K. A., & Shinn, M. M. (2002). Best practices in evaluating psychoeducational services based on student outcome data. In A. Thomas & J. Grimes (Eds.), *Best practices in school psychology IV* (pp. 265–279). Bethesda, MD: National Association of School Psychologists.

Harvey, V. S. (1996). *Guidelines for evaluating school psychological services (Revised)*. Bethesda, MD: National Association of School Psychologists.

Harvey, V. S., & Struzziero, J. (2000). *Effective supervision in school psychology*. Bethesda, MD: National Association of School Psychologists.

Huebner, E. S., & Mills, L. (1997). Another look at occupational stressors among school psychologists. *School Psychology International, 18*, 359–374.

Huebner, E. S., Gilligan, D. G., & Cobb, H. (2002). Best practice in preventing and managing stress and burnout. In A. Thomas & J. Grimes (Eds.), *Best practices in school psychology IV* (pp. 173–182). Bethesda, MD: National Association fo School Psychologists.

Hunley, S. A., Curtis, M. J., & Batsche, G. (2002). Best practices in supervision of school psychological services. In A. Thomas & J. Grimes (Eds.), *Best practices in school psychology IV* (pp. 103–114). Bethesda, MD: National Association of School Psychologists.

Montgomery County Public Schools. (2004–2005). *Psychologist evaluation instrument: Performance standards, performance criteria, and descriptive examples*. Retrieved March 18, 2007 from http://www.montgomery-schoolsmd.org/departments/development/documents/skillful/psychologist-final.pdf.

National Association of School Psychologists. (2000a). *Standards for training and field placement programs in school psychology*. Bethesda, MD: Author.

National Association of School Psychologists. (2000b). *Guidelines for the provision of school psychological services*. Bethesda, MD: Author.

National Association of School Psychologists. (2000c). *Professional conduct manual*. Bethesda, MD: Author.

National Association of School Psychologists. (2002). NASP Strategic Plan. Retrieved March 11, 2007 from http://www.nasponline.org/about_nasp/strategicplan.pdf.

National Association of School Psychologists. (2003). *NCSP renewal guidelines*. Bethsda, MD: Author.

Ysseldyke, J., Burns, M., Dawson, P., Kelley, B., Morrison, D., & Ortiz, S. (2006). *School psychology: A blueprint for training and practice III*. Bethesda, MD: National Association of School Psychologists.

Ysseldyke, J. E., Dawson, P., Lehr, C., Reschly, D., Reynolds, M., & Telzrow, C. (1997). *School psychology: A blueprint for training and practice II*. Bethesda, MD: National Association of School Psychologists.

Zins, J. E. (1990). Best practices in developing accountability procedures. In A. Thomas & J. Grimes (Eds.), *Best practices in school psychology II* (pp. 323–337). Washington, DC: National Association of School Psychologists.

Chapter 5
Consulting with Families, Schools, and Communities

Edward P. Snyder, Kim Quirk, and Frank Dematteo

Introduction

The purpose of this chapter is to provide an overview of consultation and collaboration in schools by school psychologists. Specifically, we review models of consultation that are relevant for school psychology and special education. We take a practical approach and examine consultation as it occurs in school settings. We highlight best practices but remain committed to providing a realistic look at current practices in schools. In this light, we describe problem-solving consultation focusing on interventions for academic and behavioral concerns and consultation when focusing on special education eligibility. The importance of collaboration and interpersonal skills for developing and maintaining working relationships are made clear in the discussion and case study. The case study provides a pragmatic example of how school psychologists collaborate with many different constituents and use different models of consultation depending on the needs of the school and students. Suggestions for developing professional competencies are provided and implications for future consultation and collaboration practices are described.

Consultation Overview

There is not one universally agreed-upon definition of consultation, though consultation has historically been defined as a problem-solving process between a professional and one or more consultees who provide professional services to a client (Gutkin & Curtis, 1999). Kratochwill and Pittman (2002) point out that indirect service to the client has been the primary identifying characteristic of consultation research, theory, and practice. That is, for a school psychologist providing consultation services to a teacher, the school psychologist is indirectly providing services to a student who is the client. According to Brown, Pryzwansky, and Schulte (2001), the earliest forms of consultation can be traced back to Lightner Witmer's work in the 1920s – Lightner Witmer is considered the father of school psychology. Other early forms of consultation are Lewin's field theory in 1951, Caplan's 1970 work in mental health consultation and Kratochwill and Bergan's behavioral consultation in 1990. West and Idol (1987) identified ten different consultation models:

E.P. Snyder (✉)
Department of Professional Studies, Edinboro University of Pennsylvania,
Butterfield Hall 114, Edinboro, PA 16444, USA
e-mail: esnyder@edinboro.edu

T.M. Lionetti et al. (eds.), *A Practical Guide to Building Professional Competencies in School Psychology*,
DOI 10.1007/978-1-4419-6257-7_5, © Springer Science+Business Media, LLC 2011

mental health, behavioral, organizational, human relations, organizational thinking, advocacy, process, clinical, program, education/training, and collaborative. There are other models of consultation that have been proposed; however, Kratochwill and Bergan (1990) identified three major models of consultation that are most often used in schools: mental health consultation, behavioral consultation, and organizational consultation.

Mental Health Consultation

Within mental health consultation, there are four primary models: client-centered case consultation, consultee-centered case consultation, program-centered administrative consultation, and consultee-centered administrative (Brown et al., 2001). Caplan (1970) is credited with delineating these models. Client-centered case consultation is used by mental health professionals. The consultant functions as a specialist, who assesses the client, arrives at a diagnosis, and makes recommendations concerning how the consultee might modify his or her dealings with the client (Brown et al., 2001). Examples of this type of consultation might include instances when a school psychologist is asked by a teacher to assess a student who is having academic difficulty. The consultant provides insight regarding the child's difficulty and suggests instructional approaches to help the client. Included in this approach to meeting the child's needs would be suggestions for instructional and behavioral intervention and diagnosis of a disability for special education eligibility. This type of special education consultation has been the traditional work of school psychologists since the inception of special education services.

Special education eligibility consultation parallels client-centered case consultation. Brown et al. (2001) point out the primary goal of client-centered case consultation is the development of a plan for dealing with the client's difficulties. Education or skills development of the consultee is a secondary concern. Direct assessment of the client often includes formal assessment techniques such as psychological or educational tests or clinical interviews. The focus of the assessment is on providing usable information to the consultee. Implementation of the consultant's recommendations is the responsibility of the consultee. Brown et al. point out, with this model, the consultant may meet with a teacher to discuss recommendations following the assessment and later to check on the progress of the client, which provides the consultant with a general idea of the accuracy of the diagnosis and usefulness of the recommendations. With special education eligibility consultation, the school psychologist meets with the multidisciplinary team to discuss recommendations for assisting the student, including eligibility for special education services. The school psychologist may or may not continue to consult with the individual education program (IEP) planning team depending on the state and system in which the psychologist works.

A major part of special education eligibility consultation is the identification or classification of a child with a disability. In fact, by law, students do not receive access to special education services if they do not have a disability. School psychologists have long been the specialists entrusted to help schools and families make these difficult decisions. Clearly, disability classification (diagnosis) is a critical part of the work many school psychologists perform each day. Surveys of school psychologists have revealed that they spend more than two-thirds of their work in special education eligibility determination services.

The traditional assessment for special education eligibility consultation service delivered by school psychologists has been criticized. Reschly and Ysseldyke (2002) point out several limitations of this model especially when diagnosing children with learning disabilities. One point they make is that there is disagreement over the definition of what a learning disability is. A second point they make is that some assessment techniques for identifying learning disabilities are often not directly linked to remediating academic deficits (e.g., intelligence tests). A third point is that the diagnostic approach to psychological assessment largely focuses on identifying student deficits rather than enhancing competencies. Despite these criticisms, special education eligibility consultation model of service delivery continues to be used by school psychologists because of the influence of Individuals with Disabilities Education Act (IDEA) in schools. Kauffman (2007) points out that legal models influence special education services. He describes that special education is largely impacted by legal conceptual thinking. Throughout IDEA, the legal influence is obvious. One only has to examine IDEA due process procedures to realize how legal regulations drive special education consultation practices.

Behavioral Consultation

The influence of behavioral practices in consultation is growing. There are several different models of consultation closely related to behavioral consultation. Closely related models of behavioral consultation include instructional consultation, ecobehavioral consultation, problem-solving consultation, and conjoint behavioral consultation.

In place of the special education eligibility consultation model, behavioral consultation has been emphasized as a way to develop and monitor more effective interventions for students. Behavioral consultation, according to Kratochwill and Bergan (1990), involves the consultant, consultee, and client triadic relationship. The emphasis is not placed on diagnostic concerns of the client, but rather on operationally defining the problem and implementing interventions to address the problematic behavior or behaviors. There are four primary stages to this type of consultation: problem identification, problem analysis, intervention implementation, and intervention evaluation. This type of consultation focuses the service on developing specific interventions for clients that can be implemented and evaluated. This type of consultation is in contrast to the special education eligibility consultation that provides a general description of the students functioning in diagnostic terms and makes general recommendations for interventions. Ongoing evaluation of the intervention is part of behavioral consultation but has not been part of the school psychologist's role with the special education eligibility process.

Organizational Consultation

The last type of consultation in school psychology is organizational consultation. Organizational consultation engages members of an organization in a process designed to address a presenting problem or improve the functioning of the organization. Although there are several models of organization consultation, a central component of most models is a planned and sustained effort to improve the system through self-analytic and problem solving methods (Curtis & Stollar, 1996). This approach is analogous to program-centered administrative consultation described by Caplan (1970). Schmuck (1990) points out that organizational consultation focuses on the organizational context in which a proposed program is implemented because of the norms, structures, and procedures of the setting will impose themselves on whatever plan is attempted. Organizational consultation emphasizes data collection, diagnosis, and feedback to participants as central components of both specific program implementation and overall health of the organization (Schmuck). This type of consultation has not traditionally been provided by school psychologists but the usefulness of this type of consultation is recently being realized.

There are several influences in school psychology that are helping school psychologists think about, understand, and implement organizational consultation. As a result of the provisions in the 2004 reauthorization of the Individuals with Disabilities Education Act (IDEA), response to intervention (RTI) has gained significant attention as a means of guiding decisions about school delivery (Glover & DiPerna, 2007). RTI is a potential method for ensuring that students are provided with instruction that is responsive to their educational progress. As outlined in IDEA (2004), those children who fail to respond to repeated intervention may also be considered to have a learning disability and be eligible for special education. Thus, IDEA (2004) provides changes to the definition of a learning disability. However, RTI requires changes to the general education system. RTI is not something a school psychologist can do on his or her own, but they can serve as an integral part of the process. How schools make the transition from their current state of functioning to using RTI is unclear. This potential change highlights the opportunities for using organizational consultation in schools.

Blue Print III proposed by NASP also emphasizes a model of service delivery that is prevention-oriented and shares similarities with the RTI model. Blue Print III provides a vision in which school psychology services are provided to prevent problems and enhance academic and social competencies of all students. However, the reality is that public schools function at a variety of levels. Most schools do not employ the prevention-oriented RTI model. Services of school psychologists are still likely driven by traditional special education eligibility consultation and the transition to prevention-oriented models will require considerable systems change. Clearly, school psychologists will need organizational consultation skills to help each school they serve change and enhance services for children.

Collaboration and Interpersonal Skills in Consultation

Whether consulting with a teacher, parent, or a school team, school psychologists need skills for working cooperatively with other professionals and parents. Often, school psychologists serve on teams or consult with many teachers and parents in a school district. Therefore, school psychologists need skills for collaboration with a diverse range of adults. Rosenfield (2002) describes a model of instructional consultation that has a collaborative emphasis. Collaborative consultation is defined by Rosenfield (1987) as an interchange between two or more professional colleagues in a nonhierarchical relationship, working together to resolve a problem. A working relationship is critical to collaborative consultation. According to Rosenfield (2002), the working relationship allows problem-solving to continue despite differences between the school psychologist and teacher interests, values, or perceptions. With collaborative consultation, both parties are responsible for the problem. However, the school psychologist (consultant) is responsible for monitoring the quality of the relationship and the school psychologist must be perceived as trustworthy and competent (Rosenfield, 2002).

Communication skills are a critical component of collaborative consultation. As Rosenfield points out, consultation is viewed at its core as a linguistic event. Two people must talk to each other, understand the problem, and work together to resolve the problem. However, a collaborative approach does not just happen. The words a consultant uses will influence how collaborative the consultation is. For example, when a diagnosis is involved in the consultation process (special education eligibility consultation), it can result in a teacher believing that only a specialist can address the disorder; thereby, decreasing teacher involvement and ownership of the problem. In contrast, defining the problem in terms of learning objectives and behavior is viewed by teachers as functionally related to their role (Rosenfield, 2002). When developing a collaborative relationship, question asking is downplayed because it is expert-oriented. Clarity of communication is essential. For example, a teacher-described "attention problem" with a student should be more clearly defined to such terms as out of his seat, not completing work, or shouting out. Skills for paraphrasing teacher verbalizations are also important, according to Rosenfield, to ensure that all parties are working towards a common goal.

School psychologists must have skills for working collaboratively with people for reaching different goals. What makes collaborative consultation difficult is that at some point in the consultation the consultation may switch from one of intervention to one of special education eligibility. As highlighted by Rosenfield, the medical (diagnostic) model requires an expert to make a diagnostic determination. According to many state special education regulations, the school psychologist is mandated to participate in the process of determining special education eligibility. When facilitating an eligibility determination classification, school psychologists may have to function as experts, so that the school team makes a clinically sound decision. That is, when determining whether a child has autism, the school psychologist is likely the only school professional with training on assessments and interventions for this disorder. It is interesting to point out that there is no research examining how a school psychologist's communications may change when involved in these different types of collaborative consultation services. Yet, many school psychologists know these challenges first hand. At times, role confusion – "Am I an expert or a team member?" – may seem apparent to school psychologists collaborating with school teams.

Challenges in consultation service delivery may be specific to the consultant and the system in which she or he works. Barriers experienced by one school psychologist in a particular setting may not be experienced by another psychologist. School psychologists need to consider how they interact with others. Active listening techniques are important skills. Verbal and nonverbal behaviors are part of active listening. Manner of dress and availability (face time) are also important. The school psychologist's dress should reflect his or her everyday role and function, communicate approachability, and be congruent with the general culture of the service recipient's environment. Availability or face time in the school directly improves the likelihood of interactions with others and provides potential for teachers to observe the school psychologist as being similar to them. In combination with manner of dress and availability, body language also plays an important role in communicating the service provider's "professional aura" (Preston, 2005). Approximately two-thirds of human communication is nonverbal (Brill, 1973; Sielski, 1979).

School psychologists providing consultation must continually strive to work towards mastering the art of active listening. Active listening skills are considered to be skills for nonverbal communication (eye contact, posture, body language) and verbal communication (paraphrasing, summarizing, reflecting feelings, open-ended questioning). Without active listening, interactions may be inefficient and unproductive in terms of problem solving, as the consultant risks being insensitive to underlying feelings conveyed in the teacher's messages. Insensitivity may hinder the psychologist's likelihood of effectiveness within a particular setting. As the teacher's emotional connection with the school psychologist diminishes, so may trust and creativity in the consultative process and thus the rejection of ideas generated through this process.

Integrated Case Example

In our work as school psychologists, we have regularly provided special education eligibility consultation and problem-solving collaborative consultation. Often the problem-solving collaborative consultation was provided for a student who was having difficulty in school, but was not yet formally referred for determination of special education eligibility. The following is the case of John that demonstrates how both models of consultation are provided in schools.

John is a second grade student who recently transferred into the school district in February. He is primarily having difficulty with reading. His teacher refers him to the Instructional Support Team (IST) which meets on February 20. The IST may have a designated leader who works closely with the school psychologist to manage this process. In this school, the school psychologist's job is to help manage data collection for the IST process and collaborate with team members. John's mother completes a background questionnaire and is explained the purpose of the meeting by the school psychologist or an IST teacher. Parent, teacher, IST teacher, and school psychologist meet and discuss John's needs and strengths. By using the questionnaire, informal observations, and review of records, general background information is gathered to rule out obvious developmental or medical concerns.

Problem Identification. The school team meets and the problem is defined in operational terms. John is unable to read fluently from materials used in class. He is reading more slowly and makes more errors than his peers. At the conclusion of the meeting, the school psychologist schedules the next meeting and explains that she will observe John in class and the reading specialist along with the classroom teacher will gather curriculum-based assessment (CBA) data in reading and math. After the meeting with the parent, the classroom teacher and reading specialist consult with the school psychologist regarding data collection procedures. The three educators agree on plans for data collection.

Problem Analysis. The reading specialist completes CBA probes in reading and math with John. She also gathers data regarding John's on-task behavior through direct observations. The classroom teacher also collects reading information using the Dynamic Indicators of Basic Early Literacy Skills (DIBELS). After the data is collected, the reading specialist meets briefly to review the data with the school psychologist and the classroom teacher. They all agree the data looks reliable, valid, and useful for the meeting.

The team meets again and analyzes the data found in Table 5.1. Reading probes are created from the beginning, middle, and end of the first grade and second grade reading books used in the district. The median words read correctly for the first grade probes is 31 and the median score for words reads correctly from the second grade reading probes is 27. This data indicate that he is reading below what is considered an instructional level for a second grade student. DIBELS probes were completed and indicate his letter oral reading fluency score is a 21. The CBA data suggest that John is reading at a frustrational level in the first and second grade reading probes. The DIBELS data indicates that John is reading in the at-risk range compared to other children of his age. Additionally, letter naming fluency, nonsense fluency, and phonemic segmentation fluency probes are administered from the DIBELS materials. These probes reveal a letter naming fluency score of 22, nonsense word fluency of 34, and phonemic segmentation is of 30. On-task behavior observations revealed that John was on-task for 84% of the intervals during reading, compared to peers who were on-task for 87% of the intervals. The permanent file reveals that John has a history of difficulties related to reading. He received poor grades in reading and language arts for first grade. He received tutoring in reading to help him with letter naming problems.

Intervention Design. The team meets to analyze the data on March 13. An intervention and goal is established to increase his words read correctly per minutes and to decrease his errors read per minutes. The reading specialist agrees to provide additional skills instruction for pre-reading skills with John and three other students. This instruction will occur in class during small-group skills instruction.

Table 5.1 John's curriculum based assessment (CBA) and Dynamic Indicators of Basic Early Literacy Skill (DIBELS) data for second grade

Assessment	March 13	April 30	May 20
DORF	21	25	27
CBA (first grade)	31	39	38
CBA (second grade)	27		
On-task in reading	84%		
Phoneme seg, fluency	24	32	33
Nonsense word fluency	30	29	32
Letter naming fluency	22	24	25

The team would like to provide instruction in material at John's level. The team discusses who will be responsible for which part of the intervention and when. The school psychologist and instructional team assistant document the responsibilities of each member. For example, the school psychologist administers weekly reading probes. The classroom teacher provides guided reading in small groups. The reading specialist or IST teacher provides repeated reading opportunities with John. Additionally, John's mother agrees to read with him every night and practice the alphabetic principle with John. John's mother is asked to keep a log for each night she works with John. Another meeting is scheduled to evaluate John's progress. Everyone is given a copy of the plan and their role is highlighted.

Each week, the school psychologist consults with the classroom teacher and the reading specialist to discuss the integrity of John's interventions and his progress. The teachers report that they are working hard to help John and following through consistently on the agreed-upon intervention.

Intervention Evaluation. The team evaluates John's progress after approximately 6 weeks. They evaluate data from John's reading probes, DIBELS probes, and on-task observations on April 30. The data show that John's median score on his last three CBA probes is 38 words correct per minute in probes from first grade reading book. This is an increase in seven words per minute, but still below grade level expectations. His phonemic segmentation score has increased to a median score of 32. John's mother reports that John has improved in reading fluency and letter sound correspondence. Classroom observations indicate that John is on-task during reading at a rate similar to his peers.

By examining the data, the team determines that John is making some progress, so they continue with the intervention; however, John's teacher and mother remain concerned about his difficulties. The school psychologist explains the school district's procedures for providing academic interventions to students and the legal rights of parents regarding the special education eligibility process. The team meets informally in May to discuss John's academic functioning. His teacher remains concerned about John's low reading ability compared to his classroom peers. John's mother is not interested in pursuing special education services at this time but prefers to wait and see how John does the following year. The reading specialist assists the teacher in collecting the end of the year reading information, and John's reading progress will be tracked by the reading specialist and the IST the following year.

The new school year in third grade brings a new teacher with whom the psychologist and instructional support assistant collaborate and share what was implemented the previous year. In third grade, John starts the year receiving supportive services from the reading specialist. A similar process is used this year to the one used by the IST the previous year. Interventions are created that focus on reading fluency and reading comprehension. From September through December, John continues to show some skill development, but not at a rate to match his peers in order to be successful in the third grade reading curriculum. The gap between John's reading abilities and that of his peers is increasing. At this point, the psychologist has a working relationship with John's mother.

By February of his third grade year, the data indicates that John's problems are looking to be more intensive (see Table 5.2). That is, John is responding to interventions, but his rate of progress is not able to close the gap between his skills development and that of his same age peers. In fact, DIBELS data suggest that John is still in the at-risk range (DORF=45 for beginning of third grade and 50 for middle of third grade; the school district average DORF score for the beginning and middle of third grade are 72 and 90). The team and John's mother grow frustrated with his limited progress. It is a policy in the school that the school psychologist is the primary person to handle the discussion of special education eligibility evaluations.

The school psychologist handles the transition to special eligibility consultation with the team. The school psychologist explains due process rights and the procedures for completing the special education evaluation to John's mother. Until this point in the process, assessment procedures for John were consistent with what other students in the general education received (e.g., classroom observations, weekly reading probes, services from reading specialist). The school psychologist was a collaborative consultant in this process of assessing and designing interventions for John.

Table 5.2 John's DORF data
for second and third grade

Assessment	John	District average	DIBELS bench mark
Beginning second	–	42	44
Middle second	21	66	68
End second	36	88	90
Beginning third	45	72	77
Middle third	52	90	92
End third	–	105	110

1. Permission to Evaluate is signed by parent(s) giving permission to complete a multidisciplinary evaluation (MDE).
2. Assessment information as part of the MDE is collected (e.g., observations, curriculum based assessments, psychological and academic tests, interviews, and observations).
3. The evaluation report of the MDE is prepared and signed by MDE team members. Members must indicate whether they are in agreement or disagreement with the MDE report.
4. If the students has a disability and is in need of special education, Individual Education Program (IEP) document in created by the IEP team.
5. The Notice of Recommended Education Placement (NOREP) is signed by the parents.
6. The IEP in implemented for the student.

Fig. 5.1 Pennsylvania special education eligibility steps

With the special education eligibility evaluation, the school psychologist follows the Pennsylvania-mandated procedures and timelines for completing this process (see Fig. 5.1). Parent permission is obtained by the school psychologists and allows for the school psychologist work directly with the client, John. The parent signs a permission to evaluate (PTE). On the PTE, the school psychologist describes what assessment procedures she will use and that the evaluation will be completed within 60 calendar days. The school psychologist describes that a cognitive ability test may help determine John's aptitude for learning achievement testing will assist with comparing John to national samples of other children his age, and behavioral checklists will help the team understand John's social, emotional, and behavioral difficulties. The school psychologist hypothesizes that John may have a specific learning disability in reading and has become less motivated and developed low self-esteem due to the difficulties he is experiencing.

The school psychologist observes John in reading again. Individual interviews are conducted with his teacher and she interviews his parents. DIBELS and CBA data are collected from his teacher and the reading specialist. The psychologist is careful to document input from John's teachers and his parents. Also, the school psychologist completes a thorough review of John's academic records. To test a hypothesis regarding John's cognitive difficulties, the school psychologist administers a standardized intelligence test (Wechsler Intelligence Scale for Children – Fourth Edition). The results indicate John has a Full Scale IQ of 92, indicating he is functioning in the low average range of ability compared to his same age peers. The school psychologist also notices that John is often slow to respond to questions. The school psychologist also administers a standardized norm-referenced achievement test to assess the hypothesis that John has significantly below average achievement in reading. The results show that John has a Reading Composite Standard Score of 79 indicating and verifying that John's reading composite standard scores fall in the below average range compared to his same age peers. The school psychologist substantiates the hypothesis that John has a discrepancy between his ability and achievement. John's mother reports no major medical concerns or a family history of learning difficulties, but she is concerned about his language and reading skills. Compared to his older sister and brother, John has more noticeable difficulties, according to his mother. These are primary symptoms of a learning disability.

Importantly, the school psychologist hypothesizes that John's learning difficulty is not the result of culture, language, or economic disadvantage. To test these hypotheses, the school psychologist interviews John and his parents. John reports feeling uneasy with school work. His mother reports that he has cried when discussing his school problems. According to John and his mother, he tries hard but feels like a failure. This has been going on since first grade.

The school psychologist also consults with speech and language teacher and school nurse. The speech and language teacher indicates John had some difficulties with articulation but has not received services since kindergarten as his errors were developmentally appropriate. The school nurse reports that John has no vision or hearing impairments and does not have any medical concerns, such as allergies or medication. The school psychologist rules out family stressors or adjustment issues though interviews with John's parents, but does determine that John's self-esteem is hampered based on checklists completed by John, his parents, and teacher.

At the conclusion of the special education eligibility evaluation, the school psychologist writes a report of the findings of the multidisciplinary evaluation (MDE). The school psychologist recommends the team identify John having a specific learning disability and is in need of specially designed instruction. Specifically, the psychologist suggests that the MDE team continue to provide explicit skill instruction to John at his present level of functioning. The CBA information is used to establish measurable objectives. The team also considers whether John should be fully included for all academic subjects or receive specialized instruction in a special education classroom. The MDE team recommends full inclusion with special education supports. Additional skill instruction may be needed if he does not continue to make appropriate progress. The school psychologist discusses these issues with the parents and the teacher separately. The school psychologist records the opinions of each member and finalizes the MDE report. A copy of the MDE is provided to the parents and staff and an IEP meeting is scheduled to further discuss specific interventions for John. With parents' permission, many times the MDE and IEP are held together on the same day in this school district. The school psychologist reviews the report and recommendations contained in the report; once this is completed and signed off, the team can go right into developing an IEP. The special education teacher facilitates this process and bases IEP goals on the information contained in the MDE report. The last piece of the process is the parents sign the Notice of Recommended Placement (NOREP) formally giving the school approval to provide the specialized services to John. The NOREP is signed after the IEP document is finalized. The parent chooses to agree or disagree with the recommendations.

Basic Consideration for Enhancing Consultation Competence

Understanding Intervention Options

Providing effective consultation is complicated. Problem-solving consultation requires school psychologist and the school team to determine the intervention that may work for each student under specific conditions. To make this decision, the school psychologist needs to have adequate foundational knowledge of interventions and appropriate functional skills. Thus, along with needing to be knowledgeable of theories underlying consultation and collaboration, school psychologists must understand effective interventions across populations of students and families. The process of linking consultation service to research-based interventions is described.

Effective interventions are specific. The key to a collaborative consultation intervention is to generate a specific solution to a specific problem. Effective interventions should be operationally defined and specifically tailored to meet the needs of the individual student and teacher. It must be recognized from the start that there is not one solution that can be found in a magic book of solutions. Change in student functioning is a process that is different for each case. Depending on the resources in a particular school, solutions to identified problems will often require a considerable amount of creativity. This creativity is welcomed as long as the solution directly targets the identified problem. For example, a student with difficulties getting along with peers may not need social skills training through a prepackaged social skills training curriculum. As an alternative, interventions may be designed to address the nature of the problem as it occurs in context. Teaching new skills, reinforcing desired social skills, and preventing problem behaviors from occurring are all appropriate intervention options. This intervention may likely prove to be more beneficial than automatically implementing a packaged social skills curriculum.

Solutions to common academic and behavioral problems typically lie in behavior-based assessment data, rather than norm referenced tests. Primary examples of behavior assessment are structured observations, interviews, CBAs, and functional assessments. Basic assumptions of behavioral assessment include observing the behaviors of students as they occur in the natural environment and considering the function of problematic behaviors. For example, problematic social behaviors of children may be occurring because the behaviors serve the purpose of escaping something unpleasant or gaining a positive consequence, such as attention or a tangible item. Academically, children may have problems because they lack required skills to complete in class assignments or they me be simply choosing not to complete the work. The difference between problems related to skills deficits vs. a problem of not performing a task obviously requires interventions that are quite different. School psychologists will need knowledge of learning theory (cognitive and behavioral), child development, and family functioning.

Developing Knowledge of Special Education Regulations and Disabilities

A critical job for school psychologists is special education eligibility consultant. School psychologists must have a thorough understanding of the state special education regulations in which they practice. Along with this knowledge, school psychologists must have an understanding of how the state defines different disabilities. A clear understanding of symptoms related to these defined disorders helps the school psychologist determine eligibility decisions more accurately.

Developing Knowledge of Consultation Models

School psychologists must have knowledge of consultation models. We have provided an introduction to three basic models of consultation and collaboration in school. School psychologists will need a more thorough understanding of consultation. Skills for collaboration are not likely to be developed from reading a book. These skills need to be developed in practice. This is where the lessons of human relationships are learned. Teachers, parents, and students present an unlimited variety of personalities, problems, and emotions. School psychologists will need to learn how to assist and facilitate consultation with the teachers, parent, and students they serve. A knowledgeable and experienced supervisor who is sensitive to the needs of developing professional psychologist is critical.

Developing skills for consultation is an ongoing process for each school psychologist and requires a prerequisite set of individual characteristics, explicit training, and practical experiences. In its simplest sense, the process of skill development begins with exposure to the basic theories and concepts underlying collaboration and consultation. Skills are continuously honed through practice and feedback. During this time, the school psychologist acquires increased awareness of effective interventions, the needs of the teacher, parents, and students in the schools they serve, and insight into how to consult and collaborate within the school.

As suggested in Blue Print III, building competency as a school psychologist requires time, focused effort, and ongoing perseverance (Ysseldyke et al., 2006). While acquiring daily practical experiences in the field, each school psychologist must also continually seek opportunities to enhance skills development through reading professional literature and attending trainings and conferences.

Future

Employment trends and changes in federal legislation influencing public education poses challenges for school psychology. It is anticipated there will be a shortage of school psychologists in this decade which coexists with trends in federal legislation. The passage of the No Child Left Behind Act (NCLB; United States Department of Education, 2002) and reauthorization of the Individuals with Disabilities Education Act (IDEA; United States Department of Education, 2004) have emphasized student achievement, educator accountability, and research-based interventions for all students. To sufficiently satisfy these regulations, skills from professionals specifically trained in empirical methodology, child development, and intervention effectiveness must be invoked. School psychologists have the training and expertise in each of these areas to help schools. The application of these skills needs to largely occur through consultation rather than direct service delivery.

Trends in changes to federal regulations are likely a response to the increasing complexities and diversity of today's students. Government reports suggest that up to 20% of school age children will experience a significant mental health problem (Surgeon General, 1999). Outside of adversely affecting the school climate and learning environment, these mental health issues are likely to negatively impact outcomes toward benchmarks and standards set forth by federal regulations. Thus, a continually growing need for students' access to professionals specifically trained in educational, behavioral, and social interventions is evident. Access to these professionals occurs in schools. Schools are a consistent link between children, families, and professionals. Indirect services of school psychologist are the most logical way to give out psychology to students, parents, teachers, and the community.

Summary

Consultation is considered to be a triadic relationship amongst a consultant, consultee, and a client. Often in schools, the school psychologist is the consultant, teachers are consultee, and the student is the client. Consultation is conceptualized as an indirect form of service delivery for school psychologists. The most commonly used models in schools are special education eligibility consultation, behavioral problem solving consultation, and organizational consultation. The current emphasis is on consultation that focuses on operationally defining problems, implementing interventions, and evaluating the efficacy of interventions designed to address academic and behavioral problems of students.

Let us not forget that many school psychology services are delivered because of legal mandates of IDEA. Therefore, the services provided by school psychologists exist because of legal influences on our practice. Consultation theory and interpersonal interactions are important, but a large part of the school psychologist's role in many public schools is to be cognizant of the real legal pressures they face when formally involved in the special education process. Special education eligibility determination is highly regulated and parents' rights are clearly identified. School psychologists must be able to assist with managing the legal requirements of their practice and be prepared to defend the practices used in the eligibility process. In simple terms, eligibility for special education still rests on the determination that a child has a disability. This has not changed since the inception of special education. Therefore, school psychologists must have skills necessary to complete this task.

Changes in IDEA (2004) have encouraged schools to implement RTI models. NASP has encouraged school psychologists to deliver services with more of a prevention focus than a diagnostic focus. Organization change in schools is occurring and school psychologists may play a critical role in facilitating organization change. Therefore, organizational consultation skills are likely to be needed by school psychologists in the coming years.

Consultation is an important service school psychologists provide. We have described three models commonly used by school psychologists. We believe that school psychologists will continue to use these models of consultation. Whether designing interventions or helping to determine eligibility for special education, or facilitating organization change, school psychologist need effective interpersonal communication skills and a willingness to collaborate with parent and teachers.

Chapter Competency Checklist

DOMAIN 4 – Interpersonal and collaborative skills

Foundational	Functional
Understand and explain the following: □ Consultation □ Mental health consultation □ Behavioral consultation □ Organizational consultation □ Collaboration □ Interpersonal skills □ Problem-solving model □ State-specific special education regulations □ Models of consultation	Gain practice: □ Observing various models of consultations (e.g., mental health, special education, behavioral, academic consultation) □ Providing consultation within specific school(s) with supervision □ Vary consultation experiences across settings and populations □ Asking questions and finding answers related to consultation and collaboration □ Receive feedback on consultation

References

Brill, N. T. (1973). *Working with people*. New York: J.B. Lippincott.

Brown, D., Pryzwansky, W. B., & Schulte, A. C. (2001). *Psychological Consultation: Introduction to Theory and Practice (5th ed.)*. Boston: Allyn & Bacon.

Caplan, G. (1970). *The theory and practice of mental health consultation*. New York: Basic Books.

Curtis, M. J., & Stollar, S. A. (1996). Applying principles and practices of organizational change to school reform. *School Psychology Review, 25*(4), 409–418.

Glover, T., & DiPerna, J. (2007). Service delivery for response to intervention: Core components and directions for future research. *School Psychology Review, 36*(4), 526–540.

Gutkin, T. B., & Curtis, M. J. (1999). School based consultation theory and practice: The art and science of indirect service delivery model. In C. R. Reynolds & T. B. Gutkin (Eds.), *The handbook of school psychology* (pp. 598–637). New York: Wiley.

Kauffman, J. M. (2007). Conceptual models and the future of special education. *Education and Treatment of Children, 30*(4), 241–258.

Kratochwill, T.R., & Bergan, J.R. (1990). *Behavioral Consultation in Applied Settings: An Individual Guide*. New York: Plenum Press.

Kratochwill, T. R., & Pittman, P. (2002). Expanding problem-solving consultation training: Prospects and frameworks. *Journal of Educational and Psychological Consultation, 13*(1), 69–95.

Preston, P. (2005). Nonverbal communication: Do you really say what you mean? *Journal of Healthcare Management, 50*, 83–86.

Reschley, D. J., & Ysseldyke, J. E. (2002). Paradigm shift: The past is not the future. In A. Thomas & J. Grimes (Eds.), *Best practices in school psychology* (4th ed., pp. 3–20). Bethesda, MD: National Association of School Psychologists.

Rosenfield, S. (1987). *Instructional consultation.* Hillsdale, NJ: Lawrence Erlbaum Associates, Inc.

Rosenfield, S. (2002). Best practices in instruction consultation. In A. Thomas & J. Grimes (Eds.), *Best practices in school psychology* (4th ed., pp. 3–20). Bethesda, MD: National Association of School Psychologists.

Schmuck, R. A. (1990). Organization development in schools: Contemporary concepts and practices. In T. Gutkin & C. R. Reynolds (Eds.), *The handbook of school psychology* (2nd ed., pp. 899–919). New York: Wiley.

Sielski, L. (1979). Understanding body language. *Personnel and Guidance Journal, 57,* 238–242.

Surgeon General's Report. (1999). *Mental health: A report of the surgeon general.* United States Department of Health and Human Services. Washington, DC: U.S. Government Printing Office.

United States Department of Education. (2002). *No Child Left Behind.* Retrieved March 12, 2007, from http://www.ed.gov/nclb/landing.jhtml.

United States Department of Education. (2004). *Individuals with Disabilities Education Improvement Act.* Retrieved April 6, 2005, from http://www.ed.gov/index.jhtml.

West, F. J., & Idol, L. (1987). School consultation: 1. An interdisciplinary perspective on theory, models, and research. *Journal of Learning Disabilities, 20,* 388–408.

Ysseldyke, J., Burns, M., Dawson, P., Kelley, B., Morrison, D., Ortiz, S., et al. (2006). *School psychology: A blueprint for training and practice III.* Bethesda, MD: National Association of School Psychologists.

Chapter 6
Assessing Students' Skills Using a Nontraditional Approach

Christine E. Neddenriep, Brian C. Poncy, and Christopher H. Skinner

Currently, within the field of school psychology, a shift in service delivery models is occurring. Whereas school psychology had been dominated by a refer-test-report (and place) delivery model (Reschly & Yssedyke, 2002), recent legislation has facilitated a change in service delivery to include a response to intervention (RtI) model (Brown-Chidsey & Steege, 2005). Practicing within this service delivery model both allows and requires school psychologists to expand their range of skills and the services they offer (Oakland & Cunningham, 1999), specifically increasing their use of nontraditional assessment measures. This need to increase school psychologists' competencies in nontraditional assessment measures within a problem-solving, outcome-driven model provides the context for this chapter.

This chapter focuses on the use of nontraditional assessment methods within a problem-solving context. The chapter begins with a discussion of the strengths and limitations related to the use of a traditional versus a problem-solving approach to assessment. Following the rationale for using a problem-solving approach, the chapter discusses the use of curriculum-based measurement (CBM) across basic skill areas in addition to the strengths and limitations of these measures. Finally, the chapter provides a case study example to illustrate the use of the nontraditional assessment methods within the problem-solving context.

Traditional Model

Historically, school psychologists have been limited in their role by practicing within a traditional, deficit-driven disability model (Fagan & Wise, 2000). This model assumes that variations in learning and behavior are identified within the child: these deficits are biologically based and unchanging, and these weaknesses are diagnosable through the use of traditional, norm-referenced standardized tests (Reschly & Yssedyke, 2002). By using traditional, norm-referenced standardized tests of intelligence and achievement, school psychologists have served as gatekeepers, assigning categorical labels to classify impairments and allowing access to existing special education programs based on the assumption that a given student's needs cannot be met within the general education setting.

The identification of students is guided by the diagnostic categories and the assessment guidelines described in the Individuals with Disabilities Education Act (IDEA, 2004; revision and reauthorization of Public Law 94–142). The existence of these 13 categories presupposes that diagnostic

C.E. Neddenriep (✉)
The University of Wisconsin-Whitewater, Whitewater, WI, USA
e-mail: neddenrc@uww.edu

T.M. Lionetti et al. (eds.), *A Practical Guide to Building Professional Competencies in School Psychology*, 83
DOI 10.1007/978-1-4419-6257-7_6, © Springer Science+Business Media, LLC 2011

accuracy is related to providing effective and beneficial instruction. This logical connection, however, is not supported by empirical evidence (Reschly & Yssedyke, 2002; Ysseldyke & Marston, 1999). In fact, research indicates that although specific interventions may be effective with certain groups of students, often these same interventions are effective for *all* students, with and without disabilities. Thus, accurate categorization does not necessarily improve instructional decision making (Kavale, 1990; Shinn, Good, & Parker, 1999; Ysseldyke, Algozzine, Shinn, & McGue, 1982).

With respect to learning disabilities, the traditional model has been described as a *wait-to-fail* model. Historically, educators have been required to verify a discrepancy between current level of achievement and intelligence to diagnose the presence of a learning disability. Thus, the model emphasizes waiting for achievement–ability discrepancies to become sufficiently large in order to verify a problem and provide access to remedial (i.e., special education) services. As opposed to waiting for a student to fall farther behind his/her peers, an RtI model emphasizes early identification of academic skill deficits and the immediate application of evidence-based procedures designed to enhance academic skills.

Issues have also been raised regarding the use of diagnostic labels. Labels within a traditional model serve several general purposes: they facilitate communication between providers using a common language of understanding; they verify the need for and make possible an organizational system for access to services; they provide for reimbursement for services to providers; and they provide for administrative structures for delivering services to students (Goldstein, Arkell, Ashcroft, Hurley, & Lilly, 1975). Although labels may be useful in these ways, limitations are also associated with labeling students. For example, labeling a child as having a learning disability implies that his/her academic strengths and weaknesses are similar to those of other students with learning disabilities. Although this focus on common within-student deficits may provide an explanation for these deficits, its emphasis discounts the unique contribution of the interaction between the individual student and his/her learning environment (Ysseldyke & Marston, 1999). Environments, in contrast to within-student deficits, may be assessed and modified leading to improved competencies. Labels can also be stigmatizing to the child, decreasing expectations in the learning environment. Eliminating a label does not necessarily remove the stigma associated with observed differences; however, focusing on building competencies by altering the instructional environment to support learning shifts the emphasis to capabilities rather than disabilities.

Problem-Solving Model

Whereas the traditional model emphasizes diagnosing deficits centered within the student using norm-referenced standardized measures of intelligence and achievement, the problem-solving model emphasizes the use of data to identify and solve problems centered in the environment (Deno, 2002). Within a problem-solving model, a *problem* is defined as a discrepancy between the student's current level of performance and his/her expected level of performance within the classroom setting (Tilly, 2002). Thus, a third-grade student is identified as having a problem when he is reading at the second-grade level in comparison to his peers who are reading as expected at the third-grade level. When educators actively work toward reducing this difference between a student's current level of performance and the desired level of student performance, they are engaging in a problem-solving process (Deno, 2005).

CBM has emerged as a primary source of continuous data collection used to quantify students' performance in basic skill areas and to monitor the impact of interventions on students' performance within the problem-solving model. Within this model, school psychologists act as problem solvers directing the process toward a solution.

Various problem-solving models have been proposed (e.g., Bergan & Kratochwill, 1990; Deno, 2002; Kampwirth, 2006; Tilly, 2002; Witt, Daly, & Noell, 2000). Deno (2005) describes five steps within the problem-solving process: problem identification, problem definition, designing intervention plans, implementing intervention, and problem solution that are common across most problem-solving models. During problem identification, efforts are made to observe the behavior in the environment and to determine that a problem is present (e.g., third-grade student reads aloud from a third-grade reading passage slowly and laboriously). During problem definition, efforts are made to verify that the observed behavior is truly a problem (i.e., differs significantly from expected levels of performance) and to quantify the difference. For example, the third-grade student is assessed using CBM of oral reading fluency and determined to be reading 45 words correctly in 1 minute while her average peer reads 75 words correctly in 1 minute. Within the next step, intervention plans are designed, given the assessment of the instructional environment to decrease the difference between the student's current level of performance and that which is expected. Thus, a repeated reading intervention with error correction is implemented to increase the opportunity to practice accurate reading daily for 20 minutes, increasing the number of words the student reads correctly in 1 minute. The student's progress is continuously monitored twice per week during the intervention for 6 weeks. Within the final step, the data are reviewed to determine if the intervention is solving the problem. The data reflect an increase of 2.3 words read correctly per week, indicating that the intervention is impacting the student's reading skill in the desired direction and exceeding the desired goal of 54 words read correctly in 6 weeks (See case study for further explanation).

Several advantages of the problem-solving model in comparison to the traditional model have been noted in the literature. First, the problem-solving model is a proactive process of identifying students in need of additional or different methods of instruction, designing stronger instructional programs, and realizing greater academic gains for students. Thus, the outcome is not simply identification but successful intervention. Secondly, the model requires data to inform decision making at each step of the process. Thus, the assessment process is linked to intervention continuously using data to evaluate the success of the intervention with respect to quantifiable goals. When a decision is made to change an intervention, it is based on data reflecting a lack of progress toward the identified goal. Third, the problem-solving model is also prevention focused. Given that the problem-solving model assumes that problems are defined within the context of the environment, the model requires that *all* students be provided adequate instruction within the environment. Thus, the problem-solving model ensures that scientifically validated instruction (e.g., evidence-based reading curriculum) from which all students may be expected to benefit is employed. By ensuring that *all* students are provided with high-quality instruction, some problems are prevented and students demonstrating a problem are more easily identified.

Finally, the base of research supporting a problem-solving approach is emerging as a reflection of the measures and procedures used within the model. The sensitivity, reliability, and validity of CBM measures have been consistently documented in the literature (e.g., Deno, Mirkin, & Chiang, 1982; Fuchs & Deno, 1992; Fuchs & Fuchs, 1992; Fuchs, Fuchs, & Maxwell, 1988). Strong support exists for the use of systematic formative evaluation procedures in effecting positive outcomes in student achievement (Forness, Kavale, Blum & Lloyd, 1997; Fuchs & Fuchs, 1986). Efforts to continually increase our knowledge base of evidence-based interventions for improving basic academic skills are visible within the current journals in school psychology as well (e.g., "Research into Practice" within *School Psychology Review*). Thus, the problem-solving approach incorporates scientifically based progress monitoring tools, formative evaluation procedures, and evidence-based interventions, all of which have been empirically demonstrated to contribute to the design of stronger instructional programs and to realizing greater academic gains for students (Fuchs, Fuchs, & Hamlett, 1989).

Curriculum-Based Measurement

CBM, a system of empirically validated indicators of proficiency in basic skills, was initially developed over 30 years ago by Stanley Deno and Phyllis Mirkin to aid special education teachers in making instructional decisions regarding progress toward individualized educational program (IEP) goals and objectives (Deno & Mirkin, 1977). Several characteristics of these measures make them ideally suited to the identification of students at-risk within a problem-solving model. They are brief, requiring only 1–4 minutes to administer; they are repeatable, providing alternate forms to repeatedly assess performance over time; and they are sensitive, allowing one to identify small changes in skills over time. Therefore, educators can easily incorporate them within instruction, effectively use them to identify students in need of intervention, and evaluate students' response to instructional changes.

CBM procedures have been developed for assessing a variety of skills including early literacy, reading, mathematics, spelling, and written expression (see Deno & Mirkin, 1977; Shapiro, 2004; Shinn, 1989). Each of these measures is a rate measure (Shinn, 2002); therefore, the denominator is always time whereas the numerator represents the skill that is being measured. For example, the most well-researched measure of oral reading fluency is words correct per minute (WCPM). To measure WCPM, the student reads aloud for 1 minute from a grade-level reading probe. While the student reads aloud, the examiner scores errors (e.g., mispronunciations, substitutions, omissions) and records the last word read at 1 minute. The number of errors is subtracted from the total number of words read and placed over time (1 minute). Thus, if the student read 100 words with three errors in 1 minute, then the student read 97 words correctly per minute.

Similarly, curriculum-based measures of reading comprehension reflect reading comprehension accuracy in the numerator (e.g., percent of comprehension questions answered correctly) and time in the denominator. Two CBM measures of reading comprehension are the maze technique (Fuchs & Fuchs, 1992) and reading comprehension rate (RCR); Skinner, 1998). The maze task requires students to read a grade-level passage, in which approximately every seventh word is omitted. Three choices of words are provided, from which students circle the word that best completes the meaning of the sentence. Students are given 3 minutes to complete as many sentences as possible. The number of correct replacements is placed over the denominator of 3 minutes producing the rate measure. The maze task can be group administered within a whole classroom, making administration time efficient.

Calculation of RCR requires students to read a 400-word grade-level passage, either aloud or silently. Following completion of the passage, the student then responds to ten multiple-choice questions. The percent of comprehension questions answered correctly is placed in the numerator over the denominator of the time required to read the passage. If a student read a 400-word passage in 4 minutes and answered 80% of the comprehension questions correctly, then he/she is supposed to have comprehended the passage at a rate of 20% of the passage per minute. The function or purpose of reading is almost always comprehension and students typically read silently when reading for comprehension. Therefore, assessing RCR by requiring students to read silently, as opposed to aloud, may provide the most direct measure of functional reading skills (Skinner, Neddenriep, Bradley-Klug, & Ziemann, 2002). However, researchers have shown that assessing aloud reading comprehension rates provides a more valid predictor of broad reading skill development than assessing silent reading comprehension rates by ensuring that students are actually reading (Neddenriep, Hale, Skinner, Hawkins, & Winn, 2007).

Curriculum-based measures of early literacy skills have also been developed. These rate measures are referred to as Dynamic Indicators of Basic Early Literacy Skills (DIBELS; Good & Kaminski, 2002). They include three primary measures: Initial Sound Fluency (ISF), Phoneme Segmentation Fluency (PSF), and Nonsense Word Fluency (NWF) that can be used for continuous progress monitoring. During ISF, students are shown four pictures. The examiner identifies each picture and asks the student to point to or name the picture that begins with the sound produced by the examiner. Students are also asked to identify the initial sound for several of the pictures. ISF is calculated by placing the number of correctly identified pictures or sounds in the numerator and time in the denominator. Therefore, if a student correctly identifies 21 sounds during the 3-minute administration then he/she has identified seven sounds correctly per minute.

PSF provides a measure of a student's ability to segment three- and four-phoneme words into their individual phonemes. The examiner says a word and then asks the student to identify the individual phonemes. PSF is calculated by placing the number of correct phonemes produced in the numerator over time in the denominator (2-minute administration) to reflect the number of correctly produced phonemes per minute. Finally, NWF provides a measure of letter–sound correspondence and sound blending. The student is asked to pronounce a series of random vowel–consonant or consonant–vowel–consonant combinations. NWF is calculated by placing the number of correctly identified letter sounds in the numerator and time in the denominator (1-minute administration) to reflect the number of correctly identified letter sounds per minute (see DIBELS; www.dibels. uoregon.edu).

Curriculum-based measures of mathematics assessing computational skills follow the same principles as described above. Students are provided timed math probes matched to grade-level objectives (Deno & Mirkin, 1977). These probes either contain single skills (e.g., two-digit multiplication; addition problems using numbers 1–12) or multiple skill probes containing mixed problem types. Because math skills build on one another, single-skill probes can be helpful in identifying specific skill deficits and skills mastered in determining the correct placement of a student within the curriculum. Multiple skill probes, in contrast, can be helpful in monitoring the progress of students relative to identified goals that predict proficiency (Shapiro, 2004). Students are timed for 2 minutes in grades one to three and 4 minutes for grades four to six. Accuracy of computation is represented by the number of digits correct, which is placed in the numerator over time in the denominator, to determine the rate measure, digits correct per minute (DCPM). These measures can be efficiently administered either individually or in groups.

Similar to preliteracy skills, measures of early numeracy are in development (see AIMSweb®; www.aimsweb.com). Four tasks have been developed to identify early numeracy skills – orally counting, identifying numbers, identifying the larger number from a pair, and identifying the missing number from a number line. The accuracy of each measure is assessed in 1-minute trials.

Curriculum-based measures have also been developed to assess spelling skills (Deno & Mirkin, 1977; Shinn, 1989). CBM measures of spelling can be administered individually or in groups. Spelling probes are comprised of 20 words taken from the grade-level spelling words or from standard grade-level sets (see AIMSweb®; www.aimsweb.com). Words should be dictated to the student at the rate of one word every 10 seconds for first and second grade (12 words in 2 minutes) and one word every 7 seconds for third grade and up (17 words in 2 minutes). The accuracy of words spelled is determined by counting correct letter sequences (CLS). The number of CLS is placed over time to determine the rate measure of the number of CLS per minute.

Finally, curriculum-based measures of written expression provide an indication of the student's level and type of writing skills (e.g., Deno, Marston, & Mirkin, 1982). Curriculum-based measures of writing are typically efficiently administered in group settings. Students are provided a story starter (e.g., "One day, it rained candy … "). Students are given 1 minute to think and then 3 minutes to write. Written expression can be assessed in terms of the total number of words written (TWW), providing an indication of fluency in generating words by placing the total number of words written over time; or, skill can be assessed in terms of correct writing sequences (CWS), providing an indication of correct spelling, grammar, and meaning by placing the number of correct writing sequences over time.

Limitations of Curriculum-Based Measures

With the reauthorization of IDEA, school psychologists will increasingly adopt roles congruent with RtI models and will need to use assessments that address the questions inherent to the problem-solving process. One tool that can provide data to answer questions about the problem identification and problem evaluation stages of problem solving is CBM (Deno, 1989). As CBM is used to support a variety of educational decisions, it is imperative that consumers of the assessment data (e.g., school psychologists and educators who make decisions based on CBM data) understand the purposes and questions that the data can address. Frequently, criticisms of CBM arise because of incorrect assumptions regarding what questions can be answered using CBM data (Shinn & Bamonto, 1998).

When deciding for what questions CBM can and cannot answer, educators should think about the "M" of CBM and what it stands for – measurement. CBM has been validated to *measure* the following: (1) how students compare to each other (e.g., establishing local norms), (2) a student's current level of performance (e.g., establishing a student's baseline), and (3) a student's learning rate (i.e., monitoring a student's progress). While CBM can be used to answer questions posed in the problem identification, problem definition, and evaluation of the problem solution stages of problem solving, these measures do little to directly inform the stages of problem analysis (i.e., why the problem is occurring) inherent within the plan design and plan implementation (i.e., what to do to remedy the problem) stages. To address these questions, practitioners will need to use a variety of other data collection methods (e.g., interview, observation, permanent product reviews) using other forms of curriculum-based assessment (see Howell & Nolet, 2000; Shapiro, 2004).

As stated previously, collecting data using CBM procedures has a variety of advantages (e.g., brief, easy, and repeatable); however, practitioners also need to be aware of the limitations of the measures (e.g., sources of error variance). CBM reading measures (i.e., WCPM) have been demonstrated to be a reliable measure for estimating both the level (Christ & Silberglitt, 2007; Poncy, Skinner, & Axtell, 2005) and trend (Christ, 2006; Hintze, Owen, Shapiro, & Daly, 2000) of student achievement. However, while researchers have reported high reliability-like coefficients, researchers have also showed that WCPM scores can have a large standard error of measurement (SEM; Christ & Silberglitt, 2007; Poncy et al., 2005). While WCPM scores are generally described as a specific point (e.g., Johnny is reading 55 WCPM) or a rate of learning (e.g., Johnny's reading speed is increasing by 1.2 words per week), researchers have begun to recommend using confidence intervals that represent the *estimation* of the student's level and trend of achievement (Christ, 2006; Christ & Silberglitt, 2007; Poncy et al., 2005). These studies concerning the reliability of CBM data necessitate two questions of vital importance to consumers of CBM data: (1) What are CBM data sensitive to? and (2) What can be done to reduce the amount of measurement error?

To What Are CBM Data Sensitive?

Poncy et al. (2005) conducted a study investigating the percentage of variance in student scores due to the person (i.e., student skills), items (i.e., probe difficulty), and residual (i.e., unaccounted sources of error) facets. Results showed that 81% of the variability in scores was due to the person, 10% of the variability was due to items, and 9% of the variability was caused by other factors, or the interaction of other factors not measured. The study went on to report reliability-like coefficients and the SEM depending on the number of probes administered for both relative (i.e., rank order) and absolute (i.e., intra-individual) decisions.

Other studies have investigated and confirmed variables of the testing environment that can significantly impact WCPM scores. Variables that have been identified at this point in time include the test administrator and setting (Derr-Minneci & Shapiro, 1992), administration directions

(Colón & Kranzler, 2006), the explicit exposure of a stopwatch (Skinner, Hurst, Teeple, & Meadows, 2002), and probe difficulty (Hintze & Christ, 2004).

These studies about the testing environment are of particular interest because many psychometric studies use extremely controlled testing. For example, Poncy et al. (2005) used a single test administrator, one room/setting that was used solely for testing, and one set of administration directions; they did not show students the stop watch and used a generic probe set designed to control for variations in probe difficulty. This likely is not representative of testing conditions in a school setting where multiple raters may be used, multiple settings may be used (e.g., hallway, classroom, counselors office), and administrators may "approximate" administration conditions (e.g., paraphrase administration directions). Therefore, psychometric studies may mask some of the sensitivity of CBM to extraneous variables and overestimate the reliability while underestimating the SEMs that accompany field-based data.

Research is converging to support the notion that CBM is a reliable measure with coefficients usually above 0.9, but also emphasizes that the SEM is high. For example, if a third-grade student is given three probes and his/her median score is 80 WCPM, the SEM would be 10 WCPM. This translates into saying that the student's true score would fall into a range of 70–90 WCPM 68% of the time. With a 95% confidence interval, an SEM of 20 would estimate that the student's true score would fall into a range of 60–100 WCPM. This example illustrates the notion that the sensitivity of CBM data can be a double-edged sword. CBM data are sensitive to changes in student achievement over short periods of time, which is a positive aspect of the measure; however, the bounce, or variance, observed in CBM data is likely due to a variety of other factors, which is also a limitation of the measure. In essence, CBM's sensitivity is a defining strength, but is also responsible for its most significant limitations.

Fortunately, researchers are beginning to address these issues concerning error in the data and are providing tentative recommendations about practices when using CBM to reduce bounce in CBM data due to extraneous sources of error. These recommendations will provide practitioners with data collection procedures that will increase the confidence with which educational decisions about student level and trend can be made.

What Can Be Done to Reduce the Amount of Measurement Error?

To decrease measurement error, practitioners should bear in mind four factors when using CBM data to support educational decisions: (1) characteristics of the selected probe set, (2) the type of decision being made, (3) the standardization of administration conditions, and (4) the number of behavioral samples taken. While measurement error will always be present, the following recommendations may help to circumvent some of the limitations when using CBM data and isolate the sensitivity of CBM to detect changes in student achievement. In addition, CBM data should always be employed as one of multiple sources of data to address educational questions.

Characteristics of the Selected Probe Set

Initial conceptualizations of CBM suggested creating assessment probes by directly sampling from the student's curriculum. By using the student's curriculum, content overlap was ensured between the curriculum and the assessment materials. Subsequent research, however, has consistently supported the use of generic probe sets to reflect valid outcomes (Powell-Smith & Bradley-Klug, 2001). Probe set developers, such as AIMSweb® and DIBELS, have constructed probes using

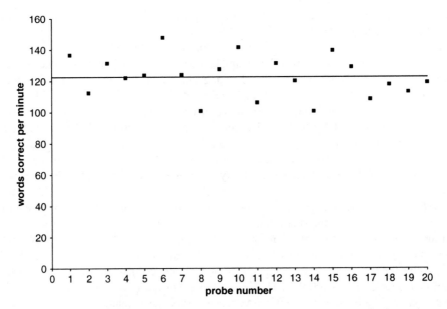

Fig. 6.1 Average performance of 37 third-grade students across 20 DIBELS progress monitoring probes

readability formulas to ensure consistent levels of difficulty across generic probes. Whereas the use of readability formulas is a substantial improvement over curriculum sampling, variability is still present. Figure 6.1 shows a progress-monitoring graph reflecting the average performance of 37 third-grade students across 20 successive third-grade probes administered across 4 days from the DIBELS progress monitoring passages (Poncy et al., 2005).

Substantial bounce is observed across the probes. Because the student achievement is not fluctuating this drastically on a daily basis, these highs and lows are representative of extraneous sources of error influencing WCPM data. The single most significant contributor, accounting for approximately half of the error, is differences in probe difficulty (Poncy et al., 2005). Simply put, for most students some probes are easier and some probes are harder. When students' reading behavior is measured using these probes, consistent highs and lows on students' WCPM scores are observed.

Recent research has demonstrated that field-testing a probe set, calculating the average score of all probes, and including only those probes that are within ±10 WCPM would reduce the amount of variability from 10 to 2% and increase the amount of variance accounted for by the student from 81 to 89%. The construction of probe sets meeting these requirements would eliminate approximately half of the 20% of the error variance observed in CBM scores and redirect this error variance toward the object of measurement (i.e., student achievement). This act would reduce the SEMs associated with CBM data and allow practitioners to more efficiently collect data to make decisions with more confidence and less error, simply by selecting and using a tightly controlled probe set. At the present time, researchers have recommended and are in the process of creating probe sets to achieve this goal (Christ & Silberglitt, 2007).

Following this logic, it is recommended that practitioners avoid using probe sets sampled from the local curriculum and identify the most tightly controlled generic probe set available. While probe sets constructed using readability formulas (e.g., DIBELS) are better than sampling from the local curriculum, probe sets using field-testing methods will virtually eliminate most of the error caused by probe difficulty, resulting in less error in the data we use to make decisions about the level and trend of student achievement.

The Type of Decision Being Made

We established that CBM are primarily used for three measurement purposes: (1) to determine how students compare to each other, (2) to estimate a student's achievement level, and (3) to estimate a student's rate of learning. Across these three purposes are two types of decisions. One type of decision is a relative one. Relative decisions focus on how a student rank orders in a measurement sample as is determined when using local norms. The other is an absolute decision. Absolute decisions focus on how a student performs independent of others as is assessed when progress monitoring or estimating a student's baseline achievement level.

Depending on whether the decision is relative or absolute will affect the amount of error in the data. Relative decisions will have less error because the variance due to differences in probe difficulty is nullified if all students in the measurement sample get the same probes. For example, if two probes are given, the first being difficult and the second being easy and a group of 100 students are given both probes, the group will be similarly rank-ordered (e.g., students that score low in comparison to peers on probe one will also score low on probe two). Thus, a student could score 55 WCPM on probe one and 85 WCPM on probe two and still be placed at a similar percentile rank. When assessing this same student's performance independent of the group, his/her baseline level of WCPM is less clear: Would it be 55 or 85 WCPM? Clearly, more samples of behavior would need to be collected to confidently estimate an absolute level of achievement.

The same data could not be used with the same level of confidence to answer these two different assessment questions. When making absolute, intra-individual decisions (e.g., comparing baseline performance to performance under a new intervention) data will need to be more precise and require more samples of behavior to confidently answer questions. This impacts decision making when estimating a student's *level* of achievement. To discriminate between relative and absolute decisions, the practitioner will need to answer the following question, "Am I estimating the student's rate of WCPM in relation to peers under the same measurement conditions or am I estimating the student's rate of WCPM independent of peers?" Fortunately, for the sake of simplicity, making decisions about student trend will almost always be absolute in nature.

The Standardization of Administration Conditions

Earlier in the chapter, we discussed the likelihood of school-based professionals using CBM across a variety of testing conditions (e.g., different rooms, different raters, paraphrasing directions) and how a variety of studies have demonstrated that these testing deviations can significantly impact WCPM outcomes. This statement is consistent with the repeated theme that sensitivity to extraneous sources of error is a limitation of CBM and that relatively minor alterations in the testing environment can significantly impact WCPM outcomes. To decrease the effect of these error sources, practitioners should emphasize to those who collect CBM data the need to explicitly follow administration procedures (e.g., not showing the stopwatch, reading the directions verbatim). Some educators may view some of these aspects of the administration conditions trivial, whereas in reality inconsistency in test administration can significantly impact scores and consequently affect the decisions made using these data.

The previous recommendation reaffirms the points made by Christ (2006) who discussed the importance of tightly controlling testing conditions and the effect on measurement error, "A smaller magnitude of standard error of the estimate (SEE) is likely to occur when measurement conditions are optimal, which means that influential extraneous variables are well controlled (e.g., quiet test setting, consistent administrator, consistent location, consistent probe difficulty, use of standardized directions)" (p. 130). Christ further demonstrated the effect of what he described as optimal, moderate, and poor measurement conditions on the standard error of the slope (SEb) when progress monitoring. Thus, the SEb differed based on qualitative evaluations of the integrity of administration conditions. These results emphasize two essential points: (1) the integrity of administration conditions will affect the confidence of the data used to support educational decisions and (2) practitioners should provide a graphic representation of the error through the use of confidence intervals in order to quantify this confidence (see Christ, 2006). (See case study for further illustration).

The Number of Behavioral Samples Taken

So far, we have discussed multiple ways to decrease the amount of error in CBM data such as strategically choosing controlled probe sets and tightly controlling administration procedures and conditions. Another method that can be used to decrease the variability in WCPM scores for both level and trend data is to increase the number of samples taken (Christ, 2006; Poncy et al., 2005). The general pattern observed across these studies is that the SEM/SEb is initially large, drops off relatively quickly, and soon flattens. Hence, while increasing the number of collected samples is helpful, it becomes counter-productive after a certain point as it does little to affect the confidence with which we can make educational decisions.

These findings suggest that there are optimal numbers of probes that should be given to make decisions about the level and trend of student oral reading fluency data that are empirically based. While this line of research is still relatively new, we will provide some tentative recommendations concerning the number of probes and SEM/SEb that should accompany these data collection procedures based on of the work of Christ (2006), Christ and Silberglitt (2007), and Poncy et al. (2005). Recommendations will be provided for the following assessment purposes: (1) comparing students (e.g., norming, screening), (2) estimating a student's level of achievement, and (3) estimating a student's rate of learning (i.e., progress monitoring).

When comparing students, a relative decision is being made. Traditionally, the recommendation when collecting benchmarking data has been to administer three probes and take the median score. Data from the Poncy et al. (2005) study would support this recommendation. If students are being considered for inclusion into a program based on screening data, students around the cutoff point may be given additional probes. However, all students around the cutoff point should be given the same additional probes. Administering over five probes becomes inefficient as the SEM is not significantly affected. Therefore, the recommendation when screening students is to give three probes to all students (SEM of 7) and to give five probes to students around defined cutoff points (SEM of 5).

Not all decisions about the level of student achievement are based on comparisons to peers. For example, a student in high school is referred for decoding difficulties and educators want to establish the student's baseline level of performance to anchor a goal line or want to compare the student's performance to a predetermined criterion (e.g., 120 WCPM). Both of these decisions are independent of other students' performance and are therefore absolute in nature. Currently, consensus is lacking regarding how many probes are necessary to establish a baseline level of performance. Some researchers recommend taking the median (i.e., middle score) of three probes administered on a single day and others recommend taking the median of nine probes administered over 3 days (Fuchs, 1989; Marston, 1989; Shinn, 1989). Data from the Poncy et al., 2005 study would suggest that practitioners give five probes (SEM of 8). While administering nine probes would provide an SEM of 6, which would decrease the SEM by 2, after giving five probes collecting additional data does little to decrease the SEM.

RtI models, as the name implies, places a premium on measuring how a student "responds" to intervention. To answer this question, educators need to accurately estimate a student's learning rate in response to defined intervention criteria. To achieve this goal, practitioners need to know how many data points to collect and over what period of time should they be collected to reliably estimate a student's rate of growth. Again, disagreements exist within the literature with various recommendations offered including the following: collecting one data point per week for 6 weeks, collecting two data points per week for 6–8 weeks, and administering three probes and taking the median each week for 6 weeks.

Initial research findings discourage the administration of only one data point per week and suggest that when progress monitoring a minimum of two data points per week should be used (Christ, 2006; Shinn, 2002). The corresponding SEb when using two data points per week for 6 weeks would be approximately 1.7, for 7 weeks would approximate 1.3, and for 8 weeks would be approximately 1.1. Research has yet to address the approach of giving three probes and taking the median once per week, which sounds promising. Practitioners should be aware that collecting one data point per week when progress monitoring is likely insufficient to produce data to accurately estimate student growth rates over short periods of time (e.g., 6–8 weeks).

After the data points are collected, practitioners need to summarize the data to estimate a student's rate of learning. To do this, Christ (2006) reviewed three methods: (1) visual analysis, (2) the split half technique, and (3) plotting a line of best fit using ordinary least-squares (OLS) regression. Research supports the recommendation that practitioners use the OLS regression approach, as visual analysis and split-half techniques will not provide as accurate as a depiction of student growth.

Conclusion

CBM procedures have been used to successfully produce data that address a variety of questions in the problem-solving model and in the process have garnered a large amount of support. While CBM has a variety of strengths, it also has limitations. The goal of this chapter of the section was to highlight the sensitivity of CBM data to a variety of error sources and provide some initial practices that can be used to reduce this error and increase the confidence with which we can support educational decisions.

Case Study Example

In the following case example, we illustrate the use of the nontraditional assessment methods within the problem-solving context. Specifically, this case study applies to the assessment of a student's reading fluency and the evaluation of an intervention for reading fluency. However, the same principles can be applied to the assessment of basic skills and the evaluation of interventions for early literacy skills, reading comprehension, math computation, spelling, and written expression.

Within a problem-solving model, the first step is to identify students at risk of failing to gain proficiency in a basic skill area. Thus, a problem must be identified through observation of behavior in the environment. To identify students at risk of failing to gain proficiency in reading fluency, the school psychologist, third-grade general education teachers, and principal at Williams Elementary met and agreed to administer a benchmark assessment program, administering generic probes of oral reading fluency from the AIMSweb® system three times per year (Fall, Winter, Spring). The school psychologist, Mr. Jones, then trained general education teachers and aides to accurately administer these three, 1-minute reading probes to each student, asking each student to read the grade-level passages aloud while the examiner scored errors and recorded the last word read at 1 minute. The examiner then determined the number of words read correctly for each passage and recorded the student's median or middle score beginning in the fall (within the first few weeks of school starting).

Mr. Jones then entered this data into a data management system (e.g., AIMSweb®, www.aimsweb.com) and provided the data in graphic form to the staff to identify the students at risk.

As noted earlier, a problem is defined as a discrepancy between the student's current level of performance and the expected level of performance. This difference can be most readily identified by comparing the student's performance to local norms of performance (established by administering progress monitoring measures to all students within a student's grade level three times per year and rank-ordering the scores) or national norms (established by administering progress-monitoring measures to a national sample of students across grade levels three times per year and rank-ordering the scores). The third-grade team reviewed their data and determined that the average third-grade student at Williams Elementary read 75 words correctly per minute in the fall. This average level of performance was found to be consistent with data the team had gathered the previous year on all third-grade students at Williams Elementary and consistent with national norm samples (e.g., AIMSweb®; $WCPM_{50th \%tile} = 78$; www.aimsweb.com). The team then identified students who performed below the 25th percentile, indicating a significant difference between current level of performance and expected level of performance in the third grade. Aimee, a third-grade student who was new to the district, was identified to be reading only 43 words correctly per minute. She was also found to be making a number of errors (six errors per minute; 88% accuracy). Her performance differed significantly from the expected levels of performance for the third grade in terms of speed and accuracy. To add confidence to the estimate of her baseline performance, two additional probes were given resulting in a median of 45 WCPM with six errors per minute.

The third step in the problem-solving process is designing the intervention plan. During this stage, Mr. Jones, in collaboration with Aimee's teacher, Ms. Brown, further assessed Aimee's reading performance within the context of the curriculum. Consistent with a model of functional academic assessment (Witt et al., 2000), Mr. Jones observed reading instruction to formulate a hypothesis accounting for her reading failure. During his observations, Mr. Jones noted the number of opportunities given to practice reading aloud, the number of times reinforcement was provided, the number of times Aimee provided correct responses, the number of errors Aimee made when reading, and the number of times Aimee was shown how to perform a skill. On the basis of this data, Mr. Jones hypothesized that Aimee had not spent enough time practicing reading and that she had not had enough help to read accurately (e.g., feedback and error correction). Mr. Jones and Ms. Brown hypothesized that given increased opportunities to practice reading and sufficient error correction to practice reading accurately Aimee's reading fluency would improve. They designed an intervention that included these components – phrase drill error correction with repeated reading (Daly, Chafouleas, & Skinner, 2005). The intervention would be implemented 20 minutes per day in the classroom with the support of a fifth-grade peer tutor. Given the empirical support for this intervention and the frequency and intensity of the intervention, they established an ambitious goal from which to evaluate progress. The average third-grade student at Williams Elementary increases her reading skill at a rate of 1 word read correctly per week based on local norms. Using ambitious rates (Fuchs, Fuchs, Hamlett, Walz, & Germann, 1993), Mr. Jones and Ms. Brown expected that Aimee would increase her reading fluency by a rate of 1.5 words correctly per week (WPW) and would decrease her errors to four or less per minute. Therefore, Aimee's reading fluency goal was stated as follows: given 6 weeks of intervention, Aimee will read 54 words correctly with 4 or less errors (>93% accuracy) from randomly selected third-grade progress monitoring probes. The aim line (dashed line) depicted on Fig. 6.2 reflects this goal anchored from her baseline performance.

The fourth step in the problem-solving process is to implement the intervention, ensuring that the intervention is implemented with integrity (accurately and consistently) and that progress monitoring data is consistently collected throughout the intervention. The phrase drill error correction with repeated reading intervention was implemented by a fifth-grade peer daily for 20 minutes during reading instruction. To ensure that the intervention was implemented with integrity, Ms. Brown

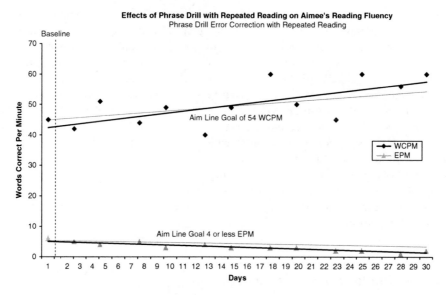

Fig. 6.2 Progress monitoring of Aimee's performance in reading fluency

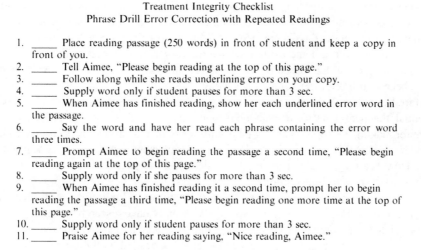

Fig. 6.3 Treatment integrity checklist phrase drill error correction with repeated readings

developed a treatment integrity checklist describing each step in the intervention. She then trained the fifth-grade peer on each step and provided practice until the peer consistently implemented each step with 100% accuracy. The peer used the checklist during implementation to self-monitor her implementation. During the intervention, Mr. Jones observed the peer's implementation 20% of the time, using a second copy of the checklist to confirm agreement in treatment implementation. Refer to Fig. 6.3 for a copy of the treatment integrity checklist.

The final step in the problem-solving process is to evaluate the data to determine if the intervention is solving the identified problem. Ms. Brown had progress-monitored Aimee's reading fluency twice per week throughout the intervention. Mr. Jones graphed this data and met with Ms. Brown to review Aimee's progress. Visual inspection of the graphed data (see Fig. 6.2) revealed that the intervention had been successful, with progress monitoring of words read correctly per minute exceeding the aim line and number of errors per minute falling in the desired direction below the aim line. Mr. Jones also added a trend line, or line of best fit, to estimate Aimee's learning rate. This line reflects an aggressive growth rate of 2.3 WPW with a confidence interval of 1.8–2.9 WPW. Ms. Brown also had noted that Aimee and her peer had been working together well and that she had observed Aimee volunteering to read aloud more frequently, appearing to gain in her confidence level. Because Aimee's response to the intervention had exceeded their goal, Mr. Jones and Ms. Brown raised the goal as a result to 75 WCPM at the end of six more weeks anticipating a continued aggressive growth rate of 2.5 WPW. They also decided to share Aimee's progress with her, giving her a role in graphing her progress-monitoring data and reinforcing her progress. This step was added to the treatment integrity checklist and Aimee's peer was trained on implementation of the self-graphing procedure.

Conclusions: Implications for Practice

When Deno & Mirkin (1977) first developed CBM procedures, their focus was on evaluating special education students' learning rates under different conditions so that we could maximize student learning. Around the same time, educators and researchers began to experiment with alternative models of service delivery that focused on providing remedial services to students before their skill deficits became so severe that special education placement was considered (e.g., pre-referral interventions, student assistance teams). Today, most RtI models have merged the two by focusing on early intervention and using repeated measurement of target skills.

In addition to merging data-based problem solving and CBM, the primary advancement of RtI models has been to use brief measures of academic responding rates (e.g., WCPM), as opposed to teacher referrals, to identify those in need of remediation. While these problem-solving models have great potential, the measures used to evaluate responsiveness have limitations. These limitations are less severe for making decision regarding eligibility for remedial service (not a primary purpose of the original measures) than they are for evaluating responsiveness (a primary purpose of the original measures). However, the success of RtI models is dependent upon quickly and precisely evaluating students' responsiveness to interventions.

We hope that the current chapter makes educators aware of the limitations associated with using these rate measures to evaluate responsiveness. Only recently have researchers begun to investigate the error associated with these measures. Clearly, these researchers have made significant strides in developing strategies and procedures to reduce the error associated with these measures. Thus, we hope that readers are as optimistic as we are regarding the progress being made.

As research on learning rate measurement systems and the measures themselves continues, we believe that we will be able to develop measures and procedures (e.g., more tightly controlled reading passages) that enhance our ability to detect small changes in skill development. Such measures will enhance our remediation procedures by allowing us to compare responsiveness across interventions and select interventions that *most rapidly* enhance each student's learning rate (Skinner, Belfiore, & Watson, 1995/2002). Such measures may also allow researchers to better evaluate group interventions, which may enhance our ability to develop and select novel strategies and procedures that can be used to enhance all students' learning (prevention). Clearly, such positive outcomes demand that researchers continue their work designed to enhance the quality of our nontraditional measures and measurement systems designed to evaluate learning rates. The quality of our data-based decisions is dependent upon the quality of our data.

Chapter Competency Checklist

DOMAIN 1 – Enhancing the development of cognitive and academic skills

Foundational	Functional
Understand and explain the following: ☐ Differences between the traditional and nontraditional approaches to assessment ☐ Problem solving model ☐ Curriculum based measurement ☐ Controlling measurement error	Gain practice: ☐ Administering CBM probes for screening ☐ Administering CBM probes for intervention progress monitoring ☐ Explaining results of CBM probes to others ☐ Administering CBM probes with a broad population of students

References

Bergan, J. R., & Kratochwill, T. R. (1990). *Behavioral consultation and therapy*. New York: Plenum.

Brown-Chidsey, R., & Steege, M. W. (2005). *Response to intervention*. New York: Guilford.

Christ, T. J. (2006). Short term estimates of growth using curriculum-based measurement of oral reading fluency: Estimating standard error of the slope to construct confidence intervals. *School Psychology Review, 35*, 128–133.

Christ, T. J., & Silberglitt, B. (2007). Estimates of the standard error of measurement for curriculum-based measures of oral reading fluency. *School Psychology Review, 36*, 130–146.

Colón, E. P., & Kranzler, J. H. (2006). Effect of instructions on curriculum-based measurement of reading. *Journal of Psychoeducational Assessment, 24*, 318–328.

Daly, E. J., Chafouleas, S., & Skinner, C. H. (2005). *Interventions for reading problems*. New York: Guilford.

Deno, S. L. (1989). Curriculum-based measurement and special education services: A fundamental and direct relationship. In M. R. Shinn (Ed.), *Curriculum-based measurement: Assessing special children* (pp. 1–17). New York: Guilford.

Deno, S. L. (2002). Problem solving as "best practice.". In A. Thomas & J. Grimes (Eds.), *Best practices in school psychology IV* (pp. 37–56). Bethesda, MD: National Association of School Psychologists.

Deno, S. L. (2005). Problem solving assessment. In R. Brown-Chidsey (Ed.), *Assessment for intervention* (pp. 10–40). New York: Guilford.

Deno, S. L., Marston, D., & Mirkin, P. (1982). Valid measurement procedures for continuous evaluation of written expression. *Exceptional Children, 48*, 368–371.

Deno, S. L., & Mirkin, P. K. (1977). *Data-based problem modification: A manual*. Reston: Council for Exceptional Children.

Deno, S. L., Mirkin, P. K., & Chiang, B. (1982). Identifying valid measures of reading. *Exceptional Children, 49*, 36–45.

Derr-Minneci, T. F., & Shapiro, E. S. (1992). Validating curriculum-based measurement in reading from a behavioral perspective. *School Psychology Quarterly, 7*, 2–16.

Fagan, T. K., & Wise, P. S. (2000). *School psychology: Past, present, and future* (2nd ed.). Bethesda, MD: National Association of School Psychologists.

Forness, S. R., Kavale, K. A., Blum, I. M., & Lloyd, J. W. (1997). Mega-analysis of meta-analyses: What works in special education and related services. *Teaching Exceptional Children, 29*(6), 4–9.

Fuchs, L. S. (1989). Evaluating solutions: Monitoring progress and revising intervention plans. In M. R. Shinn (Ed.), *Curriculum-based measurement: Assessment special children* (pp. 153–181). New York: Guilford.

Fuchs, L. S., & Deno, S. L. (1992). Effects of curriculum within curriculum-based measurement. *Exceptional Children, 58*, 232–243.

Fuchs, L. S., & Fuchs, D. (1986). Effects of systematic formative evaluation: A meta-analysis. *Exceptional Children, 53*, 199–208.

Fuchs, L. S., & Fuchs, D. (1992). Identifying a measure for monitoring student reading progress. *School Psychology Review, 21*, 45–58.

Fuchs, L. S., Fuchs, D., & Hamlett, C. L. (1989). Effects of instrumental use of curriculum-based measurement to enhance instructional programs. *Remedial and Special Education, 10*(2), 43–52.

Fuchs, L. S., Fuchs, D., Hamlett, C. L., Walz, L., & Germann, G. (1993). Formative evaluation of academic progress: How much growth can we expect? *School Psychology Review, 22*, 27–48.

Fuchs, L. S., Fuchs, D., & Maxwell, L. (1988). The validity of informal reading comprehension measures. *Remedial and Special Education, 9*(2), 20–28.

Goldstein, H., Arkell, C., Ashcroft, S. C., Hurley, O. L., & Lilly, S. M. (1975). Schools. In N. Hobbs (Ed.), *Issues in the classification of children*. San Francisco: Jossey-Bass.

Good, R. H., III, & Kaminski, R. A. (Eds.). (2002). *Dynamic Indicators of Early Literacy Skills* (6th ed.). Eugene, OR: Institute for the Development of Educational Achievement.

Hintze, J. M., & Christ, T. J. (2004). An examination of variability as a function of passage variance in CBM progress monitoring. *School Psychology Review, 33*, 204–217.

Hintze, J. M., Owen, S. V., Shapiro, E. S., & Daly, E. J. (2000). Generalizability of oral reading fluency measures: Application of g theory to curriculum-based measurement. *School Psychology Quarterly, 15*, 52–68.

Howell, K. W., & Nolet, V. (2000). *Curriculum-based evaluation: Teaching and decision making* (3rd ed.). Belmont, CA: Wadsworth.

Kampwirth, T. J. (2006). *Collaborative consultation in the schools: Effective practices for students with learning and behavior problems* (3rd ed.). Upper Saddle River, NJ: Prentice Hall.

Kavale, K. (1990). The effectiveness of special education. In T. B. Gutkin & C. R. Reynolds (Eds.), *The handbook of school psychology* (2nd ed., pp. 868–898). New York: John Wiley.

Marston, D. B. (1989). A curriculum-based measurement approach to assessing academic performance: What it is and why do it. In M. R. Shinn (Ed.), *Curriculum-based measurement: Assessment special children* (pp. 18–78). New York: Guilford.

Neddenriep, C. E., Hale, A. D., Skinner, C. H., Hawkins, R. O., & Winn, B. (2007). A preliminary investigation of the concurrent validity of reading comprehension rate: A direct, dynamic measure of reading comprehension. *Psychology in the Schools, 44*, 373–388.

Oakland, T., & Cunningham, J. (1999). The futures of school psychology: Conceptual models for its development and examples of their applications. In C. R. Reynolds & T. B. Gutkin (Eds.), *The handbook of school psychology* (3rd ed., pp. 34–53). New York: Wiley.

Poncy, B. C., Skinner, C. H., & Axtell, P. K. (2005). An investigation of the reliability and standard error of measurement of words read correctly per minute. *Journal of Psychoeducational Assessment, 23*, 326–338.

Powell-Smith, K. A., & Bradley-Klug, K. L. (2001). Another look at the "C" in CBM: Does it really matter if curriculum-based measurement reading probes are "curriculum-based? *Psychology in the Schools, 38*, 299–312.

Reschly, D. J., & Yssedyke, J. E. (2002). Paradigm shift: The past is not the future. In A. Thomas & J. Grimes (Eds.), *Best practices in school psychology IV* (pp. 3–36). Bethesda, MD: National Association of School Psychologists.

Shapiro, E. S. (2004). *Academic skills problem: Direct assessment and intervention* (3rd ed.). New York: Guilford.

Shinn, M. R. (Ed.). (1989). *Curriculum-based measurement: Assessing special children*. New York: Guilford.

Shinn, M. R. (2002). Best practices in using curriculum-based measurement in a problem-solving model. In A. Thomas & J. Grimes (Eds.), *Best practices in school psychology IV* (pp. 671–698). Bethesda, MD: National Association of School Psychologists.

Shinn, M. R., & Bamonto, S. (1998). Advanced applications of curriculum-based measurement: "Big ideas" and avoiding confusion. In M. R. Shinn (Ed.), *Advanced applications of curriculum-based measurement* (pp. 1–31). New York: Guilford.

Shinn, M. R., Good, R. H., III, & Parker, C. (1999). Noncategorical special education services with students with severe achievement deficits. In D. J. Reschly, W. D. Tilly III, & J. P. Grimes (Eds.), *Special education in transition: Functional assessment and noncategorical programming* (pp. 81–105). Longmont: Sopris West.

Skinner, C. H. (1998). Preventing academic skills deficits. In T. S. Watson & F. Gresham (Eds.), *Handbook of child behavior therapy: Ecological considerations in assessment, treatment, and evaluation* (pp. 61–83). New York: Plenum.

Skinner, C. H., Belfiore, P. B., & Watson, T. S. (1995/2002). Assessing the relative effects of interventions in students with mild disabilities: Assessing instructional time. *Journal of Psychoeducational Assessment, 20*, 345-356.15. (Reprinted from *Assessment in Rehabilitation and Exceptionality, 2*, 207-220, 1995)

Skinner, C. H., Hurst, K. L., Teeple, D. F., & Meadows, S. O. (2002). Increasing on-task behavior during mathematics independent seat-work in students with emotional disorders by interspersing additional brief problems. *Psychology in the Schools, 39*, 647–659.

Skinner, C. H., Neddenriep, C. E., Bradley-Klug, K. L., & Ziemann, J. M. (2002). Advances in curriculum-based measurement: Alternative rate measures for assessing reading skills in pre- and advanced readers. *Behavior Analyst Today, 3*, 270–281.

Tilly, W. D. (2002). Best practices in school psychology as a problem-solving enterprise. In A. Thomas & J. Grimes (Eds.), *Best practices in school psychology IV* (pp. 21–36). Bethesda, MD: National Association of School Psychologists.

Witt, J. C., Daly, E. J., III, & Noell, G. H. (2000). *Functional assessments: A step-by-step guide to solving academic and behavior problems*. Longmont, CO: Sopris West.

Ysseldyke, J. E., Algozzine, B., Shinn, N., & McGue, M. (1982). Similarities and differences between underachievers and students labeled learning-disabled. *The Journal of Special Education, 16,* 73–85.

Ysseldyke, J. E., & Marston, D. (1999). Origins of categorical special education services in schools. In D. J. Reschly, W. D. Tilly III, & J. P. Grimes (Eds.), *Special education in transition: Functional assessment and noncategorical programming* (pp. 1–18). Longmont, CO: Sopris West.

Chapter 7
Assessing Student Skills Using Process-Oriented Approaches

Susan Clements, Ray W. Christner, Amy L. McLaughlin, and Jessica B. Bolton

The idea of systematically measuring human abilities is not a new concept, as it dates back to the work of Sir Francis Galton during the late 1800s, noted as the father of the "testing movement," and the development of the first "intelligence" test by Alfred Binet in 1905 (Hale & Fiorello, 2004). Since their inception, the debate over the use and objectivity of intelligence tests has continued in the field of psychology and measurement, with the history showing examples of "IQ" tests being both mandated and banned from public education (i.e., *P.A.R.C. v. Penn*, 1971; *Larry, P. v. Riles*, 1972). Amidst the controversy of the use of intelligence tests, is the question of utility. Because of the historically strong link to placement decisions for children, many have questioned the continued value of such tests. However, recently a number of researchers have been highlighting some of the benefits of linking cognitive assessment to interventions, and the benefit of moving away from an overall IQ score to a more idiographic approach (Hale, Fiorello, Kavanagh, Holdnack, & Aloe, 2007). Like a number of topics in psychology and education, there have been differing views and opinions, not only on the structure of intelligence, but also on the idea of being able to derive useful and appropriate interventions from the assessment of cognitive abilities.

The nature of intelligence testing and the ways in which these tests are interpreted has been the topic of much debate in the field of psychology over the years. Binet proposed that interpretation of his measure be individualized for each child (e.g., looking at individual performance on tasks); however, this idea was quickly dismissed with the inception of the Intelligence Quotient (IQ). Those who supported the use of the IQ score were proponents of the general intelligence (*g*) model; a model which defines mental ability as a unitary construct. Historically, many have hailed the IQ as the best measure of overall intelligence. Those who support the *g* model do not necessarily refute the existence of other factors; however, these factors are not considered as important in conceptualizing cognitive functioning. Over time, many professionals have used global IQ as the basis for determining individual potential, making diagnostic decisions, and recommending specific educational interventions/placements.

In addition to the *g* model, there are others who support a multifactor model of intelligence (i.e., Guilford, 1967; Horn & Cattell, 1967; Thurstone, 1938). Those who support the multifactorial model emphasize the importance of explaining cognitive functioning or intelligence in terms of a variety of abilities (e.g., short-term memory, long-term memory retrieval, fluid reasoning, etc.) rather than a single concept. The debate between the *g* proponents and the multifactorial proponents continues today among practitioners and theorists (Fiorello, Hale, McGrath, Ryan, & Quinn, 2001).

S. Clements (✉)
Philadelphia College of Osteopathic Medicine, Philadelphia, PA 19131, USA
e-mail: Susancl@pcom.edu

T.M. Lionetti et al. (eds.), *A Practical Guide to Building Professional Competencies in School Psychology*, DOI 10.1007/978-1-4419-6257-7_7, © Springer Science+Business Media, LLC 2011

In practice, many clinicians go beyond simply reporting Full Scale IQ (or g) when interpreting intelligence tests. In a national survey of school psychologists, 89% of respondents indicated that they regularly utilize index scores, subtest profile analysis, or both when interpreting intelligence tests (Pfeiffer, Reddy, Kletzel, Schmelzer, & Boyer, 2000). Moreover, current theories of cognitive ability have recognized multiple component cognitive processes that make up the overall g (Hale & Fiorello, 2004).

Expanding the idea of multiple cognitive processing is the movement toward a "process-oriented approach" of assessment. A process-oriented approach not only provides an interpretation of standardized scores regarding specific processing skills, but further incorporates the clinician's detailed observations of the process by which the examinee approaches and completes the task. Although this method can be controversial to some in the field because it moves away from standardized procedures, the idea of observations and clinical judgment are not new concepts. In addition, many newer developed and renormed tests have taken into consideration the benefit of looking at the process of the examinee during assessment and have included quantitative means to process components. A few recent assessment tools fitting this model include the *Wechsler Scales* (e.g., *Wechsler Intelligence Scale for Children, Fourth Edition, Integrated [WISC-IV]* and *Wechsler Adult Intelligence Scale, Fourth Edition [WAIS-IV]*), the *Cognitive Assessment System (CAS)*, *Kauffman Assessment Battery for Children, Second Edition (KABC-II)*, and the *NEPSY, Second Edition (NEPSY-II)*. Although there is subjectivity with observation, with proper training and using observation in conjunction with other test data, this technique can be more beneficial than traditional models of test interpretation. Specifically, using this model of assessment has the potential to provide a more specific interpretation of the examinee's strengths and needs by attending to the individual's approach to a task, and ultimately, appropriate use can aid in the development of interventions to target particular areas of need.

Limitations of Cognitive Assessment

Despite the historical importance that has been placed on standardized test scores, particularly the IQ score, the idea of interpreting skills and abilities based on standardized test scores alone does not provide sufficient information to adequately conceptualize an individual's strengths and needs or to provide the most fitting interventions. Before we can move into a discussion and review of details regarding a process-oriented approach, we must first consider the limitations of cognitive evaluation in general.

Prediction

Some of the pertinent arguments of the traditional intelligence assessment involve discussions of IQ as an accurate "predictor" of academic achievement. Data from the major intelligence batteries indicates that global ability scores generally account for 45–50% of achievement variance, which means other factors account for the remaining 50–55% (Flanagan, 2006). In addition, recent statistical analysis by Hale, Fiorello, Kavanaugh, Hoeppner, and Gaither (2001) has called into question the utility of the Full Scale Intelligence Quotient (FSIQ) as a measure of global functioning for children with learning disabilities. Hale and colleagues argue that the statistical techniques utilized in studies advocating FSIQ as a better predictor of academic achievement than the factor scores (see Glutting, Youngstrom, Ward, Ward, & Hale, 1997) are flawed. In response, Hale and others suggest that FSIQ should not be interpreted in individuals with variable cognitive profiles (e.g., difference in performance on various processing tasks), as it merely provides an arithmetic mean of performance, and does not give any information about strengths and weaknesses.

Cultural Issues

Much too often the main purpose of intelligence testing has been to serve as a device that provides a sorting and labeling function. However, we must recognize the inherent flaws of many of these tests. Samuda (1998) has noted that traditional assessment measures cannot indicate the true potential of minority groups, the economically disadvantaged, or students from educationally impoverished backgrounds, as these instruments are geared toward the values, information, learning styles, and cognitive structures that are common to the middle-class lifestyle. Additionally, it is important to note that when measuring intelligence, aptitudes cannot be completely separated from academic achievement (Levine, 1999). The format of standardized tests can influence performance and should be considered, and thus, practitioners must choose tests based on student need and the referral questions. Like children with unfamiliarity with the language and the structure of the testing conditions, children with organizational problems and difficulties with output may perform poorly with open-ended formats and showcase greater abilities when the demands on organization and output (i.e., multiple choice) are reduced.

Levine (1999) further points out that IQ scores are often over-interpreted or misused and should not be thought of as an absolute measurement. Performance scores on the standardized measures merely represent a comparison with other children who participated in the testing sample. Moreover, test items are selected to show differences between age groups and correlations with school achievement, and as such, they are not necessarily reflective of how children learn or develop, particularly those from diverse cultures. Given this, practitioners must realize that merely reviewing test scores are not likely to provide useful information regarding the student, and these scores must be interpreted within the context of the situation, taking into account the student's observed behaviors, emotional reactions to the task, and problem-solving approaches (Baron, 2004).

Myths Associated with Intelligence Testing

The current dissatisfaction with the identification procedures associated with the educational diagnosis of learning disabilities has been waged by researchers and practitioners alike. Many argue that cognitive or intelligence tests have been misused and misinterpreted, which has resulted in both the over-identification and under-identification of true learning concerns. We offer, hereunder, a brief review of some of the myths that have been identified.

Myth 1: Interchangeability

Global ability scores obtained on different tests or measures are not interchangeable. Although many cognitive and intelligence tests are correlated with each other, this does not suggest that different tests measure the same construct. It would not be unusual for an individual to obtain different scores across tests due to differences in the specific cognitive process being assessed on each test, as well as the diverse modalities with which each cognitive ability or process is assessed. Scores on measures of intelligence must be interpreted with consideration given to the content processes and content knowledge necessary for each test (Hale & Fiorello, 2004). Let's consider differences on two commonly used cognitive tests – the *Woodcock–Johnson Tests of Cognitive Abilities, Third Edition* (WJ-III COG) and the *Wechsler Intelligence Scale for Children, Fourth Edition* (WISC-IV). On the WJ-III COG the overall score is the General Intellectual Ability (GIA) score, which is weighted according to the "g" loading of each subtest at the individual age levels (Sattler, 2001). This suggests that at each age level, the subtests that make up GIA have different weights. Compare this to the calculation of the Full Scale Intelligence Quotient (FSIQ) of the WISC-IV in which each of the core subtests contributes equally to the FSIQ calculations. In addition to the differences in obtaining overall scores, the nature of how different tests and subtests measure various skills and processes also varies. For example, when measuring nonverbal reasoning abilities, one of the subtests of the WISC-IV, Block Design, requires the individual to view a picture of a geometric design and use blocks to recreate the design, which involves motor dexterity and fine motor skills. On the other hand, the WJ-III COG contains a test, Spatial Relations, which measures a similar construct; however, rather than using motor skills to reproduce the designs, the Spatial Relation subtest utilizes a multiple choice format. Although both assess some similar skills, they are different in their degree of motor output demands. It is necessary for practitioners to be aware of these differences, and these should be considered whenever different tests are being used.

Myth 2: Ability-Achievement Discrepancy

The term "specific learning disability" (SLD) is defined as "a disorder in *one or more of the basic psychological processes* involved in understanding or in using language, spoken or written, which may manifest itself in the imperfect ability to listen, think, speak, read, write, spell, or do mathematical calculations, including conditions such as perceptual disabilities, brain injury, minimal brain dysfunction, dyslexia, and developmental aphasia." (IDEA 2004, 20 U.S.C. §1401 [30]). This focus on *basic psychological processes* is consistent with research indicating that many learning disorders involve deficits in neuropsychological processes (see Berninger, 2002; Collins & Rourke, 2003; Fine, Semrud-Clikeman, Keith, Stapleton, & Hynd, 2007; Hale & Fiorello, 2004; Naglieri & Bortstein, 2003; Shaywitz, Lyon, & Shaywitz, 2006; Tallal, 2006). The Learning Disabilities Roundtable (USDOR, 2002, 2004) advisory panel also supported the identification of "a core cognitive deficit" as an indicator for a specific learning disability.

By far the most significant change included in IDEA 2004 is the elimination of the requirement for a student to show a "severe discrepancy" between intellectual ability and academic achievement as a means of identifying a student as having a SLD. Before IDEA 2004, such a discrepancy had to be found in one or more of the following areas, including oral expression, listening comprehension, written expression, basic reading skill, reading comprehension, mathematics calculation, and mathematics reasoning.

The "discrepancy" requirement, which has been part of federal special education regulations since 1977, has been under attack for some time. Recognizing that the "discrepancy" approach was resulting in both late identification and misidentification of SLD, Congress included a new provision in IDEA 2004 stating that school districts are not required to take into account a severe discrepancy between ability (IQ) and achievement when determining whether a student has a specific learning disability. In fact, many argue that there may be cases where learning disabilities are validly indicated even though a discrepancy was not found (Siegel, 1999 [Flanagan presentation]; Levine, 1999). The research overwhelmingly provides little empirical support for IQ-achievement discrepancy models to diagnose learning disabilities (Ysseldyke, 2005, p. 125 [Flanagan presentation]). Levine has gone so far as to label the discrepancy formula as "misleading" and "harmful." Issues such as attention difficulties, productivity problems, higher-order cognitive weaknesses, poor understanding of syntax, working memory dysfunctions, and organizational deficits may go undetected with this type of assessment approach (Levine). Even if a student meets the eligibility criteria for special education supports, the lack of detection of other compounding difficulties could exacerbate academic and/or emotional difficulties. In addition, some students with learning problems could perform consistently across subtests, yet still possess underlying learning problems that are viewed in the classroom setting. Their difficulties may occur in areas not measured by the test or their difficulties may have led to depressed scores across all subtests.

Myth 3: Statistically Significant vs. Clinically Meaningful

Consider the example of an individual with a split of 24 points between the Verbal Comprehension Index (VCI) and Perceptual Reasoning Index (PRI) on the *Wechsler Adult Intelligence Scale, Fourth Edition* (WAIS-IV), in favor of the latter. Based on the significant discrepancy, the practitioner might conclude that the individual has impaired verbal information processing skills when compared to the norming sample of his age group. However, this would be a faulty conclusion if the individual's VCI score was 120 (Above Average range, 91st percentile) and the PRI score was a 144 (Superior range, 99th percentile). These statistical discrepancy approaches lack a means for differentiating between valuable and undesirable performance (Alloy, Acocella, & Bootzin, 1996, p. 6). In these systems, even statistically significant splits that contain a lower score within the average, high average, or even superior range can be interpreted as undesirable even though the individual shows a great deal of strength in the lower-scoring area.

Myth 4: Intra-individual Analysis and Interpretation is Independent of Inter-individual Analysis and Interpretation

Intra-individual analysis attempts to predict scores based on an individual's average performance on other subtests. Consider this example from the WJ-III in which the examinee earned a score of 98 (Average range, 45th percentile) on the Phonemic Awareness Composite. Her predicted score was a 119 (High Average range, 90th percentile). Based on the 21-point difference in scores, an intra-cognitive discrepancy of −1.71 standard deviations was calculated, which was greater than the 1.5 standard deviation that is required to interpret an information processing deficit. In this case, the practitioner interpreted the difference as evidence for a phonological processing deficit, and identified this deficit as the underlying cause of the examinee's reading disorder. Making this conclusion is an error, in that the individual's phonemic awareness score is well within the Average range. It should be noted that "flat profiles" of abilities are uncommon – that is, all scores being equal with no variation. In fact, data from the WISC-IV standardization sample indicates that only 17% of the sample population had a flat profile (Hale et al., 2001). McGrew and Knopik (1996) indicate that at least two significant discrepancies are typically found in the cognitive ability profiles of "normal" people. Therefore, these intra-individual discrepancies can be misleading and lead to unwarranted interpretation of deficient functioning.

The Evolution of the Process-Oriented Assessment

Although standardized tests of intelligence have many limitations, they still have great value in the assessment process provided that they are administered and interpreted properly. Although the interpretation of the FSIQ is not valid in many cases, factor scores, subtest scores, process scores, and process observations can provide important information about a child's functioning and can assist the practitioner in developing hypotheses regarding a child's profile of cognitive strengths and weaknesses. This is the basis for the process-oriented approach to assessment.

The process-oriented approach dates back to Heinz Werner when, in 1937 he published an article entitled, *Process and Achievement: A Basic Problem of Education and Developmental Psychology*. Werner posited that systematic observations of the examinee's problem-solving strategies could provide more useful information about the individual's cognitive functioning than scores that evaluate achievement through binary scoring. Almost every subtest of cognitive functioning is multifactorial. Therefore, in order to accurately evaluate an individual's functioning, a consideration of the component factors must occur in order to determine the underlying processes impacting performance. The implications of the multifactorial nature of cognitive subtests is that two individuals may have identical standardized scores, yet exhibit different underlying deficits which can impact diagnostic decisions, as well as the treatment interventions that are prescribed. Process-oriented scores, which are available on some standardized measures (e.g., the WISC-III PI, WISC-IV Integrated, NEPSY, Delis–Kaplan, and Children's Memory Scale [CMS]), are useful in pinpointing cognitive and processing deficits related to academic difficulties. In addition, these score may be used to evaluate whether pharmacological, behavioral, and/or educational interventions are efficacious (Kaplan, Fein, Kramer, Delis, & Morris, 1999).

Clinicians have often informally utilized testing-of-limits procedures to obtain additional information about children's performance and abilities, such as whether a child could produce a correct response with some type of modification such as a change in the stimulus modality, format of the question, or eliminating time limits. With the publication of the WISC-III Processing Instrument (Kaplan et al., 1999), clinicians were provided with a standardized way of testing the limits, and provided a structured procedure for evaluating additional information regarding a child's cognitive processing. The WISC-III PI was developed based on the process approach, that is evaluating the quality of the examinee's responses and the processes by which they were achieved. The supplemental scores provided on the WISC-III PI quantified testing-of-limits procedures already being utilized by some practitioners to test their hypotheses about a child's underlying deficits. Examples of techniques utilized in the process-oriented approach include the inclusion of a multiple choice format to help to delineate whether low scores on the initial measure are due to a problem is an expressive or receptive language issue or examining a students performance in 30-second intervals, as well as considering errors, incidental learning, and graphomotor speed to identify the underlying deficit responsible for performance issues.

Kaplan (1988) indicated that the nature and effectiveness of the strategies that a student may employ en route to either an incorrect or correct solution is of great importance, and that the student's capacities more often than not, could not be characterized in the most accurate and effective manner possible using only "global scores." For children whose global ability estimates do not match their educational achievement in specific skill areas, the clinical utility of an assessment of cognition lies in the understanding and use of specific measures of various aspects of cognitive processes. Rather than thinking that learning disabilities are reflected in the discrepancy between ability and achievement, it is necessary to understand the cognitive abilities and processes that constrain or have the greatest impact on performance in various academic areas. From this perspective, psychologists do not just derive a score that represents a child's intelligence or skill level, but rather assesses the child's capabilities and processes with various reasoning tasks and their relation to the child's achievement in the areas of concern. While it is certainly true that reasoning abilities are assessed in global measures, even the breakdown of composite scores such as Verbal Comprehension Index (VCI), Perceptual Reasoning Index (PRI), Working Memory Index (WMI), and Processing Speed Index (PSI) many times do not provide enough information to accurately and effectively characterize the student. Complex, multi-faceted tasks, such as those represented by the WISC-IV, SB-V, KABC-II, DAS, and WJ-III subtests, must be process-analyzed given the fact that successful performance on any of the reasoning tasks may require the use of multiple processes and abilities. It is also important to consider that the cognitive capacities required to perform a task can change across different items of the same task and are based on the age and ability level of the child attempting to perform the task (McCloskey, 2005). Thus close observations and monitoring of the underlying processes and strategies used by the student en route to the solution is more likely to provide useful information to understanding a student's difficulties in certain, if not all, academic areas than just composite scores.

Benefits of Using a Process-Oriented Assessment Approach

When a child is referred for a comprehensive evaluation, some practitioners continue to focus their assessment methods on a fixed battery of norm-based standardized tests and their conclusions of a child's ability and achievement represented by standard scores and Intelligence Quotients. One of the pitfalls in this traditional test interpretation approach involves the failure to call attention to the utility of the qualitative information gained from the assessment process. As suggested by McCloskey (2005) a process-oriented approach to assessment represents a different way of thinking about test content, assessment procedures, test session behavior, and test performance interpretation. The newest measures that are reflective of the latest neuropsychological research such as the *WISC-IV Integrated*, the *Kaufman Assessment Battery for Children (KABC-II)*, the *Delis–Kaplan Executive Function System (D-KEFS)*, and the *NEPSY Developmental Neuropsychological Assessment* provide a greater emphasis and inclusion of information related to simultaneous cognitive demands needed for higher level thinking, as well as the executive functioning constructs that include information about a child's cognitive flexibility in relation to problem solving, how he or she acquires and organizes visual and/or verbal information, and self monitors as opposed to just a generalized statistical representation of their performance. In addition, observations of test behavior enhances the process approach as to "how" a child obtains a score as opposed to "what" score they obtain, which ultimately contributes to pinpointing the specific difficulties in need of individualized interventions. Reitman (1964) noted that when using an "information processing approach" as a way of looking at psychological activity, we discover that even simple behaviors appear to be made up of a great many steps integrated into complex sequences. Consider the multiple steps needed to coordinate a task, whether it is selecting a strategy to use to successfully replicate a visual design, extracting information from a reading passage, or organizing the necessary problem solving steps in an algebraic equation. If one of the steps is missed or overlooked in any of the above noted tasks, there is an increased likelihood of an on-going difficulty, especially if not targeted for some means of intervention. Knowing what an individual does wrong is as important as knowing what they do right and there is an equal or greater importance in examining the nature and context of the particular errors made that may warrant further attention and help to determine appropriate intervention.

A striking case in point is provided in an excerpt from a clinical case of a 14-year old boy diagnosed with Attention Deficit Hyperactivity Disorder (AD/HD). Based on previous testing results using a traditional method of test performance analysis, Michael's visual perceptual skills were judged to be a significant area of difficulty. However, when using a process-oriented approach, the interpretation of his performance on the Processing Speed subtests of the WISC-IV revealed a contrasting viewpoint to his underlying challenges. Although Michael only earned a Scaled Score of 7 (Below Average range; 16th percentile) on the WISC-IV Symbol Search subtest, the way in which he performed this task revealed much about how he did and did not use his visual skills. Michael's performance was task analyzed by recording the number of symbol items he was able to complete in each 30-second interval of the 2-minute work period. This allowed the tracking of his productivity and the gauging of his ability to sustain attention and effort during the entire time period. Michael started working on this subtest in an extremely efficient manner. His visual discriminations were quick and accurate, as he completed 11 symbol items correctly in the first 30 seconds of work. During the second 30-second period, Michael needed to turn the page after completing four symbol items. This interruption would typically be thought of as relatively inconsequential to the flow of the activity, yet it seemed to derail Michael. With 15 more seconds left, he completed only two items in the second 30-second interval. Michael's production remained at this slower pace as he completed only three symbol items in each of the two remaining 30-second intervals. Considering his quick and efficient start with this task, it is hard to argue that his low score was the result of poor visual skills (e.g., an inability to effectively make the perceptual discrimination judgments necessary for effective performance). In fact, if Michael had continued to work at his original pace of the first 30 seconds (which most 15-year olds typically do), Michael would have completed 44 symbol items and would have earned a Scaled Score of 18 (Very Superior range; 99th percentile). Although Michael was motivated to perform well, showed definite interest in the task, and voiced confidence that he could handle this "easy" task, he was unable to sustain attention and direct his processing efforts consistently for the entire 2 minutes period.

By using a process-oriented approach to understanding Michael's test performance, observing "how" he approached and performed the various tasks eventually led to the hypothesis that Michael's difficulties with visual tasks were likely more due to his inability to sustain attention and other AD/HD characteristic behaviors than to deficits in visual skills per se. While keeping in mind the behavioral observations noted on the Symbol Search and throughout the WISC-IV assessment, and after reviewing sources of data collected through the RtI process, direct observations of the student, parent and teacher input, information provided by the student, and his performance on additional processing tasks, a general theme emerged. Taken together, the data suggested that Michael's difficulties with sustaining attention and effort for extended periods of time as well as difficulties with the selection of efficient strategies for successful task completion, and problems with self monitoring for work accuracy, emerged and accounted for a majority of the struggles he encountered in the classroom. By recording the specific observations of Michael's performance on the standardized measures, and comparing this qualitative information with other data, a pattern of performance across several tasks provided strong evidence about how Michael was using cognitive processes to perform tasks.

Specific Information Yielded in a Process-Oriented Approach

Accompanied by reasoning measures, student's performance on achievement tasks known to require the use of reasoning for successful completion should also be considered (e.g., reading comprehension tasks, written expression, mathematics problem solving). For instance, the act of reading is based on an integration of many cognitive abilities and processes and stored knowledge bases (McCloskey, 2005). In an interactive model (top-down and bottom-up processes), a reader is using multiple reasoning components to help extract the meaning from the text such as the knowledge of phoneme–grapheme associations, knowledge of particular sight words stored in the lexicon, knowledge of the syntactic and semantic aspects of language, background knowledge, and metacognitive knowledge of how to self-monitor in order to read effectively (McCloskey). To understand the possible cognitive constraints on academic achievement, information gathered from standardized measures, the child and those who know the child well (parents and other relatives, teachers, etc.), a review of the child's accomplishments and work products, and observations in various settings, should all be factored into the final description of what a child can and cannot do in relation to reasoning and academic performance. This is especially critical in the assessment of English Language Learners (ELL) and with children with cultural backgrounds that are extremely divergent from the mainstream culture. It is also equally important to gather information related to a ELL child's basic interpersonal communication skills (BICS) and cognitive academic language processing skills (CALP) which are the underlying language capacities needed for the enhancement of language based academic tasks such as reading, written expression and mathematics (McCloskey). Because of the complications that can arise in the interpretation of the scores on standardized assessment instruments the above noted multidimential approach including close observations of a student's approach to tasks should be utilized.

Kavale, Holdnack, and Mostert (2005) stated, "even if a student never enters the special education system, the general education teacher, the student's parents, and the student him or herself would receive valuable information regarding why there was such a struggle in acquiring academic content, to the point of possibly needing special education (p. 12)." Some additional information gained through a process-oriented approach utilizing assessment tools such as the *Wechsler Scales, Woodcock–Johnson achievement/cognitive tests, Kaufman measures*, and the *NEPSY* include information about how a student performs a given task (either timed or untimed) that may mirror issues related to several if not all academic and/or social skills difficulties. Issues associated with attention, executive functioning, language, memory and learning are some examples of the core areas that we assess when working with students using a targeted process-oriented assessment approach.

Attention

When we discuss attention dysfunction we actually are talking about a breakdown in one or more of the three interactive control systems over mental functioning (Levine, 1999). Many times we hear educators say, "Well he has a limited attention span" or "He is distractible." Although these general observations may be true, the breakdown of the attention control system serves a much greater diagnostic purpose. As Levine documents, some students may have specific challenges related to mental energies and effort controls (levels of concentration, alertness, initiation and maintenance of energies needed for academic productivity), while others may display dysfunction related to the processing controls (focus, distractibility, sustaining, shifting and dividing attention). In addition, specific production difficulties involving executive functions such as planning, inhibition control, emotional regulation, and self monitoring may also play a role in a child's academic difficulties. When assessing a child's attention controls it is critical to assess where the breakdown occurs. Since attention works closely with other cognitive abilities and processes, it is important to determine if breakdowns between attention and other functions such as memory and/or language are present and related. For instance, given the fundamental relevance of language processing and auditory memory in relation to school achievement, observations of a student's performance on the NEPSY Comprehension of Instructions subtest could provide valuable information pertaining to auditory and focused attention, language processing and comprehension, as well as working memory.

Additional observations and error analysis of a student's performance on the academic based measures using a process-oriented approach also provides important information pertaining to attention related challenges. Take for instance, a student's performance on the WJ-III Math Fluency subtest. On the Math Fluency subtest a student is given 3 minutes to complete as many basic math facts involving addition, subtraction, and multiplication as they can. The format of the task involves an alternation from addition to subtraction and then incorporates multiplication problems. This type of format requires more than just automaticity of math facts, but involves a student's ability to recognize the purposeful shift in attention to the operation change, an underlying component that is needed to successfully complete the task. Issues with shifting attention could directly affect the student's overall performance on any give academic task, but this difficulty is not adequately reflected when interpreting just a standard score.

Memory

Memory is a common concept that is used daily in our interactions with parents and educators alike and although ubiquitous, it does not seem to cause much confusion. Adequate understanding of the multiple components of memory and how memory is used in different task demands is important to consider when assessing for strengths and weaknesses within a student's profile. Although memory processes are crucial for effective learning, they are often not carefully explored or addressed in psychoeducational evaluations beyond mention (sometimes inappropriately) of performance on the

Letter-Number Sequencing, Digit Span, and Arithmetic subtests of the WISC-IV Working Memory Index or similar counterparts from other measures of general cognitive functions.

Despite the heavy demands of high school curricula on memory processes, assessments conducted in the upper grade levels often fail to include specific measures of memory function that are relevant to classroom learning. When memory processes are brought into discussion or incorporated as part of an assessment, the link between performance on memory tasks and classroom learning very often is poorly understood and/or poorly explained in reports (McCloskey, 2006). Memory processes that often need to be explored involve, first and foremost, the attention required for the input of the information before there is a passive encoding and initial registration into short-term memory. It is after the initial encoding and decoding of the information that working memory resources are tapped for active manipulation of information to prepare for output phases and for the storage and retrieval (immediate, short, and long delay) process. Some secondary focus includes an analysis of a student's encoding vs. retrieval processes, the memory demands presented in a free recall vs. cued recall, vs. recognition format, as well as any differences associated with recent recall of information and remote long term recall. Assessment measures such as the *Wechsler Memory Scales, Fourth Edition* (WMS-IV), *Children Memory Scales* (CMS), and specific subtests of the *NEPSY* all provide supplemental information that is pertinent to the development of hypothesis of learning challenges. Often times a student can effectively encode newly learned information but not retrieve it later from memory, or can memorize information under the right conditions (e.g., when not feeling anxious, depressed, or angry), or have greater success encoding and storing verbal but not visual material (or vice versa). It is essential to pinpoint memory weaknesses or other areas that constrain memory to provide a greater opportunity to individualize the accommodations necessary to help a student succeed with the resources they possess.

Take for instance a case of a 17-year old male student referred for a psychoeducational evaluation for behavioral challenges (disrespectful attitude toward teachers and peers), school truancy, and academic failure. As part of a thorough assessment of Zachary's processing strengths and learning challenges, in combination with the reasoning and academic measures, the auditory memory subtests of the *Wechsler Memory Scale, Fourth Edition* (WMS-IV) were administered. The WMS-IV Verbal Paired Associates Subtests required Zachary to listen to eight pairs of words and then, upon hearing the first word of a pair, immediately recall the second word of the pair. Zachary initially struggled with this task on the first and second trials which affected his overall performance, earning a scaled score of 6 (Low Average range; 9th percentile). Zachary showed a gradual improvement with each repetition of the presented words pairs, however his initial difficulty may have been attributed to his perception of the task and his own prediction of his overall performance. As indicated in the observation section of the report, as Zachary struggled with the first round of word pairs his affect and effort seemed to shift dramatically. His affect quickly changed from being verbally engaged to quiet and almost unresponsive. Zachary was observed to go from providing the examiner with well thought out responses to shrugs and head nods. In addition, his body language and mannerisms (slouched in seat, looking around the room, heavy sighs) and facial expressions suggested some anger and disinterest in the tasks. His attitude and perceived difficulty may have created a distraction which affected his initial performance and therefore overall performance. As the examiner repeated the list three additional times, Zachary began to have greater success in recalling the word pairs. As this task seemed to present as a rote memory skill for Zachary, multiple repetition proved to be effective as he earned a scaled score of 13 (High Average range; 84th percentile) on the Learning Slope measure, recording a huge benefit when Zachary is provided multiple repetitions to information to be stored in long term memory. Zachary was able to store in long-term memory six of the eight word pairs which was reflected in his recall after a 30 minutes delay. Zachary's performance on this measure resulted in scores below the average range; however, what is probably the most significant to report is the effect Zachary's perception and his mood may have on any given task. After the subtest the examiner asked Zachary about the observation of the shift in his affect, at which time Zachary acknowledged some anger and frustration about his initial performance and shared some negative personal affirmations (i.e., "I must be stupid if I can't do this."). Similar observations have been reported in the classroom setting in that his teacher shared that if she notices Zachary struggling with a task, it is best to immediately offer assistance rather than wait for him to seek out help for himself, which he does not do readily. Approaching him first seems to help prevent Zachary from becoming frustrated and potentially engaging in self destructive behaviors. One week later, Zachary was provided an informal list of word pairs generated by the school psychologist as a means of comparing his performance. Prior to presenting the list, the examiner reminded Zachary of the successes he had with repetition of the word pairs and asked to describe his feeling as he approached the task. Zachary indicated that he felt more confident and eager to try to recall the word pairs, and with that his performance improved dramatically. As documented in this example, emotions underlie all aspects of cognition and memory and therefore are inextricably bound with our psychological processes. Although Zachary demonstrated some weaknesses associated with working memory (as represented by his performance on other measures), his underlying thoughts and feelings associated with the memory, which were provoked by past struggles with "memorizing" greatly affected his performance during the evaluation process. The same issues observed during the evaluation process were also indicated by school staff which further validates how one's emotional state can constrain performance.

Language

Language plays a pivotal role in the academic and social functioning of children. Because of the volume and complexity of the linguistic expectations in school, it is essential for school psychologists to include a thorough analysis of a child's language profile in our evaluations. Language is critical for encoding information and transmitting ideas. It is needed for social interaction, and has a direct link with memory (Levine, 1999). When using a process-oriented assessment approach, many of the subtle language based problems that contribute to academic and/or behavioral difficulties can be revealed. For instance, when administering the WISC-IV an assessment of a student's lexical access can be reflected in the speed of responses, or the organization of verbal storage can be interpreted by the observed response style (specific information vs. nonspecific, rambling, etc.). In addition, how a student's performance may vary with the format of the language task (free recall vs. multiple choice) can also help to pinpoint language processing difficulties and may account for inconsistencies in class performance. Additional observations of the quality of verbal expressions (grammar/syntax of responses, vocabulary use, and organization of thoughts) can also be measured using the verbal subtests of the WISC-IV. Language facility should also be examined during informal social situations and formal testing responses. Levine suggested that by talking informally with a student, specific areas of weakness may be identified. Observations of how long it takes to pick up instructions or answer questions, the length of response time, the accuracy of the answers, and whether there is any difficulty with speech production may also help to pinpoint the etiology of academic based challenges.

Executive Functions

Executive functions are control processes that direct the use of other cognitive processes. Executive functions permeate a process oriented model in that they manage all aspects of dynamic processing, at all levels, involving all processes within language and nonlanguage (McCloskey, 2006) functions. These functions are multiple processes that, collected together, direct cognitive activity and are associated with the ability to engage in purposeful, organized, strategic, self-regulated, goal-directed behavior (Anderson, 2001). The effectiveness of these processes is often very observable during the assessment process, particularly processes involving planning, self monitoring and cognitive flexibility. Often times we observe students to have difficulty with initiation and self starting, or once started to stop and transition (cognitive flexibility), or to change an approach in response to feedback. This type of difficulties can be observed in the performances on cognitive reasoning tasks. A case in point is provided in an excerpt from a student's performance on the Block Design subtest of the WISC-IV.

On the Block Design subtest (Scaled Score 7, Low Average range; 16th percentile), Daniel seemed to have difficulty shifting problem solving methods from a detail-oriented to a pattern-oriented approach for a majority of the more challenging items that involved a nine block configuration. For this task, Daniel applied a strategy of placing the blocks together and organizing the blocks so they were first all a solid color. After that, he rotated the blocks in an attempt to match the design. With this approach, he did not provide himself with enough time to complete a majority of the items, nor did he deviate from this approach or readily learn from his mistakes. Similar difficulties were noted on the Matrix Reasoning subtest where Daniel's performance also suggested difficulty with cognitive flexibility. Daniel provided correct responses to a majority of the items in an efficient time period; however on several occasions if Daniel quickly recognized a commonality between two pictures and there were no plausible linking item on the third row, he did not change his immediate response and instead stated "nothing fits here, so I guess I have to choose this one." Similar challenges were also reported by his science teacher. Ms. P stated that despite her attempts to offer alternative ways of completing activities, Daniel often disregards her suggestions and continues with his planned approach which sometimes results in incomplete and incorrect assignments, verbal challenges and power struggles between Daniel and those who try to help.

Process-Oriented Approach and Report Writing

The use of a process-oriented approach naturally leads to a reconceptualization of reporting the results of an assessment. McCloskey (2005) suggests that the reporting of results can be organized by the assessment model rather than by the tests administered. Additional structural changes are suggested for best results when discussing findings in team meetings and parent conferences. Given the number of hats worn by educators, administrators, parents, and school psychologists, time constraints often inhibit the opportunity to read thoroughly through a comprehensive psychoeducational assessment. Therefore, it is often times effective to "frontload" the report with a summary of a student's processing strengths and challenges, following the four question format:

1. What does the student do well?
2. What does the student have difficulty doing?
3. What can be done to help with his/her difficulties?
4. Who and where can the student access the help needed (Spec Ed, Reg. Ed).

After these questions have been sufficiently answered, the interpretation section should follow, and lastly an appendix to the summary which includes standardized scores. In the interpretive section of the report the focus should be made on a description of the tasks performed, the level of performance obtained, including but not limited to norm-referenced scores, and a description of the relevant specific behaviors observed while the child was performing the tasks. It is important to remember that what a task measures can vary from one child to another depending on how the child approaches the task and therefore the learning and production strategies employed by the student are important to document. Also, when working with culturally diverse populations it is important to note whether the subtest administration was modified or adapted to accommodate English Language Learners and describe the proper interpretive approaches employed to characterize the child's abilities and skills. When a composite score is used, the description and interpretation should precede the discussion of the subtest and should only be the focus when the performance of the subtests that comprise the composite is highly consistent, not when the performance on the subtests is inconsistent. When using a process-oriented approach, McCloskey (2006) describes the general format of the interpretive section of the report to include at least five sections related to:

- Reasoning with verbal and with nonverbal information with a secondary focus related to:

  - Literal content
  - Inferential content
  - Concrete content
  - Abstract content

- Language related to receptive and expressive abilities including:

  - Information related to BICS vs. CALPS
  - Fluency
  - Speed
  - Basic (phonemic awareness and processing)

- Memory that involves initial registration, working memory, and long term storage with a secondary focus on:

  - Encoding vs. retrieval
  - Visual nonverbal vs. auditory verbal
  - Free recall vs. cued recall vs. recognition (i.e., Children's Memory Scale)

- Basic visual perception and motor production focusing on non-language processing and processing of language/orthography:

  - Integration of visual processing with motor production (i.e., performance on the Coding and Symbol Search subtests)
  - Integration of visual processing with reasoning as observed (i.e., WISC-IV Block Design subtest)
  - Completion of the organization of visual information (i.e., WISC-IV Matrix Reasoning, and the Rey Complex Figure Drawing test)

- Direction of Executive Functioning and Social Emotional Development:

  - Direction of attention (focus and sustained)
  - Initiation and modulation of efforts
  - Language production (speed and fluency)
  - Emotional regulation

RtI and Process-Oriented Assessment

The changes in the reauthorization of the Individuals with Disabilities Education Improvement Act (2004) have stirred a considerable controversy in the procedures used for the identification of students with learning and emotional disabilities. There are some extremists that advocate the sole use of cognitive assessments as the primary means of diagnosing learning disabilities on the one side, and those who are proponents of the exclusive use of a Response to Intervention (RtI) model on the other. The truth of the matter is that both approaches are neither incompatible nor mutually exclusive. As appealing as RtI and Curriculum Based Measures (CBM) may seem to be, such an approach does not, in and of itself provide enough diagnostic information relevant to identifying the "basic psychological processes" (Flanagan, 2006). These basic psychological processes noted in the IDEA definition of a "specific learning disability" (SLD) involve the fundamental areas of information processing and are related to the principal skills needed to attend, discriminate, switch cognitive sets, perceive, comprehend, memorize, plan , initiate, implement, self manage, and evaluate (Jiron, 2005). As previously stated the current federal definition continues to include the need to identify a deficit of one or more of these basic psychological processes in the classification of a learning disability, however the changes in IDEA 2004 now provide the opportunity for practioners to implement a targeted approach to assessment with students, one that can yield functionally useful results and interventions tailored to the individual child. The utilization of such an approach will serve an important role in ascertaining multiple data points that converge early on in the RtI and the CBM problem-solving multi-tiered model to support and augment diagnostic conclusions specific to the individual child.

If school psychologists are going to identify learning and/or emotional disabilities with the intention of helping a child through remediation, accommodation, or exposing them to bypass strategies to address their underlying difficulties, then we as professionals need to base our conclusions on data that supports the process of pinpointing the underlying challenges that affect a child's educational performance. As documented by Mastropieri and Scruggs (2005) the RtI models do not uncover the multidimensional nature of learning disabilities that are the basis of a student's academic challenges, nor does it identify the reasons why a student may be unresponsive to the interventions put forth in the Tier I and Tier II of the RtI model. It often times seems that by implementing research/evidence based strategies prior to the evaluation of a students specific strengths and learning needs, that school support teams are putting the cart before the horse. Through the progress monitoring probes of the pre-referral process, when a student's underachievement is documented to be unresponsive to a specific intervention, school teams often times maintain the same strategies for lengthy periods of time and are at a loss as to why a student continues to struggle. This approach is almost like constantly mounting sand bags to fight off the flood waters without ever finding the source of the leak in the dam. Furthermore, since students are supposed to be provided with the most appropriate research-based strategies available for improving academic performance, without additional information in relation to the specific nature of a student's learning difficulties, what additional methods are then justified within special education that will ultimately make a difference?

Another issue with the structure of many RtI models is the disconnect between learning and the behavioral and social/emotional challenges that may impact student learning. Many times, students present with multiple maladaptive conditions such as AD/HD, adjustment disorders, depression, anxiety, etc. which can negatively impact several areas of school achievement. Often, behavioral challenges accompany these conditions, and evidence-based behavioral interventions such as applied behavior analysis, social learning, and cognitive behavioral methods are attempted prior to a comprehensive assessment. These behavioral challenges provide only a partial picture of the student's profile, and these weaknesses may be the only traits identified resulting in labels that tell only a portion of the student's story. By using a process-oriented approach, professionals can identify individualized strengths while ruling out whether cognitive processing, executive functioning, and/or academic deficits contribute to a student's school and social struggles, or to determine if there are intense emotional, behavioral, or interpersonal issues that require more specific emotional support programming. A process-oriented approach helps the clinician to "tease out" the relationships between academic and behavioral problems to determine the cause and effect relationship.

Whether we are focusing on behavioral or academic challenges, when a child does not respond to the Tier I and II of the intervention strategies, and progress monitoring results in and of itself cannot identify the specific causes of a child's academic struggles, the next step is to attempt to create a complete and thorough learning profile of the student by uncovering any underlying psychological processing difficulties that may be affecting school success. In doing so, psychoeducational evaluations that use a process-oriented approach can help pinpoint the core reasoning, executive functioning, and social/emotional issues that may affect a child's school performance.

It is at this time that a direct measurement of a child's strengths and weaknesses using a cognitive information processing approach on standardized cognitive and/or neuropsychological measures picks up where RtI leaves off. As RtI has us looking at students' needs through a wide-lens telescope, identifying the contextual and environmental variables as viable explanations for academic difficulties, using a process-oriented approach to assessment provides a more magnified look at the individual student. Ultimately, it provides a greater chance in identifying specific problematic areas in need of remediation and an enhanced opportunity to identify tailored research-based interventions and programming.

Linking Assessment to Intervention

The value of utilizing a process-oriented approach to assessment, as mentioned throughout, lies in the ability to conceptualize a student's strengths and needs in order to make solid recommendations for intervention. Using a traditional approach, it is often difficult for practitioners to identify exactly what type of interventions are needed for the student to be successful, and thus may lead to less individualized and useful recommendations and an increased frustration among students, teachers, and parents. A process-oriented approach may help differentiate whether a student needs more intensive exposure to the curriculum, specially designed instruction, or other program modifications or accommodations.

Take for instance the case of Michael, the student with AD/HD who was highlighted earlier in the chapter. Based on Michael's score on processing speed tasks, it was originally hypothesized that he had difficulty processing visual information. Upon observing his test-taking behaviors and approach to a visual processing task, it was discovered that his difficulty was in his ability to sustain his attention and effort for the duration of the task. The interventions will greatly differ from a student who can't quickly process visual information, or for a student who demonstrates difficulties with fine motor skills, than for a student who can do the task, but can't maintain stamina. For Michael, recommendations will center on improving his efficiency and attention in order to improve his production. Consistent with other data, Michael's difficulties can be characterized as a "production" deficit rather than a skill or processing deficit (McCloskey, Van Divner, & Perkins, 2009). Resources and time will not be wasted on interventions designed to remediate skill or processing deficits. For Michael, he may just need modifications and accommodations in the classroom to help improve sustained attention and productivity.

Referring back to Daniel, the student who had difficulty finding an effective problem-solving approach to the Block Design and Matrix Reasoning subtests, another example can be derived. While it is likely that Daniel would possibly be able to replicate the designs if given unlimited time, Daniel's method was inefficient for more complex tasks. On the Matrix Reasoning task, he demonstrated an inability to attempt to find a better response when he was unsuccessful in his initial approach. Teachers also noticed that he had difficulty shifting from one to another problem-solving method in the classroom and would waste time using ineffective approaches that led to incorrect solutions. Interventions for Daniel would vary significantly from that for someone who demonstrated weaknesses with integrating visual-spatial information. With Daniel, a focus on interventions to improve cognitive flexibility and problem-solving skills may be needed. Due to his problem-solving rigidity, it will also be important to look at other areas where problem-solving is needed, such as with social friendships, to determine all targets for intervention.

Many other examples can be given about the utility of using this approach in linking assessment to intervention. Table 7.1 provides some examples of interventions that practitioners can use. However, the process-oriented approach is not only useful in examining examinee performance on cognitive instruments, but also to observe the cognitive processes and problem-solving approaches

Table 7.1 A sample of book and internet resources that provide intervention ideas for reading, writing, math, and/or behavior

Books:

Daly, E. J., Chafouleas, S., & Skinner, C. H. (2005). *Interventions for reading problems: Designing and evaluating effective strategies*. New York: Guilford.

This book provides information and intervention ideas in the areas of early literacy, phonological awareness, fluency, and comprehension. Intervention ideas presented are empirically supported. Reproducible handouts are included.

Dawson, P., & Guare, R. (2003). *Executive skills in children and adolescents: A practical guide to assessment and intervention*. New York: Guilford.

This is another book from the *Guilford Practical Intervention in Schools Series* that is a practical resource for clinicians. The authors provide a framework for assessing executive functioning difficulties in children and adolescents, and provide intervention strategies to address deficits. Reproducible worksheets are included.

Hale, J. B., & Fiorello, C. A. (2004). *School neuropsychology: A practitioner's handbook*. New York: Guilford.

This book provides a thorough review of the structures involved in cognitive processing and describes how to link assessment results to cognitive processes and academic achievement. Lists of intervention resources by reference and description are provided for each academic area discussed.

Jensen, E. (1998). *Teaching with the brain in mind*. Alexandria, VA: Association for Supervision and Curriculum Development.

While this is not an intervention book per se, *Teaching with the Brain in Mind* is a very straightforward text that helps readers better understand connections between learning and the brain. Within each chapter are intervention ideas and strategies to help promote efficient brain functioning within the classroom.

Jensen, W. R., Rhode, G., & Reavis, H. K. (1994). *The tough kid tool box*. Longmont, CO: SoprisWest.

The Tough Kid Tool Box is a great resource for clinician's working in schools. This book helps explain behavioral principles applied to classroom management in easy to understand terms. Each section includes information on the principles and techniques, in addition to examples and reproducible handouts.

Shapiro, E. (1996). *Academic skills problems: Direct assessment and intervention* (3rd ed.). New York: Guilford.

Academic Skill Problems provides instruction on how to assess academic skills and the instructional environment. Included within each instructional area are step-by-step descriptions on how to implement instructional modifications to address a variety of academic problems. A supplemental workbook accompanies this volume and includes reproducible assessment probes.

Silberg, J. (2005). *Reading games for young children*. Beltsville, MD: Gryphon House.

For young children experiencing difficulties with early literacy, *Reading Games* can provide ideas to help strengthen and support these skills. This book is not meant to provide intensive interventions or replace reading programs, but rather lends itself to supplemental activities for school or home that reinforce good reading skills such as alphabetic principle, phonemic awareness, and blending.

Internet Sites:

Florida Center for Reading Research. (2009). Retrieved October 5, 2009, from http://www.fcrr.org.

The Florida Center for Reading Research website provides empirical research on what works in reading. Intervention ideas are included as well as information on curriculum and instruction. Supplemental and comprehensive reading programs are both reviewed.

WGBH Educational Foundation. (2002). Misunderstood minds. Retrieved October 5, 2009, from http://www.pbs. org/wgbh/misunderstoodminds/.

Created as a companion website following a documentary series, this site provides information and strategies on attention problems as well as reading and math disabilities. Though the site offers an extensive list of strategies, research support is not cited. It is up to the individual reader to further examine the validity of proposed strategies. One of the most helpful aspects of the site is the resource tab, which provides books, articles, and websites for additional information.

Wright, J. (2009). Intervention Central. Retrieved October 5, 2009, from http://www.interventioncentral.org.

Intervention Central is a well-known database of intervention strategies. This website provides strategies in the areas of classroom management, behavior, and academics. Along with printable handouts on how to implement interventions, the authors provide references to research for each intervention.

(continued)

Table 7.1 (continued)

University of Buffalo. (n.d.). Reading sources for school psychologists: Assessment and intervention. Retrieved from http://gse.buffalo.edu/org/readingstrategies/read_strat.html.

  The content for this site was compiled by graduate students in school psychology. Information, assessment, and intervention strategies are organized by reading components and skills. A link for additional information or research is cited for each strategy.

used on academic achievement measures. Like task analysis of student work samples, a closer examination of the student's responses and observations of how they approach the task can give a lot of information. For example, observing student reading can tell us if a student is able to decode words phonetically but have little sight vocabulary for words with irregular patterns, or if they rely strictly on automatic recall of sight words with little phonological awareness. If relying solely on standard scores or correct words per minute using fluency probes, then a student with either problem may have two very different outcomes within the same intervention group. The clinician must have an understanding of the many complex processes used in reading in order to understand the relationships between performance and cognitive and achievement measures in his efforts to pinpoint which processes contribute to which type of deficit (Hale et al., 2008).

   It is important that practitioners are careful in making recommendations that will result in noticeable changes in student learning and behaviors in order to maintain the integrity and utility of psychoeducational assessment. The value in doing this type of careful detective work prior to intervening at the Tier III level may save time and resources in the long run, and may help ensure that a positive response to intervention can be reasonably obtained with the right interventions.

Chapter Competency Checklist

DOMAIN 1 – Enhancing the development of cognitive and academic skills

Foundational	Functional
Understand and explain the following: □ Brief history of cognitive assessment □ Strengths and limitations of cognitive assessment □ Myths associated with cognitive assessment □ Evolution of process-oriented assessment □ Benefits of process-oriented assessment □ Specific information yielded from process-oriented assessment □ How to write reports using process-oriented assessment □ How to integrate process-oriented assessment and RTI □ How to link process-oriented assessment to intervention	Gain practice: □ Administering different cognitive assessments with various populations with supervision and feedback □ Interpreting, writing, and communicating results □ Integrating results of process-oriented approaches with other assessment approaches

References

Alloy, L. B., Acocella, J., & Bootzin, R. R. (1996). *Abnormal psychology: Current perspectives*. New York: McGraw-Hill.

Anderson, V. A. (2001). Development of executive functions through late childhood and adolescence in an Australian sample. *Developmental Neuropsychology, 20*(1), 385–406.

Baron, I. S. (2004). *Neuropsychological evaluations of the child*. New York: Oxford University Press.

Berninger, V. (2002). Best practices in reading, writing, and math assessment-intervention links: A systems approach for schools, classrooms, and individuals. In A. Thomas & J. Grimes (Eds.) *Best practices in school psychology IV*. Vol 1 (pp. 851–865). Bethesda, MD: National Association of School Psychologists.

Collins, D. W., & Rourke, B. P. (2003). Learning-disabled brains: A review of the literature. *Journal of Clinical and Experimental Neuropsyclhology, 25*, 1011–1034.

Fine, J. G., Semrud-Clikeman, M., Keith, T.Z., Stapleton, L., Hynd, G. (2007). The corpus callosum and reading: An MRI family study of volume and area. *Neuropsychology, 21*(2).

Fiorello, C. A., Hale, J. B., McGrath, M., Ryan, K., & Quinn, S. (2001). IQ interpretation for children with flat and variable test profiles. *Learning and Individual Differences, 13*, 115–125.

Flanagan, D. (2006). *Identification of specific learning disability: An operational definition encompassing IDEA 2004, RTI, Assessment of cognitive processes, and culture/linguistic differences*. Presentation for the Chester County Intermediate Unit, PA.

Glutting, J. J., Youngstrom, E. A., Ward, T., Ward, S., & Hale, R. L. (1997). Incremental efficacy of WISC-III factor scores in predicting achievement: What do they tell us? *Psychological Assessment, 9*, 295–301.

Guilford, J. P. (1967). *The nature of human intelligence*. New York: McGraw-Hill.

Hale, J. B., & Fiorello, C. A. (2004). *School neuropsychology: A practitioner's handbook*. New York: Guilford.

Hale, J. B., Fiorello, C. A., Kavanaugh, J. A., Hoeppner, J. B., & Gaither, R. A. (2001). WISC-III predictors of academic achievement for children with learning disabilities: Are global and factor scores comparable? *School Psychology Quarterly, 16*, 31–55.

Hale, J. B., Fiorello, C. A., Kavanagh, J. A., Holdnack, J. A., & Aloe, A. M. (2007). Is the demise of IQ interpretation justified? A response to special issue authors. *Applied Neuropsychology, 14*(1), 37–51.

Hale, J. B., Fiorello, C. A., Miller, J. A., Wenrich, K., Teodori, A., & Henzel, J. (2008). WISC-IV interpretation for specific learning disabilities identification and intervention: A cognitive hypothesis testing approach. In A. Prifitera, D. Saklofske, & L. Weiss (Eds.), *WISC-IV clinical assessment and intervention* (2nd ed., pp. 109–171). San Antonio, TX: Pearson.

Horn, J. L., & Cattell, R. B. (1967). Age differences in fluid and crystallized intelligence. *Acta Psychologica, 26*, 107–129.

Jiron, C. (2005). Intelligent testing, not intelligence testing: To test or not to test? *Communiqué, 34*(4), 27.

Kaplan, E. (1988). A process approach to neuropsychological assessment. In T. Boll & B. K. Bryant (Eds.), *Clinical neuropsychology and brain function: Research, measurement, and practice* (pp. 125–167). Washington, DC: American Psychological Association.

Kaplan E, Fein D, Kramer J, Delis DC, Morris R. (1999). *Wechsler Intelligence Scale for Children – Process Instrument*. The Psychological Corporation; San Antonio, TX.

Kavale, K. A., Holdnack, J. A., & Mostert, M. P. (2005). Response to intervention and the identification of specific learning disability: A critique and alternative proposal. *Learning Disability Quarterly, 28*(1), 2–16.

Larry, P. v. Riles, 343 F. Supp. 1306 (D.C. N.D. Cal., 1972), *aff'd.,* 502 F.2d 963 (9th Cir. 1974), *further proceedings,* 495 F. Supp. 926 (D.C. N.D. Cal., 1979), *aff'd.,* 502 F.2d 693 (9th Cir. 1984).

Levine, M. (1999). *Developmental variation and leaning disorders* (2nd ed.). Cambridge, MA: Educators Publishing Service.

Mastropieri, M. A., & Scruggs, T. E. (2005). Feasibility and consequences of response to intervention: Examination of the issues and scientific evidence as a model for the identification of individuals with learning disabilities. *Journal of Learning Disabilities, 38*(6), 525–531.

McCloskey, G. (2005). *Neuropsychological-oriented process approach to psychoeducational assessment and intervention*. Presented at the NASP Annual Conference Anaheim, CA

McCloskey, G. (2006). *Math skills instruction, assessment and intervention: Integrating neuropsychological and RTI perspectives to develop best practices*. Presented at the Montgomery County Intermediate Unit #23, PA.

McCloskey, George, Perkins, Lisa, Van Divner, Bob (2009). Assessment and intervention for executive function difficulties; School-Based Practice in Action Series. Routledge.

McGrew, K. S., & Knopik, S. N. (1996). The relationship between intra-cognitive scatter on the Woodcock–Johnson psycho-educational battery – Revised and school achievement. *Journal of School Psychology, 34*(4), 351–364.

Naglieri, J.A. and Bornstein, B.T. (2003). Intelligence and Achievement: Just how Correlated are they? *Journal of Psychoeducational Assessment, 21*(3), 244–260.

Pennsylvania Association for Retarded Citizens (P.A.R.C.) v. Commonwealth of Pennsylvania, 334 F. Supp. 1257 (D.C. E.D. Pa. 1971), 343 F. Supp. 279 (D.C. E.D. Pa. 1972).

Pfeiffer, S. I., Reddy, L. A., Kletzel, J. E., Schmelzer, E. R., & Boyer, L. M. (2000). The practitioner's view of IQ testing and profile analysis. *School Psychology Quarterly, 15*(4), 376–385.

Reitman, W. R. (1964). Information-processing models in psychology. *Science, New Series, 144*(3623), 1192–1198.

Samuda, R. J. (1998). Cross cultural assessment: Issues and alternatives. In R. J. Samuda, R. Feuerstein, A. Kaufman, J. Lewis, R. J. Sternburg, & Associates (Eds.), *Advances in cross-cultural assessment* (pp. 1–19). Thousand Oaks, CA: Sage.

Sattler, J. M. (2001). *Assessment of children: Cognitive applications*. San Diego, CA: Jerome M. Sattler, Publisher, Inc.

Shaywitz, S.E., Lyon, G.R., & Shaywitz, B.A. (2006). Dyslexia (Specific reading disability). In F.D. Burg, J.R. Ingelfinger, R.A. Polin, & A.A. Gershon (Eds.) *Gellis & Kagan's Current*, Vol. 17. Philadelphia: W.B. Saunders.

Siegel, L. S. (1999). Issues in the definition and diagnosis of learning disabilities: A perspective of Guckenberger v. Boston University. *Journal of Learning Disabilities, 32*(4), 304–319.

Tallel, P. (2006). Dynamic auditory processing, musical experience and language development, *Trends in Neurosciences, 29*(7), 382–390.

Thurstone, L. L. (1938). *Primary mental abilities*. Chicago: University of Chicago Press.

Werner, H. (1937). Process and achievement: A basic problem of education and developmental psychology. *Harvard Educational Review, 7*, 353–368.

Ysseldyke, J. (2005). Assessment and decision making for students with learning disabilities: What if this is as good as it gets? *Learning Disability Quarterly, 28*, 125–128.

Chapter 8
Evaluating Students with Emotional and Behavioral Concerns

Barry L. McCurdy, Amanda L. Lannie, and Jennifer L. Jeffrey-Pearsall

Attending school requires that children leave the familiarity of their surroundings, many, for the first time, to interact with the larger world where they are faced with the challenge of meeting teacher demands, as well as negotiating peer-to-peer relationships. A successful outcome will depend on the degree of readiness skills and resilience fostered through early learning experiences and critical formative relationships. For most children, success is easily achieved. However, for a small percentage of children who show early signs of emotional and behavioral concerns, success will depend upon early identification and intervention.

Estimates of the number of children with emotional and behavioral concerns vary somewhat, but most authorities on the subject agree that about one in five children, or about 20%, evidence some symptoms associated with a mental health diagnosis (Burns et al., 1995; U.S. Department of Health and Human Services, 1999). Some of these children will receive services through the behavioral health system, but, sadly, for many others the only services they will receive are those provided by the school system (Hoagwood & Johnson, 2003). A subset of this larger population of children with emotional and behavioral concerns, generally about 1%, will be served through special education in the category of "emotional disturbance" (ED; Walker, Ramsey, & Gresham, 2004).

Students with ED comprise about 8% of all students identified with disabilities in the age range of 6–21 years. Recent concerns, about the rise in school violence and disruptive behaviors have led some to suggest that the percentage of students with ED, also, is on the rise (Walker, Ramsey, & Gresham, 2003/2004). However, Department of Education statistics from 1994 to 2004 have shown that the increase in students identified with ED (about 16%) has not kept pace with the increase for all students receiving special educational services (24.69%; U.S. Department of Education, 2004). While this news is certainly a cause for optimism, school psychologists and others charged with evaluating and identifying students with ED must proceed carefully as serious concerns have been raised about the identification process. For example, males with ED have always outnumbered females. However, more recent population demographics now show that students with ED are disproportionately African-American and that, different from other disability groups, less than half are identified in the elementary years, a factor that effectively prohibits the opportunity for early intervention (Bradley, Henderson, & Monfore, 2004; Kauffman, Brigham, & Mock, 2004; U.S. Department of Education, 2004). Another concern with the identification process is the fact that students designated as ED in Colorado comprise 12.79% of the total population of students with disabilities, while students designated as ED in Arkansas comprise only 1.16% (U.S. Department

B.L. McCurdy (✉)
Devereux Center for Effective Schools, 2012 Renaissance Boulevard, King of Prussia, PA 19406, USA
e-mail: BMcCurdy@devereux.org

T.M. Lionetti et al. (eds.), *A Practical Guide to Building Professional Competencies in School Psychology*,
DOI 10.1007/978-1-4419-6257-7_8, © Springer Science+Business Media, LLC 2011

of Education). This percentage difference, albeit at a macro level, is a clear indicator of the inconsistency that surrounds the identification process and points to the need for a better understanding of what is meant by the term "emotional disturbance." Given this long-standing state of confusion with regard to the evaluation of students with emotional and behavioral concerns, it is the purpose of this chapter to provide guidance and recommendations to school psychologists and others who may be charged with some portion of this task.

Seriously Emotionally Disturbed, Emotionally Disturbed, Emotional and Behavioral Disorders

Defining Emotional Disturbance

Children and youth with significant emotional and behavioral concerns were first identified as a group eligible for special education in 1975. The passage of The Education of All Handicapped Children Act (P.L. 94–142) followed by the Individuals with Disabilities Education Act (IDEA; P.L. 101-476) allowed for a designation of "seriously emotionally disturbed" for those children whose maladaptive thoughts, emotions and behaviors were so qualitatively different from the norm that they were considered in need of school-based support services (Bradley et al., 2004; Cullinan, 2004). With the IDEA amendments of 1997, the term was changed to "emotional disturbance" and in the most recent re-authorization, the Individuals with Disabilities Education Improvement Act, or IDEA 2004, the definition of ED remains unchanged:

The term means a condition exhibiting one or more of the following characteristics over a long period of time and to a marked degree that adversely affects a child's educational performance:

1. An inability to learn that cannot be explained by intellectual, sensory, or health factors
2. An inability to build or maintain satisfactory interpersonal relationships with peers and teachers
3. Inappropriate types of behavior or feelings under normal circumstances
4. A general pervasive mood of unhappiness or depression
5. A tendency to develop physical symptoms or fears associated with personal or school problems

The term includes schizophrenia. The term does not apply to children who are socially maladjusted, unless it is determined that they have an emotional disturbance (Federal Register, August, 2006, §300.8, p. 46756).

Can We Make Sense of the Confusion?

Despite the federal government's continued reliance on the above definition in identifying a student with ED, or a student with emotional and behavioral disorders (EBD) as the term is more often used in the field of special education, many professional and advocacy groups, including the Council for Children with Behavioral Disorders, have called for the use of an alternative definition (Forness & Knitzer, 1992, 2000). However, attempts to petition the Congress for a change have failed and detractors continue to express concerns regarding the applicability of the current definition for a number of reasons. Chief among the criticisms is the fact that the important features of the definition are simply too vague to be useful in providing guidance to professionals and families alike concerned with identifying an EBD (Cullinan, 2004; Kauffman et al., 2004). Phrases such as "over a long period of time," "to a marked degree" and "adversely affects academic performance" are not sufficiently operational to improve our reliability in making accurate determinations of who should and should not qualify for specially designed instruction under the ED category.

Cullinan (2004) also criticizes the federal ED definition for the use of statements that are redundant and self-contradictory. For example, while the definition confirms that "an inability to build or maintain satisfactory interpersonal relationships with peers and teachers" is one of the reasons for identifying an EBD, it also goes on to state that an EBD does not include "children who are socially maladjusted." The problem is that children in the latter category (i.e., socially maladjusted) *are* those children who have difficulty building and maintaining satisfactory relationships. Redundancy, too, is noted as the definition states that the condition must "adversely affect educational performance" and that one of the characteristics may be "an inability to learn." Is this to mean that a child may be identified with an EBD if he/she has "an inability to learn ..." that "affects educational performance?"

A third concern relates to the fact that the characteristics defining ED appear to be arbitrarily chosen and not representative of known diagnostic categories as defined by the *Diagnostic and Statistical Manual of Mental Disorders, Fourth Edition* (DSM-IV; Cullinan, 2004; Forness, 2004). Effective treatment for children and youth with ED can only occur through the convergence of special education and mental health. To the extent that these two fields do not share a common language, a barrier to effective interdisciplinary collaboration, children with and at risk for developing an EBD will not benefit from effective interventions, interventions that often involve a combination of behavioral and psychopharmacological approaches. According to Forness, this failure to take an interdisciplinary approach with children identified as EBD has negatively impacted our ability to move the field of special education forward both in terms of practice as well as research. A good example of this, as discussed by Forness, concerns comorbidity, or the occurrence of two or more disorders in one child. Considered to be a fairly common occurrence in children with emotional and behavioral concerns (Angold, Costello, & Erklani, 1999), the failure to detect comorbidity as part of the diagnostic picture for a child, will lead to errors in problem prioritization and intervention selection. This fact is further emphasized in that children with comorbid disorders are often considered to be the most treatment resistant (Gresham, Lane, & Lambros, 2001).

Probably the criticism most often levied against the federal definition is known as the "socially maladjusted" exclusion (Skiba & Grizzle, 1991; Tankersley, Landrum, & Cook, 2004). Based on the definition, children who are socially maladjusted do not qualify as having an EBD unless it is determined that they are emotionally disturbed. The exclusion is completely illogical because, by any credible interpretation of the federal definition, a student will be identified as having an EBD if he or she meets any one of the five criteria stipulated in the definition. However, by meeting any one of the criteria, that student may also be considered socially maladjusted and, thereby, excluded from services. Further, as Cullinan (2004) states, there does not seem to be a scientific basis for this exclusion.

Some critics assert that the exclusion is meant to disqualify from services those children and adolescents with chronic patterns of antisocial behavior (Walker et al., 2004). Slenkovich (1992), for example, citing three court cases upholding the exclusion clause, argued that students with various conduct and antisocial behaviors must not be identified with an EBD. Forness and Knitzer (1992) claim that the original intent of Congress was to exclude only juvenile delinquency, citing that children with disruptive behavior disorders, including conduct disorders, makeup the largest population of students in the EBD category. It may be that the best approach is the most ethical approach, particularly when legal statutes are both logically and empirically unsound (Forness, 1992).

Moving Forward: Rivers to Cross, Mountains to Climb

This brief discussion centered on the criticisms surrounding the definition of an EBD has characterized much of the debate in the field over the past several years. As Kauffman and colleagues (2004) point out, however, there are other pressing concerns that will impact the role of school psychologists moving forward, particularly regarding the evaluation of students with emotional and behavioral concerns. These include (a) personal philosophies dictating against recognizing and identifying students with EBD; (b) the related tendency to avoid early detection and, ultimately, early intervention, the most successful approach for interrupting the risk trajectory that characterizes most of these students; and (c) the avoidance of identifying students as EBD because of the 1997 reauthorization of IDEA, which stipulates that a student with a disability cannot be expelled from school for behaviors caused by that disability.

As can be seen from this discussion, the list of controversial topics is endless and, in the end, school psychologists are best advised to be at their "ethical" peak in this regard. In this chapter, we hope to provide readers with a roadmap to follow and guidance in decision-making for evaluating students with EBD.

Basic Considerations for Enhancing Research-to-Practice Connections

Prevention and Early Identification

As discussed, federal legislation and the DSM-IV provide guidelines for classification; however, there is a strong need for early identification of students with and at risk for EBD (Lane, Gresham, & O'Shaughnessy, 2002; National Association of School Psychologists, 2005). The school psychologist can play a critical role in facilitating early intervention services through systematic screening, ongoing teacher consultation, and serving as an active member of a school-based pre-referral service delivery team (e.g., Instructional Support Team, Teacher Assistance Team, Student Support Team; McConaughy & Ritter, 2002; National Association of School Psychologists, 2005).

Screening. Teacher perception may serve as the most useful first step in identifying students for early intervention. One suggested screening process is the multiple-gated procedure involved in Walker and Severson's (1992) Systematic Screening for Behavior Disorders (SSBD). The SSBD allows practitioners to identify students at-risk for externalizing and internalizing behavior disorders in grades K-6. The screening process involves a multiple-gated procedure of identification that includes: (a) the classroom teacher rank ordering all students on dimensions of externalizing and internalizing behavioral concerns, (b) the teacher completing a behavior rating scale and behavior checklist for the six students ranked highest (three with externalizing concerns, three with internalizing concerns), and (c) direct observations of student behavior in the classroom and during free-play (e.g., playground) for those students exceeding the normative level in gate 2. Students "passing through" the third gate move directly on to receive pre-referral, or early, interventions.

Role of the Pre-referral Team. As a member of the pre-referral team, the school psychologist provides the behavioral expertise to assist in assessment and early intervention planning for behavioral concerns (and typically comorbid academic concerns) before the behaviors significantly jeopardize a student's academic and social development. In doing so, the school psychologist focuses the team on gathering relevant behavioral data that serves as a baseline for monitoring student progress in response to interventions. A response-to-intervention (RtI) approach allows the team to implement and monitor a variety of strategies, ultimately identifying the strategy or strategies that result in improved outcomes for the student. Traditionally, the RtI approach has been discussed relative to students with academic concerns and the identification of a specific learning disability. More recently, however, the RtI logic has also been applied to students at risk for developing EBD (Cheney, Flower, & Templeton, 2008; Fairbanks, Sugai, Guardino, & Lathrop, 2007; Gresham, 2005; Harris-Murri, King, & Rostenberg, 2006). The goal at this stage is to maintain the student in the current setting (e.g., general education), thereby preventing behaviors from reaching a level where more intense services are needed.

Regulatory Mandates vs. Best Practice Considerations

Another best-practice consideration is the use of functional behavioral assessment (FBA) and behavior support planning across the continuum of services provided to students. FBA is the process used to identify the conditions that occasion or "set off" the behavior and those that maintain or reinforce the problem behavior. While FBA has long been supported as an assessment process with individuals with developmental disabilities, recent literature has demonstrated successful extensions of FBA to other populations including individuals with EBD (Kern, Hilt, & Gresham, 2004; Sugai, Lewis-Palmer, & Hagan-Burke, 2000).

Taking a function-based approach to assessment requires that the assessment team analyze the student's behavior in the context in which the behavior occurs. The process typically includes (a) collecting relevant information through reviewing background information, (b) conducting interviews with multiple sources, (c) developing testable hypotheses, (d) collecting direct observational data to confirm hypotheses, (e) crafting a competing pathways analysis based on the data, (f) developing a function-based behavior intervention plan and (g) implementing and monitoring student progress after plan implementation (Sugai et al., 2000). For details on how to conduct a FBA see: O'Neill et al. (1997) and Sugai et al. (2000).

Most practitioners are familiar with the role FBA has played in relation to disciplining students with disabilities based on the 1997 amendments to IDEA (now reflected in IDEA 2004), but many may not be aware of the differences in interpreting when a FBA should be conducted (Crone & Horner, 2003; Nelson, Roberts, Rutherford, Mathur, & Aaroe, 1999). The strict interpretation pertains to conducting a FBA when a student is in jeopardy of becoming subject to school discipline proceedings that might result in a change of placement (Nelson et al.). Section 300.530(d)(1)(ii) of IDEA 2004 states: "[Child must] receive, as appropriate, a functional behavioral assessment, and behavioral intervention services and modifications, which are designated to address the behavior violation so that it doesn't occur." Further, when outlining appropriate evaluation procedures, Section 300.304(b)(1) stipulates that a comprehensive assessment includes "relevant functional... information" about the student. It is this final statement that has led many in the field to develop a broader interpretation of when a FBA is necessary. The broad interpretation suggests that a FBA is appropriate at any stage throughout the special education decision-making process (Nelson et al.).

The Evaluation Process

The primary starting point when approaching an evaluation is to identify the purpose of the assessment. Has the student been referred by the classroom teacher for the purpose of receiving assistance in supporting this student in class (i.e., consultation)? Has the student been referred by the pre-referral team and/or parent for consideration of special education services (i.e., classification)? Or, is the referral for assessment guided by a request for linking the student with external behavioral healthcare services (i.e., classification/diagnosis)? The purpose for evaluation will guide the assessment tools and procedures followed; however, regardless of the referral question, the primary purpose of assessment is to guide intervention planning. Assessment results should lead to determining the student's needs and strengths, and to providing information that is useful in developing a meaningful behavior intervention plan that can be used across the multiple settings in which the student is included (National Association of School Psychologists, 2005).

When approaching an assessment where emotional or behavioral concerns are at stake, it is important to ensure that your assessment yields information about the types and dimensions of student behaviors, early in the process, as this will guide the assessment process and the measures selected (Gresham, 1999). Student behavior can be categorized as either behavioral excesses (e.g., displays of problem behavior are frequent and/or intense), behavioral deficits (e.g., displays of prosocial behavior do not occur or occur infrequently), situationally inappropriate behaviors (e.g., student has the prosocial skill within their repertoire but cannot accurately discriminate in which settings to use the skills), or some combination of the three. Additionally, it is important to determine if the student is exhibiting externalizing or internalizing problems. Externalizing problems are characterized as undercontrolled, acting-out behaviors (e.g., aggression, non-compliance, disruption) while internalizing behaviors are characterized as overcontrolled, inner-directed behaviors (e.g., depression, anxiety; Gresham, 1999).

Multidimensional assessment is the agreed upon approach to a best-practice, comprehensive assessment of emotional and behavioral concerns and aligns with the National Association of School Psychologists Professional Conduct Manual (2000); the National Association of School Psychologists Position Statement on Students with Emotional and Behavioral Disorders (2005); and the regulations surrounding assessment as stipulated in Section 300.304(b) of the IDEA 2004. The following guidelines are important when conducting a multidimensional assessment:

- Collect information from *multiple informants* – parents/guardians, teachers, student, peers, collateral contacts (e.g., involved social services or behavioral healthcare agencies)
- Assess (get to know) the behavior across *multiple contexts* – home, school, different classrooms, different times of the day
- Include *multiple methods* of assessment – direct observations, standardized rating scales, record review, interviews, FBA, and curriculum-based measurement (CBM) – across multiple informants. (Gresham, 1999; McConaughy & Ritter, 2002; National Association of School Psychologists, 2005)

Figure 8.1 shows the model for a multidimensional approach to behavioral assessment. In the figure, Gresham (1999) captures the critical elements of assessment and clarifies both direct and indirect methods for gathering data and establishing the intervention.

Eligibility Considerations

Keeping in mind the aforementioned, it is important that assessment and intervention be considered before behaviors reach a level that consideration for special education services is the only option. That said, however, some students will require evaluation for this level of intense intervention from the start. Once behaviors have reached a level warranting evaluation for special education eligibility, a comprehensive assessment is necessary to (a) make a determination based on the IDEA 2004 criteria and (b) inform intervention planning for a behavior intervention plan and the IEP (if services are deemed necessary). Eligibility for special education service hedges on two factors: (a) exceptionality and (b) degree of need (71 C.R.F § 300.306). The student must be found to meet the criteria for *exceptionality* of ED based on the definition in Section 300.8 of the IDEA 2004 and be found to demonstrate *educational need* not explained by lack of appropriate instruction or limited English proficiency (71 C.R.F § 300.306(b). A student who does not qualify for special education services through IDEA 2004 may still qualify for services under Section 504 of the Rehabilitation Act of 1973.

The following section provides detail on conducting a multidimensional assessment when the reason for referral is to determine eligibility for special education services.

Practice Implications

Linking students with EBD to the appropriate level of support is paramount in the assessment process. Although the FBA identifies function-based strategies to ameliorate the presenting issues, at times those strategies may exceed the resources available within a general education classroom.

I. Type of Behavior Problem	IV. Behavioral Repertoire	VII. Social Validation
A. Excess	A. Cognitive/Verbal	A. Social Significance of
B. Deficit	B. Overt/Motoric	Goals
C. Situationally Inappropriate	C. Physiological/Emotional	1. Consumer Opinions
	V. Methods of Assessment	2. Habilitative Validity
	A. Direct Methods	B. Social Acceptability of
II. Dimension of Behavior	1. Direct Observation	Procedures
A. Externalizing Behavior	2. Self Monitoring	1. Pretreatment
B. Internalizing Behavior	3. Physiological Monitoring	Acceptability
C. Prosocial Behavior	B. Indirect Methods	2. Posttreatment
	1. Functional Assessment	Acceptability
II. Quantification of	Interviews	3. Use and Integrity
Behavior	2. Ratings By Others	C. Social Importance of
A. Frequency/Rate	3. Self-Reports	Effects
B. Temporality	4. Permanent Products	1. Subjective Judgments
C. Duration	5. Analogue Role Play	2. Social Comparisons
D. Latency	V. Quality of Data	3. Combined Social
E. Interresponse Time	A. Reliability	Validation Procedures
F. Intensity/Magnitude	1. Interobserver Agreement	4. Visual Inspection
G. Behavior-By-Products	2. Internal Consistency	5. Percentage
(Permanent Products)	3. Stability	Nonoverlapping Data
	B. Validity	Points (PNOL)
	1. Content	6. Effect Size Estimates
	2. Criterion-Related	7. Reliable Change Index
	3. Convergent	
	4. Discriminant	
	5. Treatment	

Fig. 8.1 Critical elements of a multidimensional approach to behavioral assessment. Reprinted from Gresham (1999) with permission from Sopris West

At that point, consideration for additional support services and possible special education eligibility becomes necessary.

Assessment for the purpose of eligibility determination must be comprehensive, employing a multimethod approach to assess concerns in sufficient breadth and depth (McConaughy & Ritter, 2008). Measurement tools must demonstrate technical adequacy. With the parameters set forth by the federal government, assessment of a student with EBD spans multiple domains, including academic, social/emotional, and behavioral, utilizing both direct and indirect methods. Gathering information from parents, teachers, and the child are all integral to the assessment process. Best practice guidelines define the process as involving (a) a review of school records; (b) interviews with parents, teachers, and the student; (c) completion of behavior rating scales by parents, teachers, and the student; (d) observations of the student in the natural environment; and (e) academic achievement testing. The end goal of the assessment is to determine the need for service and the presence of barriers that interfere with the student's attainment of an education (i.e., a disability; McConaughy & Ritter; Salvia & Ysseldyke, 2004).

Record Review

As a student navigates through the educational system, numerous informational by-products of their experiences accumulate. These informational by-products, or archival records, can be instrumental in framing the referral questions for the student as well as guiding the selection of assessment measures. As archival records are permanent products of a student's school experiences, they are easy to obtain, are unobtrusive, and have limited reactivity from others (Sprague & Walker, 2005).

The primary purpose of a record review is to learn the student's history of academic achievement and problematic behavior. Reviewing academic records such as past report cards, retention notices, and state testing scores as well as work samples from the student's current teacher(s) are useful sources of information. Similarly, office disciplinary contacts, suspensions, critical incident reports, and the like are potentially valid indicators of a pattern of problematic behavior across the student's years of schooling. Structured systems of record review exist to assist the school psychologist with a standardized approach to reviewing records. One such measure is the School Archival Records Search (SARS). SARS was developed by Walker, Block-Pedego, Todis, and Severson (1991) and involves the systematic coding of variables associated with disruption, low achievement, and the need for assistance. Examples of those variables include (a) attendance at different schools, (b) data on absenteeism, (c) narrative comments depicting negative behavior, and (d) school discipline referrals (Sprague & Walker, 2005).

Interview

Gathering information via interviewing is essential to grasp the scope of the referral concerns and, ultimately, assists in diagnostic formulation. An interview often represents the next step in the assessment process after a review of records. Differing from a simple conversation with a parent or teacher, an interview has a clearly defined structure of interviewer–interviewee roles, follows a sequence and seeks to ask and answer questions for the purpose of achieving established goals (Groth-Marnat, 2003; Sattler, 2002).

Interview formats vary with the objective of the interview. That is, structured interviews often focus on psychiatric diagnosis, and follow a rigid format, permitting little latitude for follow-up questions (Sattler, 2002). Given their focus, structured interviews have limited utility in traditional school settings (Busse & Beaver, 2000). In contrast, semistructured interviews have a guiding structure but allow a degree of flexibility for the examiner to deviate from the question profile (Sattler, 2002). Although structured interviews demonstrate greater technical adequacy, semistructured interviews afford the interviewer the opportunity to explore topics relevant to the student and to probe further in areas identified by parents and teachers. Used in combination with other assessment measures, semistructured interviews can provide a wealth of valuable information.

In preparing for an interview, it is important to consider the relevant individuals in a student's life who will serve as informants. A student's parent(s) and/or guardian, and teacher are typical primary interviewees. For an elementary school student, interviewing the classroom teacher will be sufficient; whereas for middle and high school students, multiple teachers may be considered, with the teacher who has the most contact or in whose classroom the child is exhibiting problems typically selected (Busse & Beaver, 2000).

Parent and Teacher. An interview for a student presenting with EBD will cover multiple areas to permit an understanding of the biological, developmental, familial, academic, and social perspectives related to the concerns. An interview with parents should comprise a description of the current presenting problem(s) and its history, assessment of antecedents and consequences to the behavior(s), review of the student's developmental and medical history, and exploration of family factors or stressors that may be present (McConaughy & Ritter, 2008; Sattler, 2002). When interviewing teachers, similar topics can be discussed, although a teacher will likely not have the developmental and medical knowledge of the student. However, a teacher can speak of any present conditions that require accommodations in school.

Student. Conducting an interview with a student requires establishing a comfortable physical and interpersonal environment as well as flexibility with the questioning strategy in accordance with the characteristics of the child (McConaughy, 2005). Semistructured interviews are best suited for interviews with a child because of the degree of flexibility allowed (McConaughy; McConaughy & Ritter, 2008). Themes in the interview should include the child's report of problems, feelings of self, activities and interests, and academic, social, and familial issues (McConaughy & Ritter). For adolescents, it is also important to assess for information about alcohol and drugs, antisocial behavior and involvement with the law, and dating (McConaughy & Ritter). There are a number of semistructured clinical interviews for parents, teachers, and children that can be used in school settings, including the Semistructured Clinical Interview for Children and Adolescents (SCICA; McConaughy & Achenbach, 2001) for children, and the Schedule for Affective Disorders and Schizophrenia for School-Aged Children–Present and Lifetime Version (K-SADS-PL; Kaufman, Birmaher, Brent, Rao, & Ryan, 1996) for parent and child. The reader is referred to McConaughy (2005) and Sattler (2002) for further information on this topic.

Academic Assessment

Per the federal guidelines on classifying ED, an adverse impact on academic achievement must be demonstrated as a result of longstanding patterns of maladaptive behavior. Thus, an assessment of academic achievement is warranted to determine the current performance of the student, relative to typical peers in academic content areas (i.e., reading, math, and writing). Administration of a combination of norm-referenced and curriculum-based measures is recommended to pave the way for the development of interventions post-evaluation.

Standardized, norm-referenced tests (SNRTs) offer the advantage of comparing the student's performance to a sample of same-age peers. SNRTs of academic achievement abound for school-based practitioners. For the purposes of assessment and evaluation, a broad measure of academic skills should be the first course of action to obtain an overall picture of the student's academic skills. Academic achievement measures such as the Wechsler Individual Achievement Test–Second Edition (Wechsler, 2002) and the Woodcock–Johnson III Tests of Achievement (Woodcock, McGrew, & Mather, 2001) survey a student's performance in aspects of reading, math, writing, and spelling, producing overall composite scores in each area. The standard scores and percentile ranks derived from SNRTs give an estimate of the student's performance relative to same-age peers. A critical weakness of SNRTs is the limited applicability for intervention development due to the indirect nature of the assessment of basic skills.

CBM directly measures the basic skills of reading, math, writing, and spelling (Marston, 1989). Significant advantages of CBM over traditional SNRTs are its focus on observable student responses, repeated measurement of responses, sensitivity to small changes in student performance, and minimal time and cost associated with administration (Marston). At a basic level, CBM data are fundamental outcomes of daily classroom lessons. In the context of an assessment, CBM can reliably and validly determine a student's current instructional placement and more importantly, serve as means of formative evaluation of the effectiveness of instructional practices.

Social/Emotional Assessment

Assessing the social and emotional concerns of students is most efficiently accomplished by having multiple informants' complete behavior rating scales. Obtaining reports from multiple informants allows for analysis within and across raters. Moreover, best practice guidelines recommend the completion of a behavior rating scale, assessing a continuum of externalizing and internalizing behavior problems, by at least one parent and teacher (McConaughy & Ritter, 2008).

Behavior rating scales are divided into broad-band and narrow-band measures. Broad-band measures assess and screen for an array of behavioral problems, whereas narrow-band measures have a specific purpose or behavior to target (Merrell, 2000). Two commonly used broad-band scales demonstrating adequate reliability and validity are the Behavior Assessment System for Children – Second Edition (BASC-2; Reynolds & Kamphaus, 2004) and the Achenbach System of Empirically Based Assessment (ASEBA; Achenbach & Rescorla, 2001). The BASC-2 and ASEBA measure internalizing and externalizing behaviors of children and adolescents. The benefit of these measures is the breadth of behavioral issues that are addressed. Areas that may not have been identified during an interview or record review may be flagged with a broad-band measure, signifying the need for further examination. A school psychologist may then proceed with a narrow-band measure(s) to investigate a particular area of concern (e.g., depression, anxiety) in more depth.

When administering behavior rating scales, a school psychologist must judiciously select those measures which are most relevant to the presenting concerns. The selection of rating scales requires an astute understanding of the presenting concerns and information gleaned from the record review and interviews. Despite the large number of scales available for assessment of a variety of emotional and behavioral concerns, only those scales with demonstrated technical adequacy that are linked to specific referral questions should be considered for administration. An additional area worthy of exploration for a student exhibiting emotional and behavioral concerns is social skills. One component of the ED definition under IDEA pertains to social skills, or more formally described as "interpersonal relationships with peers and teachers" (IDEA, 2004). The Social Skills Improvement System (Elliott & Gresham, 2008) is a standardized norm-referenced assessment system designed to measure the social behavior of students across multiple informants.

A more direct measure of social relationships is sociometric techniques that gauge the social status of students according to peer report. Sociometric techniques directly measure the social dynamics of a defined group. Two examples of sociometric techniques are peer nomination and peer rating (Merrell, 1999). Peer nomination involves a child identifying peers according to positive and negative criteria. The information from a peer nomination procedure can be aggregated into a sociogram, a graphic depiction of the social groups. In peer ratings, children respond to one or more sociometric questions for each peer in the defined group (Merrell). Each child then receives an average rating across all respondents.

Evidence on sociometric techniques suggests adequate psychometric properties (Jiang & Cillessen, 2005; Merrell, 1999), with a possibility of utilizing sociometrics to evaluate social skills training interventions (Hansen, Nangle, & Ellis, 1996).

Behavioral Assessment

Displays of problem or disruptive behavior are hallmarks of students with emotional and behavioral concerns and are often the primary reason for referral. A pivotal part of the evaluation process is to conduct an assessment of behavior to determine the significance, severity, and discrepancy from typical peers. This is best achieved through direct behavioral observation in the natural setting (i.e., classroom, playground, etc.).

Direct observation of student behavior provides the most accurate estimate of the behavior (Cooper, Heron, & Heward, 2007). It involves recording and measuring behavior in context while a student interacts with his or her typical environment, particularly academic and social tasks. Informal modes of direct observation provide anecdotal accounts of behavior; however, such measures are subjective and cannot be replicated (Salvia & Ysseldyke, 2004). A systematic observation entails the observation of target behavior(s), operationally defined a priori. For most students, measures of academic engaged time and disruptive behavior are relevant (Walker et al., 2004). To precisely record and measure behavior, the observational assessment tool should utilize procedures of event recording, timing, and/or time sampling to measure the behavior(s) across the length of the observation period (Hintze, Volpe, & Shapiro, 2008). In contrast to anecdotal reports of problem behavior, a structured observation code produces a quantifiable number reflecting the occurrence of behavior at the end of the observation period. A series of brief observations in different settings is recommended to gain a representative sample of the student's behavior across time and settings (McConaughy & Ritter, 2008).

Using the principles of behavioral measurement, school psychologists can develop their own methods of observation. The advantage of developing one's own measure is that the observation can be tailored to specific behaviors identified by teachers and parents. Appreciating that the development can be time-consuming, commercially developed observation systems exist to assist the school psychologist with the observation of problem behavior in school settings. The Behavioral Observation of Students in Schools (BOSS; Shapiro, 2004) is an observational tool designed to measure student behavior for up to 45 minutes and samples passive and active forms of on-task behavior, as well as motor and verbal forms of disruptive off-task behavior. The BOSS includes a sample of peer behavior throughout the observation period. Obtaining comparisons of the target student's behavior to typical peers is recommended to provide a normative reference and can be incorporated into personally designed observational tools (McConaughy & Ritter, 2008).

In addition to samples of academic engaged time and disruptive behaviors, a narrative recording of antecedents and consequences of behavior allow the school psychologist to examine the environmental variables that maintain the problem behavior. Systematic measurement of these variables is critical to conducting an FBA. Outside of an FBA, data regarding antecedents and consequences are advantageous when making recommendations for relevant intervention strategies, regardless of the setting in which the student may be placed.

Diagnostic Formulation

Armed with the data from a comprehensive assessment, a school psychologist must formulate a hypothesis of the student's emotional and behavioral functioning and the resulting impact on academic achievement based on a convergence of evidence. It is then that the school psychologist, *as part of* a multidisciplinary evaluation team, will determine the student's need for service and the eligibility for a classification of ED.

Implications for Practice

While the results of a multidimensional, comprehensive assessment will drive the eligibility determination process and possible placement in special education, the results do not extend much further. The use of traditional indirect, norm-referenced assessment measures will not furnish the teacher with a summary of the student's skills that are directly applicable to the classroom. A discussion of the limitations of standardized, norm-referenced measures is beyond the scope of this chapter. However, school psychologists should avail themselves of the resources necessary to make informed decisions on the selection of assessment measures and the resulting utility of these measures in programming effectively for students. Holding school psychologists to this pursuit of evidence-based practice is the Blueprint III (Ysseldyke et al., 2006), a guiding document of the fundamental competencies in training and practice for school psychologists. Specific to the competencies outlined in the Blueprint III for evaluating students with emotional and behavioral concerns are data-based decision making and accountability, and systems-based service delivery. These competencies prescribe the actual processes of school psychology. In the context of the present topic, school psychologists must be knowledgeable in assessment methods including the type of information that can be gleaned from chosen methods and linking the results to intervention. Moreover, school psychologists must have an understanding of the role of assessment within a model of prevention and intervention, and how to promote such models in schools to enhance the delivery of services and outcomes for all students.

Building Professional Competence

For school psychologists who are new to the field and to those who are interested in developing and refining skills, there are a number of opportunities to build professional competence. These opportunities can be accessed in two general ways: local level and professional level. For further expansion, Table 8.1 presents readings and resources for school psychologists to gain competence in the area of students, with emotional and behavioral concerns.

Local Level

Assessing opportunities within one's own practicing district will apprise a school-based practitioner of those activities available at the local level. Within a school, active participation on a pre-referral team offers first-hand experience with consultation-related duties, including multi-modal assessment of problem behavior, development of function-based intervention strategies, collection of relevant, sensitive data measures, and data-based decision making within the team process. Bringing a school psychologist's knowledge base of assessment, consultation, and instructional and classroom management to the team process will be instrumental in helping pre-referral teams with intervention development. For more advanced skill development, in-district professionals who have expertise with this population of students are typically available for consultation. Consultation can

Table 8.1 Suggested readings and resources for students with emotional and behavioral concerns

Professional organizations relevant to students with emotional and behavioral concerns	Association for Positive Behavior Support
	Council for Children with Behavior Disorders
	National Association of School Psychologists
Suggested readings in specific content areas	
School-based assessment	McConaughy and Ritter (2008)
	Shapiro and Kratochwill (2000)
Functional behavioral assessment (FBA)	O'Neill et al. (1997); Sugai et al. (2000)
School-wide positive behavior support (SW-PBS)	Horner et al. (2005)
Response to intervention	Gresham (2005)

be in the form of peer mentoring networks and/or supervision. Peer mentoring networks involve pairing an early-career school psychologist with an experienced school psychologist for ongoing professional development. Supervision by senior in-district personnel may be available; however, assigned supervisors may not possess the skill with this particular population of students. It may be necessary to seek assistance from other personnel within the district or local education agencies for supervision. As the role of the school psychologist expands and the demands for services grow, more school-based professionals will be looking to enhance their skills in certain areas (e.g., students with emotional and behavioral concerns). Developing intra-district interest groups for the specific purpose of skill development is one efficient way for building the internal capacity of the district personnel. Activities for an interest group may involve quarterly meetings, sharing of professional resources, and case presentations for discussion.

Professional Level

As a school psychologist enters the field, it is important to join professional organizations to keep abreast of training opportunities, current trends in the field, public policy changes, cutting-edge technologies, and evidence-based practices, not to mention easy access to materials. For ongoing updates, many professional organizations utilize a listserv to disseminate information to its members. Various listservs are in existence at any one time, and may focus on particular areas of practice. One area may be dedicated to assessment measures. Keeping pace with revisions to assessment tools will allow a school psychologist to utilize the most current methods available. Along with assessment tools is the ability to critically evaluate new methods or procedures for assessment, including their applicability to a specific student population, intended purpose, and utility for intervention development. An additional professional endeavor for skill development is attending professional conferences. Professional conferences bring together researchers and practitioners to share new evidence-based strategies, their implications for practice, and the outcomes of the strategies employed in school-based settings. Skill-based workshops and presentations of research findings can provide valuable information to be employed in practice.

The Future Is Now: Applying a Response-to-Intervention Logic to Social-Behavioral Problems

This chapter focused on assessment of emotional and behavioral challenges as outlined in IDEA 2004. However there is a proposed alternate, better-practice approach to identifying and intervening with emotional and behavioral concerns, known as response-to-intervention (RtI). The current approach to assessment and identification follows a "refer-test-place" paradigm in which a student must demonstrate that his/her behavior is significantly discrepant from peers and that the behavior has significantly impacted school performance – thus resulting in delayed services. One could argue this approach serves as a "wait-to-fail" model of service delivery. RtI provides an alternative to this "wait-to-fail" model in which students receive immediate assistance for behavioral concerns, and interventions are carried out prior to a move towards eligibility determination (Gresham, 2005).

In a RtI model, when a behavioral concern surfaces, the concern is often taken to a grade level team or pre-referral team. The team then develops an evidence-based (and preferably function-based) plan for implementing the intervention. Once the intervention is implemented, the student's behavior is then monitored by the team to determine if there are changes in student behavior as a function of the intervention (Gresham, 2005). In addition to monitoring student behavior, the team monitors the integrity with which the intervention is implemented. Integrity of the intervention is paramount to the RtI logic (Gresham) because if the team cannot document that the intervention was carried out as intended, the team cannot establish a functional relationship between the student's behavior and the intervention. During this data-based progress monitoring of the intervention, the team looks to document a difference between the student's level of performance on a specified goal (i.e., behavioral and/or academic goal) while the intervention is in place compared to his or her level of performance prior to the intervention. If a discrepancy between pre and post-intervention levels of behavior are found, it is determined that the student has "responded to the intervention" (Gresham). The team then develops a plan to promote maintenance and generalization of the target behavior.

Within RtI logic, classification decisions are made only when the presenting problem behavior(s) persists in the light of evidence-based intervention(s) implemented with a high degree of integrity (Gresham, 1999). This approach for Learning Disability classification already appears in the federal regulations (IDEA 2004). For more detailed information on applying RtI logic to social-behavioral intervention planning and classification, see Gresham (2005).

A System-Wide Approach for Applying RtI Logic to Social-Behavioral Issues

A best-practice approach is to move beyond the application of RtI logic for individual student planning, and expand this problem solving logic to the larger system; including classroom and whole school levels. It is only when we reach the systemic application of prevention and intervention that we can be successful at preventing student difficulties before they necessitate intense and resource heavy interventions for preventing the development of more serious mental health difficulties (Gresham, 2005). Adopting RtI logic at the systems level requires a proactive, prevention-oriented approach to educational planning. Such an approach has been suggested by the National Association of State Directors of Special Education (NASDSE, 2006) for academic planning and has been demonstrated for emotional and behavioral concerns through school-wide positive behavior support (SWPBS).

SWPBS is a process for establishing consistent, predictable, positive school environments for all students and staff by providing a continuum of prevention and intervention services that match the intensity of student need to the intensity of the intervention (Horner, Sugai, Todd, & Lewis-Palmer, 2005; Sugai, et al, 2000; Sugai & Horner, 2002; Walker et al, 1996). SWPBS mirrors the three-tiered public health model with universal, secondary, and tertiary levels of prevention/intervention. At the universal level of support, all students are exposed to a school-wide intervention consisting of (a) clearly stated and posted expectations, (b) systems for recognizing appropriate behavior, and (c) a continuum of consequences for problem behavior. School teams use data (e.g., monthly reviews of office discipline referrals ODRs) to determine the success of the overall school wide system as well as the success of specific students within the universal system. Some students (e.g., students having received between 2 and 5 [ODRs]) will not "respond" to universal supports (Horner et al., 2005). These students, then, receive additional support at the secondary level. Examples include the Behavior Education Program (Crone, Horner, & Hawken, 2004) or other check-in-check-out procedures, homework club, and behavioral skill instruction. For students who do not respond support secondary level intervention, a school-based team conducts a formal FBA leading to a behavior support plan (BSP). A determination of the need for special education services is based on two factors: (a) a non-response or insufficient response to tertiary-level intervention implemented in the general educational environment, or (b) a positive response to a tertiary-level intervention that is not able to be maintained in the general education setting (i.e., there is a poor contextual fit of the intervention within the general education environment). It should be noted that not all students receiving services at the tertiary level are in need of special education services. The above provides a simple overview of the RtI process within a school-wide model.

Fairbanks and colleagues (2007) provide an exemplar extension of the RtI logic to the classroom system. Their work illustrated the data-based decision making involved with monitoring a group of students' responses to increasingly intense levels of intervention. In this study, the authors applied a universal intervention (e.g., basic classroom management strategies), a secondary level intervention (e.g., check-in-check-out) for those who did not respond to the universal intervention, and a tertiary-level intervention (e.g., FBA and function-based BIP) for those who did not respond to the universal or secondary-level interventions (Fairbanks et al.).

Early Screening

Inherent in the SW-PBS process noted above is the need for early screening procedures to identify student needs before they require more intense assessment and intervention. The SSBD was suggested earlier in the chapter as an exemplar, multiple-gated process for screening of emotional and behavior concerns (Walker & Severson, 2002). Additionally, school psychologists should take into consideration the relationship between student behavior and early academic failure and look at early literacy screening data as an additional means to prevent future emotional and behavioral concerns. One tool to facilitate this process is the Dynamic Indicators of Early Literacy Skills (DIBELS; Good & Kaminski, 2002); a standardized, norm-referenced assessment for early literacy skills that can be used for screening, intervention planning, and monitoring student progress. Recent findings by McIntosh, Horner, Chard, Boland, and Good (2006), illustrate the potential power of using a combination of academic and behavioral screening measures to identify students in need of intervention early in their educational career. Results found that poor performance on the DIBELS Phonemic Segmentation Fluency (PSF) test, in the spring of kindergarten, significantly predicted the presence of 2 or more office referrals in fifth grade (McIntosh et al.).

Prevention and early identification is the future direction for working with individuals with emotional and behavioral concerns. Such an approach requires the field of school psychology to move from direct to indirect service delivery, and consider the system (i.e., the school, classroom, group of children), as opposed to the individual only, as the level of intervention.

Summary and Conclusion

Dylan's song title, *The Times They Are a-Changin'*, seems an apt summary of recent policy changes (IDEA 2004) in eligibility determination for students with learning disabilities. As voiced by many others, it is anticipated that these changes will carry over to other high-incidence disability groups, including EBD.

Two decades have passed since Jane Knitzer and colleagues examined the programs and policies in place for children with EBD (Knitzer, Steinberg, & Fleisch, 1990). Although, many of the criticisms levied at the time remain true today, there are some improvements, particularly with regard to evaluation and identification. Knitzer et al. cautioned against the inappropriate identification of students with EBD, thereby ensuring that the "right" students receive services, by recommending a variety of preventive actions: (a) making crisis intervention and mental health services more broadly available across the general education program (i.e., preventing the inappropriate labeling of students due to an acute crisis or to problems that do not affect the student's educational progress); (b) ensuring that school teams resort to pre-referral interventions prior to assessing and determining a student's eligibility for special education services in the EBD category; and (c) providing training to all school-related personnel, including teachers, administrators and even school board members, in an effort to demystify the construct of emotional disturbance and to promote more appropriate referrals.

As reviewed in this chapter and elsewhere, progress along the lines recommended by Knitzer et al. (1990) has been made on several fronts. For example, support for a model of school-based mental health service delivery is stronger than ever, fueled by several initiatives including the President's New Freedom Commission on Mental Health (2003) and the 2006 School-Based Mental Health Empirical Guide for Decision-Makers (Kutash, Duchnowski, & Lynn, 2006). The U.S. Department of Education's Technical Assistance Center on Positive Behavior Interventions & Supports at the University of Oregon has been instrumental in introducing and disseminating systems-level school reform procedures, including SWPBS, which encompasses more efficient methods for early screening and intervention and holds implications for students at risk for EBD. Finally, we see today a greater effort on the part of researchers and professionals in the field of special education reaching out to and joining general educators, in an effort to improve services for students with, and at risk for developing, EBD through training and program dissemination (Fairbanks et al. 2007). Times are, in fact, changing in the field of behavior disorders and school psychologists, in particular, are at a critical juncture to effect a change in their professional roles that will enable them to provide improved service delivery. It is anticipated, that this chapter will be helpful in guiding school psychologists, whether new to or established in, the field to move in this new and innovative direction.

Chapter Competency Checklist

DOMAIN 2 – Enhancing the development of wellness, social skills, mental health, and life

Foundational	Functional
Understand and explain the following: □ Emotional disturbance □ Prevention and early intervention of emotional disturbance □ Evaluation process for special education services □ Eligibility considerations for special education services □ The importance of using reliable assessment methods □ The importance of using valid assessment methods □ Functional behavior assessment □ Intervention literature for treating emotional disturbance □ RtI models for providing services to children with behavioral and emotional problems	Gain practice: □ Observing children with a range of normal and abnormal functioning □ Interviewing teachers, parents, students □ Completing structured behavioral observations □ Administering and interpreting behavior rating scales □ Completing functional behavioral assessments □ Writing reports and communicating results □ Implementing interventions □ Evaluating interventions and consulting with school teams □ Providing services within an RtI model

References

Achenbach, T. M., & Rescorla, L. A. (2001). *Manual for ASEBA school-age forms & profiles*. Burlington, VT: University of Vermont, Research Center for Children, Youth, & Families.

Angold, A., Costello, E. J., & Erkanli, A. (1999). Comorbidity. *Journal of Child Psychology and Psychiatry, 40*, 57–87.

Bradley, R., Henderson, K., & Monfore, D. A. (2004). A national perspective on children with emotional disorders. *Behavioral Disorders, 29*, 211–223.

Burns, B. J., Costello, E. J., Angold, A., Tweed, D., Stangle, D., Farmer, E. M. Z., et al. (1995). Children's mental health service use across service sectors. *Health Affairs, 14*, 148–159.

Busse, R. T., & Beaver, B. R. (2000). Informant report: Parent and teacher interviews. In E. S. Shapiro & T. R. Kratochwill (Eds.), *Conducting school-based assessments of child and adolescent behavior* (pp. 235–273). New York: Guilford.

Cheney, D., Flower, A., & Templeton, T. (2008). Applying response to intervention metrics in the social domain for students at risk of developing emotional and behavioral disorders. *The Journal of Special Education, 42*, 108–126.

Cooper, J. O., Heron, T. E., & Heward, W. L. (2007). *Applied behavior analysis* (2nd ed.). Upper Saddle River, NJ: Pearson Education.

Crone, D. A., & Horner, R. H. (2003). *Building positive behavior support systems in schools: Functional behavioral assessment.* New York: Guilford Press.

Crone, D. A., Horner, R. H., & Hawken, L. S. (2004). *Responding to problem behavior in schools: The behavior education program.* New York: Guilford Press.

Cullinan, D. (2004). Classification and definition of emotional and behavioral disorders. In R. B. Rutherford Jr., M. M. Quinn, & S. R. Mathur (Eds.), *Handbook of research in emotional and behavioral disorders* (pp. 32–53). New York: Guilford Press.

Fairbanks, S., Sugai, G., Guardino, D., & Lathrop, M. (2007). Response to intervention: Examing classroom behavior support in second grade. *Exceptional Children, 73*, 288–310.

Federal Register. (2006, August). *Rules and Regulations, 71*(156), 46539–46845.

Forness, S. R. (1992). Exclusion of socially maladjusted youth from special education: Broadening the cultural-organizational perspective. *Remedial and Special Education, 13*, 55–59.

Forness, S. R. (2004). Characteristics of emotional and behavioral disorders: Introduction. In R. B. Rutherford Jr., M. M. Quinn, & S. R. Mathur (Eds.), *Handbook of research in emotional and behavioral disorders* (pp. 235–241). New York: Guilford Press.

Forness, S. R., & Kavale, K. A. (2000). Emotional or behavioral disorders: Background and current status of the E/BD terminology and definition. *Behavioral Disorders, 25*, 264–269.

Forness, S. R., & Knitzer, J. (1992). A new proposed definition and terminology to replace "serious emotional disturbance" in Individuals with Disabilities Education Act. *School Psychology Review, 21*, 12–20.

Good, R. H., & Kaminski, R. A. (2002). *Dynamic indicators of basic early literacy skills* (6th ed.). Eugene, OR: Institute for the Development of Education Achievement. August 16, 2010, from http://dibels.uoregon.edu.

Gresham, F. M. (1999). Noncategorical approaches to K-12 emotional and behavioral disorders. In D. J. Reschly, W. D. Tilly, & J. P. Grimes (Eds.), *Special education in transition: Functional assessment and noncategorical programming* (pp. 107–137). Longmont, CO: Sopris West.

Gresham, F. M. (2005). Response to intervention: An alternative means of identifying students as emotionally disturbed. *Education and Treatment of Children, 28*, 328–344.

Gresham, F. M. & Elliott, S. N.(2008). *Social skills improvement system.* San Antonio, TX: Pearson.

Gresham, F. M., Lane, K. L., & Lambros, K. M. (2001). Comorbidity of conduct problems and ADHD: Identification of "fledgling psychopaths". In H. M. Walker & M. H. Epstein (Eds.), *Making schools safer and violence free: Critical issues, solutions, and recommended practices* (pp. 17–27). Austin, TX: Pro-Ed.

Groth-Marnat, G. (2003). *Handbook of psychological assessment.* Hoboken, NJ: Wiley.

Hansen, D. J., Nangle, D. W., & Ellis, J. T. (1996). Reconsideration of the use of peer sociometrics for evaluating social skills training. *Behavior Modification, 20*, 281–299.

Harris-Murri, N., King, K., & Rostenberg, D. (2006). Reducing disproportionate minority representation in special education programs for students with emotional disturbances: Toward a culturally responsive response to intervention model. *Education & Treatment of Children, 29*, 779–799.

Hintze, J. M., Volpe, R. J., & Shapiro, E. S. (2008). Best practices in the systematic direct observation of student behavior. In A. Thomas & J. Grimes (Eds.), *Best practices in school psychology V* (pp. 319–335). Bethesda, MD: NASP Publications.

Hoagwood, K., & Johnson, J. (2003). School psychology: A public health framework I. From evidence-based practice to evidence-based policies. *Journal of School Psychology, 41*, 3–21.

Horner, R. H., Sugai, G., Todd, A. W., & Lewis-Palmer, T. (2005). Schoolwide positive behavior support. In L. M. Bambara & L. Kern (Eds.), *Individualized supports for students with problem behaviors: Designing positive behavior plans* (pp. 359–390). New York: Guilford.

Jiang, X. L., & Cillessen, A. H. N. (2005). Stability of continuous measures of sociometric status: A meta-analysis. *Developmental Review, 25*, 1–25.

Kauffman, J. M., Brigham, F. J., & Mock, D. R. (2004). Historical to comtemporary perspectives on the field of emotional and behavioral disorders. In R. B. Rutherford Jr., M. M. Quinn, & S. R. Mathur (Eds.), *Handbook of research in emotional and behavioral disorders* (pp. 15–31). New York: Guilford Press.

Kaufman, J., Birmaher, B., Brent, D. A., Rao, U., & Ryan, N. (1996). *Revised schedule for affective disorders and schizoprenia for school aged children: Present and lifetime version (K-SADS-PL)*. Pittsburgh, PA: Western Psychiatric Institute and Clinic.

Kern, L., Hilt, A. M., & Gresham, F. (2004). An evaluation of the functional behavioral assessment process used with students with or at risk for emotional and behavioral disorders. *Education and Treatment of Children, 27,* 440–452.

Knitzer, J., Steinberg, Z., & Fleisch, B. (1990). *At the schoolhouse door: An examination of programs and policies for children with behavioral and emotional problems*. New York: Bank Street College of Education.

Kutash, K., Duchnowski, A. J., & Lynn, N. (2006). *School-based mental health: An empirical guide for decision-makers*. Tampa, FL: University of South Florida, The Louis de la Parte Florida Mental Health Institute, Department of Child & Family Studies, Research and Training Center for Children's Mental Health.

Lane, K. L., Gresham, F. M., & O'Shaughnessy, T. (2002). Identifying, assessing, and intervening with children with or at-risk for behavior disorders: A look to the future. In K. L. Lane, F. M. Gresham, & T. E. O'Shaughnessy (Eds.), *Interventions for children with or at risk for emotional and behavioral disorders* (pp. 317–326). Needham, MA: Allyn & Bacon.

Marston, D. B. (1989). A curriculum-based measurement approach to assessing academic performance: What it is and why do it. In M. R. Shinn (Ed.), *Curriculum-based measurement: Assessing special children* (pp. 18–78). New York: Guilford.

McConaughy, S. H. (2005). *Clinical interviews for children and adolescents: Assessment to intervention*. New York: Guilford.

McConaughy, S. H., & Achenbach, T. M. (2001). *Manual for the semistructured clinical interview for children and adolescents* (2nd ed.). Burlington, VT: University of Vermont, Center for Children, Youth, & Families.

McConaughy, S. H., & Ritter, D. R. (2008). Best practices in multimethod assessment of emotional and behavioral disorders. In A. Thomas & J. Grimes (Eds.), *Best practices in school psychology V* (pp. 697–715). Bethesda, MD: National Association of School Psychologists.

McIntosh, K., Horner, R. H., Chard, D. J., Boland, J. B., & Good, R. H. (2006). The use of reading and behavior screening measures to predict nonresponse to school-wide positive behavior support: A longitudinal analysis. *School Psychology Review, 35,* 275–291.

Merrell, K. W. (1999). *Behavioral, social, and emotional assessment of children and adolescents* (pp. 133–151). Mahway, NJ: Lawrence Erlbaum Associates.

Merrell, K. W. (2000). Informant report: Rating scale measures. In E. S. Shapiro & T. R. Kratochwill (Eds.), *Conducting school-based assessments of child and adolescent behavior* (pp. 203–234). New York: Guilford.

National Association of School Psychologists. (2000). *Professional conduct manual*. Bethesda, MD: Author.

National Association of School Psychologists. (2005). *Position statement on students with emotional and behavioral disorders*. Bethesda, MD: Author.

National Association of State Directors of Special Education, Inc. (2006). *Response to intervention: Policy considerations and implementation*. Alexandria, VA: Author.

Nelson, J. R., Roberts, M. L., Rutherford, R. B., Mathur, S. R., & Aaroe, L. A. (1999). A statewide survey of special education administrators and school psychologists regarding functional behavioral assessment. *Education and Treatment of Children, 22,* 267–279.

O'Neill, R. E., Horner, R. H., Albin, R. W., Sprague, J. R., Storey, K., & Newton, J. S. (1997). *Functional assessment and program development for problem behavior: A practical handbook* (2nd ed.). Pacific Grove, CA: Brooks/Cole Publishing.

President's New Freedom Commission on Mental Health. (2003). *Achieving the promise: Transforming mental health care in America. Final report (DHHS Publication No. SMA-03-3832)*. Rockville, MD: U.S. Department of Health and Human Services.

Reynolds, C. R., & Kamphaus, R. W. (2004). *Behavior assessment system for children – second edition*. Circle Pines, MN: AGS Publishing.

Salvia, J., & Ysseldyke, J. E. (2004). *Assessment in special and inclusive education* (9th ed.). Boston, MA: Houghton Mifflin.

Sattler, J. M. (2002). *Assessment of children: Behavioral and clinical applications* (4th ed.). San Diego, CA: Author.

Shapiro, E.S., & Kratochwill, T.R. (2000). Conducting school-based assessments of child and adolescent behavior. New York: The Guilford Press.

Shapiro, E. S. (2004). *Academic skills problems workbook (Rev. ed.)*. New York: Guilford.

Skiba, R., & Grizzle, K. (1991). The social maladjustment exclusion: Issues of definition and assessment. *School Psychology Review, 20,* 577–595.

Slenkovich, J. (1992). Can the language "social maladjustment" in the SED definition be ignored? *School Psychology Review, 21,* 21–22.

Sprague, J. R., & Walker, H. M. (2005). *Safe and healthy schools: Practical prevention strategies*. New York: Guilford.

Sugai, G., Horner, R. H., Dunlap, G., Hieneman, M., Lewis, T. J., Nelson, C. M., et al. (2000). Applying positive behavior support and functional behavioral assessment in schools.

Sugai, G., & Horner, R. H. (2002). The evolution of discipline practices: School-wide positive behavior supports. *Child and Family Behavior Therapy, 24*, 23–50.

Sugai, G., Lewis-Palmer, T., & Hagan-Burke, S. (2000). Overview of the functional behavioral assessment process. *Exceptionality, 8*, 149–160.

Tankersley, M., Landrum, T. J., & Cook, B. G. (2004). How research informs practice in the field of emotional and behavioral disorders. In R. B. Rutherford Jr., M. M. Quinn, & S. R. Mathur (Eds.), *Handbook of research in emotional and behavioral disorders* (pp. 98–113). New York: Guilford Press.

U.S. Department of Education. (2004). *Twenty-sixth annual report to Congress on the implementation of the Individuals with Disabilities Education Act (IDEA)*. Washington, DC: Author.

U.S. Department of Health and Human Services (U.S. DHHS). (1999). *Mental health: A report of the surgeon general*. Rockville, MD: Author, Substance Abuse and Mental health Services Administration, Center for Mental Health Services, National Institutes of Health, National Institute of Mental Health.

Walker, H. M., Block-Pedego, A., Todis, B., & Severson, H. (1991). *School archival records search (SARS): User's guide and technical manual*. Longmont, CO: Sopris West.

Walker, H. M., Horner, R. H., Sugai, G., Bullis, M., Sprague, J. R., Bricker, D., & Kaufman, M. J. (1996). Integrated approaches to preventing antisocial behavior patterns among school-age children and youth. *Journal of Emotional and Behavioral Disorders, 4*, 194–209.

Walker, H. M., Ramsey, E., & Gresham, F. M. (2003/2004, Winter). Heading off disruption: How early intervention can reduce defiant behavior and win back teaching time. *American Educator, 6–21*.

Walker, H. M., Ramsey, E., & Gresham, F. M. (2004). *Antisocial behavior in school: Evidence-based practices* (2nd ed.). Belmont, CA: Wadsworth.

Walker, H. M., & Severson, H. H. (1992). *Systematic screening for behaviors disorders* (2nd ed.). Longmont, CO: Sopris West.

Walker, H. M., & Severson, H. H. (2002). *Systematic screening for behavioral disorders: User's guide and administration manual*. Longmont, CO: Sopris West.

Wechsler, D. (2002). *Wechsler individual achievement test – second edition* (2nd ed.). San Antonio, TX: The Psychological Corporation.

Woodcock, R. W., McGrew, K. S., & Mather, N. (2001). *Woodcock-Johnson III tests of achievement*. Itasca, IL: Riverside Publishing.

Ysseldyke, J., Burns, M., Dawson, P., Kelley, B., Morrison, B., Ortiz, S., et al. (2006). *School psychology: A blueprint for training and practice III*. Bethesda, MD: National Association of School Psychologists.

Chapter 9
Beyond Unproven Trends: Critically Evaluating School-Wide Programs

David N. Miller and Kristin D. Sawka-Miller

Introduction

School psychologists should be committed to enhancing the academic success and behavioral competence of all students (Ysseldyke et al., 2006). Comprehensive school-wide prevention and intervention programs designed to promote these conditions, however, are frequently not successful despite the concerted efforts of school personnel. Unfortunately, schools have historically been and largely continue to be institutions in which highly-touted interventions and prevention programs are frequently adopted despite little or no evidence of their effectiveness (Merrell, Ervin, & Gimpel, 2006). Short-term fads and unproven trends often develop and flourish, only to be eventually replaced by other well-intentioned but typically fleeting educational initiatives (Sarason, 1996). Not only are many of these faddish trends and programs (colloquially known as "bandwagons") implemented with little or no research support, in many cases they also are ineffectively evaluated or not evaluated at all (Merrell et al., 2006).

The frequency and regularity in which unproven trends and "bandwagon" approaches have been adopted by schools led Walker (2001) to the conclusion that "educators are notorious for embracing programs that look good but do no actual good" (p. 2). Consider, for example, some of the following recent trends in schools and education:

1. Substance abuse among children and youth remains a serious problem, and billions of dollars are spent annually in school-based substance abuse prevention programs (Brown, 2001). The Drug Abuse Resistance Education (D.A.R.E.) program has been the most widely implemented drug prevention program in the U.S. (Burke, 2002), despite research that has consistently demonstrated that D.A.R.E.'s effectiveness on student knowledge and attitudes is neither sustained nor leads to lower use of drugs or alcohol (Weiss, Murphy-Graham, & Birkeland, 2005). Moreover, despite the availability of other empirically-supported school-based substance abuse programs, adoption and implementation integrity of such programs appears to be low (St. Pierre & Kaltreider, 2004).

2. Low self-esteem has been viewed as such a significant problem that the California Task Force to Promote Self-Esteem and Personal and Social Responsibility (1990) stated that "the lack of self-esteem is central to most personal and social ills plaguing our state and nation" (p. 4). These and similar beliefs led to several educational and governmental initiatives designed to prevent low self-esteem and foster higher self-esteem among students (Manning, Bear, & Minke, 2006). Although it is commonly believed that self-esteem is lower among children with learning disabilities or disruptive behavior problems, there is little or no empirical support for these

D.N. Miller (✉)
University of Albany, Albany, NY, USA
e-mail: DMiller@uamail.albany.edu

T.M. Lionetti et al. (eds.), *A Practical Guide to Building Professional Competencies in School Psychology*,
DOI 10.1007/978-1-4419-6257-7_9, © Springer Science+Business Media, LLC 2011

beliefs. In fact, research suggests that aggressive children often exhibit an inflated sense of self-esteem (Manning et al., 2006).

3. During the past several decades, there has been an increased emphasis on "student-centered" approaches to reading instruction and literacy. This approach is exemplified by "whole language" instruction, which emphasizes that the best method for promoting word recognition and decoding is through reading for meaning. Although popular among teachers, this "student-centered" approach to reading has generally not been found to be as effective as "teacher-centered" approaches that emphasize phonological awareness for beginning reading instruction (Chall, 2000). Although a balanced approach involving both whole-language and phonetic approaches is preferable for most students (Pressley, 2002), for beginning and struggling readers, as well as for children of lower socioeconomic status, research clearly indicates that teacher-centered instruction emphasizing phonemic awareness and an understanding of alphabetic principles and sound-symbol relationships are the key building blocks in the development of effective reading skills (Chall, 2000; Shapiro, 2004). Teacher-centered forms of instruction, such as Direct Instruction procedures (Engelmann & Carnine, 1982), have consistently been found to be effective yet continue to be underutilized in schools.

4. Two of the most popular interventions for students who exhibit antisocial and aggressive behavior include counseling and punishment procedures (Maag, 2001; Stage & Quiroz, 1997). Despite their widespread use, research suggests that both counseling (Stage & Quiroz, 1997) and punishment (Maag, 2001) are frequently ineffective in ameliorating students' antisocial behaviors. Although some forms of cognitive-behavior therapy may be useful with some students exhibiting disruptive behavior problems (Polsgrove & Smith, 2004), effective school-based intervention typically involves the modification of environmental variables within classrooms and schools (Furlong, Morrison, & Jimerson, 2004). Moreover, punishment procedures, particularly in the form of suspension or expulsion, are actually associated with increases in disruptive behavior (Maag, 2001).

5. Many teachers appear to believe it is necessary to get students' problem behavior "under control" before effective teaching and learning can occur. Research, however, suggests that effective academic instruction and effective behavior management are reciprocally and inextricably related (Miller, George, & Fogt, 2005). For example, curricular modifications have been used successfully to promote desirable behavior by making curricula more interesting and relevant to students (Dunlap & Kern, 1996; Kern, Bambara, & Fogt, 2002). Further, research clearly indicates that improving students' academic success often has the collateral effect of enhancing student behavior and mental health (Berninger, 2006). For example, when mental health interventions were compared to a typical school treatment (i.e., regular academic program), the mental health interventions were found to be no more effective than the regular academic program in promoting mental health (Weiss, Catron, Harris, & Phung, 1999), possibly because many (though certainly not all) of the externalizing and internalizing problems experienced by students in schools are frequently a result of student frustrations at not being successful academically. Such findings strongly support the notion that effective behavior support and effective academic instruction should be viewed as complimentary and integrally related, but in everyday school practice this is often not the case.

6. Suicide prevention programs in schools have historically been of short duration, frequently follow a stress-related model (i.e., suggesting to students that suicidal behavior can occur primarily as a result of extreme stress), and often fail to assess program effects on actual suicidal behavior (Mazza, 1997). This has occurred despite research suggesting that suicide prevention programs should be of longer duration, have a mental health focus rather than a stress focus, and assess suicidal behavior (e.g., suicide attempts) rather than simply thoughts and attitude change (Berman, Jobes, & Silverman, 2006). Further, although there is empirical support for the effectiveness of self-report screening programs to prevent youth suicide (Shaffer & Craft, 1999), this model appears to be less acceptable to school principals (Miller, Eckert, DuPaul, & White, 1999), school

psychologists (Eckert, Miller, DuPaul, & Riley-Tillman, 2003), and superintendents (Scherff, Eckert, & Miller, 2005) than other more inefficient prevention programs. Although there appears to be a common belief that screening programs will increase the likelihood of suicidal behavior (Miller & McConaughy, 2005), research does not support this contention (Gould et al., 2005).

Many more examples could be provided, but the point should be clear: schools are places in which empirically unproven or unsupported practices are frequently adopted and implemented. The reasons for this unfortunate situation are numerous and complex, and it is not our intention to review them here. Instead, our purpose is to discuss procedures for critically and effectively evaluating school-wide prevention and intervention programs so that the probability of adopting, implementing, and supporting popular but unproven programs can be minimized. We begin with a review of the relevant literature in the area of school-based prevention and intervention program evaluation.

Review of Relevant Literature

Program evaluation in the schools has traditionally not been a significant role for school psychologists. Evaluating programs in schools is a broad and complex process (Merrell et al., 2006), and this is especially the case when evaluating school-wide programs. Given the greater emphasis within school psychology and education on issues such as accountability and data-based decision making, however, this is an area of increasing importance and one in which school psychologists can and should play a prominent role (Ysseldyke et al., 2006).

In particular, school psychologists can first assist in critically evaluating which school-wide programs should be considered for adoption. For example, school psychologists should be cognizant of evidence-based interventions (EBIs); that is, interventions and programs that have demonstrated empirical support for their effectiveness based on the research literature (Kratochwill & Shernoff, 2004). This requires that school psychologists be effective consumers of the research literature and that they have adequate access to it. Similarly, school psychologists should be familiar with variables common to effective school-wide prevention programs and interventions in schools. Nation and his colleagues (2003) provide several principles of effective prevention programs (see Table 9.1).

Second, school psychologists should develop competencies in the areas of *needs assessment* and *creating readiness*. A needs assessment is a form of assessment in which needs of a particular school are identified (typically through interviews with school personnel and other stakeholders) by the discrepancy between some current condition and some desired (or required) state (Nagle, 2002). Needs must be identified before they can be addressed by particular programs, and a needs assessment can serve as the foundation for program planning, implementation, and evaluation (Nagle, 2002). Similarly, readiness lays the foundation for change by developing a shared understanding of the need for and purpose of particular programs. Conveying to stakeholders the intended benefits of the program effort and a description of supports to be provided during the change process is believed to contribute to readiness for the program and greater acceptance of it (Grimes, Kurns, &

Table 9.1 Sample of multileveled service delivery for anger/aggression

Level	Sample program	Skill developed	Age range	Website for additional information
Universal	Second Step Social Skills Program	Social skills violence prevention	pre K-8	www.guide.Helpingamericasyouth.gov
Targeted	Coping Power Program	Anger management/ aggression	Late elementary-early middle school	www.copingpower.com
Intensive	Olweus Bullying Prevention Program	Intervening with bullies/victims	K-8	www.clemson.edu/olweus/ training.html

Tilly, 2006). School psychologists should conduct needs assessments and lay the foundations for creating readiness prior to the implementation of school-wide programs.

Third, once particular programs are selected, school psychologists can be integrally involved in monitoring and evaluating their effectiveness. School-wide prevention or intervention programs can be evaluated on a variety of levels. Power, DuPaul, Shapiro, and Kazak (2003) identified at least five critical questions that can be asked and should be answered about any proposed program. First, did the program get delivered, and if so how was it delivered? This question addresses factors related to the process of the program. Second, how well did the program get delivered (i.e., was it delivered as designed)? Treatment integrity is the focus of this question. Third, what effects did the program have on key assessment measures? This is the most complex question to answer as well as arguably the most important, because it addresses the program's purpose and goals. The fourth question focuses on the social validity and acceptability of the program. Specifically, what value did the program have for key stakeholders? Finally, what was the significance of the outcomes for the school? This last question addresses the overall impact of the program on the school from a broader perspective (for a more detailed discussion of these issues, see Power et al., 2003). In addition, two other variables - program sustainability and capacity building – are receiving increasing attention and should be evaluated as well. Each of these areas is described in greater detail below.

Process

The first step in evaluating a school-wide program is to determine whether the program was actually delivered to the intended student population. In other words, the process of program implementation must be assessed. To address process questions, data regarding program participants and frequency of implementation need to be collected. Records should be kept documenting when program sessions were conducted, the length of the program sessions, whether program materials were used (e.g., handouts provided to participants), and other information as needed. Audio or videotaping of the program may be useful for some of these purposes (Power et al., 2003).

Integrity

Collecting treatment integrity data involves determining if the program was implemented appropriately. Options for conducting integrity checks include direct observation of program implementation, completion of integrity checklists, and examination of permanent products generated by use of the program. Most conventional methods for conducting integrity checks focus on the content of specific programs while neglecting important process issues, such as the relationship between program participants and individuals implementing the program. For example, audiotapes of particular program sessions could be analyzed to identify key positive and negative verbal interactions between students and staff (Power et al., 2003). Conducting integrity checks is critical; for without it one cannot be sure if a program is failing, or successful, because of the program itself or because it was not properly implemented.

Outcome

Clearly, one of the most important areas in program evaluation is the need to assess the degree to which intended outcomes are achieved. Program effects on particular dependent variables are critical factors in determining whether particular programs should continue to be used. As such, dependent measures must be chosen that (a) tap behaviors and constructs reflective of program goals; (b) have adequate reliability and validity; (c) are culturally sensitive; and (d) are feasible and cost-effective. Additionally, some type of experimental design (e.g., group design; single-subject) should be employed whenever possible, and this decision needs to be made prior to program implementation. It may often be useful to evaluate programs with both descriptive and inferential statistical procedures (Power et al., 2003).

Social Validity

Social validity refers to the value placed on programs by various stakeholders. In particular, treatment acceptability is an important component of social validity that should be evaluated in any school-wide program. Treatment acceptability refers to judgments by stakeholders as to whether particular treatments are appropriate, fair, or reasonable (Eckert & Hintze, 2000). If treatments are not considered acceptable by those responsible for implementing them, treatments may not be implemented properly or with an appropriate level of integrity. Other factors to consider related to acceptability include the feasibility of program implementation, costs of the program (both in terms of financial resources as well as time and effort), and the degree to which programs are aligned with school and community values (Power et al., 2003). Program acceptability can be assessed through interviews with pertinent stakeholders, including teachers, students, administrators, related service personnel, and parents/caregivers. Other possible measures of social validity include consumer satisfaction or treatment acceptability checklists. Although acceptability data is typically collected after program implementation, ideally program acceptability should be evaluated before, during, and after programs are implemented, allowing for greater fine-tuning of program components throughout all stages of the program (Power et al., 2003).

Impact

In addition to assessing program outcomes and acceptability, it is important to determine the significance of the program for the school and for key stakeholders in it. At this level, the evaluator is not concerned as much with *statistical* significance as with *clinical* significance. That is, do pertinent stakeholders in the school view the program as leading to clinically significant change, and making a broad and important impact? For example, stakeholders could be asked to provide subjective evaluations of the degree to which programs made a meaningful difference in students' lives. Or, an evaluation could consist of determining the degree to which the program brought outcomes of an at-risk sample into the average range (Power et al., 2003).

Sustainability

Sustainable programs are programs that endure over time. Sustaining programs over time is difficult, and research clearly indicates that one should not assume that programs will be adopted and sustained based on their demonstrated efficacy alone (Schaughency & Ervin, 2006a). In many instances, programs that have been implemented successfully in schools have not been sustained when external supports (e.g., financial resources; college or university collaborators) are removed (McDougal, Clonan, & Martens, 2000).

School psychologists should be cognizant of the "common factors" of effective, sustainable programs. These include the presence of a program coordinator or committee to oversee the implementation and resolution of day-to-day problems; involvement of individuals with high shared morale, good communication, and a sense of ownership; ongoing processes of formal and informal training, including the involvement of acknowledged experts; high visibility in the school and the community; linkage to stated goals of schools or districts; and consistent support from school administrators (Elias, Zins, Graczyk, & Weissberg, 2003). Each of these variables should be monitored to ensure greater program sustainability over time.

Capacity Building

Related to the concept of sustainability is capacity building, which is the degree to which programs can continue to grow and evolve over time. The adoption, implementation, and evaluation of school-wide programs require that school personnel adopt a collaborative and systemic model of program evaluation. Collaborative strategic planning (CSP) provides school psychologists with a useful framework for capacity building and program evaluation at a school-wide level. CSP is a team-based approach that uses collaborative planning and problem solving to address individual or system-level issues (Curtis & Stollar, 2002). The effective use of CSP builds the problem-solving capacity of the system and enables it to address issues at multiple levels (Stollar, Poth, Curtis, & Cohen, 2006). The CSP is based on a five-step problem-solving model, including (1) problem definition; (2) problem analysis; (3) goal setting; (4) plan development and implementation; and (5) plan evaluation (Deno, 2002; Tilly, 2002). These steps are cyclical as well as sequential, and should be viewed as a fluid *process* rather than a static *event* (Stollar et al., 2006), because the process is ongoing as new needs and problems arise.

Basic Considerations for Enhancing the Research-Practice Connection

It is clearly important for school psychologists to be knowledgeable about EBIs, because it is these interventions that should be considered for adoption as school-wide programs. How does one determine, however, whether a particular intervention works? There are two primary models used to test the effectives of an intervention: *efficacy* and *effectiveness* models. The *efficacy* of an intervention involves implementation in "well-controlled laboratory settings where the intervention is studied under highly standardized conditions, using such procedures as randomized assignment to experimental and control groups, strict adherence to treatment protocols, and tight control over sources of extraneous variance" (Merrell & Buchanan, 2006, p.168). In contrast, examining the *effectiveness* of an intervention involves its application in "real world" settings, which tend not have the tight controls emblematic of efficacy research, or "such vaunted but unrealistic procedures as matching of samples, random assignment, and strict intervention fidelity" (Merrell & Buchanan, 2006, p. 168).

There are costs as well as benefits to both efficacy research and effectiveness research (see Power et al., 2003). For example, efficacy research generally has greater internal validity (i.e., the extent to which the results of a study can be attributed to the treatment rather than other variables), whereas effectiveness research generally has greater external validity (i.e., the extent to which the results of a study are relevant or generalizable to participants and settings beyond those in the study). The challenge for school psychologists is to effectively link efficacy and effectiveness research or, in other words, to effectively translate research into practice (Power et al., 2003).

To develop competencies in these areas, school psychologists will need to be knowledgeable regarding efficacy studies that address a variety of children's academic, social, emotional, and behavioral problems; be cognizant of contextual variables in their particular schools that will promote and/or inhibit the adoption of particular programs; implement programs in a feasible, cost-effective, socially valid and acceptable manner; and collaborate with other professionals in the implementation and evaluation of programs, including other school professionals, administrators, paraprofessionals, and (when available) college/university faculty. The importance of developing effective collaboration skills cannot be overemphasized, as effective implementation and evaluation of school-wide programs requires a team effort and will not succeed without a sustained commitment by multiple stakeholders. In developing effective partnerships, stakeholders should be engaged in a nonhierarchical, collaborative process through each stage of intervention development and outcome evaluation (Power et al., 2003).

Practice Implications: Critically Evaluating a School-Wide Targeted Intervention

School psychologists are in a unique position to lead efforts to build and maintain the capacities of systems to meet the needs of all students. In *Blueprint III: The Model of School Psychology Training and Practice* (Ysseldyke et al., 2006), the authors clearly advocated that these goals be met via a three-tiered service delivery system characterized by varying the intensity of interventions depending on the severity of student need at the universal, targeted, and intensive levels. This is consistent with positions set forth by the National Association of School Psychologists (NASP), particularly related to the current *NASP Standards for Training and Practice* (NASP, 2000). Universal interventions are implemented with all students in a particular school, grade, or classroom. For example, a universal school-wide program for the prevention of antisocial behavior involves establishing clear behavioral expectations, high rates of praise for rule-following behavior, and a well-defined systematic disciplinary response (Lewis & Sugai, 1999).

Although high-integrity universal programming is likely to positively affect and offset risk for the vast majority of students, it is expected that approximately 10–20% of students will require a more specialized group intervention with increased structure and contingent feedback to meet success. In the context of the three-tiered model and the example cited above, the goal of intervention with this targeted group of students with "at-risk" behavior would be to improve behavioral functioning and prevent the development of more serious or chronic behavioral problems. Further, although the model of service delivery for students with "at-risk" behavior is clear, selecting effective interventions for this group can be challenging. The school psychologist, acting as a coordinator for these efforts and the primary support person to the administration, must review the research literature for guidance. It is generally recommended that targeted interventions be low cost, require little effort by teachers, be consistent with school-wide expectations, and be function-based.

One evidence-based targeted intervention that is gaining momentum in research and the applied literature is the Behavior Education Program, or BEP (Crone, Horner, & Hawken, 2004). The BEP is a group intervention that addresses the needs of students whose (negative) behavior is attention-maintained through a daily check-in and check-out procedure. That is, all students in the BEP at any given time report to one "check in" person in the morning to pick up a daily report form and review their goals (consistent with the school-wide expectations). Throughout the day, students receive ratings for their behavior on defined expectations from their teachers, and at the end of the day all students in the BEP report to one "check-out" person that tallies points and provides contingent rewards (Crone et al., 2004). Although the research base for the BEP is still growing, several studies have indicated that the program can be implemented on a school-wide basis with a high degree of integrity (Hawken & Hess, 2006), and it has been associated with improved outcomes such as reduced office discipline referrals (ODRs) for approximately 60–75% of students participating in the program in elementary and secondary settings (Crone et al., 2004; Hawken & Horner, 2003; Hawken & Hess, 2006).

One coordinator oversees the BEP system in terms of identification of students in need, data monitoring, and decision-making (Crone et al., 2004). The role of the BEP coordinator is a natural fit for the school psychologist and is consistent with the *NASP Standards for Training and Practice* (NASP, 2000), as well *as Blue Print III* (Ysseldyke et al., 2006), in building competency in the domains of data-based decision making and accountability, systems-based service delivery, and interpersonal and collaborative skills. Assuming selection of the BEP as an intervention follows a needs assessment and efforts to create readiness, the school psychologist is in a prime position to monitor and evaluate the effectiveness of intervention efforts. In keeping consistent with the recommendations put forth by Power et al. (2003), examples of the school psychologist's involvement in evaluating treatment delivery and integrity, key assessment outcomes, social validity, and impact of the BEP is discussed below.

Evaluating Delivery and Treatment Integrity

Implementation of the BEP requires training of all teaching staff in how to complete the BEP form and provide the amount and type of feedback necessary for students with "at-risk" behavior, in addition to training students in all aspects of the check-in and check-out procedures. The success of this school-wide system rests on the quality of this training as well as the quality of implementation. Clearly, one can check-off and document that training occurred easily enough. Monitoring and evaluating treatment integrity, however, must occur on several levels.

Because the BEP is standardized it makes integrity of implementation more likely and monitoring such implementation easier. At the most basic level, the coordinator should monitor that the student comes back each day with a completed BEP form, suggesting a minimum level of program implementation. A higher level of integrity monitoring would require an in-class observation that the form is being filled out at the proper times (i.e., at the end of each period versus completed retrospectively at the end of the day) and accurately (i.e., that there is a correspondence between the student's behavior and the rating received). Finally, given that a student's status as "at-risk" is defined as being unresponsive to the universal intervention, treatment integrity should involve assessing the degree to which a particular teacher is implementing the universal intervention as intended (e.g., administering high rates of praise and exhibiting efficient and effective instructional and behavioral management strategies).

It is possible that the school psychologist will run into obstacles directly monitoring integrity checks at each of these levels. However, in-class data might be collected as part of routine supervisory visits, or there could be a general expectation that one teacher is selected randomly per week for an in-class observation to monitor effectiveness of the overall program. Public posting of integrity data (with positive contingencies for the teaching staff in meeting specified criteria) might be one way to increase accountability and thereby shape high-integrity implementation.

Evaluating Effect on Key Assessment Measures

Students are typically funneled into the BEP program based on their referrals to a school administrator's office. Therefore, one feasible and cost-effective system already in place for evaluating the effectiveness of the BEP program is ODR data. A review of the literature suggests that ODR data can be a valid indicator of the effects of school-wide behavior interventions (Irvin, Tobin, Sprague, Sugai, & Vincent, 2004), although this data may not adequately capture many students "at-risk" and is likely to be a better measure for students with externalizing (rather than internalizing) behavior problems (Nelson, Benner, Reid, Epstein, & Currin, 2002). Another important piece of student data that is reflective of the BEP goals is the point total on the daily report card. These two pieces of information – overall referral rates and daily prosocial behavior progress – can provide meaningful data on the effectiveness of the program in impacting disruptive behavior when couched in group or single-subject designs. As coordinator of the BEP with ongoing access to this data, the school psychologist is in an ideal position to evaluate the effectiveness of the program.

Social Validity

Equally if not more important in the evaluation of the BEP as a school-wide program is the degree to which teachers and students find the procedures acceptable. It would be important to assess this dimension as early as possible. For example, during the assessment of the readiness stage and prior to intervention, staff could be surveyed regarding what they *anticipate* they would like and not like about the program, as well as what obstacles they would predict might get in the way of implementation. Incorporating this information in designing the BEP implementation procedures might have the dual effect of improving integrity of implementation and boosting consumer satisfaction. Staff and students should also be assessed during and after the program. The *Intervention Rating Scale* (IRP; Witt & Elliott, 1985) for teachers and the *Children's Intervention Rating Scale* (CIRP-15; Witt & Elliott, 1985) are examples of treatment acceptability measures that are well-suited to intervention evaluation by school psychologists.

Impact

As a targeted intervention for students who are not responding to universal programming but do not need highly individualized, intensive programming, the purpose of the BEP system is to offset risk. As a school-wide system, it is therefore paramount to evaluate whether fewer students exhibit "at-risk" behavior following participation in the program. Data-based answers to questions such as, "Are there fewer students referred for special education evaluation for behavioral concerns?" and "What is the percentage of students placed in the BEP who exit the BEP never to return?" provide critical answers to the question of whether high-integrity implementation of the BEP resulted in meaningful differences in the lives of students and functioning of the prevention system.

For a more detailed description of the BEP, easy-to-follow implementation guidelines, and sample monitoring and data-evaluation forms, the reader is referred to Crone et al. (2004).

Building Professional Competence

Wandersman and Florin (2003) pose ten questions that should be addressed in conducting program evaluations, as well as the areas that should be considered in answering them. Their research suggests that better outcomes will be associated with adequately responding to each of these questions, and the issues they raise nicely summarize many of the topics previously described in this chapter.

Table 9.2 Ten questions of program evaluation (Wandersman & Florin, 2003)

(1) What are the needs and resources in your schools? (needs assessment; resource assessment)

(2) What are the goals, target population, and desired outcomes for your school? (goal setting)

(3) How does the prevention or intervention program incorporate knowledge of science and best practices in this area? (science and best practices)

(4) How does the prevention or intervention program fit with pre-existing programs? (collaboration; cultural competence)

(5) What capacities do you need to put this prevention or intervention program into place with quality? (capacity building)

(6) How will this prevention or intervention program be carried out? (planning)

(7) How will the quality of implementation be assessed? (process evaluation)

(8) How well did the prevention or intervention program work? (outcome and impact evaluation)

(9) How will continuous quality improvement strategies be incorporated? (total quality management; continuous quality improvement)

(10) If the intervention (or components) is successful, how will the intervention be sustained? (sustainability)

School psychologists attempting to build their professional competence in school-wide program implementation and evaluation would benefit greatly from giving careful consideration to each question (see Table 9.2).

To provide additional guidelines for building professional competence in the area of school-wide program evaluation, the following strategies are recommended: (1) Be cognizant of the research literature on EBIs and prevention programs for a variety of childhood academic, social, emotional, and behavioral problems. (2) Develop a needs assessment for your school or district. Consult Nagle (2002) for specific components of comprehensive needs assessments. (3) Create cooperative, collaborative relationships with school professionals (e.g., administrators) and other stakeholders (e.g., college and university faculty); these relationships will become important when school-wide programs are initiated. (4) Identify previously initiated school-wide programs in your particular school or district and attempt to determine what worked, what did not, and why. (5) Emphasize data-based decision making at all levels of prevention and intervention.

Finally, readers are encouraged to review the sources cited in this chapter, particularly Power et al. (2003), Schaughency and Ervin (2006b), and Weissberg and Kumpfer (2003) for more detailed information. Texts which focus specifically on issues in program evaluation may also be helpful; in particular, the reader is referred to Rossi and Freeman (1993) and Worthen, Sanders, and Fitzpatrick (1997).

Future Directions

Reforms in education, as well as scientific advances in psychology and other areas, has created the need for school psychologists who can better meet the academic, social, emotional, and behavioral needs of all students rather than simply those identified as being potentially eligible for special education services. Historically, training programs in school psychology have emphasized the assessment of children and adolescents in schools for the primary purpose of classification and special education eligibility determination (Merrell et al., 2006). More recently, there has been a greater emphasis on expanding the role of the school psychologist, including placing greater emphasis on areas such as assessment linked to intervention, EBIs, and evaluation of programs at school-wide (rather than simply individual student) levels (Merrell et al., 2006).

Preparing school psychologists for practice in the twenty-first century will require a reconceptualization of their role and function. In particular, traditional conceptualizations of school psychology have largely emphasized its role as a child-centered (i.e., individual level) profession rather than a program-centered (i.e., systems level) one (Sheridan & Gutkin, 2000). Movement toward a systems-level approach will require that school psychologists gain greater knowledge and experience in program evaluation. In fact, program evaluation has been recommended as a core domain for the training of child-oriented psychologists by the National Institute of Mental Health (NIMH), the American Psychological Association (APA), and the NASP. To engage in this process effectively and develop competencies in it, however, requires knowledge and competencies in other domains as well (e.g., empirically supported and social valid interventions; multisystemic collaboration; theory and practice of organizational change; research methods). School psychologists are challenged to become competent in each of these areas to better meet the needs of all students in schools.

Conclusion

Developing competencies in program evaluation will be one of the critical skills for school psychologists in the twenty-first century (Merrell et al., 2006). School psychologists should be knowledgeable about the evidence that supports particular programs prior to their implementation, as well how to evaluate programs across various domains (e.g., process, integrity, acceptability, impact) before, during, and after their implementation. As such, the choice school psychologists need to make is not *whether* to conduct an evaluation of school-wide programs, but rather *how* to conduct such an evaluation (Power et al., 2003). Moreover, these decisions should be made in collaboration with school personnel and other stakeholders, balancing specific needs along with feasibility and cost-efficiency issues (Power et al., 2003).

Individuals who wish to become involved in program evaluation at the school-wide level should seek information on what is already being done in this area in their school and district, and collaborate with individuals involved in these activities. School-based practitioners may also wish to consider collaborating with college and university faculty in the development and evaluation of school-wide initiatives (Merrell et al., 2006). School psychologists who are cognizant of these areas and develop competencies in them will greatly contribute to effective and efficient school-wide program evaluation.

Chapter Competency Checklist

DOMAIN 3 – Data-based decision making & accountability

Foundational	Functional
Understand and explain the following:	Gain practice:
□ School use of unproven interventions	□ Observing programs in schools
□ Literature on program evaluation in schools	□ Observing program evaluation at various levels in
□ Program evaluation process	schools
□ Needs assessment	□ Conducting needs assessment in school settings
□ Social validity	□ Implementing programs
□ Impact	□ Evaluating process, integrity, acceptability, impact
□ Sustainability	□ Communicating results of program evaluations
□ Capacity building	□ Receiving feedback on program evaluation skills
□ Evidence-based interventions	
□ Efficacy vs. effectiveness of interventions	
□ Behavior education program	
□ Treatment integrity	

References

Berman, A. L., Jobes, D. A., & Silverman, M. M. (2006). *Adolescent suicide: Assessment and intervention.* Washington, DC: American Psychological Association.

Berninger, V. W. (2006). Research-supported ideas for implementing reauthorized IDEA with intelligent professional psychological services. *Psychology in the Schools, 43,* 781–796.

Brown, J. H. (2001). Youth, drugs and resilience education. *Journal of Drug Education, 31,* 83–122.

Burke, M. R. (2002). School-based substance abuse prevention: Political finger-pointing does not work. *Federal Probation, 66,* 66–71.

California Task Force to Promote Self-Esteem and Personal and Social Responsibility. (1990). *Toward a state of self-esteem: The final report of the California Task Force to Promote Self-Esteem and Personal and Social Responsibility.* Sacramento, CA: California State Department of Education.

Chall, J. S. (2000). *The academic achievement challenge: What really works in the classroom?* New York: Guilford.

Crone, D., Horner, R., & Hawken, L. (2004). *Responding to problem behavior in schools: The Behavior Education Program.* New York: Guilford Press.

Curtis, M. J., & Stollar, S. (2002). Best practices in system-level change. In A. Thomas & J. Grimes (Eds.), *Best practices in school psychology IV* (pp. 223–234). Bethesda, MD: National Association of School Psychologists.

Deno, S. L. (2002). Problem solving as "best practice". In A. Thomas & J. Grimes (Eds.), *Best practices in school psychology IV* (pp. 37–56). Bethesda, MD: National Association of School Psychologists.

Dunlap, G., & Kern, L. (1996). Modifying instructional activities to promote desirable behavior: A conceptual and practical framework. *School Psychology Quarterly, 11,* 297–312.

Eckert, T. L., & Hintze, J. M. (2000). Behavioral conceptions and applications of acceptability: Issues related to service delivery and research methodology. *School Psychology Quarterly, 15,* 123–148.

Eckert, T. L., Miller, D. N., DuPaul, G. J., & Riley-Tillman, T. C. (2003). Adolescent suicide prevention: School psychologists' acceptability of school-based programs. *School Psychology Review, 32,* 57–76.

Elias, M. J., Zins, J. E., Graczyk, P. A., & Weissberg, R. P. (2003). Implementation, sustainability, and scaling up of social-emotional and academic innovations in public schools. *School Psychology Review, 32,* 303–319.

Engelmann, S., & Carnine, D. (1982). *Theory of instruction.* New York: Irvington.

Furlong, M. J., Morrison, G. M., & Jimerson, S. R. (2004). Externalizing behaviors of aggression and violence and the school context. In R. B. Rutherford, M. M. Quinn, & S. R. Mathur (Eds.), *Handbook of research in emotional and behavioral disorders* (pp. 243–261). New York: Guilford.

Gould, M. S., Marrocco, F. A., Kleinman, M., Thomas, J. G., Mostkoff, K., Cote, J., et al. (2005). Evaluating iatrogenic risk of youth suicide screening programs: A randomized control trial. *Journal of the American Medical Association, 293,* 1635–1643.

Grimes, J., Kurns, S., & Tilly, D. W. (2006). Sustainability: An enduring commitment to success. *School Psychology Review, 35,* 224–244.

Hawken, L., & Hess, R. (2006). Special section: Changing practice, changing schools. *School Psychology Quarterly, 21*(1), 91–111.

Hawken, L., & Horner, R. (2003). Evaluation of a targeted intervention within a school-wide system of beahvior support. *Journal of Behavioral Education, 12*(3), 225–240.

Irvin, L. Tobin, T. J., Sprague, J. R., & Sugai, G. G. (2004). Validity of office discipline referral measures as indices of school-wide beahvioral status and effects of school-wide behavioral interventions. *Journal of Positive Behavior Interventions, 6(3),* 131–147.

Kern, L., Bambara, L., & Fogt, J. (2002). Class-wide curricular modification to improve the behavior of students with emotional and behavioral disorders. *Behavioral Disorders, 27,* 317–326.

Kratochwill, T. R., & Shernoff, E. S. (2004). Evidence-based practice: Promoting evidence-based interventions in school psychology. *School Psychology Review, 33,* 34–48.

Lewis, T. J., & Sugai, G. (1999). Effective behavior support: A systems approach to proactive school-wide management. *Focus on Exceptional Children, 31*(6), 1–24.

Maag, J. W. (2001). Rewarded by punishment: Reflections on the disuse of positive reinforcement in schools. *Exceptional Children, 67,* 173–186.

Manning, M. A., Bear, G. G., & Minke, K. M. (2006). Self-concept and self-esteem. In G. G. Bear & K. M. Minke (Eds.), *Children's needs III: Development, prevention, and intervention* (pp. 341–356). Bethesda, MD: National Association of School Psychologists.

Mazza, J. J. (1997). School-based prevention programs: Are they effective? *School Psychology Review, 26,* 382–396.

McDougal, J. L., Clonan, S. M., & Martens, B. K. (2000). Using organizational change procedures to promote the acceptability of prereferral intervention services: The school-based intervention team project. *School Psychology Quarterly, 15,* 149–171.

Merrell, K. W., & Buchanan, R. (2006). Intervention selection in school-based practice: Using public health models to enhance systems capacity of schools. *School Psychology Review, 35,* 167–180.

Merrell, K. W., Ervin, R. A., & Gimpel, G. A. (2006). *School psychology for the 21st century: Foundations and practices.* New York: Guilford.

Miller, D. N., Eckert, T. L., DuPaul, G. J., & White, G. P. (1999). Adolescent suicide prevention: Acceptability of school-based programs among secondary school principals. *Suicide and Life-Threatening Behavior, 29,* 72–85.

Miller, D. N., George, M. P., & Fogt, J. B. (2005). Establishing and sustaining research-based practices at Centennial School: A descriptive case study of systemic change. *Psychology in the Schools, 42,* 553–567.

Miller, D. N., & McConaughy, S. H. (2005). Assessing risk for suicide. In S. H. McConaughy (Ed.), *Clinical interviews for children and adolescents: Assessment to intervention* (pp. 184–199). New York: Guilford.

Nagle, R. J. (2002). Best practices in planning and conducting needs assessment. In A. Thomas & J. Grimes (Eds.), *Best practices in school psychology IV* (pp. 265–279). Bethesda, MD: National Association of School Psychologists.

Nation, M., Crusto, C., Wandersman, A., Kumpfer, K. L., Seybolt, D., Morrissey-Kane, E., et al. (2003). What works in prevention: Principles of effective prevention programs. *The American Psychologist, 58,* 449–456.

National Association of School Psychologists. (2000). *Standards for training and field placement programs in school psychology.* Bethesda, MD: Author.

Nelson, J. R., Benner, G. J., Reid, R. C., Epstein, M. H., & Currin, D. (2002). The convergent validity of office discipline referrals with the CBCL-TRF. *Journal of Emotional and Behavioral Disorders, 3*(1), 181–188.

Polsgrove, L., & Smith, S. W. (2004). Informed practice in teaching self-control to children with emotional and behavioral disorders. In R. B. Rutherford, M. M. Quinn, & S. R. Mathur (Eds.), *Handbook of research in emotional and behavioral disorders* (pp. 399–425). New York: Guilford.

Power, T. J., DuPaul, G. J., Shapiro, E. S., & Kazak, A. E. (2003). *Promoting children's health: Integrating school, family, and community.* New York: Guilford.

Pressley, M. (2002). *Reading instruction that works: The case for balanced teaching (2nd edition) New York.* New York: Guilford.

Rossi, P. H., & Freeman, H. E. (1993). *Evaluation: A systemic approach* (5th ed.). Newbury Park, CA: Sage.

St. Pierre, T. L., & Kaltreider, L. D. (2004). Tales of refusal, adoption, and maintenance: Evidence-based substance abuse prevention via school-extension collaboration. *American Journal of Education, 25,* 479–491.

Sarason, S. B. (1996). *Revisiting the culture of the school and the problem of change.* New York: Teachers College Press.

Schaughency, E., & Ervin, R. (2006a). Building capacity to implement and sustain effective practices to better serve children. *School Psychology Review, 35,* 155–166.

Schaughency, E., & Ervin, R. (Eds.). (2006b). Building capacity to implement and sustain effective practices [Special issue]. *School Psychology Review, 35*(2).

Scherff, A., Eckert, T. L., & Miller, D. N. (2005). Youth suicide prevention: A survey of public school superintendents' acceptability of school-based programs. *Suicide and Life-Threatening Behavior, 35,* 154–169.

Shaffer, D., & Craft, L. (1999). Methods of adolescent suicide prevention. *The Journal of Clinical Psychiatry, 60,* 70–74.

Shapiro, E. S. (2004). *Academic skills problems: Direct assessment and intervention.* New York: Guilford.

Sheridan, S. M., & Gutkin, T. B. (2000). The ecology of school psychology: Examining and changing our paradigm for the 21st century. *School Psychology Review, 29,* 485–502.

Stage, S. A., & Quiroz, D. R. (1997). A meta-analysis of interventions to decrease disruptive classroom behavior in public education settings. *School Psychology Review, 26,* 333–368.

Stollar, S. A., Poth, R. L., Curtis, M. J., & Cohen, R. M. (2006). Collaborative strategic planning as illustration of the principles of systems change. *School Psychology Review, 35,* 181–197.

Tilly, W. D. (2002). Best practices in school psychology as a problem-solving enterprise. In A. Thomas & J. Grimes (Eds.), *Best practices in school psychology IV* (pp. 21–36). Bethesda, MD: National Association of School Psychologists.

Walker, H. M. (2001). Invited commentary on "Preventing mental disorders in school-age children: Current state of the field." *Prevention and Treatment, 4,* Article 2. Retrieved March 21, 2007, from journals.apa.org/prevention/volume4/pre004002c.html.

Wandersman, A., & Florin, P. (2003). Community interventions and effective prevention. *The American Psychologist, 58,* 441–448.

Weiss, B., Catron, T., Harris, V., & Phung, T. (1999). The effectiveness of traditional child psychotherapy. *Journal of Consulting and Clinical Psychology, 67,* 82–94.

Weiss, C. H., Murphy-Graham, E., & Birkeland, S. (2005). An alternate route to policy influence: How evaluators affect D.A.R.E. *American Journal of Evaluation, 26,* 12–30.

Weissberg, R.P., & Kumpfer, K.L. (Eds.). (2003). Prevention that works for children and youth [Special issue]. *American Psychologist, 58*(6/7).

Witt, J. C., & Elliott, S. N. (1985). Acceptability of classroom management strategies. In T. R. Kratochwill (Ed.), *Advances in school psychology* (Vol. 4, pp. 251–288). Hillsdale, NJ: Erlbaum.

Worthen, B. R., Sanders, J. R., & Fitzpatrick, J. L. (1997). *Program evaluation: Alternative approaches and practical guidelines* (2nd ed.). New York: Longman.

Ysseldyke, J., Burns, M., Dawson, P., Kelley, B., Morrison, D., Ortiz, S., et al. (2006). *School psychology: A blueprint for training and practice III*. Bethesda, MD: National Association of School Psychologists.

Chapter 10
Advocating for Effective Instruction: School Psychologists as an Instructional Leader

Brian C. Poncy, Elizabeth McCallum, and Christopher H. Skinner

Introduction

Public schools are continually faced with the challenge of responding to and meeting the demands of an ever evolving set of societal and global expectations (Friedman, 2005). Recent iterations of this responsiveness came in the wake of the No Child Left Behind Act (NCLB) and the reauthorization of the Individuals with Disabilities Education Improvement Act (IDEA) of 2004. These have converged to emphasize the data-based accountability of student achievement in public schools. While many of the professionals working in schools have received training in some areas dealing with instruction, curriculum, behavior, assessment, evaluation, consultation, and data analysis, there are few that have been trained in each of these areas. One profession that does require training in each of these areas is school psychology. The combination of school psychologists' training and skills and the evolving needs of schools to demonstrate improved student outcomes unveil a context for school psychologists to be increasingly active and influential participants on instructional leadership teams. The goal of this chapter, is to explore recent developments that are impacting professional practices in schools and identify ways that school psychologists can use their skills and knowledge to support effective instruction.

Review of Literature

While all students have access to the public education system, data continually confirm that an achievement gap exists between groups of students (NAEP, 2007). For example, the National Assessment of Educational Progress (NAEP) results from 1992 to 2005 show that Caucasian and Asian students have consistently and significantly outperformed African American, Hispanic, and American Indian students in the areas of reading, math, and writing across grade levels. Similarly, students from high-income families have significantly higher scores than students from low-income families. As a result, many lawmakers and student advocates believe that some schools are failing to meet the educational needs of their students. In addition, many believe that the parents of students enrolled in failing schools should have choices to ensure that their children receive a high-quality education. This current state of the United States educational system was the impetus for the proposal and enactment of NCLB with its focus on data-based accountability for all students.

B.C. Poncy (✉)
Oklahoma State University, 420 Willard Hall, Stillwater, OK 74078, USA
e-mail: brian.poncy@okstate.edu

T.M. Lionetti et al. (eds.), *A Practical Guide to Building Professional Competencies in School Psychology*, DOI 10.1007/978-1-4419-6257-7_10, © Springer Science+Business Media, LLC 2011

No Child Left Behind

The No Child Left Behind Act (2002) was devised to meet four primary goals: (1) Make schools accountable for student achievement, (2) Increase flexibility for schools to spend their money, (3) Focus resources on proven educational methods, and (4) Expand choices for parents if their local school is failing. Since its inception, NCLB has had its supporters and dissenters. The goal of this section is not to evaluate NCLB but to describe what this piece of legislation proposes and consequently the context (including both supports and challenges) that schools are presently operating within.

Under NCLB, states are required to clearly define standards in reading and math in grades three to eight, define baseline levels of achievement, and set goals for achievement gains, known as annual yearly progress (AYP). To answer questions about whether schools are meeting these goals, states specify standardized assessments of achievement to measure student performance in the form of state tests. The results of these state tests can then be used to provide feedback about the performance of schools with regard to both students' aggregate achievement levels *and* the achievement levels of the following subgroups: Caucasian, African American, American Indian, Asian/Pacific Islander, Latino, students with an individualized education plan (IEP), students from low-income families (i.e., students receiving free and reduced lunch), and English language learners (ELL).

NCLB was created with the vision that schools should have increased flexibility over how to use funds to best meet their needs, allowing schools to use up to 50% of their non-Title 1 funds at their discretion. For example, school A may have a large ELL population, while school B has an 80% free and reduced lunch population. Given the difference in the needs of each school, it makes sense not to tie up monies to pre-determined programs but to allow schools to differentiate funds toward high priority areas in an effort to increase achievement in the most efficient manner possible.

NCLB also increased funding to support research-based approaches to improving student achievement. These federal funding sources are provided to individual states who then determine how to distribute these resources. In many cases, this means that states channel these monies to schools with significant needs due to poor achievement or the presence of high risk populations, such as ELL. Many schools who are meeting their goals do not receive any additional money as this money often goes to schools who are not meeting state AYP trajectories. While NCLB purports to provide increased funding and flexibility to schools in need, some question the extent to which funding and support is being given to schools in need of assistance.

If a school or any of the before mentioned subgroups continually fail to meet AYP goals, a variety of options are open to parents of students attending the failing school. These include being able to transfer their child to a higher achieving school or use Title 1 funds to pay for supplemental services (e.g., outside tutoring, after school programs, or summer school). NCLB also encouraged the development of charter schools as an avenue for innovative new practices that deviate from traditional K-12 public school settings, such as corporations and universities.

In summary, policymakers and advocates have sent a clear message to schools that they expect increased achievement results for all students. In order to help schools accomplish these goals, NCLB has presented states and schools with an increased amount of flexibility to funnel funding to the areas of their schools, which they feel will result in the greatest overall achievement gains. Also, NCLB increased spending to support research-based academic programs. If schools fail to progressively increase achievement on state tests, then repercussions could include intervention from the state, a loss of Title 1 funds for supplementary services, or face restructuring which involves a change in governance where management of the school is taken over by the state or a private entity.

The Individuals with Disabilities Education Act 2004

NCLB was not the only piece of recent legislation to stress the importance of student achievement data. In 2006, the final regulations of the reauthorization of the Individuals with Disabilities Education Act were published. Two changes in IDEA that will certainly impact the roles and functions of school psychologists are the increased emphasis on eligibility determination based on students' response to intervention (RtI) and the increased amount of IDEA Part B funds available to supplement early intervention services. These changes encourage the prevention and remediation of student difficulties before special education eligibility determinations, as well as decrease the importance of de-contextualized (i.e., away from the classroom) assessments using published standardized norm referenced tests.

The sheer number of students that are receiving special education services in the learning disabled category stresses the importance of IDEA's emphasis on using a RtI approach to determining special education eligibility. In the past, nearly all state rules and regulations used some form of an IQ/achievement discrepancy to determine special education eligibility for students identified with learning disabilities. With the enactment of IDEA 2004, states can no longer require the use of the discrepancy model and must allow evaluation processes focusing on student RtI. This, when combined with a focus on demonstrating that the student received scientifically based instruction in his or her area of need, necessitates the use of assessments explicitly tied to classroom instruction and the measurement of the student's RtI. Instead of assessing to determine within-child strengths and weaknesses, evaluations will primarily gather information about a student's learning rate as it relates to factors such as instruction (i.e., how to teach), curriculum (i.e., what to teach), and the environment (i.e., physical arrangements).

Prior to the reauthorization of IDEA 2004, schools were allowed to use 5% of Part B funds to assist students not identified for special education, but who demonstrate educational need in academic and/or behavioral areas. Uses of these funds might include staff professional development in scientifically based interventions or providing educational and behavior evaluation, supports, and services to struggling students, as is done in student/teacher assistance teams. With IDEA 2004, schools can now use up to 15% of their Part B funds for these early intervention services. Increased funding for early intervention services combined with an emphasis on using RtI as a major component in diagnosing learning disabilities converge to focus school psychologists on collaborating with all school staff concerning instruction across the educational setting.

In the past decade, much discourse has taken place concerning the identification of learning disabilities. While past policy and practice have largely employed a discrepancy model to special education eligibility determination, both NCLB and IDEA emphasize the use of early intervention services coupled with an RtI approach to identify students with learning disabilities. Furthermore, these new provisions place the burden of proof on intervention-based student outcomes and should, consequently, focus discussion on the student-instruction-curriculum match and not on the aptitudes of the student.

Recent legislation has significantly impacted the way in which schools are structuring themselves to meet the diverse needs of their students. Today's climate of high-stakes testing and data-based accountability places a premium on making sound decisions that result in the efficient use of school resources to increase student achievement, not only with at-risk populations, but across the board. To support schools in meeting the lofty demands of NCLB and IDEA 2004, the roles and functions of school psychologists must evolve from those of determining eligibility and placement, to those of identifying and preventing academic and behavioral difficulties before special education placements become necessary (Reschly & Ysseldyke, 2002). Major components of achieving these goals are (1) properly identifying problems, (2) having knowledge and skills in identifying, constructing, implementing, and evaluating interventions across the school setting, and (3) being able to effectively incorporate these interventions into school systems.

It is evident that schools are progressively moving toward a system in which data is driving educational decisions. While many policy makers and community members are focusing on student outcome data, practitioners in the schools are well aware that a variety of factors, in addition to data-based decision making, must be in place if we are to see achievement gains. These include factors such as scientifically-based instruction, systematic curricular alignment, age-appropriate social and interpersonal skills, and continual systemic improvement. Unfortunately, as popular trends continue to have an impact on practices in the schools, some school personnel may be compelled to follow the latest promises by publishers and/or organizations that focus on a particular method of teaching (e.g., whole language and constructivist approaches to mathematics).

School Psychologists Role on Instructional Leadership Teams

Given the pressures of NCLB to increase student achievement across all students, including those groups that traditionally struggle, administrators are actively seeking quality programs that are effective, efficient, and easy to implement. Unfortunately, one-size-fits-all approaches, or easy answers, are not available. Schools do have a variety of data that they can use to determine which instructional methods result in increased levels and rates of student achievement.

As a practitioner working alongside school districts on school improvement initiatives, it was apparent to me that a variety of district wide assessments (e.g., the state tests) were used to collect data on student achievement. However, it was unclear whether the school linked data from these assessments to specific questions regarding instructional practices. It seemed that the primary purpose of collecting such large amounts of data, usually from state tests, was to report out to the state on AYP goals. While these data could be used to identify groups not reaching AYP and items could be analyzed in an attempt to hypothesize what skills were missing, the annual administration of these broad band tests appeared to provide little data to meaningfully inform instruction. Some of the reasons that it is difficult to glean this information from these broad band achievement tests include a lack of fluency based items, number of items per skill, and selection-type responses; for a more detailed critique, see Marston (1989).

These reasons lead to why school leadership teams may have difficulty using district assessment data to impact decisions about instruction and curriculum. They have general data that can identify a problem, but they often do not have sufficient data to determine why the problem is occurring, to directly link data to intervention strategies, or to efficiently monitor student progress. For example, a district's aggregated subgroup data shows that only 30% of the students receiving free and reduced lunch are meeting AYP in reading, but without the aid of supplemental and targeted assessments, they could not say whether it was caused by phonemic awareness skill deficiencies, inaccurate decoding (i.e., phonics), a lack of fluency, low vocabulary, or an absence of using comprehension strategies. Without this information, or the capacity of the system to provide other sources of data to address these issues, it is difficult for administrators to work with teachers and delineate instructionally what needs to be altered.

Given the training experiences of school psychologists, we could be a valuable resource to use our skills of assessment, instruction, program evaluation, and systems to help schools collect and analyze data that directly link to recommendations for instructional practices and materials targeting identified problems. One approach to assisting schools in accomplishing these goals is to raise assessment questions inherent to the problem solving model. While schools are currently mandated to gather data that will, once a year, identify problems, these data do very little to efficiently answer questions about why the problem is occurring, what should be done to fix it, and when a treatment is decided on – if the treatment is working. The goal of the next section is to discuss ways in which school psychologists can increase their role in supporting schools in organizing and collecting systemic data to align these data with the purposes of the problem solving model.

Research to Practice

Deno (1989) emphasized the importance of the marriage of assessment and evaluation and how this can help practitioners answer questions focused on alterable variables in the interaction between the educational environment and student achievement. School psychologists have combined this ecological focus with the problem solving model to successfully make instructional decisions for individual students through RtI as well as systems, using a variety of methods (e.g., CBM and positive behavioral supports (PBS)). The core ingredient of these approaches is the use of data with the problem solving model to drive decision making. The problem solving model consists of four parts: (1) problem identification; (2) problem analysis; (3) plan implementation; and (4) plan evaluation (Bergan, 1977; Heartland Area Education Agency, 2002). Each of these steps contextualizes a series of educationally relevant questions that need to be answered.

Step 1 – Problem Identification: What is the Problem?

Before problem solving can commence, data needs to be identified or collected to set a standard and answer the question, "what is expected." Without this, identifying what the problem is cannot be completed and a system emphasizing data-based accountability will fall flat on its face. Screening may seem to some a fairly simple task of data collection where everyone gets tested and their scores are compared, but there are some key elements that must be met. With screening, in order to compare "apples-to-apples," so to speak, the more standardized the testing materials (e.g., probes) and procedures (e.g., directions, timing), the better. This uniformity in how and what you test allows you to make reliable and valid rank-order comparisons between students, in the testing group (Poncy, Skinner, & Axtell, 2005). For example, Shinn (1989) explains different procedures for use depending on whether the goal is to collect data for a district-wide, school-wide, or class-wide norm. Depending on the questions that will eventually be answered with these data, the team will need to decide about how far-reaching to set up their screening assessments, especially in larger school districts that may have multiple elementary, middle, and high school buildings. These data will ultimately determine what types of problems will be possible to identify and define.

Steps that accompany the problem definition stage include problem identification, problem definition, and problem validation (Deno, 1989; Heartland Area Education Agency, 2002). A majority of the data used to make these decisions come from the normative data of a standardized test (e.g., a state test or CBM). Traditionally, these data are collected once per year for state tests, while CBM data are usually collected three times over the course of a school year in the fall, winter, and spring. These data can be presented in the form of a raw score, standard score, and/or percentile rank. These allow for the establishment of an expected criterion (e.g., the 50th percentile) from which to identify if a problem exists, define the magnitude of the problem (e.g., expected words correct per minute (wcpm) is 120, student behavior is 46 wcpm, so the problem discrepancy is 74 wcpm), and validate where in the system the problem exists (i.e., at the district, school, classroom, supplemental, or individual student level).

The importance of correctly identifying problems has been emphasized in the literature. Given the finite amount of resources available in schools coupled with the intense pressure of documenting achievement increases across students, schools need to efficiently invest resources. While school psychologists have traditionally used normative achievement data with individual students to identify and define problems, these same data can also be used to identify and define systemic achievement issues as well. This is accomplished by looking at patterns in the district level data to rule out problems that may not be at the child level. For example, in Poncy, Skinner, and O'Mara (2006), a third grade student was referred for low achievement in math, however, before delving into an individual evaluation, the school psychologist reviewed relevant sources of data to rule out the presence of systemic problems, namely low achievement across the classroom and/or grade level. In this case, the low achieving student was one of many, and a class-wide intervention was selected, implemented, and evaluated.

In the previous case, without the collection of a grade level standard, the practitioner may have implemented an individualized intervention due to the misidentification of the problem. School psychologists serving on instructional leadership teams need to discuss the importance of investigating district wide data to understand what the problem is and, just as importantly, *where* it is occurring. Answering these questions can aid teams in preventing the inefficient misappropriation of instructional resources to misidentified problems. Depending on patterns in the data, the problem should be identified and defined at its highest level of occurrence (the highest level being the district and lowest being the individual student). This will allow schools to appropriately match resources (e.g., teachers, money, and instructional time) to the most relevant problem. Once the problem is correctly identified and defined, the instructional team can turn its collective focus to the next question of the problem solving model – why is the problem occurring.

Step 2 – Problem Analysis: Why is the Problem Occurring?

The assessment data collected during the problem analysis stage, provides information to support inferences about why the identified problem is happening with the goal of linking data to an intervention (Heartland Area Education Agency, 2002). This process consists of asking educationally relevant questions that focus on the interactions of alterable variables of the educational environment. Heartland recommends focusing on four primary areas: (1) Instruction; (2) Curriculum; (3) Environment; and (4) Learner. The instructional domain pertains to *how* behaviors are taught. The curricular domain focuses on *what* is taught and addresses the question of the match between what behaviors/skills are expected and the actual skills of the student(s). The environmental domain investigates the physical and affective components of schools and how these can be altered to increase the rate of student skill development (e.g., reinforcement and classroom management). Aspects of the learner include interests and preferences as well as constructs such as task perseverance and self efficacy. These four domains encompass the crucial facets of the interaction between the student and the educational environment and serve as a tool to organize the alterable variables that impact student achievement.

Howell, Fox, and Morehead (1993) propose that the goal of this stage of problem solving is to link data to a provable hypothesis (e.g., Cale reads slowly but accurately, therefore, he needs repeated practice in instructional level material to build fluent decoding skills). To aid in the development of assessment questions, practitioners should break down skills and curricular objectives into their component parts (i.e., task analyze the target behavior and the student's corresponding skills and/or knowledge). This approach has traditionally been done with individual students but can also be applied to groups. For example, a review of a district's CBM data indicates that 55% of the students are reading below the criterion of 120 wcpm, however, nearly all of these students are making only 1–2 errors. This would suggest that while students were learning appropriate decoding strategies to read grade level material, they need increased repetition with reading. If, on the other hand, 55% of the students were reading below the criterion of 120 wcpm and a majority of these students were making 5+ errors, then the team would likely need to investigate the ability of students to use phonics skills to decode unknown words. Based on the identified error patterns, the team would have to explore empirically-validated instructional practices and materials and match these to the identified skill deficiencies (e.g., using re-reading strategies to build fluency), implement an intervention plan, and measure the impact of the treatment on student achievement.

Using the Instructional Hierarchy to Aid Hypothesis Generation

This chapter has recommended that school psychologists work with instructional leadership teams to emphasize functional assessment and the alterable variables of the educational setting. Functional assessment seeks to provide an educationally relevant context to prompt patterns in student responding to the academic tasks expected in the classroom. Furthermore, identifying these patterns (e.g., slowly and inaccurately, slowly but accurately, or quickly in a fixed context) can be helpful in suggesting instructional strategies to remediate the identified deficit (Howell et al., 1993). One approach that has been used to "functionally" match students' academic responding to classroom based tasks to intervention selection is the Instructional Hierarchy (IH; Haring & Eaton, 1978).

Haring and Eaton (1978) described a learning hierarchy of skill development that included acquisition (the goal is to increase accuracy), fluency building (the goal is to increase speed and maintenance of accurate responding), and generalization/adaptation (the goal is to enhance discrimination and creative responding). Many traditional assessment (e.g., teacher exams) and intervention procedures (e.g., demonstration) focus on accuracy. More recently, educators and researchers also have become focused on assessing (e.g., CBM, DIBLES, AIMSweb) and increasing fluency or speed of accurate responding (AIMSweb Progress Monitoring and Response to Intervention System, 2006; Daly, Chafouleas, & Skinner, 2005; Deno & Mirkin, 1977; Good & Kaminski, 2002). The final two stages are more difficult to define as they require students to learn other conditions where their skills can be applied (generalization) and/or adapted (creativity). Generalization requires teachers to provide students with numerous opportunities to respond along with feedback about when specific skills can, and cannot, be applied to similar tasks. During this stage of learning, students are given assignments that require the application of multiple skills, thereby providing students with opportunities to learn to discriminate when skills can be applied and, just as importantly, when they cannot be applied. Adaptation is similar, but now the stimuli require students to adapt or engage in novel responding. Both of these advanced and essential stages of skill development are most likely to be successful when students can apply their basic skills rapidly, resulting in numerous discrimination, generalization, and adaptation trials with a short period of time.

The goal of problem analysis is to go beyond knowing what the problem is. Specifically, the goal is to focus on understanding why the problem is occurring. Data about how a student, or students, respond to curriculum-based tasks can be an integral source of information for instructional teams to generate hypotheses about why skill deficiencies exist and what instructional procedures and materials could be implemented to remedy skill deficiencies. For example, a significant group of students (perhaps 30%) are reading slowly and inaccurately. The team would hypothesize that fluency rates weren't reached due to inaccurate decoding (i.e., they were spending time breaking down words). Using a combined approach of using curriculum-based assessment (CBA), the IH, and ICEL, the team would need to use data to hypothesize about what *instructional* strategies could be used to increase accurate decoding, common error patterns that would guide the selection of *curricular* objectives, adaptations that could be made to the instructional *environment* (e.g., increasing reinforcement), and what aspects of the *learner(s)* could be used to increase relevance and interest in instructional materials. While evidence-based programs are available in reading, math, and written expression, teachers and/or interventionists will need to know why and how to differentiate their instruction practices based on student needs. Below we will discuss several strategies which have been shown to enhance learning across these levels of skill development. This system linking student responding to instructional strategies should be a valuable heuristic for instructional teams to conceptualize, how teaching can be changed to match patterns in student responding.

When discussing teaching, we often focus on techniques which increase accuracy such as demonstration, description, modeling, prompting, and immediate corrective feedback (Haring & Eaton, 1978). The teaching behaviors, or events, that occur prior to the student responding (e.g., modeling, demonstration, description) are critical and necessary in that they allow someone who cannot respond accurately to begin responding accurately. However, it is equally important that students receive feedback concerning the accuracy of their responses as this may reinforce the future use of the response. Providing immediate corrective feedback following errors can prevent students from practicing these errors while ensuring that their last response is accurate (Skinner & Smith, 1992). Finally, errors can be analyzed and used to guide teaching (e.g., a student who subtracts the smallest numeral from the largest in all subtraction problems will need additional demonstrations, descriptions, and models that focus on the skills and concepts of regrouping (Skinner & Schock, 1995).

Skills differ from knowledge in that both speed *and* accuracy of responding are important (Skinner, 1998). For example, cognitive limitation theories suggest that students who read slowly and accurately will struggle to comprehend what is read because their cognitive resources (e.g., working memory) are being used to decode words (Breznitz, 1987; Daneman & Carpenter, 1980; LaBerge & Samuels, 1974; Perfetti, 1977; Rasinski, 2004; Stanovich, 1986). These theories have been supported by numerous correlational findings showing a relationship between rates of accurate responding and achievement (e.g., Marston, 1989). Additionally, behavioral research suggests that those who respond accurately and slowly will be required to expend more effort and receive poorer reinforcement (e.g., lower rate, less immediate) for their responding (Billington, Skinner, & Cruchon, 2004; Binder, 1996). These variables make it less likely that slow but accurate responders will choose to engage in academic behaviors that require these resources (Skinner, Pappas, & Davis, 2005). These theories have been supported by numerous studies that show a relationship between rates of responding and choosing to engage in assigned academic behaviors (see Skinner, 2002).

Given that demonstration, modeling, and practice with immediate feedback can enhance student accuracy, research has examined whether *demonstrations* of rapid and accurate responding can enhance the speed of accurate responding (i.e., fluency). Unfortunately, these results suggest that such *antecedent* procedures are not efficient with increasing fluency (Skinner, Logan, Robinson, & Robinson, 1997). However, researchers investigating opportunities to respond (Greenwood, Delquadri, & Hall, 1984), academic learning time (Berliner, 1984), and learning trial rates (Skinner, Belfiore, Mace, Williams, & Johns, 1997) have applied Ebbinghaus' (1885) independent variable of repeated practice and found that an emphasis on repetition not only enhances the maintenance of accurate responding but also the speed of accurate responding. This suggests that after students have acquired a degree of accurate responding, educators should reduce the time they spend teaching (e.g., demonstrating and describing) and allot time to activities that allows students to engage in high rates of active, accurate, academic responding (AAA responding). Procedures which have enhanced response rates include altering the topography of the response (Skinner et al., 1997), reinforcing more rapid responding (Skinner 1997, Bamberg, Smith, & Powell, 1993), using explicit timing procedures (Rhymer, Skinner, Henington, D'Reaux, & Sims, 1998), and the rapid presentation of new stimuli (Skinner, Fletcher, & Henington, 1996).

Educators can develop and assign work designed to occasion high rates of AAA responding (e.g., homework, worksheets), however, these assignments will only be effective if students choose to engage in those activities. Students who must expend a lot of time and effort to respond accurately are less likely to choose to engage in these assignments. Therefore, the students who most need the addition trials to enhance their fluency and maintenance may be the least likely to choose to engage in assigned academic tasks. These students may need stronger or additional reinforcement for engaging in these activities than other students (Skinner et al., 2005). Interdependent group oriented contingencies (Popkin & Skinner, 2003; Sharp & Skinner, 2004), altering long assignments to multiple brief assignments (Wallace, Cox, & Skinner, 2003) and interspersing additional brief problems (McCurdy, Skinner, Grantham, Watson, & Hindman, 2001; Skinner, 2002; Skinner, Hurst, Teeple, & Meadows, 2002) have all been shown to be effective procedures for enhancing the probability that students will choose to engage in assigned work, by increasing the strength and/or rate of reinforcement for choosing to engage in assigned work (Skinner, Wallace, & Neddenriep, 2002).

While there is a significant amount of research about the instructional strategies that accompany the acquisition and fluency building stages of the IH, information concerning generalization/

adaptation stages is less abundant. These stages emphasize the application of skills across settings and problem types. An example of this would be a student using his or her fluent computation skills to solve a multi-step story problem. Educators can assist by demonstrating, describing, and modeling strategies and behaviors that enhance discrimination and generalization as well as modeling adaptation attempts. Thus, both acquisition strategies (e.g., demonstration, modeling) and fluency building strategies (high rates of AAA responding) may be needed to enhance skill development during these final two stages. Another way to think about this is to acknowledge that many "problem solving" activities require procedural (i.e., how to) scripts. While the accurate and fluent use of skills is necessary, this is not sufficient to ensure the generalization and/or adaptation of skills. Therefore, teachers may need to use acquisition building strategies (e.g., modeling and demonstration) to build procedural knowledge and provide ample opportunities for students to use a combination of skills and procedures (e.g., problem solving) to apply skills to novel contexts.

The IH poses a heuristic to link patterns of academic responding to instructional strategies. While it may be easy for instructional teams to become overwhelmed with district wide problems, the IH can be used to match interventions (e.g., repeated practice and increased reinforcement to build fluency in basic math facts) to student responding (e.g., students compute basic facts in subtraction slowly but accurately). While doing this, the IH provides direction for the instructional leadership team to answer such questions as, why is the problem occurring? and the answer provides the foundation to the third stage of the problem solving model, what should be done to fix the problem?

Step 3 – Plan Implementation: What Should Be Done to Fix the Problem?

Once problems have been identified, defined, and analyzed, the team is ready to link the assessment data to an intervention plan that will be implemented and evaluated. Teams can take several approaches to arriving at an intervention. Treatments can be created and constructed, published programs can be selected, or current programs can be altered. Each of these will have strengths and weaknesses. For example, if the team creates and constructs the intervention it should be tightly matched to the identified skill deficiencies but will also be costly in terms of staff time. Also, this task becomes more difficult the larger and more heterogeneous the group becomes. Published programs can be selected that generally reflect a skill need (e.g., SRA Reading Mastery for beginning phonics) but still may re-teach previously learned skills and be somewhat inefficient. Also, teachers may not be familiar with the program and will need training as well as time to learn how to deliver the program. Adapting generic instructional strategies would require the least amount of change to classroom routines, but will also be susceptible to poor intervention integrity. Furthermore, differentiating learning needs with broad curricular objectives for heterogeneous groups poses a variety of challenges.

Previously in the chapter we have discussed the intense pressures schools face to increase achievement. While some schools qualify for extra funding through Reading First and other funded programs, a majority of schools are carefully distributing a limited amount of resources across their district. This places a premium on decisions that not only increase achievement, but increase it efficiently. The question every instructional leadership team should ask is, "How can we get the most achievement growth, given our resources?" The problem identification process should allow the team to identify the highest level of the problem (i.e., district, building, classroom, supplemental, and student level). The problem analysis stage should have helped the team collect data to understand why the problem was occurring and used patterns of student responding to drive instructional decisions. Together, these two stages should set the stage for confidently made educational decisions. However, before deciding on an intervention plan, teams will want to discuss a variety of issues to ensure the efficiency of interventions. First, it is important to not spend instructional time teaching students items they have mastered or items that are too advanced. Teaching without a proper instructional match will stifle learning rates and waste valuable instructional time. In line with the argument of knowing how much learning you gain per instructional minute (Poncy, Skinner, & Jaspers, 2007), schools should investigate student-to-teacher ratios. It makes little sense to teach to a group of three students if you can get similar achievement results teaching a group of six. It is simply not enough to do an intervention; instructional teams need to take into account student learning rates in relationship to resource expenditures. In other words, we need to get the best for our buck.

While these questions may appear overwhelming, educational professionals have continually conducted research to empirically-validate specific interventions that increase student learning. In education and other fields, researchers have proposed various criteria that allow one to classify a treatment as being empirically-validated (Chambless & Hollon, 1998; Drake, Latimer, Leff, McHugo, & Burns, 2004; Kazdin, 2004; Kratochwill & Shernoff, 2004; McCabe, 2004). Although these criteria are not identical, they are designed to meet the same goal. Empirically-validated interventions are to have gone through a process that increases both researchers' and practitioners' confidence that an intervention has altered student behavior (e.g., enhanced learning rates). Given that a strategy, procedure, or intervention has been proven to work in a particular instance suggests that it may also be effective in preventing or remedying the presenting problem across students (i.e., it worked before, it will work with other students). This common, and foundational, purpose of empirically validating interventions requires researchers to establish the validity of the intervention and practitioners to consider the contextual/pragmatic issues. This information will be crucial to teams who are selecting and/or recommending educational treatments.

An intervention is said to have internal validity when scientific procedures demonstrate a cause-and-effect relationship between the intervention and the change in behavior. Research methods including design, analysis, and measurement procedures allow researchers to establish internal validity by ruling out other known and unknown variables (i.e., variables other than the intervention) that may have caused the measured change in the dependent variable (Campbell & Stanley, 1966; Skinner, 2004). Some suggest that designs must be true-experiments, meaning that they must include random assignment of participants (subjects) to conditions. However, much of what we know about what works was established using other research procedures, such as single subject designs.

After establishing that an intervention can enhance learning or skill development, the next issue is whether it will have a similar effect across subjects, target behaviors, and environments. This is referred to as external validity and provides us with confidence that the intervention will work again, and more specifically with presenting target behavior(s). One of the most common fallacies associated with large N statistical research is that using many subjects automatically enhances external validity. In some cases it may, but in other cases a larger number of subjects may not enhance external validity (Michael, 1974). Thus, another common component of criteria that is needed to classify an intervention as being empirically validated is replication (Chambless & Hollon, 1998; Kazdin, 2004). Replication studies can provide additional evidence for internal validity while also demonstrating effects across treatment agents (e.g., across teachers), settings (e.g., across classrooms), target behaviors, time, and students.

While establishing the internal and external validity of an intervention is important, from a practitioners' standpoint, it is not enough. For an intervention to benefit educators and students, it also must be pragmatic. Many variables effect whether an intervention can be applied to a presenting problem including: (a) the amount of training needed to implement it; (b) the degree of implementation precision (e.g., treatment integrity/fidelity) needed for the treatment to be effective; (c) possible negative side effects of the intervention; and (d) the amount of resources needed to carry it out. Finally, the degree with which the intervention can be implemented within the current context of the classroom is an important pragmatic concern. For additional resources, information, and forms supporting the documentation and implementation of interventions see Heartland Area Educational Agency (2002).

The profession of school psychology has continually worked to develop (a) a data-base on what works with respect to intervention development (Berliner, 1984), (b) numerous theories regarding why these things work, (c) assessment procedures designed to allow us to measure skill development levels and within learning strengths and weaknesses, and (d) numerous models of linking assessment to intervention. These data and criteria may allow school psychologists to identify skill deficits (e.g., acquisition vs. a fluency problem) and develop or select interventions based on the skill characteristics we want to improve (e.g., provide more demonstration and modeling to enhance accuracy vs. reinforcing high rates of AAA responding to enhance fluency). However, the science and practice driving school psychologists practice has not developed to the point where data is collected and can be used to determine with any certainty that intervention X will remedy a presenting problem (Daly et al., 2005). Researchers have offered numerous reasons for this state of affairs, sometimes deriding others for wasting efforts, resources, and time on inappropriate models of linking assessment to intervention.

Our opinion regarding our progress in this area is that we have done remarkably well considering we are attempting to address (a) an extremely complex phenomenon (i.e., human behavior change), (b) that is not stable (i.e., human behavior change is constant), (c) is susceptible to many known and many more unknown variables, and (d) is difficult to study (just ask those trying to run large N double blind studies in educational environments). Regardless, as researchers continue to pursue this line of research we are faced with the same qualified conclusion that aptitude-treatment interaction researchers have offered: the data on student skill development levels *may guide* educators in their formation of *hypothesizes* regarding which interventions are *more likely* to be effective in preventing and remedying skills. While new methods of linking assessment to intervention have taken a behavioral, and arguably a more direct, approach to observing variables that account for student learning, a hypothesis testing model to validate what works for which students continues to be needed. For this reason, intervention evaluation is critical.

Step 4 – Intervention Evaluation: Did the Plan Work?

RtI models have increasingly garnered support, in part, to the realization that practitioners need to demonstrate how students interact with the classroom environment. In RtI models, many of the same brief assessment procedures used for screening and identification of target behaviors can also be used to evaluate the effects of interventions (Fletcher, Coulter, Reschly, & Vaughn, 2004). These brief measures often allow for repeated assessment of skill development and are sensitive enough to allow researchers and practitioners to evaluate the effects of interventions on learning rates. Thus, educators can conclude not only whether the intervention is working, but also how quickly the intervention is working. These formative data help educators arrive at many formative decisions including whether to continue the intervention, adapt the intervention, change interventions, and/or cease remediation procedures (Deno & Mirkin, 1977).

There are at least three ways in which practitioners can assess student progress. Two of these are formative in nature and consist of using general outcome measures (GOM) and sub-skill mastery measures (SMM). Another is the use of summative assessment via a pre–post test method. Each is useful for different reasons and is accompanied by strengths and weaknesses. A GOM, such as oral reading fluency, is useful because it strongly correlates with broad tests of achievement, as is seen in reading. Researchers have demonstrated that decisions about a student's learning rate in response to an intervention can be estimated within as little as 8 weeks (Christ, 2006). Unfortunately, this still takes approximately 25% of the school year to have reliable and valid data to support growth rate estimates. Another option is to use SMMs, such as single digit subtraction probes or a list of five sight words, to quickly detect immediate gains in student achievement (see Poncy et al., 2007). However, SMMs fail to generalize to broad tests of achievement. Although we can be sure that an intervention increased single digit subtraction fluency, whether this significantly helps the student across mathematical tasks (e.g., algebra) is doubtful.

Both GOMs and SMMs are forms of formative assessment and present feedback to practitioners while instruction is occurring. Summative assessment, on the other hand, is conducted before and after the intervention and does not provide information about intervention effectiveness, until the intervention has concluded. It is our opinion that formative assessment is the better option of the two for evaluating the effects of interventions; however, summative assessments can be useful if the treatment is a systemic change (i.e., curriculum). In this case, it would be hoped that the new curriculum would meet the needs of a large portion of the students (e.g., 80%). An example of the use of summative assessment to aid in program evaluation can be observed by using state test data to compare and evaluate a curricular change. A district may review past data and determine that student achievement levels and progress are not at a desired level. A team uses data to select a new curriculum and implements it. After a year of the new curriculum, the instructional team could compare achievement gains of the year of the initial curriculum to that of the newly implemented curriculum, evaluating what worked best for their students.

Depending on the nature and purpose of the particular program under investigation, an appropriate method to evaluate the success of the intervention will need to be selected. This chapter has attempted to define several approaches to collecting data to address the success of an intervention. For more information on formative assessment practices, see Chap. 6 of this book. This final stage completes a cycle of the problem solving model, which is a process with the end goal of continuous improvement. When schools are successful in remedying problems and improving the system, it is hoped that educators will be continually reflective and search for new and innovative ways to improve student achievement.

Practice Implication

We propose three ways in which school psychologists can meaningfully impact instructional leadership teams. They are: To (1) Organize and present data in a purposeful and meaningful manner; (2) Support school professionals in using data to answer the questions posed in the problem solving model; and (3) Assist with the methods and interpretation of evaluating instructional practices. To guide practitioners through this process, we have constructed an assessment matrix that aligns assessments used in districts with the questions from the problem solving model (see Fig. 10.1). To demonstrate how this

---

Sunset Heights Elementary School staff is working hard to increase the reading skills of all our students. The purpose of the current assessment matrix is to define the assessments given to students and how we can use this information to provide answers about how to continually increase reading scores. As building principal, I want to personally applaud the Sunset staffs' professionalism and commitment to helping each of our students meet their potential. Below is a quick description of each of the assessments used in our building in the area of reading.

Iowa Test of Basic Skills (ITBS). The ITBS is a standardized broad band achievement test that investigates several areas of achievement. It reports out a percentile rank comparing students to a national and state based norm. Student progress concerning AYP is reported out using the results of the ITBS. Students are considered proficient if they score at or above the 40th percentile when compared to the national norm. This test is given once per year to both 3rd and 4th grade students in the month of February.

Measures of Academic Performance (MAP). The MAP test provides data similar to the ITBS and was chosen as an additional measure to report to the state concerning student achievement in the areas of reading, mathematics, and language usage. Students are deemed proficient if they score above the 33rd percentile versus the national norm. This test is given twice per year to both 3rd and 4th grade students, once in the fall and spring.

Dynamic Indicators of Basic Early Literacy Skills (DIBELS). The DIBELS is a set standardized achievement tests specifically investigating reading skills such as phonemic awareness, alphabetic understanding (i.e., phonics), and oral reading fluency. This data from these tests are used to screen students a minimum of three times per year with achievement scores being classified in the benchmark, strategic, or intensive range. Students that score in the strategic and/or intensive range receive increased intervention services focusing on need areas through classroom instruction and Title 1 services. Furthermore, these students are monitored weekly to assess how students respond to intervention services. If students fail to make significant progress, the student is referred to the Sunset Success Team, where a multidisciplinary team meets to review data and systematically attempt to solve the problem.

Fig. 10.1 The Soap Creek Assessment Matrix: Reading (SCAM-R)

Curriculum-Based Assessment (CBA). While state tests and DIBELS allow teams to identify, define, and monitor progress, they do little to address why students are failing to meet the task demands of the educational setting. To assist in answering these questions teachers and other educational professionals are encouraged to summarize data derived from a variety of classroom/curriculum based assessments. Information can be obtained from reviews of student products, interviews of teachers, parents, and the student, classroom observation, and tests. These data need to be collected to answer pre-specified questions about student performance (e.g., what types of decoding errors does the student make?).

Each of these assessments provides data that can be used to answer questions about our how our instruction is impacting student achievement in some form or another. The goal of Sunset Heights is to have a minimum of 80% of our students scoring in the proficient and/or benchmark range of the district wide assessments (ITBS, MAP, & DIBELS), a maximum of 15% of our students to receive supplemental services on a consistent basis, such as Title 1 reading, and to use our most intensive services (i.e., special education) for the bottom 5% of our students. The proceeding Reading Assessment Matrix aligns building assessment with the four stages of the problem solving model and places an "X" when the data from the assessment provides data to address the question.

Soap Creek Assessment Matrix: Reading

Assessments	DIBELS			ITBS		MAP	CBA
Subtests	PSF	NWF	ORF	VOC	COMP		
Grades	K	K-1	1-4	3-4	3-4	3-4	K-4
Schedule	Bi-Ann	Tri-Ann	Tri-Ann	Annual	Annual	Bi-Ann	Daily
Problem Identification	X	X	X	X	X	X	
Building	X	X	X	X	X	X	
Classroom	X	X	X	X	X	X	
Supplemental	X	X	X	X	X	X	
Student	X	X	X	X	X	X	
Problem Analysis							X
Instruction	X	X	X				X
Curriculum	X	X	X	X	X	X	X
Environment							X
Learner							X
Instructional Hierarchy							X
Plan Implementation							X
Empirically-Validated							X
Intervention Integrity							X
Intervention Evaluation	X	X	X	X	X	X	X
Summative	X	X	X	X	X	X	X
Formative	X	X	X				X

Fig. 10.1 (continued)

tool may be used by psychologists, a case study of how an instructional leadership team used this matrix to influence decisions about a building wide reading model is presented.

The goal of the Assessment Matrix is to identify the assessments administered at a particular school, specify when the assessments are given, and identify questions that the data from the assessments can answer (i.e., their purpose). In cannot be emphasized enough that the final goal of this process should not be to simply document the different assessments, but to specify the purpose of each assessment as well as the questions that can be answered from the collected data. In order for this process to not be overwhelming to the school staff, it is suggested that this process be broken down by area (e.g., reading, math, written expression); in the forthcoming case study reading, when used. The ultimate goal of the assessment matrix is to present teams with a heuristic to support the understanding of the relationship between the data collected and educational questions that need to be answered. Once this is organized, the school psychologist, with a combination of other qualified team members, should be able to increase the confidence with which the team can make instructional recommendations

Soap Creek Elementary School is a K-4th grade building and educates approximately 350 students. Student demographics show that approximately 90% of the students are Caucasian, 36% receive free and reduced lunch, 10% are ELL, and 8% receive special education services. The Soap Creek staff consists of 14 general education teachers, two special education teachers, two reading interventionists, one behavioral interventionist, and a half time position for a math interventionist and ELL teacher. Class sizes are approximately 22 students. To report AYP goals, Soap Creek Elementary uses results from the Iowa Test of Basic Skills (ITBS) for their fourth grade students. In addition, data are collected from the Measures of Academic Performance, the Dynamic Indicators of Basic Early Literacy Skills (DIBELS), and a variety of CBAs (see Fig. 10.1 for expanded descriptions). These assessments and the questions they address are identified and described on the Soap Creek Assessment Matrix: Reading (SCAM-R; see Fig. 10.1). The completed SCAM-R is meant to provide an example of one method to describe and summarize the alignment of district assessments and the purposes of the problem solving model.

At the end of the 2005–2006 year, the instructional team gathered and organized their reading data using ITBS, MAP, and DIBELS data. The instructional team consisted of the principal, school psychologist, title 1 reading teacher, and one classroom teacher from each grade. The team members were happy given the outstanding performance of the students on the state tests. Soap Creek's data in the area of reading had 92% of the third grade and 90% of fourth grade students scoring at or above the 40th percentile when compared to the national norm of the ITBS. These data placed Soap Creek's achievement results above their AYP and building goals. MAP data also supported these data with 94% of the fourth grade students scoring in the proficient range, which for the MAP was above the 33rd percentile when compared to the national norm. DIBELS data confirmed exemplary achievement in grades K-1, however trends in the data suggested that as students progressed through second and third grade that an increasing amount of students were being specified in the some risk to at risk range (see Fig. 10.2). While general achievement rates were extremely high, especially when compared to

Grade	K			1st			2nd	3rd	4th
DIBELS Test	LNF	PSF	NWF	PSF	NWF	ORF	ORF	ORF	ORF
Established (low risk)	84%	93%	89%	100%	95%	94%	82%	65%	77%
Emerging (some risk)	14%	7%	7%	0%	5%	6%	8%	28%	15%
Deficit (at risk)	5%	0%	4%	0%	0%	0%	11%	7%	8%

Fig. 10.2 Soap Creek Elementary end of the year DIBELS results

national norms, DIBELS data demonstrated a pattern of 90% or more students scoring in the low risk range in grades K-1, 80% in second grade, and 65% in grade three, and 77% in grade four.

The team convened, reviewed the data, and was not surprised by the test results. In the past, given the relatively high achievement rates of the district (usually around 85–90% of the students scoring in the proficient range) the team provided more support services to kindergarten and first grade students. For example, the Title 1 teachers would see anywhere from 30 to 50% of the kindergarten students at some point through the course of the year, some for a short time for a "boost" and others more consistently. This decision to concentrate resources in kindergarten and first grade to prevent reading problems may have been affecting fluency gains in students in second and fourth grades. As the team reviewed these patterns in student achievement, they asked the following questions, "Should we lessen our focus on prevention in kindergarten and first grade to bolster instruction in grades two to four and what would be the most efficient way to deliver the needed interventions for each group?" Ultimately, the team needed to figure out how to keep student achievement rates in kindergarten and first grade from dipping, while they increased oral reading fluency rates for students in second, third, and fourth grades.

The Soap Creek Elementary School instructional team established that they wanted a minimum of 85% of their students scoring at benchmark. While approximately 90% of students in kindergarten and first grade were meeting the reading benchmarks, the percentage of students meeting bench marks for second through fourth grade was declining. This decline was most evident with the third grade, where they had only 65% of the students meeting the reading benchmark of 110 words/minute. Further assessments using DIBELS and classroom data indicated that a majority of the students not meeting benchmark were reading accurately (i.e., above 95%) but slowly and these data were consistent across classrooms. Furthermore, students who were reading slowly and inaccurately were receiving support from the Title 1 teachers. At this point, the problem was defined (see Fig. 10.3) and patterns in student responding were identified and compared to the IH. These data converged to show decreasing student performance in reading fluency.

The team met with the Soap Creek teaching staff with a plan to increase ORF rates. The group decided on using a classroom based set of fluency building interventions for grades two, three and four and an intensive professional development program for the teachers emphasizing interventions to increase reading fluency. Specifically, the intervention plan was composed of combining and using a variety of fluency building reading interventions including repeated reading, emphasized phrasing, and readers theater, cooperative learning groups (paired reading and peer assisted learning), and the incorporation of various options for feedback and reinforcement using performance feedback and interdependent group contingencies (Daly et al., 2005; Rasinski, 2003). In addition, the cessation of round robin reading was discussed and the aforementioned replacement strategies were reiterated. These interventions were to be implemented daily in a pre-determined 15 minutes block. To address the needs of students who are identified as reading slowly and inaccurately, the Title 1 teachers continued to work to build decoding/phonics skills. In addition they identified the struggling student's instructional level and selected material for them to use in the rereading interventions. The plan was to be

Grade	K			1st			2nd	3rd	4th
DIBELS Test	LNF	PSF	NWF	PSF	NWF	ORF	ORF	ORF	ORF
Expected Performance	85%	85%	85%	85%	85%	85%	85%	85%	85%
Actual Performance	84%	93%	89%	100%	95%	94%	82%	65%	77%
Problem Definition	1%	–	–	–	–	–	3%	20%	8%

Fig. 10.3 Problem definition data

implemented at the beginning of the next school year with progress being monitored using oral reading fluency scores from DIBELS assessments. The instructional leadership team will continue to meet next year to discuss professional development efforts with the teachers from grades two, three, and four and will review data, as they are collected and will make decisions accordingly.

Future Issues

Participating on instructional decision making teams provides a context for school psychologists to use their skills in data collection and analysis, consultation, learning theory, and program evaluation to influence student achievement on a large scale. However, given the relative newness of this role, there will be a variety of issues for practitioners to consider. As school psychologists transition into this role, two basic issues will need to be initially confronted: (1) role advocation and (2) time allocation.

Role Advocation

With the inception of IDEA in 1974, school psychologists spent a majority of their time in testing activities using a battery of aptitude and achievement tests to determine if students were eligible for special education services. As the profession has evolved, researchers and practitioners have emphasized that assessment and intervention activities should be concretely tied to demonstrable increases in student achievement. These principles have been the impetus for the development and implementation of RtI models. While school psychologists have generally embraced this transition, administrators and teachers may still adhere to traditional conceptions of school psychologists and view school psychologists as "gatekeepers" to special education eligibility.

If administrators and teachers continue to see school psychologists as professionals who diagnose within student deficits of disabled populations, they will rarely be asked to join an instructional leadership team focusing on the entire student population. However, given their breadth of training, many school psychologists posses novel skills that would assist teams in using the problem solving process to collect and/or analyze data to identify and define problems, figure out why they are occurring, select empirically validated treatments, and evaluate the effects of the interventions on student achievement. As legislation changes to provide a platform for these activities, practitioners and researchers will need to advocate for a shift from traditional roles to new roles, such as instructional decision making teams. Given the importance of data-based accountability with NCLB and the emphasis on documenting improved student achievement, school psychologist's skill sets with data collection and analysis could be a valuable asset to district administrators. However, for this to happen, school personnel need to be aware of how a school psychologist could assist instructional decision making teams.

Time Allocation

As state rules and regulations change to support RtI approaches, school psychologists will likely spend an increased amount of time conducting and interpreting data (i.e., CBA) that are directly linked to the curricular objectives and expectations of the district. In addition, practitioners will likely begin to spend more time consulting with teachers and intervening with students. This exposure and immersion in the instructional milieu will provide school psychologists with knowledge about the scope and sequence of district curricula, data concerning the level, trend, and distribution of student achievement, and will assist in building personal relationships with teachers, staff, and students. However, finding time to conduct these activities will be difficult if school psychologists continue to spend their time administering published norm referenced aptitude and achievement tests. Therefore, agencies and schools who employ school psychologists will not only need to acknowledge a shift in the role of school psychologists, but also allot the time for the training and implementation of these activities.

Conclusion

As the needs of schools continue to change, school psychologists will be faced with a plethora of new challenges and changing roles. One area that school psychologists will likely be called upon to increasingly participate in is the area of instructional decision making. The goal of this chapter was to present readers with methods and ideas for how psychologists can support schools with their alignment of assessments with the problem solving model to drive data-based educational decisions concerning instructional practices and materials. The Assessment Matrix was designed to focus the attention of instructional teams to the specific purposes of the problem solving model. Specifically, teams will be looking at (1) identifying problems; (2) analyzing why they occur; (3) implementing instruction; and (4) evaluating the effects of the intervention. While districts are directed to collect achievement data, these data are usually in the form of broad-band achievement tests and usually produce data that is useful to identify and define problems, but does little to produce data that informs the other questions of the problem solving model that answer what needs to be done and how well it works for students. It is the goal of the Assessment Matrix to prompt teams to assess with purpose and collect data to specifically answer the questions of the problem solving model. The systematic application of these principles and methods should direct teams to use data to efficiently match resources to school needs and to demonstrate how the implemented interventions are impacting student learning.

Chapter Competency Checklist

DOMAIN 1 – Enhancing the development of cognitive and academic skills

Foundational	Functional
Understand and explain the following: ☐ Legal pressures on public education ☐ Roles of school psychologists on instruction leadership teams ☐ Linking assessment and intervention through problem solving ☐ Instructional hierarchy ☐ Role of state curricula standards and NCLB ☐ How to access state curricula standards in the state in which you practice	Gain practice: ☐ Consulting with individual teachers regarding instruction ☐ Consulting with school teams regarding instruction ☐ Collecting data via system-wide intervention packages (DIBELS, AIMSWEB) ☐ Using data to make instructional decisions for individual students ☐ Using data to make instructional decisions within an RtI system

References

AIMSweb Progress Monitoring and Response to Intervention System. (2006). Retrieved August 24, 2006, from www.AIMSweb.com

Bergan, J. R. (1977). *Behavioral consultation*. Columbus, OH: Merrill.

Berliner, D. C. (1984). The half-full glass: A review of research on teaching. In P. L. Hosford (Ed.), *Using what we know about teaching* (pp. 51–85). Alexandria, VA: Association for Supervision and Curriculum Development.

Billington, E. J., Skinner, C. H., & Cruchon, N. M. (2004). Improving sixth-grade students perceptions of high-effort assignments by assigning more work: Interaction of additive interspersal and assignment effort on assignment choice. *Journal of School Psychology, 42*, 477–490.

Binder, C. (1996). Behavioral fluency: Evolution of a new paradigm. *The Behavior Analyst, 19*, 163–197.

Breznitz, Z. (1987). Increasing first graders' reading accuracy and comprehension by accelerating their reading rates. *Journal of Educational Psychology, 79*, 236–242.

Campbell, D. T., & Stanley, J. C. (1966). *Experimental and quasi-experimental designs for research*. Chicago, IL: Rand McNalley.

Chambless, D. L., & Hollon, S. D. (1998). Defining empirically supported therapies. *Journal of Consulting and Clinical Psychology, 66*(1), 7–18.

Christ, T. J. (2006). Short term estimates of growth using curriculum-based measurement of oral reading fluency: Estimating standard error of the slope to construct confidence intervals. *School Psychology Review, 35*, 128–133.

Daly, E. J., Chafouleas, S., & Skinner, C. H. (2005). *Interventions for reading problems: Designing and evaluating effective strategies*. New York: The Guilford Press.

Daneman, M., & Carpenter, P. A. (1980). Individual differences in working memory and reading. *Journal of Verbal Learning and Behavior, 19*, 450–466.

Deno, S. L. (1989). Curriculum-based measurement and special education services: A fundamental and direct relationship. In M. R. Shinn (Ed.), *Curriculum-based measurement: Assessing special children* (pp. 1–17). New York: Guilford Press.

Deno, S. L., & Mirkin, P. K. (1977). *Data-based problem modification: A manual*. Reston, VA: Council for Exceptional Children.

Drake, R. E., Latimer, E. A., Leff, H. S., McHugo, G. J., & Burns, B. J. (2004). What is evidence. *Child and Adolescent Psychiatric Clinics of North America, 13*, 717–728.

Ebbinghaus, H. (1885). *Uber das Dedachtinis* (*Memory*, H. A. Ruger & C. E. Bussenius, Trans., New York: Teachers College, 1913; reprinted by Dover, 1964). Leipzig: Duncker & Humbolt.

Fletcher, J. M., Coulter, W. A., Reschley, D. J., & Vaughn, S. (2004). Alternative approaches to the definition and identification of learning disabilities: Some questions and answers. *Annals of Dyslexia, 54*, 304–331.

Friedman, T. L. (2005). *The world is flat: A brief history of the twenty-first century*. New York: Farrar, Straus and Giroux.

Good, R. H., & Kaminski, R. A. (Eds.). (2002). *Dynamic indicators of basic early literacy skills* (6th ed.). Eugene, OR: Institute for the Development of Educational Achievement.

Greenwood, C. R., Delquadri, J., & Hall, R. V. (1984). Opportunity to respond and student academic performance. In W. Heward, T. Heron, D. Hill, & J. Trap-Porter (Eds.), *Behavior analysis in education* (pp. 58–88). Columbus, OH: Charles E. Merrill.

Haring, N. G., & Eaton, M. D. (1978). Systematic instructional procedures: An instructional hierarchy. In N. G. Haring, T. C. Lovitt, M. D. Eaton, & C. L. Hansen (Eds.), *The fourth R: Research in the classroom* (pp. 23–40). Columbus, OH: Merrill.

Heartland Area Education Agency. (2002). *Program manual for special education*. Johnston, IA: Author.

Howell, K. W., Fox, S. L., & Morehead, M. K. (1993). *Curriculum-based evaluation teaching and decision making* (2nd ed.). Columbus, OH: Charles E. Merrill.

Kazdin, A. E. (2004). Evidence-based treatments: Challenges and priorities for practice and research. *Child and Adolescent Psychiatric Clinics of North America, 13*, 923–940.

Kratochwill, T. R., & Shernoff, E. S. (2004). Evidence-based practice: Promising evidence-based interventions in school psychology. *School Psychology Review, 33*, 34–48.

LaBerge, D., & Samuels, S. J. (1974). Toward a theory of automatic processing in reading. *Cognitive Psychology, 6*, 293–323.

Marston, D. B. (1989). A curriculum-based measurement approach to assessing academic performance: What it is and why we do it. In M. R. Shinn (Ed.), *Curriculum-based measurement: Assessing special children* (pp. 18–78). New York: Guilford.

McCabe, O. L. (2004). Crossing the quality chasm in behavioral health care: The role of evidence-based practice. *Professional Psychology: Research and Practice, 35*, 571–579.

McCurdy, M., Skinner, C. H., Grantham, K., Watson, T. S., & Hindman, P. M. (2001). Increasing on-task behavior in an elementary student during mathematics seat-work by interspersing additional brief problems. *School Psychology Review, 30*, 23–32.

Michael, J. (1974). Statistical inference for individual organism research: Mixed blessing or curse. *Journal of Applied Behavior Analysis, 7*, 647–653.

National Assessment of Educational Progress. (2007). *Nations report card*. Retrieved March 13, 2007, from http://nces.ed.gov/nationsreportcard

No Child Left Behind Act. (2002). U.S.C. 115 STAT. 1426.

Perfetti, C. (1977). Language comprehension and fast decoding: Some psycholinguistic prerequisites for skilled reading comprehension. In J. Guthrie (Ed.), *Cognition, curriculum, and comprehension* (pp. 20–41). Newark, DE: International Reading Association.

Poncy, B. C., Skinner, C. H., & Axtell, P. K. (2005). An investigation of the reliability and standard error of measurement of words read correctly per minute. *Journal of Psychoeducational Assessment, 23*, 326–338.

Poncy, B. C., Skinner, C. H., & Jaspers, K. E. (2007). Evaluating and comparing interventions designed to enhance math fact accuracy and fluency: Cover, copy, and compare versus taped problems. *Journal of Behavioral Education, 16*, 27–37.

Poncy, B. C., Skinner, C. H., & O'Mara, T. (2006). Detect, practice, and repair (DPR): The effects of a class-wide intervention on elementary students' math fact fluency. *Journal of Evidence Based Practices for Schools, 7*, 47–68.

Popkin, J., & Skinner, C. H. (2003). Enhancing academic performance in a classroom serving students with serious emotional disturbance: Interdependent group contingencies with randomly selected components. *School Psychology Review, 32*, 282–295.

Rasinski, T. V. (2003). *The fluent reader: Oral reading strategies for building word recognition, fluency, and comprehension*. New York: Scholastic Professional Books.

Rasinski, T. V. (2004). Creating fluent readers. *Educational Leadership, 61*, 46–51.

Reschly, D. J., & Ysseldyke, J. E. (2002). Paradigm shift: The past is not the future. In A. Thomas & J. Grimes (Eds.), *Best practices in school psychology IV* (pp. 1–20). Washington, DC: National Association of School Psychologists.

Rhymer, K. N., Skinner, C. H., Henington, C., D'Reaux, R. A., & Sims, S. (1998). Effects of explicit timing on mathematics problem completion rates in African-American third-grade students. *Journal of Applied Behavior Analysis, 31*, 673–677.

Sharp, S., & Skinner, C. H. (2004). Using interdependent group contingencies with randomly selected criteria and paired reading to enhance class-wide reading performance. *Journal of Applied School Psychology, 20*, 29–46.

Shinn, M. R. (Ed.). (1989). *Curriculum-based measurement: Assessing special children*. New York: Guilford Press.

Skinner, C. H. (1998). Preventing academic skills deficits. In T. S. Watson & F. Gresham (Eds.), *Handbook of child behavior therapy: Ecological considerations in assessment, treatment, and evaluation* (pp. 61–83). New York: Plenum.

Skinner, C. H. (2002). An empirical analysis of interspersal research: Evidence, implications and applications of the discrete task completion hypothesis. *Journal of School Psychology, 40*, 347–368.

Skinner, C. H. (2004). Single-subject designs: Procedures that allow school psychologists to contribute to the intervention evaluation and validation process. *Journal of Applied School Psychology, 20*(2), 1–10.

Skinner, C. H., Bamberg, H., Smith, E. S., & Powell, S. (1993). Subvocal responding to increase division fact fluency. *Remedial and Special Education, 14*, 49–56.

Skinner, C. H., Belfiore, P. J., Mace, H. W., Williams, S., & Johns, G. A. (1997). Altering response topography to increase response efficiency and learning rates. *School Psychology Quarterly, 12*, 54–64.

Skinner, C. H., Fletcher, P. A., & Henington, C. (1996). Increasing learning trial rates by increasing student response rates. *School Psychology Quarterly, 11*, 313–325.

Skinner, C. H., Hurst, K. L., Teeple, D. F., & Meadows, S. O. (2002). Increasing on-task behavior during mathematics independent seat-work in students with emotional disorders by interspersing additional brief problems. *Psychology in the Schools, 39*, 647–659.

Skinner, C. H., Logan, P., Robinson, S. L., & Robinson, D. H. (1997). Myths and realities of modeling as a reading intervention: Beyond acquisition. *School Psychology Review, 26*, 437–447.

Skinner, C. H., Pappas, D. N., & Davis, K. A. (2005). Enhancing academic engagement: Providing opportunities for responding and influencing students to choose to respond. *Psychology in the Schools, 42*, 389–403.

Skinner, C. H., & Schock, H. H. (1995). Best practices in mathematics assessment. In A. Thomas & J. Grimes (Eds.), *Best practices in school psychology* (3rd ed., pp. 731–740). Washington, DC: National Association of School Psychologists.

Skinner, C. H., & Smith, E. S. (1992). Issues surrounding the use of self-managed interventions for increasing academic performance. *School Psychology Review, 21*, 202–210.

Skinner, C. H., Wallace, M. A., & Neddenriep, C. E. (2002). Academic remediation: Educational application of research on assignment preference and choice. *Child and Family Behavior Therapy, 24*, 51–65.

Stanovich, K. E. (1986). Matthew effects in reading: Some consequences of individual differences in the acquisition of literacy. *Reading Research Quarterly, 21*, 360–406.

Wallace, M. A., Cox, E. A., & Skinner, C. H. (2003). Increasing independent seat-work: Breaking large assignments into smaller assignments and teaching a student with retardation to recruit reinforcement. *School Psychology Review, 23*, 132–142.

Chapter 11
Facilitating Mental Health Services in Schools: Universal, Selected, and Targeted Interventions

Ray W. Christner, Rosemary B. Mennuti, Mary Heim, Kathrine Gipe, and Justin S. Rubenstein

Over the past 20 years, a growing amount of research has been conducted, and strategies have been implemented to determine the most effective ways to ensure that all youth achieve positive outcomes from the school system. It is widely accepted that the purpose of schools is to promote learning and provide students with the skills necessary to become productive members of society. Although there is no question of the responsibility for schools to develop student's academic learning, there continues to be some disagreement and debate around the role of schools in promoting mental health and addressing students with mental health needs. Students with good mental health have the potential to be more successful in school; however, students who exhibit mental health difficulties may be less successful in accessing the curriculum. As such, these children and adolescents often have higher absenteeism, more difficulty completing assignments, and increased conflicts with both peers and adults (Skalski & Smith, 2006). These students are at much greater risk for dropping out of school and suffering from long-term difficulties, which reduces their quality of life and results in them being less productive adult citizens (National Institute of Mental Health, 2001). There is compelling evidence that there are strong, positive associations between mental health and academic success and that emotional and behavioral health problems are significant barriers to learning (Adelman & Taylor, 2006; Paternite, 2005). Therefore, mental health is essential for healthy development, individual success in life, and the welfare of the community (Power, 2003).

Operational Definition of Mental Health

It is important to create an operational definition of mental health so that stakeholders involved in improving mental health programs in schools are functioning from the same understanding. Too often, preconceived notions and the stigma of the term "mental health" lead professionals and community members to view mental health only through the lens of "disorders" or "problems." In contrast, the U.S. Surgeon General defined mental health as "the successful performance of mental function, resulting in productive activities, fulfilling relationships with other people, and the ability to adapt to change and cope with adversity" (U.S. Department of Health and Human Services, 2001, p. 7). Other definitions reflect the emotional, behavioral, and cognitive processes that influence personal health and success in life (Weist, 2003). It is important to note that the key component of these definitions call into account the need to address cognitive, emotional, and behavioral functioning, and assist individuals to experience positive life experiences.

R.W. Christner (✉)
Cognitive Health Solutions, LLC, Unit 2, 1201 West Elm Avenue, Hanover, PA 17331, USA
e-mail: rwc@cognitivehealthsolutions.com

T.M. Lionetti et al. (eds.), *A Practical Guide to Building Professional Competencies in School Psychology*, DOI 10.1007/978-1-4419-6257-7_11, © Springer Science+Business Media, LLC 2011

Mental Health and School Systems

Mental health problems oftentimes have their root in childhood, and when these problems do not receive thenecessary attention, more serious and prolonged problems can develop. Some research has shown that when these issues are not addressed, they lead to more extensive problems later in life (Kessler, Berglund, Demler, Jin, & Walters, 2005), and subsequently, the need for prolonged and expensive services. The number of children and adolescents with unaddressed mental health needs has reached a crisis level in the USA, with well below 50% of children with mental health disorders actually receiving any kind of treatment to address their needs (Power, 2003). Research estimates that at least 20% (with some approximations reaching 38%) of youth present emotional and behavioral problems severe enough to warrant intervention, yet less than one-fifth of these students receive mental health services (Paternite, 2005; Power, 2003; Prodente, Sander, & Weist, 2002). Failure to address the mental health needs of children can have profound effects on the individual, family, community, and society. Untreated mental health problems in youth are associated with increased rates of teen pregnancy, risk taking behavior, substance abuse, criminal offenses, incarcerations, psychiatric hospitalization, persistence of problems into adulthood, and even early death (Prodente et al., 2002). It has been estimated that the USA loses $192 billion in combined income and tax revenue with each cohort of students who fail to complete high school (Skalski & Smith, 2006). Given the detrimental contextual effects of untreated mental health problems facing our society, we must find ways to prevent and treat the mental health needs of children and adolescents during the time when children are developing and resilient; therefore, creating a window of opportunity during which interventions are most likely to be successful.

Schools offer access to children as a point of engagement for addressing educational, emotional, and behavioral needs (Paternite, 2005), and they are a natural entry point for the delivery of mental health services (Mennuti & Christner, 2005; Mennuti, Christner, & Freeman, 2006; Christner, Forrest, Morley, & Weinstein, 2007). In fact, numerous research studies show that insofar as children receive any mental health services, schools are the major providers. Whereas only 16% of children receive any mental health services, the overwhelming majority (70–80%) receive them within the school setting (Rones & Hoagwood, 2000). Evidence of the critical need to provide mental health services in schools is furthered by studies showing that 96% of families offered school-based mental health services initiated treatment, while only 13% of families offered services in other community settings followed through with the referral (Prodente et al., 2002).

Given that schools are a place with access to students, families, and communities, the logical conclusion is to provide mental health services, at least partly, in the school setting. It is important to note that, as delineated by Adelman and Taylor (2006), "school systems are not responsible for meeting every need of their students, but when the need directly affects learning, the school must meet the challenge." Difficulties in implementing school-based mental health programs stem from many barriers that are inherent in most school systems, such as funding for programs and trained personnel, space, and resources. In addition, there is no one blueprint or set of guidelines for schools wishing to implement school-based mental health programs.

We are currently facing a paradigm shift in providing mental health services in the schools. Traditional approaches have focused on reacting to pathology and servicing children with uncoordinated efforts within isolated systems (Weist, 2003). Reactive models comprise referrals to Child Study Teams, followed by the assessment and placement into special education and searches for pathology, rather than attempting to prevent these issues in children. A significant challenge is to coordinate efforts among the fields of mental health and education in order to promote a paradigm shift that will focus on the prevention and reduction of future risk. Alternate strength-oriented models are based on research related to resilience and positive psychology, and emphasize the importance of promoting competence and strengthening the contexts in which children function (Power, 2003).

This ecological systems model focuses on understanding the developing child in the context of multiple systems in which he or she exists (e.g., family, community, school, society, etc), identifying protective factors and contexts that support healthy development, and strengthening individual and systemic assets (Power, 2003). In order to fully understand the implications of this philosophical shift in school-based practice, it is essential to review mental health models that currently exist.

Legislation and School-Based Mental Health Initiatives

Beginning with the Education of All Handicapped Children Act (PL 94–142) passed in 1975 and continuing as the Individuals with Disabilities Education Act, federal legislation has mandated the need for schools to deliver mental health services as needed to the students they serve (Kutash, Duchnowski, & Lynn, 2007). The original act placed a larger responsibility on the education system to meet the mental health needs of students with an emotional disturbance and required that all support services needed to help educate students with disabilities must ultimately be supplied by the education system (Kutash et al., 2007). This federal mandate blurred the lines of who is responsible for providing mental health services to children and adolescents and raised the important question of funding. The resulting mental health services that are most often provided to students in the school setting are piecemeal and not collaborative with outside community resources. IDEA (2004) regulations apply only to students who have an identifiable disability that may affect various life domains and interfere with the student's educational achievement. However, research shows that the educational disability "emotional disturbance" is an underidentified population, with 1% of students receiving services, despite prevalence estimates closer to 5%. Based on the population of school-aged children, the number of children who have a significant emotional disturbance is about three million while only about a half million are served in special education programs (Kutash et al., 2007).

No Child Left Behind

The No Child Left Behind (NCLB) federal mandate was signed into law in 2002 by President Bush. The emotional well-being of students is addressed in Title V of this act and outlined initiatives aimed at ensuring the emotional well-being of youth (Kutash et al., 2007). While no clear guidelines exist within NCLB, the act offers some examples of strategies including character education, safe and drug free school initiatives, violence prevention programs, and specific programs for at-risk students (Kutash et al., 2007).

The Maternal and Child Health Bureau

In 1995, the Maternal and Child Health Bureau (a branch of the Department of Health and Human Services) began funding two centers for school-based mental health, located at UCLA and the University of Maryland. The focus of these centers was to improve how schools address barriers to learning and enhance healthy development, especially mental health (Kutash et al., 2007). Detailed information about these programs is located on the respective Web sites: UCLA at http://smhp.psych.ucla.edu and University of Maryland at http://csmh.umaryland.edu.

Presidents New Freedom Commission on Mental Health (NFC)

Finally, a noteworthy federal initiative toward promotion of school-based mental health is the *President's New Freedom Commission on Mental Health: Achieving the Promise: Transforming the Mental Health Care in America* (NFC, 2003). Prior to the NFC, the country's most recent Presidential Commission on mental health was in 1978. The NFC highlights the need for early mental health screening, assessment, and referral. In addition, it sets forth the following recommendations: Promote the mental health of young children, improve and expand school mental health programs, screen for cooccurring mental and substance use disorders and link with integrated treatment strategies and screen for mental disorders in primary health care across the lifespan, and connect to treatment and supports (NFC, 2003). Clearly, federal support is provided to schools and community mental health centers for children. However, little direction is offered as to the content of the collaboration between schools and mental health agencies, how it is to be accomplished, or how it will be funded (Mills et al., 2006). Therefore, standing theories and current research findings must be utilized to develop effective models of school-based mental health services.

Current Theories and Research Findings

School psychologists play an important role in prevention, identification, and interventions geared toward student mental health. The National Association of School Psychologists (NASP) has issued *Blueprint III*, a guide for training programs and practice that calls school psychologists to improve competencies for all students, building and maintaining the capacity of systems to meet the needs of students as they traverse the path to successful adulthood (NASP, 2006). In addition, school psychologists are called upon to be mental health practitioners who can guide parents and teachers in learning how to create environments where children and youth feel protected and cared for, as well as sufficiently self-confident to take risks and expand their range of confidence. *Blueprint III* asks that psychologists advocate for a service delivery system characterized by varying the intensity of interventions depending on the severity of student need (NASP, 2006). This service delivery system has a long history in the prevention and public health literature and includes three levels of service. The service delivery is a tiered model, often represented as a triangle, with the majority of student needs being addressed at the base of the triangle through Universal Interventions and Prevention Services. The base can be conceptualized as broad mental health promotion and environmental enhancement programs (Weist, 2005). Children and adolescents who are at-risk for the development of emotional or behavioral disorders either due to familial or environmental conditions require more selective interventions, known as secondary prevention or targeted interventions for at-risk students (Kutash et al., 2007). These interventions are aimed at preventing the onset of behavior or emotional problems. Finally, a small number of students will require tertiary or indicated treatment, usually employed once the disorder or condition has been established. These are referred to as intensive interventions.

Literature Review

The state of current practice is reactive, and most often waits for behavior or emotional problems to arise before treatment is provided. Mental health in schools have historically been restricted, limited primarily to assessment, clinical consultation, and treatment services for students in or being referred to special education (Paternite, 2005). The field of mental health has long followed a medical model by perceiving emotional and behavior difficulties as inherent deficits in individuals. This deficit-oriented approach minimizes the role of ecological factors in the development of psychopathology.

Conversely, the science and practice of prevention is based largely upon research related to developmental psychopathology and resilience and indicate that mental health outcomes are determined by the number and extent of risk factors as well as by protective factors in a child's life (Power, 2003). Risk and protective factors that school psychologists should be cognizant of include: Qualities of the individual child (cognitive, social, and self control skills) as well as characteristics of the systems in which children develop (parenting skills of caregivers), attachment with a primary caregiver, and relationships with educators and community members (Power, 2003).

Research describes how cumulative risk factors contribute to adjustment problems and mental disorders (National Institute of Mental Health, 2001), while enhancing factors have been identified (e.g. contact with positive adults, opportunities for meaningful life involvement) that protect youth against emotional or behavioral problems (Weist, 2003). By ignoring risk and protective factors, we rely on reactive approaches that serve to overwhelm the mental health system with cases that are time consuming, expensive, and difficult to treat (Power, 2003). Current models in the school system most often become activated in response to a referral, which often comes after the family and individual is already in crisis, resulting in services that are expensive, disruptive, and often rendered in a context in which a majority of children are not healthy (Power, 2003). Treatments delivered in such settings have not only been shown to be ineffective, but also possibly harmful, and rarely lead to lasting improvements after the child returns to the community (National Institute of Mental Health, 2001). Providing mental health services in schools is a challenge that calls upon many fields of research and stakeholders, and requires collaborative efforts and innovative programming.

Part of the difficulty in implementing school-based mental health services centers around the lack of consensus on how to best design and implement these services. Researchers and practitioners often assert that one model is better than another based on their theoretical perspectives. Several models of implementing mental health programming in the schools have emerged and will be discussed. Several important factors are indicated as important considerations, regardless of the model being proposed. Specifically, most models ascribe to some variation of the public health model of prevention discussed above. Additionally, it is important to study the school's readiness for change and objectively identify the needs of a particular school. Data may be informal or school-wide and may include voluntary screenings for mental health problems or formal surveys (Skalski & Smith, 2006). Programs require an adequate level of support, trained personnel, and technical assistance to promote effective implementation (Weist, 2003). They should involve and empower key stakeholders, and utilize limited resources efficiently (Mills et al., 2006). Finally, school-based mental health programs should promote and adhere to evidence based practice and documented outcomes (Weist, 2005). Despite this recommendation, Mills et al., (2006), states that the use of passive eclectic treatments devoid of empirical support remains prominent, and Tashman et al., (2000), note that although many clinicians working in an educational setting identify themselves as scientist-practitioners, the gap between research and practice in the field remains as wide as ever. Furthermore, although mental health clinicians express a favorable attitude toward research and recognize the value of empirically supported interventions, few clinicians indicate that they are actively combining research and practice in their professional roles for a variety of reasons, including training issues, differing values, time constraints, funding issues and limited dissemination of research (Tashman et al., 2000). Barriers and strategies to overcome them will be discussed in more detail in a later section of this chapter.

School-Based Mental Health Models

Different approaches to school-based mental health services emerge based on the theoretical approach to which the clinician or researcher ascribes. The result is a literature base that provides many ideas to school-based mental health services, but no one model has been shown to be superior in the community.

The three prevailing models to implementing mental health services in the schools are discussed in detail in the monograph, *School-based Mental Health: An Empirical Guide for Decision Makers* (Kutash et al., 2007). The first is a model put forth in publications by Mrazek and Haggerty (1994), and Weist (2005), termed, "spectrum of mental health interventions and treatments." This can be viewed as implementing traditional mental health interventions in a school setting. The methods used in this model have their roots in the psychological and mental health literature. Prevention and treatment services focus on identifying diagnostic categories, and selecting interventions based on intervention methods designed for that specific problem. Prevention, treatment, and maintenance are addressed in a variety of settings (ranging from home to inpatient units) (Kutash et al., 2007).

The second prevailing model to implementing school-based mental health services is one supported by UCLA and University of Maryland federally funded programs discussed earlier. This model is referred to as the Interconnected Systems Model, and is guided by a public health strategy and based on collaboration between systems. This model reflects the idea that schools must address the mental health needs of students, but recognizes the effectiveness of combining resources in the school and the community. The three levels included in this model are: Systems of prevention (universal interventions that encourage parent and community involvement), systems of early intervention (at-risk and moderate needs targeted), and systems of care (framework of an integrated and collaborative continuum of services provided by the various child-serving agencies, aimed at children with the most intensive needs). Systems of care is a conceptual philosophy of community care that includes school-based services. These services should be child-centered, family-focused, community-based, culturally competent, and provide children access to a wide variety of services tailored to their individual physical, emotional, social, and educational needs (Rones & Hoagwood, 2000). Finally, a systems of care is a comprehensive approach that addresses both the internal (specific to child) and external (environmental) causes of psychosocial barriers to learning (Kutash et al., 2007)

The third model that has emerged is a Positive Behavioral Supports model (PBS). This model has theoretical underpinnings in Applied Behavior Analysis and was originally developed as an alternative to aversive control of extremely serious and often dangerous behaviors of people who were developmentally disabled (Kutash et al., 2007). Its application has expanded to include students with a wide range of academic, social and behavior challenges in the home, school, and community. PBS uses educational and environmental redesign to enhance quality of life and minimize problem behavior (Kutash et al., 2007). PBS utilizes a triangular, three tiered model with 80–90% of students requiring only universal preventions. The middle tier consists of 5–15% of students who are at risk for behavior problems and the top tier consists of the remaining 1–7% of students with chronic and intense problem behavior that require intensive prevention. The percentages conceptually being served at each level correspond to the children's mental health epidemiological findings that 20% of children, at any point in time, have a diagnosable disorder that meets DSM criteria and about 5% have a more serious and persistent disorder.

Gaining Support for Systems Change

Given the reality that schools have been called on to increase access and delivery of mental health services to children, questions regarding program selection, implementation and structure arise. A tiered model of prevention and intervention is a hallmark signifying a comprehensive approach to mental health that aims to teach all students the skills necessary to address the challenges that life may present (Christner et al., 2007). Although program selection at each tier may be slightly unique, key components of program selection can be applied throughout the full model to ensure that quality programs are being chosen. However, before delving into program selection, the importance of gaining support for the necessity of programming and implementation must be addressed.

Prior to examining specific programs, the first phase of program selection must include concrete steps to establish institutional support for program implementation. Building support can be approached systematically and will ultimately prove to increase effectiveness of selected programs. Establishing new programs within schools is not an easy feat, and certainly a task that does not occur instantaneously. The UCLA Center for Mental Health addresses the necessity for systematic change and articulates four main overlapping stages. First, *readiness to change* involves reaching out to stakeholders and fostering a climate that is motivated for change. Secondly, *initial implementation* is executed in stages with built-in support and guidance for program implementation. Third, *institutionalization* involves the establishment of the program with safeguards to maintain, monitor, and adjust as necessary. Finally, *ongoing evaluation* provides the opportunity to improve quality and affords stakeholders the chance to increase sense of community through ongoing learning. The nature of systemic change is complex, tedious, and requires ongoing analysis and adjustment. Consequently, systemic change can be a laborious and lengthy process. Therefore, careful attention must be given to the initial step, *creating readiness*, since without adequate consideration, many attempts at change may be debunked (Adelman & Taylor, 2006).

Considering the concept of *readiness to change* as a primary focus, the first step is to build interest and support for the creation of the system (Adelman & Taylor, 2006). Within the framework of the public schools, teachers, counselors, principals, and parents are individuals whose support should be sought. Providing examples of how programs could improve student learning, classroom, and school climate, as well as parent–child interaction, will illustrate the need for increased services and display a foundation for increasing support. The discussion of increased need for school-based programs will be strengthened by providing data to illustrate key points. Later in the process, specific data will be utilized to drive program selection, yet while vying for support it may be useful to present data that focuses on the need for programming. Examples of such data include the number of office referrals, number of suspensions, attendance records, occurrences of violent acts, and referrals for special education assessments. At this stage, data collection need not be an arduous process, but it should be incorporated into the discussion of need since it helps convey your point in a powerful manner.

As support for programming is established, the second element will begin to surface, and the introduction of the basic concepts and elements of the selected program will be communicated to stakeholders. Introduction of the basic concepts is an integral part of increasing the momentum for change, and for reinforcing the baseline of interest established in the first step. As stakeholders begin to grasp the basic concepts being introduced, the framework for programming can begin to take shape. Although individual needs will be met, it is necessary to initially view programming from a more general perspective, which will enable the first tier, Universal Prevention and Intervention, to take form. Finally, as support is being built by engaging individuals and stakeholders, it is appropriate to ensure that high-level school leaders are aware and invested in the process. The investment of school and district level leaders is necessary to ensure that commitments to programming are upheld.

Elements of Effective Programs

Program selection at each level of intervention, involves consideration of several elements. Regardless of the tier on which the program will be implemented, the integration of theory, research, and practice should be evident, and the program should embody an ecological framework, be collaborative in nature, and provide for the evaluation opportunity (Plyumert, 2002). Programs that integrate theory, research and practice should be selected to increase the likelihood of positive outcomes. This cyclical approach involves learning, planning, implementing, and evaluating practice as theory develops, and research is evaluated. Secondly, effective programs will embody an ecological framework in which the needs of the individual, as well as the needs of the unique school system are met. Background work conducted when evaluating readiness to change will prove useful in understanding the system, and in understanding the relationships of system components. Effective programs encourage a collaborative approach in which all members of the community participate and are invested in positive outcomes. Within the school context, a collaborative approach would entail participation opportunities for students, teachers, guidance counselors, school administration and support staff, parents and community agencies. Finally, for a program to be effective, it is imperative that opportunity for evaluation be integrated within the framework of the program, or be possible through supplemental means.

Tiers of Intervention

Universal Intervention and Prevention

Universal Intervention and Prevention (UIP) services, which compose the first tier of the proposed model, can be operationally defined as interventions and preventative measures within the general population. The goal of UIP services is to prevent the onset of a disorder, or mental health problem (Levitt, Saka, Romanelli & Hoagwood, 2007). When influencing systematic change and attempting to introduce and integrate mental health programs in the schools, initial energy and efforts should be placed at this level, with an understanding that as this first tier becomes an integral part of the school community, the needs for second and third tiers will become apparent. Examples of UIP services include programs that address violence prevention, bullying prevention, social skills training, and the promotion of a supportive learning school environment (see Resilient Classrooms by Doll, Zucker, & Brehm, 2004, for more information).

Program Selection

The unique needs of the school community must be identified in order to select a program, and therefore should be assessed. The use of data presented to stakeholders, during the readiness to change phase, could be subsequently used to assist in program selection. Additionally, universal screenings can be conducted with the general population to determine the need, regardless of presenting mental health concerns or risk factors (Levitt et al., 2007). Examples of standardized universal screening tools include the Pediatric Symptom Checklist and the Strength and Difficulties Questionnaire. However, noteworthy is the concept of devising your own survey to assess the mental health needs of the general population. A cautionary note should be extended that approval and or parent permission for data collection may be necessary as mandated by the local school district and ethical principles (Jacob & Hartshorne, 2003). Other informal measures include focus groups consisting of parents, teachers or students, in which targeted preplanned questions are posed to the group.

   Once the general concept of need is identified, program selection can begin. Keeping in mind the tenets of effective programming, it may be helpful to utilize resources such as the Collaborative for the Advancement of Social and Emotional Learning (CASEL), an organization whose goal is, in part, to "facilitate the implementation, ongoing evaluation and refinement of comprehensive social and emotional programs." (Elias et al., 1997).

Program Implementation

At the UIP, teachers, paraprofessionals, and peer educators typically deliver the service and rein-forcement of curriculum, since delivery will target all students within the general education setting (Nastasi, 1998). However, parents may be involved as partners in the process, or parents may be called on to assist in bolstering skills. The selective and indicated level skills, which are aimed at smaller groups of children, are where parents may be included as a part of the therapeutic process or as deliverers of the curricula (Kutash et al., 2007).

Targeted Interventions for At-Risk Students

Participant Selection

Universal screenings have been employed to drive program selection at the UIP level. For 80–90% of the population, the exposure to UIP services will be sufficient in meeting mental health needs. Yet, students who are considered at-risk, approximately 5–15% of students, more intensive ser-vices at the Targeted Intervention for At-Risk Students (TIARS) level will be necessary (Christner et al., 2007). Risk factors are defined as, "scientifically established factors or determinants for which there is strong objectionable evidence of a casual relationship to a problem" (National Youth Violence Prevention Resource, 2001). Conversely, protective factors can be described as those contributors that commonly decrease the likelihood of developing problematic behavior and lead to resiliency. Environmental risk factors such as poverty, substance abuse, domestic violence, divorce, abuse and neglect, death or suicide, and the developmental and educational transitions have been linked to the development of emotional or behavioral disorders (Kaiser, Cai, Hancock, & Foster, 2002). Likewise, inconsistent parenting, as well as divorce, large family size, and aca-demic difficulties have been linked to emotional and behavioral difficulties (Walker & Shinn, 2002, p. 7).

This smaller percentage of students will need to be identified, as will their presenting needs. Data collection may be less disruptive since a smaller portion of the population will be involved (Levitt et al. 2007). Reevaluation of previously collected data may be useful by examining rates and frequencies of discipline referrals, suspensions, and conduct infractions. Additional screenings for At-Risk factors should be conducted, and can be done informally by reviewing records, and talking with parents, teachers, and students. Data can be analyzed for patterns and themes of reoccurring issues among individual students. Results of data collection should be used to select programs that target the area of need (Levitt et al., 2007).

Students selected for TIARS will have continued the exposure to the UIP; however, an additional layer of intervention and support will be provided. Selected students will have been identified as At-Risk, through the data collection process. However, it is important to note that at the TIARS level, risk reduction is the focus, and while some students may be demonstrating symptomology that sets them apart from the general population, not all students will outwardly demonstrate the need.

Program Selection and Delivery

At the TIARS level, program selection will become narrower in approach. The goal of TIARS is to reduce or prevent adjustment difficulties through teaching coping skills, and building competence by maximizing and building protective factors (Nastasi, 1998). The presenting and prevailing risk factors of the population will drive program selection. Although programming is becoming more restrictive in scope, the same guidelines applied at the UIP level should be followed to ensure that effective programs are selected.

The nature of the small group service delivery will provide opportunity to offer more than one targeted program within the school system. This, at-risk population, will have the added benefit of interaction with mental health professionals such as the school psychologist, guidance counselor, social worker, or school nurse, any of whom may be involved in service delivery. Provided in a small group setting, programming will aim to build competence, teach coping skills, and maximize protective factors (Nastasi, 1998).

Intensive Intervention

Participant Selection

Approximately 20% of children and adolescents in the USA meet criteria for psychiatric diagnoses that are serious enough to merit treatment (NASP, 1997). The Intensive Intervention level should draw from this 20% of children and encompass approximately 1–7% of children, previously identified at the TIARS level. Although a child may be diagnosed with an emotional or behavioral disorder, such a diagnosis does not exclusively identify an individual for Intensive Intervention. Children who carry a diagnosis of an emotional or behavioral disorder may be very well served at the UIP or TIARS level, and should not be identified to participate in an Intensive Intervention solely on the basis of a psychiatric diagnosis.

Methods of identification include more specialized instruments such as the Behavior Assessment System for Children (BASC-2), the Child Behavior Checklist (CBCL), and Systematic Screening for Behavior Disorders, which are screening tools that can be completed by classroom teachers or parents. Students who demonstrate clinically significant behaviors on these rating scales could be considered for Intensive Intervention. Additionally, more specified instruments can be utilized to identify specific emotional or behavioral concerns, after significant results are identified using screening tools. Examples of more specialized instruments include the Beck Depression Inventory-II, the Conners Rating Scales, Children's Depression Inventory, Beck Anxiety Inventory and the Personal Experience Screening Questionnaire. Caution regarding the reliability of respondents should be exercised when administering the rating scales, and using the results as selection criteria. When appropriate, multiple respondents should be used, and rating scales should not be used as the sole decision-making determinant. Additional measures that should be used to help guide decision-making include comprehensive interviews with the individual, with his/her family, and with other appropriate school personnel.

At the Intensive Intervention level, a case conceptualization and treatment plan will be formulated, and ultimately, the criteria for diagnoses will be explored through additional data collection and analysis. When an individual has progressed to this concentrated level of intervention, it has been suggested that programming be viewed as treatment (Munoz, Mrazek & Haggerty, 1996).

Program Selection and Delivery

Program selection should be based on the necessity of meeting established treatment goals. Treatment goals, and subsequently program selection, for some students may be fairly straightforward.

However, students requiring Intensive Intervention display the most significant and intricate presenting problems. Therefore, employing a cognitive behavioral therapy (CBT) Case Conceptualization Model may prove useful. A specialized CBT model designed for use with children and adolescents in the school setting allows for integration of developmental considerations unique to children (Murphy & Christner, 2006). Additional information may be necessary to formulate a treatment plan and select interventions, and psychoeducational evaluations may be appropriate at this time.

Intensive interventions may be delivered on an individual basis, or in small groups. Mental health professionals should be involved at this level of intervention and could include both school-based professionals, as well as involvement from community-based resources. Duration and intensity of program delivery should be determined through progress monitoring and ongoing assessments.

Practice Implications

Building competence in the area of school-based mental health services will enable school psychologists to expand their repertoire of service delivery, and prevent the development of emotional and behavioral problems in children. In addition, they can intervene to reduce the impact of risk factors for at-risk students, promote resiliency, and increase collaboration and consultation skills. NASP published a model for how practice and training in school psychology should be executed. The draft titled, *A Blueprint for Training and Practice III*, outlines eight basic domains of competence that are interrelated and require lifelong learning. The domains of competence are broken into functional and foundational competencies. Functional competence addresses the processes and context through which the work of a school psychologist is carried out. Foundational competences serve as basic principles that support functional groups. *Blueprint III* calls on school psychologists to address the mental health needs of children in the schools. Enhancing the development of wellness, social skills and life competencies are considered functional competencies that purport, "school psychologists should be the leading mental health experts in schools" (NASP, 2006). Furthermore, school psychologists are faced with the challenge of using such expertise to design and implement programming focused on prevention and intervention, as well as to promote wellness and resiliency.

Foundationally, school psychologists will need to call on the domains of professional, legal, ethical and responsibility, and interpersonal collaborative skills to support the charge of the functional domain. Within the foundational domains, school psychologists will rely on their unique collaborative and consultative skills to partner with community agencies, school staff, and parents to meet the identified goal of delivering comprehensive school-based mental health services.

Design and Implementation

Design and implementation of school-based mental health programs have far reaching effects. Effective programming has been shown to improve school climate, reduce disciplinary infractions, and decrease suspension rates (Knoff & Batasche, 1995). Comprehensive models, such as the three tiered intervention model have reduced referral rates for special education, increased academic performance, and decreased the impact of risk factors in the development of emotional and behavioral disabilities. In addition to behavioral concerns, the strong link between mental health and academic success has been well established (Paternite, 2005). Mental health prevention efforts, such as UIP, have proven to increase academic successes, while early intervention has reduced mental health issues and enabled students to focus on academics.

Examining the Effectiveness of School-Based Programs

Mental health service delivery varies widely across the nation, and little attention has been dedicated to examining the effectiveness of school-based mental health services (Rones & Hoagwood, 2000; Slade, 2002). Environmental factors vary widely between school systems, which in turn compromise the external validity of program analysis. However, although there have been some questions as to the generalizability of findings, several studies have demonstrated some favorable results. For example, after 3 years of implementation, Project Achieve demonstrated a 75% reduction in special education referrals, and a 67% reduction in special education placement. Disciplinary referrals were reported to decline by 38%, while suspensions decreased by 64%, and there was a 90% reduction in grade retention (Knoff & Batasche, 1995). Likewise, Rones & Hoagwood (2000) reported that the PATHS program (Greenberg, Kusche, Cook, & Quamma, 1995) resulted in high emotional vocabularies, increased levels of comfort in discussing emotions, and increased the understanding of others' feelings. More specific programs targeting issues with anxiety, depression, substance abuse, conduct disorders, and emotional problems have also shown favorable outcomes (Rones & Hoagwood, 2000). Finally, the overall climate of schools has been reported to be more positive with the implementation of school-based mental health programs, including an increase in job satisfaction and more positive student–teacher relationships.

Barriers to School-Based Mental Health Programs

Despite the best intentions to improve student mental health through providing comprehensive, preventative programs, many barriers to program implementation may still exist. Often, teacher and administrative "buy-in" must be established to convince them of the benefits in implementing effective mental health prevention programs in the schools. Given the increased pressure for students to achieve academic standards and perform in the classroom, mental health programs are often seen as a competing, and are a less important focus. Such an attitude may result in teachers not wanting students to leave class for mental health help, because of the perceived conflict between mental health services and educational goals (Prodente et al., 2002). Especially given the significant pressure to promote academic achievement (as expressed in NCLB), teachers and administrators might view mental health needs as secondary to academic needs (Weist, 2005). School psychologists can begin to overcome this perception and help to advance the paradigm shift by educating staff about the negative academic outcomes that students face when they are struggling emotionally. Generally, teachers may be more receptive to mental health programs in the schools when they are reframed as programs that will reduce and remove barriers to student learning.

Once internal support is gained for the implementation of these programs, another barrier that may impede upon the process is funding. School systems are often viewed as businesses, and expensive programs that do not deliver results immediately have difficulty competing with academic programming for funding. School psychologists must begin to form collaborative relationships and advocate for funding for such programs. Often, as seen in an integrated model of service, the community and schools can work together to deliver services and reduce costs by sharing programs, space, and staff. As another approach, school psychologists can help educate and reach a wide range of decision-making stakeholders who may allow for funding, by becoming involved in school board meetings and practices.

School psychologists should be aware of interpersonal difficulties and "turf-problems" that might arise as a result of implementing mental health programs in the schools (Prodente et al., 2002). Using interdisciplinary approaches (e.g., shared decision making, peer supervision and support, true collaboration with stakeholders, etc.) will serve to reduce the likelihood of duplicating services, give students access to a broad range of mental health expertise, and ultimately use a non-hierarchical approach to service delivery that will decrease resistance due to turf issues (Prodente et al., 2002).

Weist (2005), described several barriers that are inherent to school systems, including fluidity in personnel, struggles to develop and sustain family–school partnerships, an over extended academic schedule, and environmental factors such as space. Additionally, Tashman et al. (2000) pointed out that issues pertaining to the training of school-based personnel, differences in agendas, time constraints, and limited dissemination of research, hinder efforts to deliver mental health services in the schools.

The aforementioned barriers cannot be overcome by any one person in the system. A collaborative and consultative effort must be made, and needs must be agreed upon by stakeholders. Because school psychologists have extensive training in mental health, collaboration, and collecting needs and outcome-driven data, they are good candidates to lead the effort toward increasing mental health services in the schools. By establishing connections with key stakeholders, enhancing the dialog between invested parties, and collecting outcome data to show that programming is valuable and cost-effective, the transition toward school-based mental health programs can begin.

Building a Professional Competence

According to the ethical principles set forth by NASP, Responsible Caring refers to the obligation of school psychologists to "work within the boundaries of their professional competence and accept responsibility for their actions" (Jacob, 2002). However, not all school psychologists enter the field with practical training and experience necessary to independently take on the challenge of creating systems change and implementing mental health services within the framework of their school system. Therefore, it is the responsibility of the individual to seek out additional training, support, and practical resources to ensure that their functioning is within the guidelines of responsible caring. The need for additional guidance and information should not be a deterrent, since several feasible options exist for accessing the necessary support and resources.

Peer Supervision

Peer supervision is an excellent avenue through which professionals can connect, share ideas, gain experience and problem solve. Peer supervision can be initiated by the individual who seeks to connect with established professionals within the field or peer supervision can be sought through more formalized channels. Established peer groups can be accessed through local professional organizations, such as state associations or local trainings. Additionally, NASP provides a wide range of interest groups via the internet in which members can interact and engage in meaningful conversations. Currently, NASP offers an interest group for members titled, "Character Education and Social Emotional Learning." This group aims to provide a forum in which members converse and build a knowledge base grounded in research supported strategies. The interest group also seeks to explore the role of the school psychologist in initiative development and program implementation (see www.nasponline.org).

Resources

In addition to connecting with other professionals, it is incumbent upon the individual to stay current regarding programming, best practices, as well as legislation and policy. A plethora of information is accessible via the internet as well as through professional publications and texts (see Table 11.1).

Ethical Considerations

In addition to the importance of operating within the framework of responsible caring, additional ethical considerations exist. As students progress through the tiers of intervention and prevention, additional attention must be given to ethical considerations, including informed consent, confidentiality, and the duty to protect.

Informed consent. At the UIP level, it is not necessary to secure informed consent for student participation. Services are delivered to all students as an integrated part of the traditional curriculum. However, as students are selected from the general education population to participate in more selected and targeted interventions and treatments, it may be necessary to secure parental consent.

Table 11.1 Resource list of regarding school-wide mental health

Source	Description
Center for Advancement of Social Emotional Learning (www.casel.org)	CASEL is a collaborative effort that works to advance the science and evidence-based practice of social and emotional learning (SEL)
The National Technical Assistance Center on Positive Behavior and Intervention Supports (www.pbis.org)	The National Technical Assistance Center on Positive Behavior and Intervention Supports was established to address the behavioral and discipline systems needed for successful learning and social development of students. The Center provides capacity-building information and technical support about behavioral systems to assist states and districts in the design of effective schools
National Center for Mental Health Promotion and Youth Violence Prevention (www.promoteprevent.org)	Seeks to increase the capacity of schools and communities to meet the mental health needs of students and their families, create and expand coalitions to prevent youth violence, suicide, substance abuse and other mental health and behavioral problems, and prevent violence in schools
National Association of School Psychologists (www.nasponline.org)	Contains a database and publications regarding the practice of school psychology, legislation, policy, mental health, etc.
Promoting Social and Emotional Learning: Guideline for Educators (Elias, et al. 1997)	A practical guide to designing and implementing quality social and emotional education programs

Consultation with administration may be advantageous to ensure that school-based policies and safeguards are also being followed.

Confidentiality. At the TIARS and the Intensive Intervention levels, students will be participating in small groups and possibly by themselves. As interventions become more specific, the reality becomes that sensitive information may be shared with the facilitator and the group. Therefore, it is essential that the facilitator addresses the issue of confidentiality with the group, in developmentally appropriate terms, and that every effort is made to maintain confidentiality regarding sensitive personal matters.

Duty to protect. Finally, it is the legal obligation of school personnel to ensure the safety of students who are under school supervision. Just as therapists have a legal obligation to take action when clients are a risk to themselves or others (e.g., *Tarasoff v. Regents of California,* 1976), school personnel have a similar obligation to disclose confidential information if a student is a danger to himself or others (Thomas & Grimes, 2002). Likewise, students may disclose behaviors that are not indicative of imminent danger, but have the potential to be dangerous, such as substance abuse, eating disorder, self-injurious behaviors, risky sexual behavior or abuse (Jacob & Hartshorne, 2003). Disclosure of such information can present a difficult situation for the school psychologist, and deciding on a course of action can be precarious. However, in the event that confidentiality must be broken, it is advised that the situation first be discussed with the student (Jacob, 2002).

Future Considerations

National statistics, federal mandates, and common sense make clear the need to further unify mental health services in the schools. Apart from homes, schools are the most universal, natural setting to reach a large number of students. Professionals in the school setting are in the unique position to identify risk factors and future mental health problems before they begin. Once the risk factors are ignored and go untreated, the academic, social, and emotional outcomes for these students are poor and become exponentially more difficult to remediate.

School psychologists should actively work to build a public awareness and open dialog surrounding children and adolescent mental health. By integrating their research and consultative skills, school psychologists can help schools identify needs, and help choose and implement the most research-sound school-based approaches. Collaborative efforts must reach all stakeholders in the process in order to garner support from communities and administrators, address family, caregiver, and teacher concerns, and advocate for a stable and growing funding base (Prodente et al. 2002).

Central to the cause of increasing school-based mental health services will be opening the dialog between researchers and educators so that the fields are unified, and working toward providing the best services for children. In opening this dialog, researchers who support varying theoretical models must work together to form consensus on a "best practices" model of mental-health promotion and school-based services. This model will serve to increase the continuity of services and provide practitioners with a solid framework from which to begin implementing mental health services in their school. Several organizations discussed (i.e., UCLA; University of Maryland) have begun to put forth recommendations and committees to further work in this area.

Schools are responsible for providing mental health services to students when their needs directly impact their learning and school success. However, schools should not be the only mental health providers for America's youth. The field of education and community mental health must form nonhierarchical and collaborative partnerships to seamlessly integrate services and promote mental health for all students.

Chapter Competency Checklist

DOMAIN 4 – Systems-based service delivery

Foundational	Functional
Understand and explain the following: ☐ Rationale for mental health services in schools ☐ Definition of mental health ☐ Legislation influencing mental health services in schools ☐ IDEA ☐ NCLB ☐ Maternal child health bureau ☐ Presidents New Freedom Commission on Mental Health ☐ Prevention of mental health problems ☐ School-based mental health models ☐ Systems change ☐ Elements of effective programs ☐ Universal interventions and prevention – Tier 1 ☐ Targeted intervention – Tier 2 ☐ Intensive intervention – Tier 3 ☐ Barriers to school-based mental health services ☐ Family systems theory ☐ Normal child development milestones ☐ Consultation and collaboration ☐ Ethical concerns: informed consent, confidentiality, duty to protect	Gain practice: ☐ Observing universal, targeted, and intensive mental health programs (RtI) at the local level ☐ Assessing current school system and mental health services ☐ Consulting and collaborating with community mental health providers ☐ Designing mental health programs in an RtI model ☐ Implementing mental health programs in an RtI model ☐ Evaluating mental health programs in an RtI ☐ Conducting needs assessments ☐ Creating systems change at the local and community level

References

Adelman, H., & Taylor, L. (2006). *The current status of mental health in schools: A policy and practice brief*. Los Angeles: University of California at Los Angeles: UCLA School Mental Health Project.

Christner, R. W., Forrest, E., Morley, J., & Weinstein, E. (2007). Taking CBT to school: A school-based mental health approach. *Journal of Contemporary Psychotherapy, 37*, 175–183.

Doll, B., Zucker, S., & Brehm, K. (2004). *Resilient classrooms: Creating healthy environments for learning*. New York: Guilford.

Elias, M. J., Zins, J. E., Weissberg, R. P., Frey, K. S., Greenberg, M. T., & Haynes, N. M. (1997). *Promoting social and emotional learning: Guidelines for educators*. Alexandria, VA: Association for Supervision and Curriculum Development.

Greenberg, M., Kusche, C., Cook, E., & Quamma, J. (1995). Promoting emotional competence in school-aged children: The effects of the PATHS curriculum. *Development and Psychopathology, 7*, 117–136.

Jacob, S. (2002). Best practices in utilizing professional ethics. In A. Thomas & J. Grimes (Eds.), *Best practices in school psychology IV* (Vol. 1, pp. 77–90). Bethesda, MD: The National Association of School Psychologists.

Jacob, S., & Hartshorne, T. S. (2003). *Ethics and law for school psychologists* (4th ed.). Hoboken, NJ: Wiley.

Individuals with Disabilities Education Act. (2004). Public Law 108–446 (20 U.S.C. 1400 et seq.). Retrieved November 10, 2007, from: http://edworkforce.house.gov/issues/108th/education/idea/conferencereport/confrept.htm.

Kaiser, A. P., Cai, X., Hancock, T. B., & Foster, E. M. (2002). Teacher-reported behavior problems and language delays in boys and girls enrolled in head start. *Behavioral Disorders, 28*, 23–39.

Kessler, R. C., Berglund, P., Demler, O., Jin, R., & Walters, E. E. (2005). Lifetime prevalence and age of-onset distributions of DSM-IV disorders in the National Comorbidity Survey Replication. *Archives of General Psychiatry, 62*, 593–602.

Knoff, H., & Batasche, G. (1995). Project ACHIEVE: Analyzing a school reform process for at-risk and underachieving students. *School Psychology Review, 24*, 579–603.

Kutash, K., Duchnowski, A. J., & Lynn, N. (2007). *School-based mental health: An empirical guide for decision-makers*. Tampa, FL: University of Southern Florida.

Levitt, J. M., Saka, N., Romanelli, L. H., & Hoagwood, K. (2007). Early identification of mental health problems in schools: The status of instrumentation. *Journal of School Psychology, 45*, 163–191.

Mennuti, R., & Christner, R. W. (2005). School-based cognitive-behavioral therapy (CBT). In A. Freeman (Ed.), *International Encyclopedia of Cognitive Behavior Therapy*. New York: Springer/Kluwer.

Mennuti, R. B., Christner, R. W., & Freeman, A. (2006). An introduction to a school-based cognitive behavioral framework. In R. B. Mennuti, A. Freeman, & R. W. Christner (Eds.), *Cognitive-behavioral interventions in educational settings* (pp. 37–62). New York: Routledge.

Mills, C., Stephan, S.H., Moore, E., Weist, M.D., Daly, B.P., & Edwards, M. (2006). *Clinical child and family psychology review,* Retrieved online from http://ezproxy.pcom.edu:2139/content/j2841010x22mwmv2/fulltext.html.

Mrazek, P. J., & Haggerty, R. J. (Eds.). (1994). *Reducing risks for mental disorders: Frontiers for preventative intervention research*. Washington, D.C.: National Academy Press.

Munoz, R., Mrazek, P., & Haggerty, R. (1996). Institute of Medicine report on prevention of mental disorders: Summary and commentary. *The American Psychologist, 51*, 1116–1122.

Murphy, V. B., & Christner, R. W. (2006). A cognitive behavioral case conceptualization approach for working with children and adolescents. In R. B. Mennuti, A. Freeman, & R. W. Christner (Eds.), *Cognitive-behavioral interventions in educational settings* (pp. 37–62). New York: Routledge.

NASP. (2006). *School psychology: A blueprint for training and practice III*. Bethesda, MD: National Association of School Psychologists.

Nastasi, B. K. (1998). A model for mental health programming in school communities: Introduction to the miniseries. *School Psychology Review, 27*(2), 165–175.

National Institute of Mental Health. (2001). In National Advisory Mental Heatlh Council (Ed.), *Blueprint for change: research on child and adolescent mental health*. A report of the national advisory mental health council's workgroup on child and adolescent mental health intervention development and deployment. Washington, D.C.: National Institute of Mental Health.

National Youth Violence Prevention Resource Center. (2001). *Risk and protective factors for youth violence [Fact Sheet]*. GA: U.S. Department of Health and Human Services, Centers for Disease Control and Prevention.

NFC. (2003). *Achieving the promise: Transforming mental health care in America: Final report*. Rockville, MD: New Freedom Commission on Mental Health.

Paternite, C. E. (2005). School-based mental health programs and services: Overview and introduction to the special issue. *Journal of Abnormal Child Psychology, 33*, 657–663.

Plyumert, K. (2002). Best practices in developing exemplary mental health programs in schools. In A. Thomas & J. Grimes (Eds.), *Best practices in school psychology IV* (Vol. 2, pp. 963–975). Bethesda, MD: The National Association of School Psychologists.

Power, T. J. (2003). Promoting children's mental health: Reform through interdisciplinary and community partnerships. *School Psychology Review, 32*, 3–16.

Prodente, C. A., Sander, M. A., & Weist, M. D. (2002). Furthering support for expanded school mental health programs. *Children's Services: Social Policy, Research, and Practice, 5*, 173–188.

Rones, M., & Hoagwood, K. (2000). School-based mental health services: A research review. *Clinical Child and Family Psychology Review, 3*, 223–241.

Skalski, A.K., & Smith, M.J. (2006). Responding to the mental health needs of students. Retrieved March 29, 2008, from www.nasponline.org.

Slade, E. P. (2002). Effects of school-based mental health programs on mental health service use by adolescents at school and in the community. *Mental Health Services Research, 4*(3), 151–167.

Tarasoff v. Regents of California, 118 Cal.Rptr. 129, 529 P.2d 553 (Cal. 1974). Tarasoff v. Regents of California, 131 Cal.Rptr. 14, 551 P.2d 334 (Cal.1976). Tarasoff II).

Tashman, N. A., Weist, M. D., Acosta, O., Bickham, N. L., Grady, M., Nabors, L., et al. (2000). Toward the integration of prevention research and expanded school mental health programs. *Children's Services: Social Policy, Research, and Practice., 3*, 97–115.

Thomas, A., & Grimes, J. (Eds.). (2002). *Appendix I: NASP Principles for Professional Ethics*. Bethesda, MD: The National Association of School Psychologists.

U.S. Department of Health and Human Services. (2001). *Mental health: culture, race, and ethnicity: a supplement to mental health: a report of the surgeon general*. Rockville, MD: U.S. Department of Health and Human Services.

Walker, H. M., & Shinn, M. R. (2002). Structuring school-based interventions to achieve integrated primary, secondary, and tertiary prevention goals for safe and effective schools. In M. R. Shinn, H. M. Walker, & G. Stoner (Eds.), *Interventions for academic and behavior problems II: preventative and remedial approaches* (pp. 1–26). Bethesda, MD: National Association of School Psychologists.

Weist, M. D. (2003). Commentary: Promoting paradigmatic change in child and adolescent mental health and schools. *School Psychology Review, 32*, 336–341.

Weist, M. D. (2005). Fulfilling the promise of school-based mental health: Moving toward a public mental health promotion approach. *Journal of Abnormal Child Psychology, 33*, 735–741.

Chapter 12
Preventing and Intervening in Crisis Situations

Melissa A. Reeves, Amanda B. Nickerson, and Stephen E. Brock

Over the past 30 years, the role of school psychologists in school-based crisis intervention has increased significantly. In fact, it has reached a point where following a crisis these interventions are expected by the public (Brock, Sandoval, & Lewis, 2001). In addition, they have become a school psychology training standard (National Association of School Psychologists (NASP), 2000).

Crises are sudden, uncontrollable, and extremely negative events that have the potential to impact an entire school community (Brock, 2002a). School-based crisis intervention is designed to address events that range from relatively common nonfatal accidents and injuries to extremely rare school shootings. More recently, hurricane Katrina demonstrated the need for crisis intervention and response services following natural disasters.

The importance of school psychologists being involved in crisis prevention, preparedness, intervention, and recovery is highlighted by the fact that children are a particularly vulnerable population who may demonstrate more adverse crisis reactions than those observed among adults. Further, it is now clear that childhood trauma has many short- and long-term consequences. It can, for example, affect a child's cognitive and personality development and coping abilities (Barenbaum, Ruchkin, & Schwab-Stone, 2004).

The purpose of this chapter is first to review the school crisis intervention literature, including its history, current status, and the need for training. Next, recommendations for crisis prevention and intervention practice are provided. Finally, the importance of these activities is emphasized, and resources to consult to improve competence in this area are offered.

Review of the Literature

This review begins by examining the history of crisis intervention. Next, it explores the current status of these services by discussing several available models of school-based crisis intervention. It concludes with a summary of recent studies that have documented the continued need for school crisis intervention training.

M.A. Reeves (✉)
Winthrop University, 135 Kinard Hall, Oakland Avenue, Rock Hill, SC 29733, USA
e-mail: MEREEV@aol.com

T.M. Lionetti et al. (eds.), *A Practical Guide to Building Professional Competencies in School Psychology*, DOI 10.1007/978-1-4419-6257-7_12, © Springer Science+Business Media, LLC 2011

The History of Crisis Intervention

The origins of modern community-based crisis intervention can be traced to the pioneering work of Lindemann (1944, 1979) following the Coconut Grove fire. His work with the survivors of this nightclub fire and subsequent contributions by Caplan (1964) provide the foundation upon which our current understanding of crisis reactions and interventions is built (Brock et al., 2001).

Some of the first descriptions and conceptualizations of school-based crisis intervention appeared in the literature in the 1970s and 1980s. For example, Meyers and Pitt (1976) provided a detailed discussion of the consultation procedures they followed after two separate student deaths. Their approach, which might be considered psycho-educational, involved a workshop designed to help teachers understand student reactions and to facilitate teachers' examination of their own feelings about the deaths.

One of the first descriptions of how a school psychological services staff responded to a mass disaster (i.e., a terrorist attack) was offered by Klingman and Ben-Eli (1981). Making use of Caplan's (1964) preventive mental health model, a school psychological services staff in Israel developed and implemented "primary" and "secondary" school crisis interventions for the victims of a terrorist attack. The primary prevention activities included what might be termed psycho-education, as well as the enhancement of the natural caregiving environment and caring for the caregivers. Secondary prevention included what might be termed psychological triage and psychological first aid. It is interesting to note that the interventions first documented by Meyers and Pitt (1976) and Klingman and Ben Eli (1981) are still among the primary services offered by school crisis teams today and play a central role in NASP's model of crisis intervention and recovery (Brock et al., 2009; Brock, 2006).

Models of Crisis Intervention

Until relatively recently, there have been few, if any, models of crisis intervention dedicated to the *school*-based response. The need for such models is highlighted by Brown and Bobrow (2004), who state: "As outside providers enter the school setting specifically to provide mental health services, a clear understanding of the school structure and culture is warranted" (p. 212). Without such knowledge, even the most experienced community-based crisis intervener will make mistakes (e.g., not accounting for the school bell schedule when providing services).

Previously, Brock and Poland (2002) reviewed a selection of five crisis intervention models available in the literature at that time (i.e., Brock et al., 2001; Johnson, 1993; Petersen & Straub, 1992; Pitcher & Poland, 1992; Poland & McCormick, 1999). Common to all of these models was the concept of multiple crisis intervention teams. Specifically, all these models suggest that each district have their own district-level crisis team, as well as multiple school-site teams. Among the district team, responsibilities would be to provide direct crisis services following the events that overwhelm available school resources. In addition, the district team would be available to consult with school-site crisis teams as they independently provide crisis services. Finally, the district-level team would have crisis preparedness training responsibilities. In the Brock et al. (2001) model, school teams are considered the first line of defense. To the extent possible, this model recommends that schools respond independently to their own crisis events. Obviously, this expectation calls for significant crisis preparedness.

Brock and Poland (2002) also found specific guidance for crisis preparedness and response to be common among these models. For example, both Petersen and Straub (1992) and Brock et al. (2001) offered checklists designed to facilitate crisis planning and to guide the crisis response. Primarily, the planning checklists involve the identification of specific individuals to fill specific crisis intervention roles. The response protocols typically suggest that the first step is to determine crisis facts and estimate the impact of the crisis on the school. Then, the team begins to make decisions about what and how crisis facts will be disseminated to faculty, students, parents, and the community. In addition, the team begins to identify and respond to psychological trauma victims. Finally, these protocols often conclude with an acknowledgement of specific logistical details (e.g., establishing an emergency operations center), the need for debriefings, and memorial development considerations.

A final common element of school-based crisis intervention models identified by Brock and Poland (2002) is an acknowledgment of the importance of caring for caregivers. For example, both Johnson (1993) and Bolnik and Brock (2005) acknowledge that crisis intervention takes its toll on those providing these services. Thus, these models also include the discussion of debriefings designed to prevent and/or detect burnout among crisis interveners and to assist with stress management.

Most recently, NASP developed one of the first training curricula specifically designed to develop the crisis prevention, preparedness, intervention, and recovery skills of the school-based mental health professional (Brock, 2006; Brock, Nickerson, Reeves, Jimerson, Lieberman, & Feinberg, 2009; Reeves, Nickerson, & Jimerson, 2006). The *PREPaRE School Crisis Prevention and Intervention Training Curriculum* (PREPaRE) provides school-based mental health professionals training on how to best fill the roles and responsibilities generated by their membership on school crisis teams. *PREPaRE* is based on the assumptions that: (a) The skill sets of school psychologists are best used when embedded within a multidisciplinary team that provides crisis prevention, preparedness, intervention, and recovery, (b) school crisis response is unique and as such requires its own model, and (c) school psychologists are best prepared to address the psychological issues associated with school crises. Specifically, *PREPaRE* emphasizes that, as members of a school crisis team, school psychologists are involved in the following hierarchical and sequential activities: (a) *Prevent* and prepare for psychological trauma, (b) *Reaffirm* physical health and perceptions of security and safety, (c) *Evaluate* psychological trauma risk, (d) *Provide* interventions *and Respond* to psychological needs, and (e) *Examine* the effectiveness of crisis prevention and intervention.

Consistent with the guidance offered by the U.S. Department of Education (2003), *PREPaRE* views crisis team activities as occurring during the four stages of a crisis: (a) prevention, (b) preparedness, (c) response, and (d) recovery. Adhering to the U.S. Department of Homeland Security (2004), it also incorporates the U.S. Department of Education's Emergency Response and Crisis Management (ERCM) guidance, and the Incident Command Structure (ICS) as delineated by the National Incident Management System (NIMS).

The Need for Crisis Intervention Training

There is a growing body of legislation mandating schools to engage in crisis prevention and intervention. PL 107-110, The No Child Left Behind Act, though primarily concerned with academic progress, also mandated that all schools have a safety plan. In addition, schools are required to report crime and safety statistics each year and schools designated as "persistently dangerous" must inform parents of this label and provide the parents the choice of moving their child to another school. There are also several federal acts, such as the Schools Safety Enhancement Act of 1999, Goals 2000 Educate America Act, the School Anti-Violence Empowerment Act of 2000, and the Improving America's Schools Act of 1994 that provide funds to states to develop violence and crisis prevention programs. In addition, the U.S. Departments of Education and Homeland Security strongly suggest (and require, for grant recipients) that school crisis prevention and intervention efforts use the structure of the NIMS ICS, which is described in more detail in this chapter.

It is clear that professionals, legislators, and the general public place great importance on school crisis prevention and intervention. Despite this, survey results have consistently found that less than 10% of responding school psychologists has taken a course specific to crisis prevention and intervention (Allen et al., 2002; Wise, Smead, & Huebner, 1987). Although school psychologists report that they are more likely to obtain information about crisis prevention and intervention through school district or local trainings and consultation with colleagues than from graduate school (Nickerson & Zhe, 2004), 45% (Furlong, Babinski, Poland, Munoz, & Boles, 1996) to 58% (Allen et al., 2002) of school psychologists report feeling minimally prepared to respond to crisis situations, suggesting a need for further preparation.

Basic Considerations for Enhancing the Research-Practice Connection

Effective crisis prevention and response involves a comprehensive multidisciplinary team approach. This section describes the role of the school psychologist within the multidisciplinary crisis team. The role of the school psychologist within a 3-tiered model of prevention is then discussed.

It is important that school crisis teams conform to the NIMS and its ICS so that these teams can communicate in a common language with the many other agencies and response personnel that may be involved in responding to a crisis at school (Brock, Jimerson, & Hart, 2006; Nickerson, Brock, & Reeves, 2006). Homeland Security Presidential Directive (HSPD) 5-Management of Domestic Incidents of 2003, indicates that all federal departments and agencies must adopt the NIMS, including its ICS to receive federal emergency assistance (U.S. Department of Homeland Security, 2004). The NIMS allows for a common set of concepts, principles, terminology, and organizational processes to be used in planning, preparing, and responding to a crisis. Use of the ICS allows for public health, mental health, law enforcement, public safety, and local governments to collaborate and communicate using the same organizational system (U.S. Department of Education, 2006). From the experiences of educational professionals who have implemented the ICS, the structure and consistency it generates between agencies is suggested to be a very important contribution to this system (Reeves et al., 2006). As shown in Fig. 12.1, the ICS has five major functions: Command, Intelligence, Operations, Logistics, and Finance.[1]

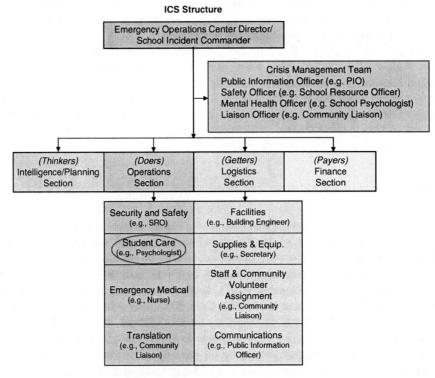

Fig. 12.1 School crisis teams roles/responsibilities within incident command structure (ICS). This figure illustrates the structure of the National Incident Management System's Incident Command System (U.S. Department of Homeland Security, 2004). Examples of school personnel who may assume the different roles within this system are included in parentheses. ©2006, National Association of School Psychologists, PREPaRE WS1: Crisis Prevention & Preparedness: The Comprehensive School Crisis Team

---

[1] For more detailed information about the ICS, see the U.S. Department of Education website, Brock et al., 2009, or Nickerson, Brock, and Reeves (2006), all of which are described in Table 12.1.

Command includes the Incident Commander, and if necessary, a crisis management team comprised of a Public Information Officer (PIO), Safety Officer (SO), and Liaison Officer. The Incident Commander is the person who coordinates the crisis response and assigns responsibilities. If the response entails involvement from a local or federal agency (i.e., police, fire, Department of Homeland Security), a representative from the agency usually serves as the Incident Commander, or a unified command structure is used. In a unified command, the Incident Commander from the school district and the Incident Commander from the local or federal agency work together in a unified fashion. As crises create overwhelming demands, there is a need for the commander(s) to be highly directive and decisive in responding. Within the command staff, the PIO communicates relevant and accurate crisis-related information to the public, the media, and other agencies. The Safety Officer ensures the safety of the response personnel, students, and staff; conducts ongoing assessments of hazardous environments; coordinates safety efforts among different agencies; and advises the incident commander on safety matters. The Liaison Officer is the point of contact for representatives of other government agencies, nongovernmental organizations, and private entities. In addition to this traditional command structure, the Los Angeles County Office of Education (n.d.) suggests adding a Mental Health Officer, who assesses and coordinates mental health services for students, staff, and families.

The Intelligence function is comprised of "the thinkers" (California Governor's OES, 1998), who collect, evaluate, and disseminate the information about the crisis to the Incident Commander or unified command. Referred to as "the doers" by the California Governor's Office of Emergency Services (OES, 1998), Operations is responsible for immediate response needs, such as reducing immediate hazard, saving lives, establishing situational control, and restoring normal operations (U.S. Department of Homeland Security, 2004). This function is most relevant for school psychologists, as activities we consider to be "crisis intervention," or the immediate response to the psychological challenges generated by a crisis event, fall under the control of Operations. The Logistics section or "getters" obtain all resources needed to manage the crisis (California Governor's OES, 1998), such as personnel, equipment and supplies, and services, including transportation. The Finance section consists of "the payers" (California Governor's OES), who keep a record of all expenses.

The school psychologist most likely fulfills the "Student Care" role, which is subsumed under the "Operations" section. The primary responsibilities include crisis prevention, preparedness, response, and recovery priorities established by the Incident Commander(s). In addition to ICS duties assigned, the school psychologist also serves a vital role within a 3-tiered crisis intervention model (see Fig. 12.2). This model emphasizes the importance of providing a continuum of services, including universal prevention, targeted/selected interventions, and intensive/indicated interventions, which are described further in the following sections.

Tier 1: Universal Crisis Planning, Preparedness, and Evaluation

At the universal level, it is important for the school psychologist to strive to prevent and prepare for crises, reaffirm physical health, and ensure perceptions of safety and security. This is done by comprehensive crisis planning and preparedness which addresses both physical and psychological safety. In addition, members (primarily mental health professionals) of the multidisciplinary crisis team need to receive training in how to evaluate the impact of psychological trauma in order to help identify and deliver appropriate interventions at the targeted/selected and intensive/indicated levels of response. In order to successfully achieve all of these, the school psychologist should serve on a multidisciplinary school crisis team and help facilitate the development of crisis roles and responsibilities according to the ICS.

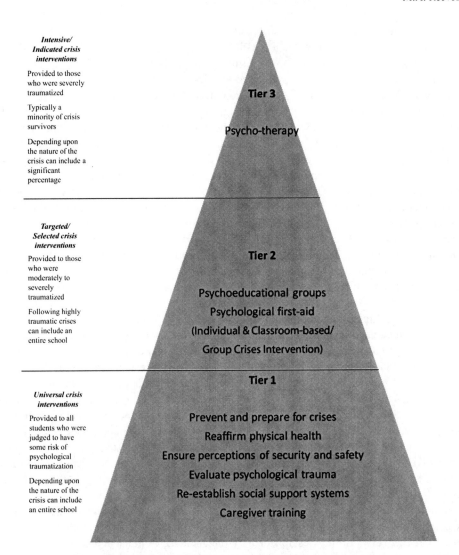

Intensive/
Indicated crisis
interventions

Provided to those
who were severely
traumatized

Typically a
minority of crisis
survivors

Depending upon
the nature of the
crisis can include a
significant
percentage

Tier 3

Psycho-therapy

Targeted/
Selected crisis
interventions

Provided to those
who were
moderately to
severely
traumatized

Following highly
traumatic crises
can include an
entire school

Tier 2

Psychoeducational groups
Psychological first-aid
(Individual & Classroom-based/
Group Crises Intervention)

Tier 1

Universal crisis
interventions

Provided to all
students who were
judged to have
some risk of
psychological
traumatization

Depending upon
the nature of the
crisis can include
an entire school

Prevent and prepare for crises
Reaffirm physical health
Ensure perceptions of security and safety
Evaluate psychological trauma
Re-establish social support systems
Caregiver training

Fig. 12.2 Crisis prevention and intervention roles within a 3-tiered crisis intervention model
Source: Brock, S.E., Nickerson, A.B., Reeves, M.A., Jimerson, S.R., Lieberman, R.A., & Feinberg, T.A. (2009).
School crisis prevention and intervention, the PREPaRE model. Bethesda, MD: National Association of School
Psychologists

Physical and psychological safety. From a crisis prevention and preparedness standpoint, it is critical that planning takes into account the needs for both physical and psychological safety. In our experience, administrators often focus on the physical safety of a school and do not always address the psychological safety. School psychologists can consult with administrators to be sure that both physical and psychological safety are being addressed and that data-driven decision-making is being used to implementing appropriate interventions. It is common for parents, community members, and legislators to advocate for high security or "get-tough" approaches such as zero tolerance policies. Research has not supported the use of zero tolerance policies, as students who are suspended are more likely to be referred for disciplinary actions in the future (Tobin & Sugai, 1999), a disproportionate number of males and children from low SES/ethnic minority backgrounds are referred for disciplinary actions leading to questions of social justice and fairness (Skiba, Peterson, & Williams, 1997), and most behavior problems resulting in suspension and expulsion can be prevented through proactive prevention programs such as School-Wide Positive

Behavior Support (Horner, Sugai, Todd, & Lewis-Palmer, 2005; Sprague & Horner, 2006). Instead, school psychologists can lead the way in promoting physical and psychological safety by helping their school and/or district develop a plan, with corresponding policies and procedures, that is sensitive to the needs of students, families, and community context (Reeves et al., 2006).

Physical safety involves activities that are focused on the physical structures of the school environment. Sprague and Walker (2005) in *Safe and Healthy Schools: Practical Intervention Strategies* note the importance of the architectural design of the school building and grounds, and how this may be the most neglected source of vulnerability facing schools. To address these safety concerns, a set of principles known as Crime Prevention Through Environmental Design (CPTED), which focuses on natural surveillance, natural access control, and territoriality, has been established (Schneider, Walker & Sprague, 2000). Natural surveillance is the ability to see what is happening in a school and involves such efforts as staff and volunteer supervision of activities, appropriate lighting, employment of school resource officers, and two-way communication between staff and front office. Natural access control involves having one point of entry while keeping others locked, a uniform visitor screening policy, identification badges that are consistently worn, and strategically placed surveillance cameras. Territoriality involves a shared sense of ownership and pride in the school by faculty and students, a clean and attractive school, and a confidential reporting system.

Psychological safety includes activities that are focused on the emotional and behavioral well-being of students and staff and include such models as positive behavior supports at the universal level. Entire school environments can be reengineered to create positive and lasting behavior change among students, the use of research-based strategies to achieve positive social and learning outcomes (e.g., www.pbis.org) and the use of data for decision making. Positively stated behavioral expectations that include clear definitions of problems and expectations are provided, and students are directly taught the skills that allow them to meet the expectations, effective incentives and motivational systems are provided, and administrators and staff are committed to implementing the expectations and incentives on a consistent basis. Studies have found that using comprehensive approaches that include training, supervision, restructuring, and teaching expectations and skills decrease antisocial behavior and office discipline referrals (Meltzer, Biglan, Rasby, & Sprague, 2001; Sprague et al., 2001), as well as increase protective factors, such as school engagement and achievement (O'Donnell, Hawkins, Catalano, Abbott, & Day, 1998). It must be noted that school-wide positive behavioral supports should include interventions at every level of a multi-tiered service delivery system (universal, targeted, and intensive). For example, good crisis planning and preparedness involves the identification of at-risk students that may need additional support. There must be well-developed suicide and risk assessment process for those demonstrating warning signs, and staff and students must know how to access this process. Students may also need and benefit from educational groups to teach social skills, anger management, conflict resolution, foster self-esteem/resiliency, and reduce substance abuse. Individuals more likely to need individualized plans can benefit from the school psychologist conducting a Functional Behavioral Assessment (FBA), and developing a Behavior Intervention Plan. In addition, meaningful consequences and alternatives to suspension should be identified.

By focusing on psychological safety and building internal and external resiliency factors, we can also increase connectedness to school. This results in increased teacher efficacy, work enjoyment, morale and attendance, increased academic interest/achievement, and decreased student misbehavior and dropout (McNeely, Nonnemaker, & Blum, 2002). It is important for school mental health professionals and administrators to recognize that building a positive school climate, in addition to addressing physical safety, is a process that takes time, effective leadership, and cohesive teamwork.

Evaluation and crisis response activities. The aforementioned activities are necessary to prevent crises, such as student-to-student violence or a threat to self; however, it is unrealistic to expect all crises to be prevented. Therefore, at the universal level, there are a variety of crisis intervention activities that should be conducted with all students if a crisis occurs, including ensuring physical safety, evaluating psychological trauma, reuniting social support systems, and providing caregiver training.

For almost all students and staff, clearly, the most essential task at the universal level of crisis intervention is to ensure physical safety. In addition, one of the primary postcrisis roles for the school psychologist is to evaluate psychological trauma (i.e., to conduct psychological triage). This involves considering trauma risk factors (e.g., emotional proximity to the crisis event; personal vulnerabilities such as preexisting mental health, family stressors; threat perceptions) and warning signs (i.e., crisis reactions). For example, if a student is killed in a car accident, other students who knew the victim well, witnessed the accident, had a close family member or a friend who had died in an accident in the recent past are likely to need a greater degree of intervention than students who did not know the child who died and who did not have first-hand experience with this or other motor vehicle accidents.

It is also critical to make use of and empower the child's natural support systems by reunifying children with parents and providing caregiver training to support natural recovery and adaptation (Yorbik, Akbiyik, Kirmizigul, & Söhmen, 2004). Information to be shared with teachers and parents may include: general information about crises, children's responses, and ways to help children cope (Brock & Jimerson, 2004). As mentioned in Table 12.1, the NASP Web site contains a variety of resources that may be helpful in these trainings. Allowing opportunities for parents to receive information, ask questions, and consult with school staff about how to help their children after a crisis situation results in better coping and fewer problems for children over time (Pynoos, Steinberg, & Goenjian, 1996). School psychologists should also advise caregivers to minimize repeated exposure to the trauma, as such has been correlated with increased symptomatology (e.g., repeated media exposure; Hoven et al., 2004; Pfefferbaum et al., 1999).

Table 12.1 Suggested readings and resources on crisis prevention and intervention

Resource	Description
Books, article, and government documents	
Brock, S. E., Sandoval, J., & Lewis, S. (2001). *Preparing for crises in the schools: A manual for building school crisis response teams* (2nd ed.). New York: John Wiley.	Provides guidance on how to establish, implement, and maintain a school crisis team. Information provided on the early detection of trouble, how to develop crisis plans, and how to provide crisis intervention.
Brock, S. E., Lazarus, P. J., & Jimerson, S. R. (Eds.). (2002). *Best practices in school crisis prevention and intervention.* Washington, DC: National Association of School Psychologists.	The 37 chapters in this edited book provide detailed information about crisis theory, the characteristics of responsive schools, primary prevention, crisis response, long-term treatment of traumatized students, and research-based practices that promote safe schools.
Brock, S.E., Nickerson, A. B., Reeves, M.A., Jimerson, S.R., Lieberman, R.A., Feinberg, T.A. (2010). *School crisis prevention and intervention: The PREPaRE model.* Washington, DC: National Association of School Psychologists.	This book provides in-depth information on the school-based PREPaRE crisis prevention and intervention model. It was written to complement and reinforce the PREPaRE workshops and provides school-based professionals with specific strategies and interventions to help prevent, prepare for, and respond to a variety of crisis situations.
Jimerson, S. R., & Furlong, M. J. (Eds.). (2006). *Handbook of school violence and school safety: From research to practice.* Mahwah, NJ: Lawrence Erlbaum.	The 41 chapters in this edited handbook address the full range of school violence from harassment and bullying to serious physical assault. It also examines existing school safety programs and the research and theories that guide them.
National Institute of Mental Health. (2001). *Mental health and mass violence: Evidence-based early psychological intervention for victims/survivors of mass violence. A workshop to reach consensus on best practices.* Washington, DC: Author.	Provides a summary of the National Institute of Mental Health workshop that included 58 disaster mental health experts from six countries. Addresses the impact of early psychological interventions, what works and what does not work, and identifies gaps in our current knowledge.

(continued)

Resource	Description
Nickerson, A. B, Brock, S. E., & Reeves, M. A. (2006). School crisis teams within an incident command system. *The California School Psychologist, 11*, 63–72.	This article describes the function and structure of school crisis teams using the Incident Command System. Specific case studies are presented.
Reeves, M.A., Kanan, L.M., & Plog, A.E. (2010). *Comprehensive planning for safe learning environments: A school professional's guide to integrating physical and psychological safety- prevention through recovery.* New York: Routledge Publishing.	This book provides school-based professionals with the guidance and tools needed to balance both physical and psychological safety with a multi-tiered intervention approach covering all 4 crisis management phases. Case examples and user-friendly sample forms are provided throughout the book and on a supplemental CD.
U.S. Department of Homeland Security. (2004). *National incident management system.* Retrieved September 9, 2005, from www.fema.gov/pdf/nims/nims_doc_full.pdf	Delineates the basic elements of the National Incident Management System (NIMS). The system is designed to provide a consistent nationwide template to enable federal, state, local, and tribal governments, private sector, and nongovernmental organizations to work together to prevent, prepare for, respond to, and recover from crisis events.
U.S. Department of Education, Office of Safe and Drug Free Schools. (2003). *Practical information on crisis planning: A guide for schools and communities.* Washington, DC: Author. Available from http://www.ed.gov/admins/lead/safety/emergencyplan/crisisplanning.pdf	Provides key principles for effective crisis planning and discusses mitigation/prevention, preparedness, response, and recovery in-depth. Includes directory of state emergency management offices and provides specific information on aspects of crisis management, including examples from school districts.
Training curriculum	
National Association of School Psychologists. (2006). *PREPaRE crisis prevention, preparedness, and intervention training curriculum.* Bethesda, MD: Author. Training information available at http://www.nasponline.org/prepare/index.aspx	This curriculum includes a 1-day training overview of the comprehensive school crisis team appropriate for a school crisis team member, as well as a 2-day training specifically oriented toward the school-based mental health professional and specific interventions.
Internet resources	
U.S. Department of Education, Safe and Drug Free Schools http://www.ed.gov/admins/lead/safety/edpicks.jhtml?src=ln	This Web site is updated regularly and includes current information regarding initiatives and publications related to promoting safe schools.
National Association of School Psychologists, Crisis Resources http://www.nasponline.org/resources/crisis_safety/	This Web site offers an exceptional collection of school crisis prevention and intervention resources (e.g., publications, handouts, links to other Web-based resources) specifically developed for school psychologists and other educational professionals.
U.S. Department of Education, Readiness & Emergency Management for Schools (REMS), http://rems.ed.gov/	This Web site offers newsletters and handouts regarding. Formerly called Emergency Respone and Crisis Management for Schools (ERCM), this website offers newsletters, handouts, helpful hints, and lessons learned regarding all facets of school crisis planning and preparedness. Specific emphasis is placed on integrating the NIMS/ICS into schools and collaboration with FEMA (Federal Emergency Management Agency).
U.S. Office of Special Education Programs, Positive Behavioral Interventions and Supports (PBIS) www.pbis.org	This Web site gives schools capacity building and technical assistance to identify, adapt, sustain, and affect school-wide discipline practices. Information and specific practices are shown for all grade levels.

In addition, the information is provided to parents about signs that may indicate the need for more targeted crisis interventions. As indicated in the *PREPaRE* curriculum, psychological triage is a dynamic process. Thus, secondary evaluation takes place as these initial immediate crisis interventions are provided, and the school psychologist and other caregivers evaluate the student's response and crisis reactions to these initial interventions. If a student is exhibiting warning signs of psychological trauma, then additional interventions are provided (Brock, 2006).

Tier 2: Selected/Targeted Crisis Interventions

For students and staff more directly impacted, a targeted/selected level of interventions may be necessary. At this level, psycho-education groups and psychological first aid (individual and group crisis interventions) are provided. Psycho-education groups are designed to teach students how to best cope with a given stressor (e.g., stress management strategies). It includes specific elements such as answering questions and dispelling rumors about the crisis, preparing students for common crisis reactions, teaching them how to manage reactions, and developing a crisis reaction management plan.

Psychological first aid deals directly with students to facilitate the initiation of adaptive coping skills. In the *PREPaRE* model, individual psychological first aid, now currently referred to as individual crisis intervention (ICI), involves (a) establishing rapport, (b) identifying and prioritizing crisis events, (c) addressing crisis problems, and (d) reviewing progress to ensure immediate coping has been reestablished. The school mental health professional addresses crisis problems by asking about coping attempts already made, facilitating the exploration of additional coping strategies, and proposing other alternatives. Whether the mental health professional takes a facilitative or directive stance depends on the level of risk of harm to self or others being exhibited by the student.

Like other group crisis intervention approaches (e.g., Mitchell & Everly, 1996), the *PREPaRE* model of group psychological first aid, now currently referred to as classroom-based/group crisis interventions (CCI), includes the following steps: (a) An introduction to the group, (b) providing facts and dispelling rumors about the crisis, (c) sharing crisis stories, (d) sharing crisis reactions, (e) empowerment and identifying adaptive coping strategies, and (f) a closing. This is designed to actively explore individual crisis experiences and reactions and to help students feel less alone and more connected to classmates by normalizing experiences and reactions (Brock, 2002b). It should be noted that some studies have demonstrated that among acute trauma victims, one-time psychological debriefing techniques that explore crisis experiences and reactions in adults fail to prevent posttraumatic stress disorder and may even be related to increased long-term symptomatology (Bisson, 2003; Deahl, 2000). With this limitation in mind, the *PREPaRE* model recommends that group psychological first aid/classroom-based crisis intervention be: (a) voluntary, (b) not provided to acute trauma victims (these individuals will need more individualized assistance), (c) offered within a more integrated approach that may include large group meetings, family counseling, and referrals for outside therapy (Brock & Jimerson, 2004; Everly, Flannery, & Eyler, 2002), (d) conducted with groups that are homogeneous in terms of having had vicarious crisis exposure and, (e) focused primarily on facts and sharing of adaptive coping rather than on specific details and reminders of the trauma. These precautions are intended to decrease the likelihood that children and adolescents will experience vicarious traumatization.

As the crisis intervention progresses, the dynamic process of psychological triage continues. Tertiary evaluation identifies those individuals who require professional mental health intervention (Brock, 2006). School mental health professionals must be attuned to students whose posttraumatic symptoms are severe (e.g., severe hyperarousal, flashbacks, suicidal ideation or attempts; Cook-Cottone, 2004) and/or do not diminish with the passage of time. At this level, the student is typically referred to an appropriately trained mental health professional that specializes in working with persons impacted by a crisis.

Tier 3: Intensive/Indicated Crisis Interventions

There is empirical support for psychotherapy in children with posttraumatic stress disorder, particularly cognitive-behavioral approaches (March, Amaya-Jackson, Murray, & Schulte, 1998). These are more formal mental health interventions, and although some school psychologists may be dually licensed as a private mental health therapist or clinical psychologist, this is typically not within their scope and practice of school psychology within the school setting. Cook-Cottone (2004) suggests that the stress management and cognitive restructuring techniques of this treatment are appropriate; however, exposure, a critical component of treatment, is not appropriate for school settings because it may exacerbate symptoms (Cook-Cottone, 2004).

Obviously, providing these services can be mentally and physically exhausting for the school-mental- health professional. It is crucial the school crisis plan address "Caring for the Caregiver" by being sure that caregivers take care of themselves and each other. This can be done by individuals having a personal stress management plan, debriefing with other crisis responders, continuing to enhance professional skills through ongoing staff development, mentor/mentee relationships, and having time off to relax both emotionally and physically (Brock, 2006).

Lastly, it should be emphasized that evaluation of the crisis response is crucial. As Pagliocca, Nickerson, and Williams (2002) suggest, developing an "evaluation mindset" when engaging in crisis prevention and intervention is essential to improving practice. These authors suggest that crisis teams adopt this mindset by continually asking and answering important questions about how the response was implemented and whether or not it accomplished its purpose. This allows the school and/or district crisis team to make improvements in the plan to better prepare for the next crisis that may occur. Consistent with this "mindset," the *PREPaRE* model offers specific guidance on how to evaluate the effectiveness of a crisis- intervention response.

Practice Implications

School psychologists are often the most highly trained mental health professionals in schools. In addition, their unique training in education and psychology places them in the ideal position to assume leadership roles in preventing student crises, advising school leaders on how to safely and effectively plan for responding to crises, providing direct interventions after a crisis, and evaluating current crisis response capabilities (Furlong, Morrison, & Pavelski, 2000; Knoff, 2000). As stated in *School Psychology: A Blueprint for Training and Practice III* (NASP, 2006), though school psychologists are not expected to be experts in every area, they should have "basic competency in a broad array of crisis situations, know how to access resources to address these issues, and understand how to work with others to bring effective services to students and school staff" (p. 20). School psychologists are most often involved in implementing different crisis prevention and response strategies, yet are less likely to be involved in developing or designing these efforts and evaluating them (Nickerson & Zhe, 2004). By obtaining skills in the crisis prevention and intervention area, school psychologists can enhance their skills and marketability. In addition, possessing these skills helps school psychologists expand their role and function within a school to include more than just "test and place" for learning and emotional issues. Crisis planning and intervention is a great avenue for school psychologists to become leaders in the school, become involved at the system level to impact school-wide change, and promote a positive school climate.

School psychologists need to advocate to be a central component to crisis planning and intervention. Although there are barriers being involved in this type of work, the most commonly cited being the lack of time and not in being the same school every day (Nickerson & Zhe, 2004); it is possible to remind school leaders that prevention is an intervention. Developing and implementing evidence-based prevention and preparedness, it is likely that less time will be spent in time-consuming reactive approaches.

Although the large majority of school personnel have expertise in the academic realm, the school psychologist is one of the few who have expertise in understanding the psychological effects of a crisis on an individual and the necessary interventions to promote resilience in times of distress. If the capacity to respond to a crisis is developed at the school level, there is a decreased likelihood that administrators will need to turn to external consultants and mental health professionals who may have the necessary expertise in trauma, but may not have the understanding of how schools work to implement the response most effectively.

Building Professional Competence

Given the aforementioned findings indicating that school psychologists do not tend to receive specific training on crisis prevention and intervention in graduate school, an obvious implication is that more graduate programs need to incorporate this coursework into the curricula. Although adding a class in this area is ideal, it is also possible for crisis training to be infused in the curriculum. For example, lectures on suicide risk assessment and threat assessment can be integrated in a course on social-emotional assessment and school-based crisis intervention can be a component of a psychotherapy or intervention course.

For the majority of school psychologists who have not obtained this information in graduate school, there are a variety of ways to gain such knowledge and skill. As shown in Table 12.1, several books, government documents, training curricula, and internet resources provide comprehensive and research-based coverage of these topics. Based on existing theory and research, the *PREPaRE* Crisis Prevention and Intervention Curriculum targets many of the specific competencies critical to the school psychologist's crisis preparedness and intervention role.

Future

Increased attention to school safety issues has created the need and opportunity for school psychologists to transform their roles and assume leadership roles in preventing and intervening in crisis situations (Furlong et al., 2000; Knoff, 2000). Recent surveys have shown that school psychologists are often active members of school crisis teams (Allen et al., 2002; Bramlett, Murphy, Johnson, Wallingsford, & Hall, 2002), which is encouraging. School psychologists, with their training in psychology, mental health, and education, are in a unique position to take a lead in prevention and interventions that complement the skill sets of other important crisis team members. With the availability of resources and training in this area, school psychologists are in a ripe position to embrace this role.

Summary/Conclusion

As highlighted in this chapter, school psychologists have unique training that allows them to expand their job role and be a leader in school crisis preparation, preparedness, intervention, and recovery. By emphasizing both physical and psychological aspects of developing safe schools, in addition to adopting a team approach utilizing the NIMS/ICS, school psychologists can present a balanced, team approach to crisis planning and become a vital part of any school's crisis planning and response activities. Current legal statutes require that schools be prepared and develop crisis plans, therefore, further emphasizing that "prevention is an intervention." School psychologists are in a position to help all students reach their full potential academically, socially, and emotionally by providing services and interventions to mitigate the negative impact of a crisis. As more and more school psychologists embrace this role, we can prevent further acts from occurring and provide quality support for those situations that are not preventable.

Chapter Competency Checklist

DOMAIN 2 – Enhancing the Development of Wellness, Social Skills, Mental Health, and Life

Foundational	Functional
Understand and explain the following:	Gain practice:
□ Brief history of crisis intervention	□ Observing the three level of crisis intervention
□ Models of crisis intervention	□ Providing three levels of crisis intervention
□ Factors driving the need for crisis intervention in schools	□ Evaluate crisis intervention services in schools
□ Physical and psychological safety	□ Making improvements to crisis intervention services
□ Internal and external resiliency factors	
□ Normal child development milestones	
□ Prevention - Tier 1	
□ Selected/targeted intervention - Tier 2	
□ Intensive interventions - Tier 3	
□ Suicide & homicide threat assessment	

References

Allen, M., Jerome, A., White, A., Lamb, S., Pope, D., & Rawlins, C. (2002). The preparation of school psychologists for crisis intervention. *Psychology in the Schools, 39*, 427–439.

Barenbaum, J., Ruchkin, V., & Schwab-Stone, M. (2004). The psychosocial aspects of children exposed to war: Practice and policy initiatives. *Journal of Child Psychology and Psychiatry, 45*, 41–62.

Bisson, J. I. (2003). Single-session early psychological interventions following traumatic events. *Clinical Psychology Review, 23*, 481–499.

Bolnik, L., & Brock, S. E. (2005). The self-reported effects of crisis intervention work on school psychologists. *The California School Psychologist, 10*, 117–124.

Bramlett, R. K., Murphy, J. J., Johnson, J., Wallingsford, L., & Hall, J. D. (2002). Contemporary practices in school psychology: A national survey of roles and referral problems. *Psychology in the Schools, 39*, 327–335.

Brock, S. E. (2002a). Crisis theory: A foundation for the comprehensive crisis prevention and intervention team. In S. E. Brock, P. J. Lazarus, & S. R. Jimerson (Eds.), *Best practices in school crisis prevention and intervention* (pp. 5–17). Washington, DC: National Association of School Psychologists.

Brock, S. E. (2002b). Estimating the appropriate crisis response. In S. E. Brock, P. J. Lazarus, & S. R. Jimerson (Eds.), *Best practices in school crisis prevention and intervention* (pp. 355–365). Bethesda, MD: National Association of School Psychologists.

Brock, S. E. (2006). *Trainer's handbook workshop #2: Crisis intervention and recovery: the roles of the school-based mental health professional.* (Available from National Association of School Psychologists, 4340 East West Highway, Suite 402, Bethesda, MD 20814).

Brock, S. E., & Jimerson, S. R. (2004). School crisis interventions: Strategies for addressing the consequences of crisis events. In E. R. Gerler Jr. (Ed.), *Handbook of school violence* (pp. 285–332). Binghamton, NY: Haworth Press.

Brock, S. E., Jimerson, S. R., & Hart, S. R. (2006). Preventing, preparing for, and responding to school violence with the National Incident Management System. In S. R. Jimerson & M. J. Furlong (Eds.), *Handbook of school violence and school safety: From research to practice* (pp. 443–458). Mahwah, NJ: Erlbaum.

Brock, S. E., Nickerson, A. B., Reeves, M. A., Jimerson, S. R., Lieberman, R. A., & Feinberg, T. A. (2009). *School crisis prevention and intervention: The PREP_aRE model*. Bethesda, MD: National Association of School Psychologists.

Brock, S. E., & Poland, S. (2002). School crisis preparedness. In S. E. Brock, P. J. Lazarus, & S. R. Jimerson (Eds.), *Best practices in school crisis prevention and intervention* (pp. 273–288). Bethesda, MD: National Association of School Psychologists.

Brock, S. E., Sandoval, J., & Lewis, S. (2001). *Preparing for crises in the schools: A manual for building school crisis response teams* (2nd ed.). New York: Wiley.

Brown, E. J., & Bobrow, A. L. (2004). School entry after a community-wide trauma: Challenges and lessons learned from September 11th, 2001. *Clinical Child and Family Psychology Review, 7*, 211–221.

California Governor's Office of Emergency Services. (1998). *School emergency response: Using SEMS at districts and sites*. Sacramento, CA: Author.

Caplan, G. (1964). *Principles of preventive psychiatry*. New York: Basic Books.

Cook-Cattone, C. (2004). Childhood posttraumatic stress disorder: diagnosis, treatment, and school reintegration. *School Psychology Review, 33*, 127–139.

Deahl, M. (2000). Psychological debriefing: Controversy and challenge. *Australian and New Zealand Journal of Psychiatry, 34*, 929–939.

Everly, G. S., Flannery, R. B., & Eyler, V. A. (2002). Critical incident stress management (CISM): A statistical review of the literature. *Psychiatric Quarterly, 73*, 171–182.

Furlong, M., Babinski, L., Poland, S., Munoz, J., & Boles, S. (1996). Factors associated with school psychologists' perceptions of campus violence. *Psychology in the Schools, 33*, 28–37.

Furlong, M., Morrison, G., & Pavelski, R. (2000). Trends in school psychology for the 21st century: Influences of school violence on professional change. *Psychology in the Schools, 37*, 81–90.

Goals 2000 Educate America Act. Pub. L. 103-227. (March 31, 1994). §§ 101 and 102 of the Act are codified as 20 USC 5811 and 5812. Retrieved November 18, 2009, Available http://lamar.colostate.edu/~hillger/laws/goals-2000.html.

Horner, R., Sugai, G., Todd, A., & Lewis-Palmer, T. (2005). School-wide positive behavior support. In L. M. Bambara & L. Kern (Eds.), *Individualized support for students with problem behaviors: Designing positive behavior plans*. New York: Guilford Press, pp. 359–390.

Hoven, C. W., Duarte, C. S., Wu, P., Erickson, E. A., Musa, G. J., & Mandell, D. J. (2004). Exposure to trauma and separation anxiety in children after the WTC attack. *Applied Developmental Science, 8*, 172–183.

Improving America's Schools Act of 1994, Retrieved H. R. 6. November 18, 2009, Available http://www.ed.gov/legislation/ESEA/toc.html.

Johnson, K. (1993). *School crisis management: A hands-on guide to training crisis response teams*. Alameda, CA: Hunter House.

Klingman, A., & Ben-Eli, Z. (1981). A school community in disaster: Primary and secondary prevention in situational crisis. *Professional Psychology, 12*, 523–533.

Knoff, H. M. (2000). Organizational development and strategic planning for the millennium: A blueprint toward effective school discipline, safety, and crisis prevention. *Psychology in the Schools, 37*, 17–32.

Lindemann, E. (1944). The symptomatology and management of acute grief. *American Journal of Psychiatry, 101*, 141–149.

Lindemann, E. (1979). *Beyond grief: Studies in crisis intervention*. New York: Aronson.

Los Angeles County Office of Education, Safe Schools Center, Division of Student Support Services. (n.d.). *Managing a school crisis using the standardized emergency management system: An administrator's guide to complying with California government code 8607 (SEMS)*. Retrieved February 24, 2007, from http://156.3.254.236/lacoeweb/DocsForms/20010917013712_MSCpg19.pdf.

March, J. S., Amaya-Jackson, L., Murray, M. C., & Schulte, A. (1998). Cognitive-behavioral psychotherapy for children and adolescents with posttraumatic stress disorder after a single-incident stressor. *Journal of the American Academy of Child and Adolescent Psychiatry, 37*, 585–593.

McNeely, C. A., Nonnemaker, J. M., & Blum, R. W. (2002). Promoting school connectedness: Evidence from the National Longitudinal Study of Adolescent Health. *Journal of School Health, 72*, 138–147.

Meltzer, C. W., Biglan, A., Rasby, J. C., & Sprague, J. R. (2001). Evaluation of a comprehensive behavior management program to improve school-wide positive behavior support. *Education and Treatment of Children, 24*, 448–479.

Meyers, J., & Pitt, N. W. (1976). A consultation approach to help a school cope with the bereavement process. *Professional Psychology, 7*, 559–564.

Mitchell, J. T., & Everly, G. S. (1996). *Critical incident stress debriefing: An operations manual for the prevention of traumatic stress among emergency services and disaster workers (2nd ed. rev.)*. Ellicott City, MD: Chevron.

National Association of School Psychologists. (2000). *Standards for training and field placement programs in school psychology. Standards for the credentialing of school psychologists*. Bethesda, MD: Author.

National Association of School Psychologists. (2006). *School psychology: A blueprint for training and practice III*. Bethesda, MD: Author. Retrieved November 18, 2009, Available http://www.nasponline.org/resources/blueprint/FinalBlueprintInteriors.pdf.

Nickerson, A. B., Brock, S. E., & Reeves, M. A. (2006). School crisis teams within an incident command system. *The California School Psychologist, 11*, 63–72.

Nickerson, A. B., & Zhe, E. J. (2004). Crisis prevention and intervention: A survey of school psychologists. *Psychology in the Schools, 41*, 777–788.

O'Donnell, J., Hawkins, D., Catalano, R. F., Abbott, R. D., & Day, E. (1998). Preventing school failure, drug use, and delinquency among low-income children: Long-term intervention in elementary schools. *American Journal of Orthopsychiatry, 65*, 87–100.

Pagliocca, P. M., Nickerson, A. B., & Williams, S. (2002). Research and evaluation directions in crisis intervention. In S. E. Brock, P. J. Lazarus, & S. R. Jimerson (Eds.), *Best practices in school crisis prevention and intervention* (pp. 771–790). Bethesda, MD: National Association of School Psychologists.

Petersen, S., & Straub, R. L. (1992). *School crisis survival guide: Management techniques and materials for counselors and administrators*. West Nyack, NY: Center for Applied Research in Education.

Pfefferbaum, B., Nixon, S. J., Tucker, P. M., Tivis, R. D., Moore, V. L., & Gurwitch, R. H. (1999). Posttraumatic stress responses in bereaved children after the Oklahoma City bombing. *Journal of the American Academy of Child and Adolescent Psychiatry, 38*, 1372–1379.

Pitcher, G., & Poland, S. (1992). *Crisis intervention in the schools*. New York: Guilford Press.

Poland, S., & McCormick, J. (1999). *Coping with crisis: Lessons learned. A complete and comprehensive guide to school crisis intervention*. Longmont, CO: Sopris West.

Pynoos, R. S., Steinberg, A. M., & Goenjian, A. (1996). Traumatic stress in childhood and adolescence: Recent developments and current controversies. In B. A. van der Kolk, A. C. McFarlane, & L. Weisaeth (Eds.), *Traumatic stress: The effects of overwhelming experience on mind, body, and society* (pp. 331–358). New York: Guilford Press.

Reeves, M., Nickerson A., & Jimerson, S. (2006). *Trainer's handbook workshop #1: Prevention and preparedness: The comprehensive school crisis team*. (Available from National Association of School Psychologists, 4340 East West Highway, Suite 402, Bethesda, MD 20814).

Schneider, T., Walker, H., & Sprague, J. (2000). *Safe school design: A handbook for educational leaders: Applying the principles of crime prevention through environmental design*. Eugene, OR: ERIC Clearinghouse on Educational Management.

School Anti-Violence Empowerment Act of 2000, H. R. 1895. Retrieved November 18, 2009, Available http://frwebgate.access.gpo.gov/cgi-bin/getdoc.cgi?dbname=106_cong_bills&docid=f:h1895ih.txt.pdf.

Schools Safety Enhancement Act of 1999, H. R. 1898. Retrieved November 18, 2009, Available http://www.govtrack.us/data/us/bills.text/106/h/h1898.pdf.

Skiba, R. J., Peterson, R. L., & Williams, T. (1997). Office referrals and suspension: Disciplinary intervention in middle schools. *Education and Treatment of Children, 20*, 295–315.

Sprague, J. R., & Horner, R. H. (2006). School wide positive behavioral supports. In S. R. Jimerson & M. J. Furlong (Eds.), *Handbook of school violence and school safety: From research to practice* (pp. 413–427). Mahwah, NJ: Lawrence Erlbaum Associates.

Sprague, J. R., & Walker, H. M. (2005). *Safe and healthy schools: Practical prevention strategies*. New York: Guilford Press.

Sprague, J., Walker, H., Golly, A., White, K., Myers, D. R., & Shannon, T. (2001). Translating research into effective practice: The effects of a universal staff and student intervention on indicators of discipline and school safety. *Education and Treatment of Children, 24*, 495–511.

The No Child Left Behind Act of 2001, Pub. L. 107–110. 115 STAT. 1425. Retrieved November 18, 2009, Available http://www.ed.gov/policy/elsec/leg/esea02/107-110.pdf.

Tobin, T. J., & Sugai, G. M. (1999). Using sixth-grade school records to predict school violence, chronic discipline problems, and high school outcome. *Journal of Emotional and Behavioral Disorders, 7*, 40–53.

U.S. Department of Education. (2006). *Emergency management for schools training*. Washington, DC: Author.

U.S. Department of Education, Office of Safe and Drug-Free Schools. (2003). *Practical information on crisis planning: A guide for schools and communities*. Washington, DC: Author. Retrieved September 9, 2005, from www.ed.gov/admins/lead/safety/emergencyplan/crisisplanning.pdf.

U.S. Department of Homeland Security. (2004). *National incident management system*. Washington, DC: Author. Retrieved September 9, 2005, from www.fema.gov/pdf/nims/nims_doc_full.pdf.

Wise, P. S., Smead, V. S., & Huebner, E. S. (1987). Crisis intervention: Involvement and training needs of school psychology personnel. *Journal of School Psychology, 25*, 185–187.

Yorbik, O., Akbiyik, D. I., Kirmizigul, P., & Söhmen, T. (2004). Post-traumatic stress disorder symptoms in children after the 1999 Marmara earthquake in Turkey. *International Journal of Mental Health, 33*, 46–58.

Chapter 13
Developing Competent Written and Oral Communication

Timothy M. Lionetti and Susan Perlis

Introduction

Because of the nature and importance of the information garnered from assessment, oral and written communication is taking on an increasingly important role in the daily life of the school psychologist. In scenarios that follow, the school psychologists' task is to explain the data that answer the myriad of questions that parents or an attorney poses in an attempt to address the fears of parents for the future of their child. In either scenario, you are faced with the most daunting and difficult of all tasks that school psychologists face: explaining the results of your evaluation so that the data are useful, clear, understandable, and defensible. Any seasoned school psychologist will tell you that he/she has faced these kinds of situations with trepidation.

For instance, imagine that you have just completed an evaluation, and a meeting has been scheduled with your team and the student's parents in order to discuss the team's results. You are about to tell the parents that their child meets the criteria which identifies the child as a student with a specific learning disability, an emotional disturbance, or perhaps mental retardation. Parents frequently have misconceptions about these terms and may not know what this means for their child. Parents' minds begin to race, "What does this mean for my child's future?" "Will he go to school beyond high school?" "Can he or she get a good job?" or "Will he, or she be able to live independently?"

In another situation, you may find yourself facing a due process hearing related to the process of the diagnosis and/or educational plan for a student. You enter the court confident in the accuracy of your report. The lawyer begins his questioning by stating, "This report is flawed from beginning to end." The attorney is trying to put you on the defensive. Yet you have to stay calm and explain the report you have written. The barrage of questions continues.

As these examples illustrate, much of the need for competent communication is likely related to the number of audiences to whom these results are available. Obviously, parents and other school personnel will need to understand the results in order to make informed instructional decisions. Beyond these audiences, other psychologists, parent advocates, lawyers, and judges may have the opportunity to review the results. Misconceptions and biases within all these audiences, like the fascination and misperceptions with overall IQ, demand clear oral and written communication of results.

To further complicate parents' understandable emotional response to the results presented by the school psychologist, an evaluation report becomes part of the students permanent school file, and will follow him or her throughout their school career and perhaps beyond. As such, the initial report

T.M. Lionetti (✉)
College of Social and Behavioral Sciences, Walden University, Minneapolis, MN 55401, USA
e-mail: timothy.lionetti@waldenu.edu

T.M. Lionetti et al. (eds.), *A Practical Guide to Building Professional Competencies in School Psychology*, DOI 10.1007/978-1-4419-6257-7_13, © Springer Science+Business Media, LLC 2011

may be valuable for subsequent evaluations. The report, for example, may provide a premorbid baseline for mental illnesses that arise in adolescence, or of their cognitive functioning prior to a traumatic brain injury. Based upon the longevity of these data, the clarity and accuracy of the report are imperative to both school personnel and parents alike. The future of a child depends on the accuracy and utility of the report.

Despite the incredible importance of communicating results, a paucity of research has been conducted on the topic of report writing and oral communication of results (Groth-Marnat, 2006). The purpose of this chapter is to help school psychologists and students of school psychology to understand the importance of effective communication in general with particular emphasis on report writing due to its potential for lasting impact into the future.

What Is Communication?

It seems appropriate to define communication prior to discussing more practical aspects of written and oral communication. Wood (2004) defines communication as "a systemic process in which individuals interact with and through symbols to create and interpret meanings (p. 9)." There are four main parts to this definition that are worth further explanation. By using the term "process," Wood implies that communication is never ending, ongoing, and forever changing. Systemic means that each part of the communication chain is interrelated and affects the other. Perhaps one of the more readily identifiable ideas of the definition is the term symbols. Symbols such as the words we use or nonverbal behaviors are ambiguous or abstract representation of something else. Through this systemic process of symbols, we create meaning, the last important term in the definition. In our oral or written communications with parents, teachers, students, and others, we are trying to convey and the recipient is trying to construct meaning.

Based on the above definition, it is easy to see how school psychologists' success rests on the shoulders of communication. Our success will be based on our communication with a variety of constituencies. We will be judged as professionals on our ability to communicate, and perhaps more significantly, our ability to create helping relationships will be judged based on our communication. The remainder of this chapter is devoted to helping you develop into a more effective communicator both in writing and orally. First, this chapter will discuss effective communication. Second, a brief discussion of ethical and legal considerations ensues. Finally, a review of typical components of a written report is delineated.

Effective Communication of Results

Communication is the ability to convey one's thoughts clearly in verbal or written form. The role of the school psychologist is to review data that have been collected in a clear and understandable manner, and share the results of that data with all parties concerned. The concerned parties include school professionals, the judicial system, the medical community, and of course parents of the student under study. The results of the data collection or evaluation process will be used to create an optimum educational experience for the student. Given the emotionality of the test results in some cases, school psychologists need to be prepared to present the results in a clinical and unemotional manner so that parents will not be confused with the presentation. This should not be misconstrued to be a callous or dispassionate presentation of data, but rather continued maintenance of support of the child and parents without exhibiting inappropriate emotional responses. As advocates for students and their families, school psychologists needs to convey the information in a manner that is useful and understandable to the family.

The National Association of School Psychologists makes the following recommendations for Reporting Data and Conference Results in the association's *Professional Conduct Manual* (National Association of School Psychologists, 2000a, b, c) under Competency IV: Professional Practices – General Principles:

1. School psychologists ascertain that information about children and other clients reaches only authorized persons.

   a. School psychologists adequately interpret information so that the recipient can better help the child or other clients.
   b. School psychologists assist agency recipients to establish procedures to properly safeguard confidential material.

2. School psychologists communicate findings and recommendations in a language readily understood by the intended recipient. These communications describe potential consequences associated with the proposals.
3. School psychologists prepare written reports in such a form and style that the recipient of the report will be able to assist the child or other clients. Reports should emphasize recommendations and interpretations; unedited computer-generated reports, pre-printed "check-off" or "fill-in-the-blank" reports, and reports that present only test scores, or global statements regarding eligibility for special education without specific recommendations for intervention are seldom useful. Reports should include an appraisal of the degree of confidence that could be assigned to the information. Alterations of previously released reports should be done only by the original author.
4. School psychologists review all of their written documents for accuracy, signing them only when correct. Interns and practicum students are clearly identified as such, and their work is co-signed by the supervising school psychologist. In situations, in which more than one professional participated in the data collection and reporting process, school psychologists assure that sources of data are clearly identified in the written report.
5. School psychologists comply with all laws, regulations, and policies pertaining to the adequate storage and disposal of records to maintain appropriate confidentiality of information (pp. 28–29).

However, in addition to the information above about the specifics of writing and reporting results, NASP addresses a variety of Standards for Practice and Training covering a wide variety of domains in which school psychologists become competent. Interestingly, none of these domains specifically address effective communication. Despite not having any one specific standard that addresses communication, as one reads the Standards, you will gather that there is an underlying assumption that this skill is a prerequisite for many of the other competencies. Standard 2.2 (Consultation and Collaboration) states, "School psychologists have the knowledge and skills necessary to facilitate communication with children and youth among teams of school personnel, families, community professionals, and others" (p. 24). Blueprint III (Ysseldyke et al., 2006) more directly emphasizes the communications skills. In fact, it is considered a "Foundational Competency." The first foundational competency is Interpersonal and Collaborative Skills. This document specifies that the "school psychologist's repertoire must include the ability to communicate well and disseminate information clearly to diverse audiences" (p. 15).

As denoted by the inclusion of communication as a Foundational Competency, it is clear that communication is vital to many areas of the day–to–day functioning of school psychologists. Some areas that school psychologists must be able to use effective communication are instructional consultation, problem-solving consultation with teachers and parents, collaboration, using assistive technologies, promoting educational reform, reporting outcomes of large-scale assessments, with culturally diverse populations, and building partnerships with families. In each of these areas, basic communication skills noted before are used, but each requires special attention. Each of these topics is covered in other chapters in this volume. Suffice it to say, the list is quite extensive and encompasses a wide array of situations. The sheer amount of activities that will involve effective communication can be overwhelming to the novice practitioner. The task through our careers is to work continually toward the end goal, with hope, of becoming effective communicators.

Oral Communication

Often parents are given feedback through oral communication. This typically occurs after an evaluation or as part of a child study team meeting. A team of professionals may gather, each providing feedback about their results. However, the school psychologist is often the major player in these sessions, as he/she frequently has the bulk of the material to present. This can be a daunting situation for parents as they are in a room full of professionals who, like written reports, often present information at a level that is not easily understood by nonprofessionals. Possibly, compounding the intimidation factor is the language we use in these meetings. Parents are bombarded with information that may include professional jargon, and a base knowledge of psychometric properties are lacking. The sheer amount of information coupled with the jargon often makes it difficult for parents to question the "experts." Lavine (1986) noted other factors that may prevent effective communication. One such factor is the length of the meeting as well as the quality of the interactions. Simply stated, Lavine concluded that oral communication needs to be "demystified" and "stated in simple English" (p. 616).

Kamphaus (2005) has also cited a number of "hints" to facilitate information sharing with parents. For a full accounting of these tips, the interested reader is referred to Kamphaus. Here, a select number are presented as they are useful in communications beyond the scenario presented above with parents, and extend to teachers and other community members. First, be honest. Lack of honesty is likely to result in distrust and may damage the relationship between yourself and the parties involved both presently and in the future. Second, practice communicating with a variety of constituencies. As with any skill, practice will help you be more comfortable in the real situation. It is often difficult to provide the useful information that you have to parents and community members in a cogent fashion. The difficulty may be from nervousness, or not knowing the material sufficiently. Practice will allay your concerns as well as help find the gaps in your knowledge base. Third, use your basic counseling skills. This will convey a sense of interest and empathy that helps in building relationships. In addition to these, I add, be yourself. No one can tell you how to present information as there is no right way. There is certainly specific information that needs to be conveyed. However, as practitioners, we must develop our own sense of how to present information that is in keeping with who we are as individuals. When not internalized, communications can become stilted and robotic. Too often, students present information the way it is modeled in a class or the way a mentor has suggested. These models are useful, but are not intended to be taken wholesale. Instead, take the model and use language that you would use and in a style that is natural for you. With time, these skills will be developed and honed as your competency develops.

Legal and Ethical Implications

As is often the case, ethics and law are important aspects of our practice. Communication is no different. Although it is not the driving force for being an effective communicator, it does play an important role. This important role of law and ethics applies to written reports as they are often used in legal proceedings (Sattler 2001). As previously stated, the IDEA requires that parents are given a copy of their child's report. The NASP code of ethics also states that information is delivered in terms that are "readily understood by the intended recipient" (p. 29). The ethical code further states that reports should emphasize recommendations and interpretations and not simply test scores. This is quite a difficult task, especially for the beginning school psychologist, but seasoned practitioners are not beyond reproach in this matter. The veracity of the information is also the obligation of the school psychologist. School psychologists sign the report only when the information is deemed accurate (NASP-PPE, IV, D, #4).

Although practicum and intern supervisors are responsible to cosign reports, practicum and intern students are still responsible for signing reports and ensuring accuracy (NASP-PPE, IV, D #4). It is suggested that practicum and intern students ensure the accuracy as changes to the report should be done by the original author of the report (NASP-PPE, IV, D, #3). As previously discussed, reports should be in a language understandable to the parents, and "strive to propose a set of options that takes into account the values and capabilities of each parent" (NASP-PPE, III, C, #1, p. 20). Suggestions also need to "show respect for the ethnic/cultural values of the family" (NASP-PPE, III, C, #5). As if this is not difficult enough, the NASP ethical code also requires us to discuss outcomes with the students, as the code clearly states that students should participate in the decision-making process.

Protecting Student Information

Any discussion of reporting results necessitates a discussion of protecting the privacy of student information. Experience has shown that protecting student information is a difficult matter in the school system. It is incumbent on the school psychologist to be a leader in maintaining a student's privacy. Privacy and confidentiality in the context of this chapter is applicable to oral and written communication. The focus, however, is on written materials because of its lasting nature and its potential to be viewed by many. A full discussion of this vital topic is beyond the scope of this text and is covered in greater detail in other volumes such as Jacob and Hartshorne (2007). What follows is, however, a brief synopsis of this material.

According to Jacob and Hartshorne (2007), privacy has both ethical and legal meanings. Legally speaking, privacy has been defined by case and statutory law. Merriken v. Cressman (1973) and New Jersey v. T.L.O. (1985) are the two primary court cases that have addressed the issue of privacy. They address the right to be free from invasion of family privacy and from unreasonable search and seizures. Neither specifically address communications, but remain important as they help distinguish confidentiality from privacy. Ethically, privacy is concerned with allowing individuals the freedom to decide which personal information is to be disclosed to others. NASP's code of professional conduct also addresses privacy by encouraging psychologists to not only try but also make every effort to minimize intrusions on privacy, and to only obtain information that is needed for the provision of services (NASP-PPE, III, B, #1).

Confidentiality, on the contrary, is almost solely an ethical matter (Jacob & Hartshorne, 2007). At its core, it is a decision to not reveal any information without prior agreement from a client regarding the conditions of disclosure. However, these authors do warn that legal proceedings can be pursued in some states for breaches of confidentiality. As psychologists, we must "respect the confidentiality of information obtained during their professional work" (NASP-PPE, III, A #9). This principal further states that we cannot release information without "informed consent …except in those situations in which failure to release information would result in clear danger to the client or others" (NASP-PPE, III, A #9, p. 19).

Given this set of guidelines, it is easy to see how oral communications in consultation and written communication in the form of reports make this decision a tricky matter. In consultation with a teacher, school psychologists are advised to make clear the boundaries of confidentiality from the outset. Written communications are particularly troublesome as reports are part of the student's file. In 1974, the Family Educational Rights and Privacy Act (FERPA) was passed. FERPA specifically addresses the privacy of student records and the access to them. It is a case law how-ever, that requires the information from psychologists that is relevant to educational decisions to be placed in students' files. The concern in the school setting is that school personnel follow FERPA's restrictions which permits only those who have "legitimate educational interests" to have access to the student's file without parental or student permission. It is easy to see why school psychologists must be judicious when deciding what information to include in their reports. The next section will describe the contents of reports and as such is intended to help psychologists make judicious decisions.

Written Report Content

At first glance, one would think that report writing is easy. All that is involved is communicating the compiled data in a coherent fashion, interpreting the data, making decisions based on the data, and most importantly making suggestions on how to help. It is, however, often not so easy. Zins and Barnett (1983) stated that written reports was one of the most "underestimated problem areas facing school psychologists" (p. 219). Compounding the difficulty is that there is no consensus on how to structure the information. Similarly, some departments of education, such as Pennsylvania Department of Education, have formats that must be followed, while others do not. No matter how a report is structured, the field has come to agreement on what information should be included in reports. Typically, reports include the following information: identifying information, assessment procedures, reason for referral, background information, behavioral observations, results, summary, recommendations, and signatures.

Because of the fuzzy nature of report writing, it is not uncommon for budding school psycholo-gists to ask questions about what type of information they should include in reports. Students might ask about how to report scores if at all, which scores do I report first and which scores do I use, do I need to explain tests, and what information do I include? Seemingly, in response to these types of questions Goldfinger and Pomerantz (2010) formulated guiding questions that psychologists can ask themselves when writing reports that provide guidance and answer these common questions. They posed four guiding questions that can be used to frame reports. They are "how much back-ground information should I include, how should I organize the results of a particular method, should my report include specific test scores as opposed to summaries, and to what extent should my report incorporate behavioral observations?" In general, these authors suggest brief explanations of the tests the first time it is mentioned, and beginning with the broadest results and then other scores in decreasing order. Similarly, Goldfinger and Pomerantz suggest that there are two options for reporting scores. The writer can either include the scores with a brief explanation of them or can substitute written summaries instead of the score, and use a table of scores rather than in the text. They especially think the latter is an option if the psychologist is concerned about the reader being confused by all the numbers within the text. Indeed, the writing style should always consider the effect on the reader.

In 1983, Zins and Barnett challenged the field to write reports that "engage" the people working with a student and increase the probability that that student's needs will be met. This can be quite challenging for the writer(s) of reports, especially if one considers the readability, length, and use of tables in reports. What follows is a brief description of information typically included in each section of the report, and samples from reports are included for illustrative purposes. Also addressed in this section will be a discussion on each of the "controversial" aspects of report writing.

When writing reports, Goldfinger and Pomerantz (2009) urge psychologists to write reports for both primary and secondary audiences. According to these authors, primary audiences consist of the person to whom the report will be sent (likely the parent in school settings), and secondary audiences are all others who may read the report now or in the future. The future for school-aged children could be from preschool through age 21 years. It is the primary audience for whom the report should be written. This has large implications for the style of writing a school psychologist would choose to use. This will be discussed in more detail later. In general, school psychologists' reports must be written in a fashion that is understandable for parents and school personnel. Goldfinger and Pomerantz suggest defining the primary audience by relationship to the client and to writer the report with this audience in the forefront of your mind, but also being sure that the report is written so that the language is accessible to all.

Identifying Information

At the top of most reports and prior to any other information is delivered, the agency (e.g., school) identifies itself and will often include some statement regarding the confidentiality of the information presented. After that, this section includes information that identifies the student who has been evaluated, such as their name, age, school currently attending, and parents' name. Some may also include other demographic information such as a student's ethnicity or their address.

Assessment Procedures

In this section, a list of all procedures to gather information is delineated. For the purposes of this text, an exhaustive list of the possible procedures that would be included in this section would be unwieldy. It is not uncommon to include interviews, rating scales, cognitive tests, achievement tests, observations, or tests of personality. Most often this is written in a bulleted list and not in narrative form. Each of the categories may also have more than one and should therefore have a separate listing. For example, an interview of the parent and child is typical and should be listed separately, and not just as interviews. The following is an example of a listing of assessment procedures.

- Woodcock Johnson Tests of Cognitive Ability – Third Edition (WJ-III Cog)
- Woodcock Johnson Tests of Achievement – Third Edition (WJ-III Ach)
- Behavioral Assessment System for Children, Second Edition Parent Rating Scales-Child (BASC-2-PRS-C)
- Behavioral Assessment System for Children, Second Edition Teacher Rating Scales-Child (BASC-2-TRS-C)
- Behavioral Observations
- Student Interview
- Teacher Interview
- Parent Interview
- Record Review.

Reason for Referral

This is seems rather straight forward, and it is. Its importance, however, is significant. This reason for referral impacts the manner in which the evaluation is conducted and is often overlooked (Tallent, 1998). To help direct the evaluation, the reason for referral is often represented in the form of a question. By stating the reason for referral as a question, the problem-solving process previously discussed in Chap. 1 is begun. A question leads the school psychologist to the kinds of information needed, the types of procedures to gather that information, and then lastly to the specific procedures. Furthermore, the school psychologist should steer away from yes or no questions. For example, say, a student was referred because of attentional concerns. A likely resulting question is, "does the student have attentional problems?" Questions like this one, a "yes or no" question, will likely result in a school psychologist using procedures that will rule in or out attention problems without addressing the multitude of potential causes of inattention. In contrast, asking a broader question like "what factors are affecting the students attention?" will likely lead to varied procedures that will include information that takes into account the many factors that can contribute to inattention (e.g., depression, anxiety, cognitive factors, and environment). The reason for referral may not always be apparent and may indeed be different from the stated reason. It is wise to contact the referral source to help clarify the reason(s) for referral (Tallent, 1998). We would also suggest that one very common question that parents and school personnel have but rarely state outwardly is "what can be done to help?" Including this question will help the psychologist keep in mind that we assess to create intervention and not to diagnose.

Goldfinger and Pomerantz (2010) remind us that the referral question(s) are not always simple and straight forward. They may also not be what the stated issue of concern is either. In fact, one of the key factors that these authors include in considering the formulation of a referral question is that referral questions can be either implicit (questions that are discovered or not directly stated by the client) or explicit (clearly stated by the client). Goldfinger's and Pomerantz's contention is that the full understanding of the referral questions guides the psychologist's work.

The following excerpt from a report is provided to demonstrate what might be included in a reason for referral.

> Mr. and Mrs. Smith referred their daughter Sara for a psychological evaluation due to concerns with her reading. Sarah is struggling in reading, especially in the area of comprehension. Comprehension is also a concern in Math word problems. The Smiths are also concerned with Sara's ability to sustain effort and/or attention. Finally, Sarah's parents are concerned with the amount of time Sarah needs to complete her work. The questions to be answered are: does Sarah meet the criteria as a student with a specific learning disability, what may be causing Sarah's difficulty with reading comprehension, what factors may be impacting Sarah's attention span, and what interventions may be used to help Sarah improve academically?

Background Information

On some reports, this is referred to as relevant information. By using the word relevant, it allows school psychologists latitude to include only the information that is likely to impact interpretation. During the evaluation, the school psychologist will garner a lot of information, and all of it may not be relevant. For example, I have read reports that read like verbatim transcripts of interviews. This is not the intent of this section. Instead, it should only include information gathered that helps to make sound decisions. In addition, Teglasi (1983) suggested not including information that may invade the student's privacy. Lichtenberger, Mather, Kaufman, and Kaufman (2004) suggested a general rule: "only include information that relates to the interpretation of the person's scores or test behaviors or is relevant to the referral questions" (p. 39). Similarly, Zins and Barnet urged the exclusion of irrelevant information that "may be detrimental or which has questionable bearing on the outcomes" (p. 224). It is up to the individual to decide what information is relevant. For example, that a student broke his arm may or may not be relevant. It would be relevant if the student broke his arm when he was 5 years of age, as it may be part of a pattern of injuries due to engaging in risky behaviors. It is not likely relevant if the student is being evaluated for an enrichment program.

Information for this section is collected from a variety of sources. It typically includes information gathered during interviews of students, parents, and teachers; and a review of educational, mental health, or medical records. As a result of this data collection, the psychologist generates a significant amount of information about a student's educational, medical, developmental, family, service, and social histories. As previously discussed, more information than you need may be gathered, and only pertinent information from each source should be included (Kamphaus, 2005).

When writing this section, it is important to clarify the sources of information. For example, if a student's mother reports that her daughter is depressed, a statement such as "According to Ms. Smith, her daughter is depressed." Similarly, information from a review of records should be sure to reference that record. For example, "The report dated May 25, 2002 by Robert E. Smith, Ph.D., psychologist, indicated that Jonny is depressed." By identifying the source of information, the source's perceptions are clarified and the reader's interpretation may be altered based on to whom the statement was attributed. Kamphaus (2005) and Lichtenberger et al. (2004) provide further examples on how to clarify sources of information.

Beyond attributing statements to specific sources, organizing the background information can also be troublesome. A simple yet effective way to organize the information is by topic (e.g., development, medical, and educational). Each of these topics is usually written in separate paragraphs, with an attempt to keep each paragraph on just one topic or domain. Similarly, each paragraph generally follows in chronological order.

The following provides an example of how one paragraph within background information would read.

> Jonny anticipates attending the 12th grade at Eastern High School. According to Mrs. Smith, Jonny has attended the Eastern School District since Kindergarten after attending Kindergarten in catholic school. A second year of Kindergarten was deemed necessary as Jonny was "not ready" academically to advance to first grade. By not ready, Mrs. Smith noted that Jonny wasn't reading or grasping concepts, did not know his letter sounds, and did not know "enough" numbers. Prior to Kindergarten, Jonny attended preschool. According to Mrs. Smith, Jonny received all A's until the 8th grade. After this Jonny's grades have been mostly A's, B's and C's. Jonny has earned an F and a D the past two years in geometry.
>
> In the second grade Jonny was evaluated by the school psychologist and was identified with a specific learning disability and in need of specially designed instruction. Jonny was evaluated by Dr. Susan Williams, school psychologist, on 11/25/95. The results of that evaluation indicate that Jonny's overall cognitive functioning was in the high average range (WISC-III FSIQ = 113). His Reading and Mathematics Composite scores on the WIAT were 75 and 88 respectively. It was determined that Jonny met criteria as a student with a specific learning disability in reading and math. In addition, the evaluation noted that Jonny would benefit from counseling to help control his anxiety about academics. According to the well organized records of Mrs. Smith, no further cognitive testing has been conducted. In the third grade, Jonny was reevaluated using the Woodcock Reading Mastery Test on 2/28/97.

Behavioral Observations

In this section, the psychologist reports observations made during the testing situation and in other settings. Both provide important information in very different settings. During the testing situation, the school psychologist is one-on-one with the student, and attempts to elicit the student's best performance with little distraction. These observations, however, may not represent typical behavior of the student in the classroom. Many assessment procedures available today (e.g., Woodcock-Johnson Tests of Cognitive Abilities) have specifically indicated the types of information to be observed. These may include, attention span, activity level, appearance, distractibility, language use, mood, response to failure, persistence, cooperation, and rapport.

Observations outside the formal testing situation, such as in the classroom, or during recess are also included in this section. Behavioral observations of this kind can be obtained in a structured format, such as the Behavioral Observation of Students in Schools (Shapiro, 2003) or the State-Event Classroom Observation System (Saudargas, 1997), or in narrative form. The advantage to using published observation codes is their reliability and validity. The down side is that one must be trained in the specific code. Of course, school psychologists can also create their own structured observation codes. The interested reader is referred to Shapiro & Kratochwill (2000) to learn more about developing observational codes. These observations are vital as they provide additional information about how the student interacts in and acts upon their environment.

As before, only include those observations that are useful in understanding the student. Lichtenberger et al. (2004) suggest including observations that are consistent, and leaving out those that are isolated, or not substantiated by other data. After you have decided which observations to include, be sure to back up your observations with specific examples. Providing examples helps the reader gain a clearer picture of the student.

Test Results and Interpretation

This section is one of the most important of all sections as decisions often rely heavily on the gleaned from standardized tests. Here is where the test results from standardized testing such as cognitive ability tests, tests of achievement, and data from behavioral ratings scales are reported and explained. Generally, writing information from each type of assessment instrument follows a sequence. First, an explanation, or introduction of the instrument is given. This does not need to be long, but should include the purpose of the test and some explanation of the kinds of scores. By doing so, the reader can get a sense of the scores' meaning. Of course, you will be describing the scores in greater detail. After the general description, the sequence is usually from the broadest scores to the narrower scores. For example, on a cognitive assessment instrument, the global or full-scale score is generally followed by composite scores and then individual test or subtest scores. Standard scores, percentile rank, and confidence intervals are usually included. In addition to the scores, be sure to define your terms. Beginning school psychologists often assume the reader has some understanding of terms. A statement like "Johnny's Verbal Comprehension Index score is in the average range," will not be clear to many audiences. Instead, include a simple definition. For example, "Johnny's Verbal Comprehension Index, or his general fund of information, is in the average range" is likely to be understood by a variety of audiences. This is at first difficult to do, but with experience it becomes more common place. Although this is common practice, the debate continues regarding the interpretation of any score beyond the Full Scale IQ or global score. Ipsative or subtest scatter analysis has received significant attention in the past. It is beyond the scope of this chapter to review this debate. Suffice it to say, some absolutely discourage the practice, McDermott, Fantuzzo, and Glutting (1990), for example, wrote an article entitled "Just say no to subtest analysis." Others, however, have taken exception to this line of research (Hale, Fiorello, Kavanagh, Hoeppner, & Gaither, 2001).

What follows is an excerpt from a report that follows the pattern described above, reporting the broadest scores first followed by narrower scores using data from the Wechsler Individual Achievement Test-Second Edition.

Results from the WIAT-II revealed Suzie's overall reading skills to be within the Average range (Reading Composite = 101, 53rd percentile). Her word reading and word decoding skills were efficient (Word Reading = 104, 61st percentile). She used multiple strategies to identify words (e.g., sight word knowledge, phonological decoding); however, for most of the words presented, she read them automatically from sight knowledge. When she needed to use decoding skills for unfamiliar words, her phonetic decoding was efficient and within the High Average range (Pseudoword Decoding = 118, 88th percentile). In contrast to her strong word knowledge skills, Suzie had trouble with reading comprehension. While her score remains in the lower portion of the Average range (Reading Comprehension = 90, 25th percentile), this was observably a more difficult task for her. The reading comprehension test was comprised of passages that Suzie had to read and then answer orally presented questions

Summary

As the name implies, this section is an overview of the major findings of your evaluation results. This chapter should be used to help the reader understand the conclusions you have drawn. Beginning report writers often simply rehash the test results. This is not the intended purpose of this section. Information from all data sources (e.g., record reviews and interviews) is included and synthesized. Teachers have been found to not garner much information from test data (Ysseldyke & Mirkin, 1982), but are interested in your professional opinion about the synthesis of the data (Salvano & Teglasi, 1987). The reader should be able to follow your thinking in how you came up with the conclusions. Goldfinger and Pomerantz have created a matrix to help organize and integrate the data into domains of functioning. The interested reader is referred to the source for a complete description of this tool. Unfortunately, *all* the data do not always fit with your conclusions and, in fact, some may even be contradictory. Your job is to resolve the contradictory data using your judgment. This is difficult because multiple sources of data often do not coincide for a number of reasons. These reasons include data are inaccurate, information may be unreliable, differences exist between reporters on rating scales, and the impact of syndromes are inconsistent (Goldfinger & Pomerantz). Several suggestions were offered to deal with inconsistent data. These include throw out unreliable or invalid data, look at patterns of data and make inferences, check the research literature, pay attention to situational factors, and do not feel obligated to make definitive statements (Goldfinger & Pomerantz).

In addition, beginning report writers often include new information that has not been included before. Kamphaus (2005) bluntly and plainly states to not include new information in the summary. Including new information in the summary may be confusing. Readers should be able to identify the source of the information from the previous sections of the report. Interestingly and anecdotally, there is a recent trend of leading the full report with a summary report. Leading with a summary may increase the likelihood of it being read, as report length is a concern as discussed later in this chapter.

Finally, the summary should answer the referral question(s). To answer the question(s), it is the clinicians' responsibility to sort out and analyze the data. Goldfinger and Pomerantz liken this part of the process to a jigsaw puzzle, as the psychologist requires logical analysis of the patterns of data and keeps in mind the purpose of the evaluation.

The following is an excerpt from a summary that illustrates inclusion of a variety of data and resolving of contradictory information.

Regarding the question of inattention, John continues to meet the criteria for ADHD, combined type. This diagnosis is justified based on his history of hyperactivity and inattention throughout his school and home life. The results of both the student and parent structured interview met DSM-IV criteria for ADHD. In addition, the results of two structured observations revealed John to be on task a significantly lower percentage of the intervals. On both the broadband and narrowband measures, his mother consistently rated John as having significant difficulties with attention and hyperactivity-impulsivity. Similarly, the house parent's ratings on the broadband measure also indicated that John has difficulty sustaining attention. Contrary to the majority of the evidence, the teacher's and house parent's ratings on the narrowband scale are not indicative of those students with ADHD. However, John has primarily been observed while on psychostimulant medication, both in the class and in the student home. The low ratings by the teacher and house parent may be a reflection of the utility of the medication.

Recommendations

Because the point of evaluating students is to help, this section takes on primary importance. Oddly enough, some reports exclude recommendations, leaving treatment suggestions up to staff who did not conduct the evaluation or may not have training in data-based decision making. As a psychologist, recommendations based on your data should always be included by you. This seems self-evident, but sadly it is not always the case. Similarly, recommendations are often too broad or nonspecific for the treatment provider to implement. The lack of specificity is likely to result in an intervention being implemented, if at all, without integrity or the way it was intended. Suppose you went to your physician for an ear infection and the doctor prescribed you an antibiotic. Typically, the prescription says something like "Take 1 tablet twice a day for the next ten days." It does not just say "Take these." Our recommendations need to be equally specific and clear (Teglasi, 1983). Goldfinger and Pomerantz offer a number of suggestions which include the following: be realistic and practical, only make recommendations within your area of expertise, cover the referral questions, and make recommendations that are appropriate to the referral source.

One difficulty beginning school psychologists may encounter is not "knowing" what interventions to suggest among the myriad of interventions that are available. Throughout your training, you will, or you have already, learned numerous interventions that have empirical support for their use. Issues such as treatment integrity, acceptability, and effectiveness become prominent when considering which intervention to suggest. Elliot, Witt, Kratochwill, and Stoiber (2002) provide an excellent review of the literature pertaining to these concerns, as well as providing other means to aid in intervention selection. The point these authors make is that all three issues must be considered when selecting an intervention to increase the likelihood that an intervention would have the desired effect. Although treated as separate entities in their discussion, each influences the other. For example, if an intervention is not acceptable to a teacher or parent, it is less likely to be implemented as planned. Similarly, an intervention's effectiveness influences its acceptability. In short, teachers prefer recommendations that are concrete and easy to implement (Salvano & Teglasi, 1987). With that said, Elliot et al. noted that perceptions will change with the type and severity of the behavior being assessed. The greater the severity, the more likely teachers will find more intensive interventions acceptable. Similarly, parents' perceived barriers/benefits of the intervention are related to intervention compliance (Human & Teglasi, 1993). An in-depth discussion of these issues is beyond the scope of this chapter. The interested reader is encouraged to read Elliot et al. for a more detailed discussion of these topics.

Despite the abundance of interventions available, no matter how long a school psychologist has been practicing, you will likely come across a case with which you are unfamiliar and do not know what interventions are effective. Remember you are learning broad-based skills, such as research skills, that can help you access interventions. Similarly, the Internet has helped tremendously and there are a number of websites that specifically address interventions (e.g., Intervention Central and What Works Clearing House). Colleagues are also a good source of information.

Signatures

Finally, the finishing touches of the report. At the end, signatures are required. In addition to signatures, one's credentials are used. This includes your level of educational attainment and other titles such as practicum student or intern. If you are a student, your immediate supervisor will also sign the reports. Remember, however, that as a student or intern, you are obligated to the same guidelines and ethical principals as your supervisors. It is incumbent on you, therefore, to insure the accuracy of your work.

Controversial Aspects of Report Writing

As previously stated, there is widespread agreement on what is included in the reports. There still exists, however, some aspects of report writing that do not have wide spread agreement. Some of these areas include use of tables, computer generated reports, length, inclusion of test scores, and readability (for a comprehensive review, see Groth-Marnat & Horvath, 2006). The purpose of this section is go beyond what is included in reports, and should be considered additional guidelines for improving your written communication.

Readability

The importance of writing clear psychological reports was underscored when the Family Educational Rights & Privacy Act of 1974 and the Education of All Handicapped Act of 1975 expanded the conditions under which parents can view reports. At this point in time, school personnel routinely give reports to parents as well as one place in the student's file. Not only are parents entitled to the reports, but many parents have difficulty in reading reports written at a high level. According to the US Bureau of Census (1994), approximately 72% of parents of children referred for psychological services are unlikely to read above a 12th grade level. Harvey (1997), however, found that reports are often written at a level higher than 12th grade in schools and other settings. Similarly, in 1984, Weding found that the mean grade reading level of reports was 14.66. Reports in school settings, on average were written somewhat above the 13th grade level. This result was found for practitioners at the doctoral and master's level.

There are a number of possible reasons why psychological reports are written at such high levels. Harvey (1997) suggested that psychologists may be trying to bolster their prestige by writing at high levels. Psychologists may also think that other professionals are their primary audience when in fact they are not. Harvey also pointed out that the level of readability may be related to their level of education. Given that less than 10% of the population obtains a graduate degree, it is likely that psychologists' writing level is commensurate with their education, and is above many parents who are their primary audience.

The good news is that making reports readable so that they are understood by a wide variety of readers is a goal that can be readily achieved. Training programs often focus on oral communication, but provide less in report writing. As a result Lavine (1986) and Harvey (1997) suggested that the writing of readable reports must first be addressed at the graduate level. Shortening sentence length, and minimizing difficult words and jargon help reduce the readability. Kamphaus (2005) and Sattler (2004) have also made the same suggestion. Other opportunities to reduce readability include, rereading and rewriting your reports. It may be helpful to seek feedback from clients, peers, or faculty about your reports (Ownby, 1987). Specifically, have these groups read your reports, and seek comments about the readability. Readability statistics are also available in most word processing programs. Providing students with opportunities to "reduce the density" of their reports can involve having them rewrite their own reports, and/or providing students with models of sample reports at a variety of readability levels. An exercise that can be utilized is to review the reports and purposely attempt to decrease the readability without compromising necessary/relevant information.

Computer Generated Reports

Technological advances continue to aid many of the areas of school psychological practice (see Chap. 7 in this volume), and report writing is no different. Many new assessment procedures have the capability to be scored by computer (e.g., Wecshler Intelligence Scale for Children-Fourth

Edition) and some must be scored by computer (e.g., Woodcock-Johnson Tests of Cognitive Abilities-Third Edition). In addition to scoring, many of these computer programs generate a report. These reports vary in comprehensiveness, but can lead to cutting and pasting the entire computer generated report into the final written report. Besides ethical concerns (NASP-PPE, III, E #3), concerns of interpretive accuracy, length, and practitioner overreach are raised by such a practice (Lichtenberger, 2006). Because of perceived accuracy of computers, psychologists may assume the interpretation is equally accurate. However, researchers have questioned the validity of these interpretations (Garb, 2000). Because of this perceived accuracy of computers, the concern of overreach is raised as we may be tempted to use procedures that are beyond our expertise. Finally, Lichtenberger noted that computer generated reports also can be lengthy as they tend to generate too much information. Despite the potential problems with computer generated reports, they are here to stay and Groth-Marnat and Horvath (2006) remind us that we are responsible for the content and interpretation of our reports no matter how these are generated.

Length

There exists considerable variation in the length of reports. Donders (2001) reported that the average length of a psychological report is between 5 and 7 pages, single spaced. Many, however, are much longer. The length of a report may depend on the setting in which it is written, and may depend on the orientation of the psychologist (Groth-Marnat & Horvath, 2006). Reports that are too long may not be read or understood by parents and/or teachers. Reports that are too short may not include sufficient information to be useful in making recommendations. The dilemma for a school psychologist then is to strike a balance between including enough information so that the reports are of use, and being read by various audiences.

As previously mentioned, Pennsylvania, like other states, has a prescribed evaluation report format that school systems are required to use. The form is 5 pages in length prior to any data being imported or typed. As a result, an Evaluation Report (ER) in Pennsylvania is likely to be lengthy, and it is not unforeseeable that ERs in Pennsylvania will be longer than the average length of reports. Length, however, is related to the above discussion on readability and the need to keep in mind the potential audiences who may read the report. Based on this dilemma, some have adopted writing a summary report in addition to the full length report as noted above.

Inclusion of Test Scores

One contributing factor to the overall length of the report is the decision to include test data. Often, test scores are included in text as part of the narrative, and in a table. Sometimes the tables are included in the body of the report and other times, the tables are appended. At the heart of this controversy, however, is the extent to which potential readers will misinterpret the data.Matarazzo (1995) believes that including test data is helpful to other psychologists, while others caution that non-psychologists will misinterpret the data especially if the scores are "meaningful to the general public" (Groth-Marnat & Horvath, 2006), such as IQ scores. These authors also caution including test data because psychologists may misinterpret the data in the absence of data from other sources of information.

Building Professional Competence

The importance of continued professional development of skill sets for good written and oral communication reports cannot be minimized. As difficult as it is at first it is a skill that you will develop and with which you will become comfortable as you practice, gaining experience through supervision and consultation with other psychologists (Goldfinger & Pomerantz, 2009). Imbedded in these skill sets for written and oral reports is the development of exceptional intercultural skills and overall cultural competence. The NASP website has extensive information available for developing your own cultural perspective as well as enhancing your understanding of others cultural perspectives. Attend as many seminars and in-service trainings on the groups that are represented in your school district, or geographical area. Talk to parents and be open with them. Ask them questions to gain as much information as possible and whenever possible, ask them for their approval. A question as simple as "Will this work at home for Michaela?" could open the discussion. Ask questions about how the suggested intervention will fit within their daily family life and if it poses any problems. Be prepared to revisit your plan in a short timeframe to see if the plan needs some adjusting. Be open to the cultural realities of others by first understanding your cultural perspectives or world view. Once you clearly understand how you see the world, you can better understand how others who do not share your race, gender, religion, socioeconomic status, or sexual orientation see their world. Then, be willing to work together to create the best plan for the success of the child.

Conclusions

The purpose of this chapter is to provide a basis for effective oral and written communication with an emphasis on written communication. The emphasis has been on writing reports, as it is often the most visible and long-lasting form of communication. The potential for public scrutiny and perhaps legal scrutiny makes written communication an important competency for the school psychologist to develop. Ethical and legal implications abound, as well as other concerns such as readability make this skill difficult to develop. Compounding the issue is the scarce research on the topic, and training programs often do not spend a significant amount of time on this competency. Yet, oral and written communication underlies most of our work. The underlying tone of many of NASP's standards assumes that this skill set is developed and Blue Print III has included it as a foundational competency. Communication will continue to be one of the most important skills in the future. As we become more technologically advanced, we are likely to become more reliant on these technologies (see Chap. 14). Computer scoring software and computer generated reports are likely to become more commonplace. It is up to each of us to continue to develop our communication skills and to keep up with advancing technologies while keeping in mind our readers and ethical concerns that arise from such practices. In the end, effective communication is often a skill that school psychologists are assumed to possess. It is, however, a skill that must be learned in order to be an effective communicator. This chapter is intended to promote the process of becoming competent communicators. Table 13.1 is a top ten list of ways to be an effective communicator either orally or in writing.

Table 13.1 Top ten ways to be effective communicators

1. Be yourself/genuine
2. Listen
3. Convey Understanding
4. Avoid use of jargon & Explain Terms/Acronyms
5. Increase Readability of reports
6. Include relevant information only
7. Assure Confidentiality
8. Be concise, yet thorough
9. Emphasize recommendations and interpretations
10. Review for Accuracy
11. Remember your audience(s)

Chapter Competency Checklist

DOMAIN 1 – Professional, legal ethical and social responsibility domain

Foundational	Functional
Understand and articulate:	Gain practice:
☐ Communication	☐ Reviewing reports of others and develop questions
☐ Effective Communication of Results	
☐ Cultural Competence	☐ Writing results of psychological assessments
☐ Oral Communicating	☐ Receiving feedback on written reports
☐ Purpose of psychoeducational reports	☐ Writing different types of psychological reports
☐ Legal mandates for written reports	☐ Evaluating the range and types of students with whom you work
☐ Ethics concerning reporting results of psychological evaluations	
☐ Ethics concerning protecting student information	☐ Observing oral communication of results completed by others
☐ Content of Reports of psychological evaluation reports	☐ Delivering oral results to others and receive feedback
☐ Controversial aspects of report writing	

References

Donders, J (2001). A survey of report writing by neuropsychologists, II: Test data, report format, and document length. *The Clinical Neuropsychologist, 15,* 150–161.

Education for All Handicapped Children Act of 1975, Pub. L. 94-142 (20 U.S.C. and 34 C.F.R.).

Elliot, S. N., Witt, J. C., Kratochwill, T. R., & Stoiber, K. C. (2002). Selecting and evaluating classroom interventions. In: M. A. Shinn, H. M. Walker, G. Stoner (Eds.). *Interventions for academic and behavior problems II: Preventive and remedial approaches.* Bethesda, MD: National Association of School Psychologists.

Family Educational Rights and Privacy Act of 1974, Pub. L. 93-380 (U.S.C. and 34 C.F.R.).

Garb, H. N. (2000). Computers will become increasingly important for psychological assessment: Not that there is anything wrong with that! *Psychological Assessment, 12,* 31–39.

Goldfinger, K. & Pomerantz, A.M. (2010). Psychological assessment and report writing. Los Angeles, CA:Sage

Groth-Marnat, G., & Horvath, L. S. (2006). The psychological report: A review of current controversies. *Journal of Clinical Psychology, 62,* 73–81.

Groth-Marnat, G. (2006). Introduction to the special series on psychological reports. *Journal of Clinical Psychology, 62,* 1–4.

Hale, J. B., Fiorello, C. A., Kavanagh, J. A., Hoeppner, J. B., & Gaither, R. A. (2001). WISC-III predictors of academic achievement for children with learning disabilities: Are global and factor scores comparable? *School Psychology Quarterly, 16,* 31–55.

Harvey, V. S. (1997). Improving readability of psychological reports. *Professional Psychology: Research and Practice, 28,* 271–274.

Human, M. T., & Teglasi, H. (1993). Parents' satisfaction and compliance with recommendations following psycho-educational assessment of children. *Journal of School Psychology, 31*, 449–467.

Jacob, S., & Hartshorne, T. S. (2007). *Ethics and law for school psychologists.* Hoboken, NJ: Wiley.

Kamphaus, R. W. (2005). *Clinical assessment of child and adolescent intelligence.* NY: Springer.

Lavine, J. L. (1986). De-mystifying professional evaluations. *Academic Therapy, 21*, 615–617.

Lichtenberger, E. O. (2006). Computer utilization and clinical judgment in psychological assessment reports. *Journal of Clinical Psychology, 62*, 19–32.

Lichtenberger, E. O., Mather, N., Kaufman, N., & Kaufman, A. S. (2004). *Essentials of assessment report writing.* Hoboken, NJ: Wiley.

Matarazzo, R.G. (1995). Psychological report standards in neuropsychology. The Clinical Neuropsychologist, *9*, 249–250.

McDermott, P. A., Fantuzzo, J. W., & Glutting, J. J. (1990). Just say no to subtest analysis: A critique on Wechsler theory and practice. *Journal of Psychoeducational Assessment, 8*, 290–302.

Merriken v. Cressman, 364 F. Supp. 913 (D.C. E.D. Pa 1973).

National Association of School Psychologists. (2000a). *Professional conduct manual: Principles for professional ethics and guidelines for the provision of school psychological services.* Bethesda, MD: Author.

National Association of School Psychologists (2000b). *Standards for training and field placement programs in school psychology. Standards for credentialing of school psychologists.* http://www.nasponline.org. Accessed 21 May 2007.

National Association of School Psychologists (2000c). Principles for professional ethics. Guidelines for the provision of school psychological services. *Professional conduct manual* (pp. 13–62). Bethesda, MD: Author. Available from: http://www.nasponline.org

New Jersey v. T.L.O. 469 U.S. 325 (1985).

Nuijens, K. L., & Klotz, M. B. (2004). *Culturally competent consultation in schools: Information for school psychologists and school personnel.* National Association of School Psychologists. http://www.nasponline.org.

Ownby, R. L. (1987). *Psychological reports: A guide to report writing in school psychology* (2nd ed.). Brandon, VT: Clinical Psychology Publishing Company.

Sattler, J. M. (2001). *Assessment of children: cognitive applications* (4th ed.). San Diego, CA: Author.

Sattler, J. M. (2004). *Assessment of children: Cognitive applications* (5th ed.). San Diego, CA: Author.

Salvano, M., & Teglasi, H. (1987). Teacher perceptions of different types of information in psychological reports. *Journal of School Psychology, 25*, 415–424.

Saudargas, R. A. (1997). *State-Event Classroom Observation System (SECOS). Observation manual.* Knoxville: University of Tennessee.

Shapiro, E.S. & Kratochwill, T.K. (2000). Behavioral assessment in schools, second edition: Theory, research, and clinical foundations. NY: The Guilford Press.

Shapiro, E. S. (2003). Behavioral observation of students in schools. In E. S. Pearson Shapiro, & T. R. Kratochwill (Eds.) (2000). *Conducting school-based assessments of child and adolescent behavior.* New York, NY: Guilford.

Tallent, N. (1998). *Psychological report writing.* Englewood Cliffs, NJ: Prentice Hall.

Teglasi, H. (1983). Report of a psychological assessment in a school setting. *Psychology in the Schools, 20*, 466–479.

US Bureau of Census (1994)

Weding, R. R. (1984). Parental interpretation of Psychoeducational reports. *Psychology in the Schools, 21*, 477–481.

Wood, J. T. (2004). *Communication theories in action: An introduction* (3rd ed.). Belmont, CA: Wadsworth/Thomson Learning.

Ysseldyke, J. E., & Mirkin, P. K. (1982). The use of assessment information to plan instructional interventions: a review of the research. In C. R. Reynolds & T. B. Gutkin (Eds.), *The handbook of school psychology.* New York: Wiley.

Ysseldyke, J. E., Burns, M., Dawson, P., Kelly, B., Morrison, D., Ortiz, S., et al. (2006). *School psychology: A blueprint for training and practice III.* Bethesda, MD: National Association of School Psychologists.

Zins, J. E., & Barnett, D. W. (1983). Report writing: Legislative, ethical, and professional challenges. *Journal of School Psychology, 21*, 219–237.

Chapter 14
Using Advancing Technologies in the Practice of School Psychology

Dan Florell

Technology, broadly defined, is applying scientific knowledge to practical tasks. Technology use is rapidly increasing in a variety of work settings, including the areas of education and psychology (Czaja, Charness, Fisk, Nair, Rogers, & Sharit, 2006). Starting with the rapid adoption of personal computers in the 1980s, advanced technologies (e.g., computers) have made a significant impact on the practice of school psychology. The early use of computers allowed school psychologists to more efficiently complete assessment reports and reduced the need to laboriously rewrite common sections of reports. The early experience of those who adopted personal computers in the 1980s encapsulates the promise of advanced technologies for education and more specifically for school psychology.

Advanced technology magnifies and enhances any practice that it touches. Though the term advanced technologies is fairly generic, it tends to refer to items that use electronic devices to enhance our productivity and communication capacity. As such, it can be a school psychologist's best friend provided that it is used in an optimal manner. Advanced technology has made school psychologists more productive and efficient in all areas of the field including assessment, consultation, and intervention. Immense amounts of information can be stored and modified in computers, thus both time and money are saved. Computers and related technology are less prone to computational errors than humans, and communication between clients and professionals is much more feasible with the use of technology. However, technology brings in a host of problems that stand in the way of increased efficiency. Such problems include legal and ethical issues that clearly must be addressed by the school psychologist (Harvey & Carlson, 2003). Such issues will be a part of the present, and will inevitably be a part of the future of school psychology (Macklem, Kalinsky, & Corcora, 2000).

The need for school psychologists to be proficient in advanced technologies has slowly become an expectation in various domains of practice. The first Blueprint for Training of School Psychologists published in 1984 did not mention technology as an influential domain of practice for school psychology (Ysseldyke, Reynolds, & Weinberg, 1984). By the time Blueprint-II was released in 1997, the importance of technological competence was more evident. By 1997, most school psychologists were using computers to write reports, score protocols, communicate with other school personnel, and find clinical information on the Internet. Though technological competence was noted as being one of the changes in the field and an important component in the training of school psychologists, it still was not considered an essential part of practice (Ysseldyke, Dawson, Lehr, Reschly, Reynolds, & Telzrow, 1997). However, the increased technology usage by school psychologists was noted in the release of the National Association of School Psychologist's (NASP)

D. Florell (✉)
Eastern Kentucky University, Richmond, KY 40475, USA
e-mail: Dan.Florell@EKU.EDU

T.M. Lionetti et al. (eds.), *A Practical Guide to Building Professional Competencies in School Psychology*, DOI 10.1007/978-1-4419-6257-7_14, © Springer Science+Business Media, LLC 2011

Standards for the Provision of School Psychological Services, which specifically endorsed technological support for school psychologists (NASP, 1997). In between the second and third editions of the Blueprint, the Futures Conference was held to discuss what school psychologists' jobs would look like in the future. One of the themes from the conference was "the use of technology as a tool for dissemination and communication" (Dawson, Cummings, Harrison, Short, Gorin, & Palomares, 2004). The use of technology was noted as having the powerful ability to shape school psychologists future job descriptions. Blueprint-III acknowledged the increased importance of technological competence by making it a foundational competency. The foundational competencies are essential skills that support all of the other competency domains. Technological Applications is included because technology has quickly become embedded into every aspect of school psychological practice (Ysseldyke et al., 2006).

The remainder of this chapter will focus on how school psychologists decide to adopt new technology into their jobs. Based on the diffusion of innovation and technology adoption models, two categories of advanced technology competencies will be presented. The first type of competency highlights essential technological competence for today's school psychologists. The second type focuses on emerging technological competence for the practice of tomorrow. The integration of these technological competencies into school psychologists' practice will be presented, including a look into the future of technology usage in school psychology.

Review of Relevant Literature

One of the most important changes in work settings is the use of computers and, in particular, the Internet. Even though the Internet has been implemented in workplaces rapidly, little guidance has been given as to how computers and the Internet should integrate into a professional's work routine. Since technology is continually advancing, it is helpful to have a framework in mind before school psychologists decide to adopt a new technology into practice.

There are two particular models that can assist practitioners in deciding upon adoption of new technology. The first model is the diffusion of innovations paradigm, which assists in providing an explanation of why a new technique is accepted or rejected by a specific population. According to Rogers (2003), there are five characteristics of innovation that influence the adoption decision. The first, *relative advantage* is when an innovation is perceived as more useful than that which came before. The second is *compatibility* in which the innovation is consistent with existing practices and needs. *Complexity* is the third characteristic and refers to the ease of use of the innovation. Fourth is *observability*, where the innovation is shown to have value to others. The fifth characteristic is *trialability*, which is the extent a person can experiment with the innovation on a limited basis.

These five characteristics can apply to school psychologists' adoption of technology. An example would be the adoption of the word processor. The first school psychologists who used word processing programs found that they were quicker and easier to use than using a typewriter to write a report (relative advantage). The computer and word processing program resembled the typewriter as it had the same keyboard and did many of the same functions (compatibility). As word processing evolved, it became easier to use (complexity). This led school psychologists to see how more efficient school psychologists were in writing their reports (observability), which led to those school psychologists who were not using the word processing program to try it out (trialability). Soon, all school psychologists were writing reports using word processing programs.

The second model is the Technology Adoption Model (TAM; Davis, 1989). TAM narrowed the five characteristics of the diffusion of innovations to two characteristics that impact a person's attitude and behavior towards adopting new technology. The first characteristic of TAM is *perceived usefulness*, which closely parallels *relative advantage* in the diffusion of innovations model.

Table 14.1 Questions to ask before adopting a new advanced technology

1. How will this technology help me do my job better?
2. How much time will I need to devote to learn this technology?
3. Have I seen this technology used before by other school psychologists?
4. Have I tried the new technology and found it useful?
5. Is the new technology consistent with best practice standards?
6. What is the cost of adopting the new technology?

If the new technology will help increase productivity, not take long to learn, generally easy to use, relatively low cost, and is consistent with best practices, then adoption should be considered

The other characteristic of TAM is *perceived ease of use*, which parallels the *complexity* characteristic in the diffusion of innovations (Davis, 1989; Vishwanath & Goldhaber, 2003). Perceived usefulness/relative advantage and perceived ease of use/complexity appear to be the most influential characteristics in a person's decision to adopt a new technology (Chau, 1996; Melenhorst, Rogers, & Bouwhuis, 2006).

The influence of the characteristics of the diffusion of innovation and TAM are reflected in Table 14.1, which presents questions that school psychologists should consider when adopting new technology. These questions, a review of the relevant literature, and my own experiences in using technology in school psychology are the basis of the next section regarding advanced technology competencies for school psychologists.

Practice Implications

Overall, the introduction of advanced technology to school psychology has had a positive impact on the field. School psychologists have been able to greatly increase their productivity and efficiency in completing assessments, designing interventions, and enhancing their consultation skills. Underlying the increased use of advanced technology is the development of the computer and the melding of the computer with communication devices. One example would be the melding of the phone and computer to result in the cell phone. There are two types of advanced technology competencies for school psychologists. The first is essential technology competencies, which consist of products that are used by most school psychologists and are needed for them to do their jobs. The second type is emerging technology competencies. These consist of relatively new products that have not enjoyed widespread use in school psychology, but have the capability to enhance school psychologists' productivity and have a positive impact on service provision. All of the following technologies cut across the various competency domains as outlined in Blueprint-III (Ysseldyke et al., 2006). Table 14.2 provides an overview of the two types of technological competencies and how they tie in with the Blueprint-III domains of competence. A brief review of the two types of technological competencies and their use in school psychology today follows.

Essential Technology Competencies

The essential technology competencies allow school psychologists to enhance their productivity. Most of these technologies have been around for over a decade, and enough school psychologists have adopted them to be considered essential competencies. In some instances, such as scoring programs for assessment instruments, it is impossible to score by hand, thus making it necessary to use computer-scoring programs. The rest of this section will give an overview of the essential technology competencies for school psychologists.

Table 14.2 The essential and emerging advanced technology competencies of school psychology and how they apply to the Blueprint-III domains of competence

BP-III domains[a]	1	2	3	4	5	6	7
Essential competencies							
Word processing				X			
Spreadsheets			X	X			
Presentation					X	X	X
Scoring programs				X			
E-mail	X	X				X	X
Web browser		X				X	X
Emerging competencies							
Cell phones	X						
PDA				X		X	X
Dictation				X			
Statistical programs			X	X	X		
Listservs	X	X				X	X
Instant messaging (IM)	X						
Voice over internet protocol (VoIP)	X						
Blogs	X	X				X	X
Social bookmarking	X				X	X	X
Real simple syndication (RSS)	X					X	X
Tracking /intervention websites				X	X	X	X

[a]School psychology: A Blueprint for training and practice-III competence domains:
1. Interpersonal and collaborative skills
2. Diversity awareness and sensitive service delivery
3. Professional, legal, ethical, and social responsibility
4. Data-based decision making and accountability
5. Systems-based service delivery
6. Enhancing the development of cognitive and academic skills
7. Enhancing the development of wellness, social skills, and life competencies

Assessment and Report Writing

Word Processing: Assessment and Report Writing

Word processing was one of the first computer applications utilized by school psychologists. Word processing programs enabled school psychologists to develop report templates, allowing flexibility to complete sections of reports as information came in. Word processing permits easy storage of reports and a way to share content with other school personnel. In independent practices, Rosen and Weil (1996) found that 69% of psychologists used word processing. In the 2007 preliminary Kentucky School Psychologist Technology (KSPT) study, I surveyed 127 school psychologists from Kentucky on their use of various technologies in practice. Of the school psychologists surveyed, 96% indicated using word processing. Most (93.7%) use the programs to create report templates. The most common word processing programs are Microsoft Word and Corel WordPerfect. Another option is Writer in Open Office, which is a free word processing program that is compatible with Word and WordPerfect. Google and other companies have recently released word processing software that allows word processing on a central server, which allows documents to be completed by multiple contributors without the need to send files back and forth via e-mail.

Scoring Programs: Assessment and Report Writing

Not long after the adoption of word processing programs by school psychologists, various test publishers began to offer scoring programs for their assessment products. The scoring programs require school psychologists to enter the raw data, which then results in a fully scored protocol with an accompanying report. Computer scoring and interpretation are available for behavior rating scales and all major objective personality, achievement, and intelligence tests. Computer scoring allows a large number of scales and composite scores to be viewed at once. Professionals generally accept these applications as valid. Rosen and Weil (1996) reported that 26% of their sample used computer-scoring programs for psychological tests. As a sign of the growth of the use of computer-scoring program, the KSPT study found that 96.8% indicated using scoring programs. Computer scoring and interpretation are useful because of the computers' capacity to calculate, apply decision rules, and to display results in many different forms, all in an accurate, reliable, and fast manner. The programs save school psychologists time, and thus increase efficiency (Murphy, 2003).

Though scoring programs were acknowledged as being useful, the report writing capabilities of these programs have caused some controversy as they generated generic reports that were not tailored to the individual student. This issue was settled as guidelines have been created and there is general agreement regarding the appropriate usage of scoring programs (Carlson & Harvey, 2004; Jacob & Hartshorne, 2003; NASP, 2000; Snyder, 2000). Today, there are assessment instruments that do not have hand scoring protocols as an option. This reliance on computer-scoring software is a natural evolution, though it leaves school psychologists at the mercy of the test publishers to have accurate scoring programs.

Interventions, Consultation, Research

Spreadsheets: Interventions, Consultation, Research

Spreadsheets are flexible programs that allow school psychologists to effectively manage data and conduct basic statistical analysis. School psychologists typically use spreadsheets to keep accountability data, track caseloads, and monitor intervention effectiveness. Some examples of activities that utilize spreadsheets include Curriculum Based Measurement (CBM), activity logs, and case management. The graphing capability of spreadsheets allows school psychologists to present data in an easy-to-understand format. For example, a school psychologist could present growth and learning curves to parents and teachers when measuring intervention effectiveness in CBM. It could also make school psychologists aware of how they are spending their time by creating a pie chart regarding the percent of time spent in assessment, consultation, and intervention activities. The KSPT study indicated that 73.2% of school psychologists use spreadsheet software. The most common spreadsheet programs are Microsoft Excel and Corel Lotus. Calc in Open Office and Docs & Spreadsheets offer a free alternative to Excel and Lotus.

Presentation: Interventions, Consultation, Research

Presentation software allows school psychologists to present information in a visually appealing manner that is often lacking when presenters use overheads or other projection means for their information. The software also allows for the integration of text, pictures, audio clips, and video clips (Cummings, 2002). In addition, presentation software can be uploaded to web sites and become continuing education modules. This allows for presenters to train and inform many more people than would be possible in a single training session. An example of this capability would be presenting on Functional Behavior Assessments (FBA) at the beginning of the school year for all special education personnel. However, some personnel are hired after the training. With presentation software, the training can be put on a school's website and even include comprehension questions at the end of the training to ensure that the new school personnel have understood the material. The most common presentation software is Microsoft PowerPoint. Impress in Open Office is a free alternative to PowerPoint. The KSPT study indicates that 81.4% of school psychologists use PowerPoint for their trainings and presentations.

E-mail: Interventions, Consultation, Research

E-mail was one of the first Internet capabilities used widely. School psychologists are able to communicate and consult with colleagues worldwide. Previously, they would need to call and hope that the colleague was available. The information could also be disseminated to multiple colleagues for little expense (Cummings, 2002; Kanz, 2001; Kruger, Maital, Macklem, Weksel, & Caldwell, 2002). All of the school psychologists on the KSPT survey indicated that they used e-mail to consult with colleagues. In addition, e-mail allowed for the sharing of documents and other information. E-mail is widely available through both desktop and Internet applications. The advantage of Internet applications such as Google's Gmail and Microsoft's Hotmail are that they are available wherever a school psychologist has access to the Internet and not bound to a particular computer.

Web Browser: Interventions, Consultation, Research

The web browser allows school psychologists to access the relatively unlimited information on the Internet. The browser allows for users to access websites and be continually updated on the latest information on a variety of topics. Almost all (97.6%) of the school psychologists in the KSPT study were provided Internet access by schools. Today's browsers all have the same basic forms and functions, but less popular browsers can create problems with some website content. The most common web browsers are Microsoft's Internet Explorer, Mozilla's Firefox, and Apple's Safari.

Emerging Technology Competencies

Emerging technology competencies differ from essential competencies in a couple of ways. First, emerging competencies are relatively new developments. Most of the essential competencies are well established, and have typically existed for well over a decade. Second, emerging technologies have not been adopted by as many school psychologists as the essential technologies. The lone exception is the use of cell phones, which will be addressed later. Each emerging competency has the potential to be an essential competency in the future. Some emerging competency technologies are more likely to make this move based on the promise of increasing school psychologists' efficiency and productivity. One example is the cell phone and its ability to make school psychologists available as they travel to various schools. Its increasing functionality also makes cell phones a likely candidate to move to an essential competency. Another technology that is likely to be adopted rapidly is tracking/intervention websites, due to changing legislation and legal requirements. Others competencies can enhance school psychologists' learning and information gathering capabilities. These competencies offer school psychologists opportunities to increase their awareness of new issues and options for completing continuing education requirements. Though some emerging competencies will never likely become essential technology competencies, such as blogging or Real Simple Syndication (RSS) aggregators, they are still important in the evolution of the field. The following are emerging technology competencies for school psychologists.

Dictation: Assessment and Report Writing

While not as common as other software, dictation software can allow school psychologists to dictate reports. Programs such as Dragon Naturally Speaking have evolved over the last decade to allow a 99% degree of accuracy. In addition, dictation can be up to three times faster than typing. The programs are typically integrated into word processing, spreadsheet, and web browser software (Nuance, 2007). Dictation software can greatly enhance a school psychologist's speed at writing reports and communicating via e-mail and instant messaging. Even though dictation software has been available for over a decade, only 56.3% of school psychologists reported using dictation services in the KSPT study.

Cell Phones: Interventions, Consultation, Research

Cell phones have become more prevalent in the past decade. The technology quickly replaced pagers as a way to communicate while away from home or office. The sophistication of cell phones continues to increase. In addition to using the cell phone for its basic phone capabilities, it can be used for a myriad of other tasks such as to keep a list of contacts, have a calendar of events, answer e-mail, instant message, surf the net, play songs, and take pictures and video. The use of cell phones by school psychologists increases their availability to other school personnel even when they are not in the building. According to the KSPT survey, most (91.3%) school psychologists reported using cell phones to communicate with colleagues though only 22% reported that school districts provided them with cell phones.

Personal Data Assistants: Interventions, Consultation, Research

Personal Data Assistants (PDA) were the forerunner for information storage regarding contacts, phone numbers, and addresses. They evolved into being portable computers capable of running e-mail, word processing, spreadsheet, and presentation software. The PDA gave school psychologists the ability to do practically everything they did on their computer in a device that fit into the palm of a person's hand. Scoring and observational software were also offered for PDA's. The advantage of having a small computer in the classroom while observing a child eliminates the need for transcribing observation sheets and allows for a more complex breakdown of observed behaviors. The Behavior Observation of Students in Schools (BOSS) and the BASC-2 Portable Observation Program are two examples of this type of PDA software (Harcourt Assessment, 2007; Pearson Assessment, 2007). Despite the utility of PDAs, only 22% of school psychologists reported school districts providing them in the KSPT study. The PDA and cell phone are gradually joining together in capabilities as seen in the Palm Treo and Blackberry phones.

Statistical Programs: Interventions, Consultation, Research

The use of statistical programs beyond spreadsheets is limited for practicing school psychologists. Training programs are typically where school psychologists are exposed to and use statistical programs. However, competence in the use of statistical programs will probably gain a larger role. There is an increased emphasis on empirically based interventions including ways in proving that interventions and programs are effectively treating problem behaviors. The best way to ensure that interventions are appropriately evaluated is to collect data and enter it into a statistical program for analysis. The most common statistical packages used at university training programs are SPSS and SAS (SAS, 2007; SPSS Inc, 2007).

Listservs: Interventions, Consultation, Research

Listservs are programs that allow large groups of people to communicate via a general forum. They are typically subscribed to through e-mail. The listserv then distributes a school psychologist's response to the whole group through a central server. Listservs are generally easy to respond to and usually require a simple reply to an e-mail to distribute it to the group. However, the ease of listservs can inadvertently result in having personal e-mail communications relayed to the whole listserv if a person does not carefully monitor to whom the e-mail is being sent. State school psychology associations, trainers of school psychologists, and various interest groups have all formed listservs so as to disseminate information broadly and to get feedback quickly. NASP has several special interest listservs and communities on a variety of topics, including computers and technology (see http://www.nasponline.org/communities.aspx).

Instant Messaging: Interventions, Consultation, Research

Instant Messaging (IM) is popular among the younger generation of technology users. Students in the public schools use IM frequently on their cell phones. The IM capability can allow school psychologists to send messages to others while in meetings or other venues where phone calls would be inappropriate. IM can also allow for school psychologists to quickly communicate with each other while they are at their computers and need immediate feedback on an issue. There are several instant message programs available, and many have overlapping voice over Internet protocol (VoIP) capabilities. Unlike web browsers, different instant messaging programs tend to be incompatible with one another.

Voice Over Internet Protocol: Interventions, Consultation, Research

A fairly recent technology is the ability to talk through the Internet to people who are all over the world for free. Depending on the bandwidth of the user, audio and video conferencing is possible with the right software and an inexpensive camera (Carroll, 2004; Mohamed, 2006). The use of this technology has significant implications for school psychologists practicing in rural settings as they can confer on cases, or set up supervision without having to travel long distances for face-to-face meetings (Cummings, 2002; Kanz, 2001; Rule, Salzberg, Higbee, Menlove, & Smith, 2006). Services such as Skype and Sight Speed allow for the free long distance and video conferencing capabilities.

Blogs: Interventions, Consultation, Research

Weblogs or blogs are relatively new on the Internet landscape. They are sites that allow users to keep an ongoing journal that is accessible and searchable on the Internet. School psychologists can utilize blogs to write about issues that are of a particular interest to them, such as autism or ADHD. Another example would be school psychologists writing blogs regarding frequently asked questions about situations and problems that commonly occur. Blogs are typically searchable, which allows people to find specific content quickly. There are several places to search for blog content, including Technorati, Feedster, and Blog Pulse. While blogs can be a quick resource for people of similar interests, there are a few words of caution. First, what is written on a blog is on the public domain, and the content could violate laws such as FERPA or issues of confidentiality. Second, the validity of the content found on blogs is less likely to be accurate when compared to information published in other venues.

Social Bookmarking: Interventions, Consultation, Research

Social bookmarking is the ability to keep a person's bookmarks online, and share them with others. For instance, if a school psychologist happens to be an expert in Autism and has collected a number of sites on the subject, then she could have those posted on a social bookmarking site, such as Del. icio.us, and others could access the bookmarks when seeking information on Autism. They could also contact the school psychologist and start a group with an Autism focus.

Real Simple Syndication: Interventions, Consultation, Research

Real simple syndication (RSS) allows for school psychologists to be alerted when new content is available from sites that they frequent. For instance, APA has RSS feeds available for its story headlines. A user would subscribe to the RSS feed and then access those feeds on a RSS aggregator site such as Bloglines, Google Reader, and News Gator. The use of RSS allows school psychologists to keep updated on trends in psychology and education without having to visit numerous websites continually to check for new content.

Tracking/Intervention Websites: Interventions, Consultation, Research

Tracking/intervention websites are an outgrowth of spreadsheets and information databases. The recent focus on the Response to Intervention (RTI) model in IDEA 2004 has driven a couple of websites that use spreadsheet capabilities to focus on assisting schools in tracking student academic progress. One site is the Dynamic Indicators of Basic Early Literacy Skills (DIBELS) which assesses early literacy progress and is a form of CBM. The DIBELS site provides information on setting up the program including ways to measure progress, and a data system where schools can enter data and compare the results on an individual, school, district, and/or national basis (University of Oregon Center on Teaching and Learning, 2007). Another site, AIMSweb, is similar to DIBELS but has a broader focus on early numeracy, mathematics, spelling, and written expression in addition to early literacy and reading within a CBM framework (AIMSweb, 2007). Both sites are compatible with the RTI model.

Technology Awareness: Assistive Technology: Interventions, Consultation, Research

One area that is often overlooked by school psychologists is that of assistive technologies (AT). Although AT are not considered an essential or emerging advanced technology competency for school psychologists, it is an area that school psychologists should have some knowledge of. AT are used by school psychologists to help families support their children's development and learning. AT consist of three components: adaptations and devices, services to identify adaptations and devices, and teaching children and families to use the adaptations and devices successfully. Some adaptations are low cost and generally available, while others are limited in availability and designed for specific disabilities. Low-technology items tend to be more readily available, such as bath seats, spoons, Velcro, and toys. Advanced technology devices include specialized switch interfaces, power wheelchairs, and computerized toys (Lane & Mistrett, 1996). In order for advanced technology devices to be successful, some instruction is needed for the family and child. Most research on AT describes strategies to teach activation of switch interface devices. A switch is motorically activated by the child that is tied to an outcome that results in the movement of a toy or an interaction that is believed to be reinforcing for the child (King, 1999). Computer AT devices teach children learning skills and increase their interaction with other children (Campbell, Milbourne, Dugan, & Wilcox, 2006).

While many advances have been made in public schools in the last decade to provide traditional students with access to computers and technology, the same is not true for special education students. Special education teachers are not given the training needed to teach advanced assistive technology skills to students. Assessment instruments exist that help to determine the fit between a user and the AT. One such assessment is the Matching Person and Technology (MPT) assessment process. The instrument includes a set of person-centered measures that determine the self-reported perspectives of adult consumers regarding strengths/capabilities, needs/goals, preferences and psychosocial characteristics, and the expected benefit of technology. It is given before the techno‑logy is selected in order to provide a better fit between the user and the AT (Jackson, 2003). While AT is not typically a part of a school psychologist's role in the schools, it is an important part of special education, and school psychologists should be familiar with the concepts of AT.

Professional Issue: Ethics and Law Meet Technology

While becoming competent in both the essential and emerging technology competencies is desirable, there needs to be an awareness of how ethics and law might apply when using advanced technology. Ethical concerns are a major disadvantage to advanced technology use in the field of school psychology. Psychologists are often hesitant to try new technologies, and research has shown that part of that hesitancy is attributed to ethical concerns (Murphy, 2003).

The main legal and ethical issue with technology is the assurance of confidentiality. Student confidentiality is a key part of the school psychologist's role and technology can threaten this due to its ease of use and ability to distribute information quickly (McMinn, Buchanan, Ellens, & Ryan, 1999). E-mail and other Internet communication are not private, and confidentiality of e-mail or any other Internet content is not guaranteed (Rosik & Brown, 2001; Shapiro & Schulman, 1996). The use of school district networks can create ethical problems related to confidentiality because of the availability of student files through centralized record keeping (McMinn et al., 1999). There have been several cases where the use of technology has resulted in the dissemination of confidential records. In one case, a school psychologist's reports were inadvertently moved from a school district's intranet and put onto the Internet without the school psychologist's knowledge. This type of occurrence stresses the importance of using encryption when working on confidential material. Many of the more recent computers have automatic encryption capabilities. At a minimum, school psychologists should use the 128 bit Advanced Encryption Standard (National Institute of Standards and Technology, 2001).

The Global School Psychology Network (GPSN), a website support group for school psychologists, developed a set of guidelines for participants to follow when dealing with ethical concerns. The guidelines suggest making all important decisions in face-to-face meetings; using e-mail to generate possible alternatives only; remembering that electronic phrases could be misconstrued as being critical, insulting, or dismissive; clarifying brief issues by telephone instead of using e-mail; not using identifying information; and using a computer that does not allow others to log on to your account (Macklem et al., 2000).

Technology failure in regard to record keeping is another prominent ethical concern. Computer-storage devices such as CDs, DVDs, jump drives, and hard drives have a limited life expectancy, so data are likely to be lost when the storage device eventually fails (McMinn et al., 1999). The record keeping laws of various states would dictate that the school psychologist and school district are at fault. This underlies the importance of backing up records in a secondary location in case of storage device failures. Any records kept on a computer should be protected by passwords, and the use of non-networked computers should be employed. Encrypting can also be used to avoid personal identifiers (Harvey & Carlson, 2003). School psychologists should know about the security provided by their e-mail system and inform recipients about the level of security. One can also never be sure of exactly who is receiving and sending messages on the Internet. The absence of visual or vocal cues makes it easy for someone to pose as someone else (Kruger et al., 2002; Macklem et al., 2000).

The rapid evolution of technology guarantees that there will always be new ethical questions raised. A good summary of guidelines for responsible ethical use of computer technology is provided by Harvey and Carlson (2003). The guidelines summarize ethical principles and how they apply to many of the advanced technology competencies described in this section.

Building Professional Competence

All of the essential and emerging technology competencies enable school psychologists to become more effective in the practice of school psychology. In this section, these competencies will be reviewed within the areas of school psychology practice which consists of assessment, consultation, supervision, and training (Table 14.3).

Assessment

Traditional assessment is one school psychology domain where advanced technology has become thoroughly integrated into the process. Though most assessment administrations still rely upon paper and pencil tests, advanced technology dominates the scoring of the assessment and the writing of the report. Scoring programs are used to convert the raw scores of the assessment into standard scores. Scores can also be compared to other respondents and compared between intelligence and achievement tests. Graphs as well as generic reports are created. The school psychologist takes this information, and can cut and paste parts of these reports into a report template. After the scores have been entered into the template, the school psychologist individualizes the report. After writing a summary of the findings, the school psychologist can access the Internet for possible intervention suggestions.

Even the paper and pencil assessment administration can be given on a computer. Internet-based assessments electronically calculate responses leading to rapid and practically errorless scores.

Table 14.3 Websites for building professional competence in school psychology

School psychology:
National Association of School Psychologists – http://www.nasponline.org/
School Psychology Resources Online – http://www.schoolpsychology.net
Global School Psychology Network – http://www.dac.neu.edu/cp/consult/index.html

Word processing, spreadsheets, and presentation:
Google Docs & Spreadsheets – http://docs.google.com
Open Office – http://www.openoffice.org/

Blog sites:
Technorati – http://technorati.com
Feedster – http://www.feedster.com
Blog Pulse – http://www.blogpulse.com

Real simple syndication aggregators:
Bloglines – http://www.bloglines.com
Google Reader – http://www.google.com/reader
News Gator – http://www.newsgator.com/home.aspx

Social bookmarking:
Del.icio.us – http://del.icio.us

VoIP:
Skype – http://www.skype.com
Sight Speed – http://www.sightspeed.com

Tracking/intervention websites:
DIBELS – http://dibels.uoregon.edu
AIMSweb – http://www.aimsweb.com/
Intervention Central – http://www.interventioncentral.org/
What Work's Clearinghouse – http://www.whatworks.ed.gov/

Supervision:
Internet Logging System – www.internetloggingsystem.com

Human mistakes are prevented, and feedback is immediate and completely objective. Internet assessments are convenient because they can be taken anytime and anyplace where there is an Internet connection. The advantage of conserving time is particularly valuable to the school psychologist who needs time to devote to other services, such as direct interventions (Kruger et al., 2002). One example of a computer-based assessment is the continuous performance test (CPT). CPTs use simple stimuli and response monitoring that requires automation. They are used as part of assessments for attention deficit disorders and are relatively inexpensive.

Computer-based interviews are a different type of assessment that may reduce cost, but have been criticized for having more impediments than benefits. Critics suggest that online interviews cannot be assumed to yield the same results or have the same sound psychometric qualities as traditional applications (Kruger et al., 2002; Murphy, 2003).

Part of the assessment process also entails filling out paperwork and forms for special education. Special education paperwork and forms are legendary in their complexity and length. The reduction of special education paperwork was a focus of the renewal of IDEA (Council for Exceptional Children, 2004). One way states and school districts have begun to address the paperwork is to put the forms in electronic format. Now, Individualized Education Plan (IEP) meetings can be completed electronically and stored in school district databases in virtual folders. Many possible interventions and IEP goals have been stored on district databases to allow special education teachers, regular education teachers, and school psychologists' access when creating learning goals (Wilson, Michaels, & Margolis, 2005).

Consultation

Consultation is another school psychology domain that can be impacted by advanced technology. Consultation is an indirect service delivery model that focuses on problem solving. Often, school psychologists are not allowed the amount of time they would like to perform consultations because of various factors, including not being available for face-to-face consultation due to assessment demands. The Internet, e-mail, instant messaging, and VoIP can supplement face-to-face consultation (Harvey & Carlson, 2003).

Internet communication programs such as e-mail, instant messaging, and VoIP are useful in obtaining information, monitoring the implementation and troubleshooting when problems arise. The different communication programs can work in concert with their own distinct advantages. E-mail allows for asynchronous communication which means there is no longer a need to coordinate schedules to find a meeting time. IM can allow teachers to ask quickly a series of questions that might be too time consuming to complete via e-mail. VoIP can have the feel of face-to-face interaction, which would be especially beneficial in rural settings. In addition, if messages are securely saved, they provide a way to record the consultation process. Records are important for consultation, training, and research (Kruger et al., 2002).

In the consultation and assessment process, school psychologists are often asked to find the most effective type of research-based intervention for an individual. The Internet is making that type of information much more accessible to school psychologists. Websites such as *Intervention Central*, *School Psychology Resources Online*, and the *What Work's Clearinghouse* are three examples of intervention sites that school psychologists might utilize. The speed and flexibility provided by Internet links to related resources can allow school psychologists to find an array of intervention material.

However, the sheer amount of information can become problematic as the time spent finding relevant information can be prohibitive. Another issue is accurately identifying the validity of the information on websites. There are currently no standards or regulatory agencies for psychology or education websites. Therefore, school psychologists need to pay careful attention to the source of information. Typically, government agencies and well-known non-profit organizations websites provide valid information.

Consulting and collaborating with other school psychologists increase competence and enhance school psychologists' provision of services. Unfortunately, some school psychologists, such as those in rural areas, lack access to others in the profession (Kruger et al., 2002). One way to minimize this isolation is to join an online community through listservs and websites such as the Global School Psychology Network (GSPN). The GSPN provides professional development options and resources for practitioners, including links to other sites (Macklem et al., 2000). It also allows school psychologists to join mentoring programs and to discuss professional issues with others. This type of support has been shown to have positive reactions and a high level of satisfaction from school psychologists with how much they learned from their experience (Kruger et al., 2002).

Supervised Practice

The use of technology for the provision of supervision (telesupervision) mirrors many of the techniques used by school psychologists who informally collaborate. The difference is that telesupervision is more formalized with a hierarchical relationship, while collaboration is an equal relationship. The use of telesupervision allows more frequent contact between supervisees and their supervisors when distance is an issue. Like the use of technology in consultation, the use of technology in supervision is a way to supplement face-to-face supervision. An integrated telesupervision model with four modules has been proposed by Wood, Miller, and Hargrove (2005). The first module requires supervisees to participate in both instructive and hands-on training in the various telecommunication applications that will be used for telesupervision. The supervisees will also learn the legal and ethical issues involved with telesupervision. Once the supervisees gain knowledge of and comfort with the equipment, they complete the next three modules in the order that best fits their needs. The second module includes hypothetical case studies used for practice and discussion. This module is particularly helpful in demonstrating ethical problems that might arise during practice in the schools. The third module involves group supervision by one supervisor at a separate site. Supervisors are able to work with trainees through live interactive teleconferencing. The fourth module offers traditional face-to-face supervision in the clinical setting. The telesupervision model uses a combination of e-mail, instant messaging, VoIP, web sites, and face-to-face contact to accommodate professional, legal, and ethical guidelines.

Telesupervision has been shown to lower the social inhibitions of students, eliminate communication barriers, and offer students a variety of instructional formats for supervision. Split-screen technology allows students and supervisors to observe clinical interviews, or monitor the administration of psychological assessments (Wood et al., 2005). A weakness of this approach is in the possible loss of visual cues, which could lead to depersonalized communication. Other weaknesses were previously mentioned in the ethics and law section of this chapter.

Another use of technology that provides supervision and enhanced accountability is the creation of an activity logging system for the supervisee. One such system is the Internet Logging System (ILS). ILS provides a cumulative and detailed view of the amount of time and services that the supervisee provides. It allows the collection of both qualitative and quantitative data for program evaluation, and to ensure that the supervisee is receiving a well-rounded training experience (Hinkle, 2003). The system eliminates the need for paper and pencil tracking and allows the supervisor real time access to review supervisee activities so that experiences can be monitored and if need be, modified. Supervisors and supervisees who have used ILS believe it to be a significant improvement over paper-and-pencil methods of tracking service hours, and is effective in organizing training experiences (Hinkle, 2005).

E-Learning and Continuing Education

In most states, school psychologists are required to complete a certain amount of continuing education hours. A problem arises when there is a lack of continuing education opportunities in the area, or those that are offered do not apply to the school psychologist. E-learning is an additional technology used by school psychologists to receive required training that increases their domains of expertise. E-learning focuses specifically on electronic applications like: Web-based learning, computer-based learning, virtual classrooms, and digital collaboration (Principles, 2002). The major advantages of e-learning are flexibility and timing. While problems are frequent, such as difficulties with delivering material, the demand for e-learning appears to outweigh the difficulties (Harris & Gibson, 2006). Around 56% of all nationally accredited colleges and universities offer classes through e-learning. In addition, associations such as NASP offer continuing education in a wide variety of areas. The KSPT study indicated that while few school psychologists (36.2%) have used e-learning, most (81.9%) believe they will in the next 5 years.

The impact of technology on the practice of school psychology has been significant. In the KSPT study, 84% indicated they were comfortable with using technology and 95% believe that technology helps improve their job. The outlined advanced technology competencies should ensure school psychologists with the ability to practice in an efficient and productive manner for the next few years. However, technology is a quickly changing area. The next section will discuss how technology may be used in the future.

Futures Section

The future of advanced technology use in school psychology is difficult to predict. However, there are some trends that can be identified. One trend is called Web 2.0. Web 2.0 is a phrase used to reflect the use of collaborative social networks rather than individual computers with their own programs and storage. Advances such as blogs, social bookmarking, wikis, and podcasts are all reflections of Web 2.0 (Cong & Du, 2007; Connolly, 2007). The impact on school psychology could be significant. A typical day for a school psychologist a decade from now could look something like the following scenario.

The school psychologist comes to work and accesses a report from the school's central server. The server is utilizing a Web 2.0 platform that allows various school professionals to write specific sections of a student's report. The school psychologist is then notified when all sections have been completed, and edits the report. Graphs of the student's learning progress have been inserted from various learning software and websites that track the student's growth in academic areas. The interventions for the report are generated using several empirically-based intervention sites. In addition, video observations are hyperlinked to the report demonstrating the behavior of concern. The observations were gathered from cameras in the classroom that utilize VoIP.

The school psychologist is working on another report when a reminder pops up on her computer reminding her of a teleconference IEP meeting. While pulling up the VoIP feed of the IEP meeting, the school psychologist accesses the special education paperwork to fill out the appropriate sections. During the IEP meeting, there are concerns regarding a student's medical condition. A nurse practitioner joins the IEP meeting to fully explain the medical condition and forwards recommendations for the condition. The whole conference is recorded and everything is saved in the student's secured e-portfolio.

Once the IEP meeting concludes, the school psychologist checks her RSS aggregator for the latest updates on assessment instruments and changing regulations. Based on the latest information, she logs on to her blog to distribute the information to the other school psychologists in her district. She also updates her social bookmarking with a few useful intervention websites she has come across.

Of course, there are many social, legal, and ethical issues to be addressed before this scenario can be a reality. However, the technological tools are already in place. While many in school psychology have hopes of strengthening the field by improving efficiency, accuracy, and quality with the use of technology in the future, others' attitudes are more bleak (Power, 2006). Not all psychologists are comfortable with technology. In fact, a survey by Rosen and Weil (1996) found that 54% of psychologists would prefer to wait to use new technology until it is proven, 28% wait until they must use it, and 8% avoid new technology all together. Of the survey participants, 54% rated themselves as either mildly, moderately, or highly technophobic. However, it appears that attitudes have started to change from 1996. In the KSPT study, 57% indicated that they were typically the first to embrace new technology, while only 32% believed that technology was changing way too quickly. While school psychologists' positive attitude toward technology is promising, they will not be able to embrace the newest technology unless school districts provide more support (Williams & Kingham, 2003).

Summary

This chapter has reviewed the gradual integration of technology into the role of a school psychologist. The integration of technology can be predicted using the diffusion of innovation and technology adoption models. The factors of perceived usefulness, perceived ease of use, compatibility, observability, and trialability influence the decision to adopt advanced technology. Based on these criteria, an extensive literature review, and my own experience, I created two types of advanced technology competencies.

The first type of competency is considered as essential skills for today's school psychologists. Most of these technologies have been around for a decade or longer, and are well integrated into the practice of school psychology. These competencies include word processing, spreadsheets, scoring programs, e-mail, and web browsers.

The second type of competencies is considered emerging skills that could complement today's school psychologist and could become essential skills in the future. Most of these technologies are relatively new and still need to be adopted by most school psychologists. These competencies consist of hardware such as cell phones, PDAs; desktop software such as dictation and statistical programs; communication programs such as VoIP, listservs, IM, and blogs; and information programs such as RSS, and tracking/intervention websites.

The use of technology can be integrated into the domains of school psychology. Assessment is the prime example of how school psychology has embraced technology. Consultation holds promise in the integration of technology into the consultative process. Advanced technology and the Internet can also assist school psychologists in regard to supervision, professional collaboration, and e-learning. Despite all the promise of technology, legal and ethical issues have arisen.

The future of technology use in school psychology is relatively limitless. It will be difficult to imagine how the practice of school psychology will have changed a decade from now based on the change in technology.

Chapter Competency Checklist

DOMAIN 2 – Technological Applications

Foundational	Functional
Understand and explain the following: ☐ Technology and Advanced Technology ☐ Computers and internet ☐ Innovations and adoption of technology ☐ Technology Adoption Model ☐ Word Processing Software ☐ Scoring software for psychological tests ☐ Software for spreadsheets ☐ Presentation software ☐ Communication software ☐ Web browsers ☐ Emerging technologies ☐ Ethics concerning recording keeping	Gain practice: ☐ Observing software and hardware for administering and scoring psychological assessments ☐ Using software for administering and scoring psychological assessments ☐ Using hardware for administering and scoring psychological assessments ☐ Using advanced technologies to communicate with other regarding psychological services ☐ Exploring new technologies

References

Aimsweb. (2007). Aimsweb progress monitoring and response to intervention system. Retrieved February 12, 2007 from http://www.aimsweb.com.

Campbell, P. H., Milbourne, S., Dugan, L. M., & Wilcox, M. J. (2006). A review of evidence on practices for teaching young children to use assistive technology devices. *Topics in Early Childhood Special Education, 26*(1), 3–13.

Carlson, J. F., & Harvey, V. S. (2004). Using computer-related technology for assessment activities: Ethical and professional practice issues for school psychologists. *Computers in Human Behavior, 20*(5), 645–659.

Carroll, J. (2004, May). Not your parent's telephone. *CA Magazine,* 12–17.

Chau, P. Y. K. (1996). An empirical assessment of a modified technology acceptance model. *Journal of Management Information Systems, 13*(2), 185–204.

Cong, Y., & Du, H. (2007). Welcome to the world of web 2.0. *CPA Journal, 77*(5), 6–10.

Connolly, J.M. (2007, April). Tech turns to web 2.0. *B to B, 92*, 24–27.

Council for exceptional children. (2004). *The new IDEA: CEC's summary of significant issues.* Retrieved December 6, 2004, from http://www.cec.sped.org.

Cummings, J. A. (2002). A school psychological perspective on the consulting psychology education and training principles. *Consulting Psychology Journal, 54*(4), 252–260.

Czaja, S. J., Charness, N., Fisk, A. D., Nair, S. N., Rogers, W. A., & Sharit, J. (2006). Factors predicting the use of technology: Findings from the center for research and education on aging and technology enhancement (CREATE). *Psychology and Aging, 21*(2), 333–352.

Davis, F. D. (1989). Perceived usefulness, perceived ease of use, and user acceptance of information technology. *MIS Quarterly, 13*(3), 319–340.

Dawson, D., Cummings, J. A., Harrison, P. L., Short, R. J., Gorin, S., & Palomares, R. (2004). The 2002 multisite conference on the future of school psychology: Next steps. *School Psychology Review, 33*(1), 115–125.

Harcourt assessment. (2007). Behavioral observation of students in schools (BOSS). Retrieved March 6, 2007 from http://harcourt.assessment.com/hai/ProductLongDesc.aspx?ISBN=015-8048-601&Catalog=TPC-USCatalog&Category=AchievementBasicSkills.

Harris, M. L., & Gibson, S. G. (2006). Distance education vs. face-to-face classes: Individual differences, course preferences, and enrollment. *Psychological Reports, 98*, 756–764.

Harvey, V. S., & Carlson, J. F. (2003). Ethical and professional issues with computer-related technology. *School Psychology Review, 32*(1), 92–107.

Hinkle, K. T. (2003). Internet loggingsystem.com: An analytical tool for student and program evaluation. *Trainer's forum: Periodical of the trainers of school psychologists, 22*(4), 1–4.

Hinkle, K. T. (2005). Perceptions of school psychology trainers and students on the use of an electronic data base for practicum and internship documentation and supervision. *Trainer's forum: Periodical of the trainers of school psychologists, 24*(4), 12–16.

Jackson, V. L. (2003). *Technology and special education: Bridging the most recent digital divide.* (ERIC Document Reproduction Service No. ED 479685)

Jacob, S., & Hartshorne, T. S. (2003). *Ethics and law for school psychologists* (4th ed.). Hoboken, NJ: Wiley.

Kanz, J. E. (2001). Clinical-supervision.com: Issues in the provision of online supervision. *Professional Psychology: Research and Practice, 34*(4), 415–420.

King, T. W. (1999). *Assistive technology: Essential human factors.* Boston: Allyn and Bacon.

Kruger, L. J., Maital, S., Macklem, G., Weksel, T., & Caldwell, R. (2002). The internet and school psychology practice. *Journal of Applied School Psychology, 19*(1), 95–111.

Lane, S. J., & Mistrett, S. G. (1996). Play and assistive technology issues for infants and young children with disabilities: A preliminary examination. *Focus on Autism and Other Developmental Disabilities, 11*(2), 96–105.

Macklem, G. L., Kalinsky, R., & Corcoran, R. (2000, July 17). *International consultation, professional development and the Internet: School psychology practice and the future.* Paper presented at the XXIII Annual Colloquim of the International School Psychology Association, Durham, New Hampshire.

McMinn, M. R., Buchanan, T., Ellens, B. M., & Ryan, M. K. (1999). Technology, professional practice, and ethics: Survey findings and implications. *Professional Psychology: Research and Practice, 30*(2), 165–172.

Melenhorst, A., Rogers, W. A., & Bouwhuis, D. G. (2006). Older adults' motivated choice for technological innovation: Evidence for benefit-driven selectivity. *Psychology and Aging, 21*(1), 190–195.

Mohamed, A. (2006, September). The voip revolution. *Computer Weekly,* p. 32.

Murphy, M. J. (2003). Computer technology for office-based psychological practice: Applications and factors affecting adoption. *Psychotherapy: Theory, Research, Practice, Training, 40*(1/2), 10–19.

National Associate of School Psychologists. (1997). Standards for the provision of school psychological services. *School Psychology Review, 26*(4), 677–692.

National Association of School Psychologists. (2000). *Professional conduct manual.* Bethesda, MD: Author.

National Institute of Standards and Technology. (2001, November 26). *Advanced encryption standards* (Federal Information Processing Standards Publication 197). Washington, DC: U.S. Government Printing Office.

Nuance. (2007). Dragon Naturally Speaking 9 Preferred. Retrieved February 21, 2007 from http://www.nuance.com/naturallyspeaking/preferred/

Pearson Assessment. (2007). BASC-2 Portable Observation Program. Retrieved March 6, 2007 from http://ags.pearsonassessments.com/group.asp?nGroupInfoID=a38206

Power, T. J. (2006). School psychology review: 2006–2010. *School Psychology Review, 35*(1), 3–10.

Principles of good practice in distance education and their application to professional education and training in psychology. (2002). Report of the task force on distance education and training in professional psychology. American Psychological Association.

Rogers, E. M. (2003). *Diffusion of Innovations* (5th ed.). NY: Free Press.

Rosen, L. D., & Weil, M. M. (1996). Psychologists and technology: A look at the future. *Professional Psychology: Research and Practice, 27*(6), 635–638.

Rosik, C. H., & Brown, R. K. (2001). Professional use for the internet: Legal and ethical issues in a member care environment. *Journal of Psychology and Theology, 29*(2), 106–120.

Rule, S., Salzberg, C., Higbee, T., Menlove, R., & Smith, J. (2006). Technology-mediated consultation to assist rural students: A case study. *Rural Special Education Quarterly, 25*(2), 3–7.

SAS. (2007). Business Intelligence and Analytic Software – SAS. Retrieved March 7, 2007 from http://www.sas.com

Shapiro, D., & Schulman, C. E. (1996). Ethical and legal issues in e-mail therapy. *Ethics and Behavior, 6*(2), 107–124.

Snyder, D. (2000). Computer-assisted judgement: Defining strengths and liabilities. *Psychological Assessment, 12*, 52–60.

SPSS Inc. (2007). SPSS Home Page. Retrieved March 7, 2007 from http://www.spss.com

University of Oregon Center on Teaching and Learning. (2007). Official DIBELS Home Page. Retrieved February 12, 2007 from http://dibels.uoregon.edu

Vishwanath, A., & Goldhaber, G. M. (2003). An examination of the factors contributing to adoption decisions among late-diffused technology products. *New Media & Society, 5*(4), 547–572.

Williams, H. S., & Kingham, M. (2003). Infusion of technology into the curriculum. *Journal of Instructional Psychology, 30*(3), 178–184.

Wilson, G. L., Michaels, C. A., & Margolis, H. (2005). Form versus function: Using technology to develop individualized education programs for students with disabilities. *Journal of Special Education Technology, 20*(2), 37–46.

Wood, J. A. V., Miller, T. W., & Hargrove, D. S. (2005). Clinical supervision in rural settings: A telehealth model. *Professional Psychology: Research and Practice, 36*(2), 173–179.

Ysseldyke, J., Burns, M., Dawson, P., Kelley, B., Morrison, D., Ortiz, S., et al. (2006). *School psychology: A blueprint for training and practice III*. Bethesda, MD: National Association of School Psychologists.

Ysseldyke, J. E., Dawson, P., Lehr, C., Reschly, D., Reynolds, M., & Telzrow, C. (1997). *School psychology: A blueprint for training and practice II*. Bethesda, MD: National Association of School Psychologists.

Ysseldyke, J. E., Reynolds, M. C., & Weinberg, R. A. (1984). *School psychology: A blueprint for training and practice*. Minneapolis, MN: National School Psychology Inservice Training Network.

Chapter 15
Making a Career of School Psychology

Leigh D. Armistead and Diane Smallwood

Overview

At first glance, the need for a chapter on "making a career of school psychology" might not be obvious. After all, why else would someone devote 3–5 years or more to obtain a graduate education in school psychology without intending to have a career in it? It would seem that earning an appropriate degree and getting a position as a school psychologist would result in a career. Careers simply happen – if you have the right training and work hard. In some professions that may be the case. A novice advertising executive, for example, may expect to work her way up a "career ladder" by acquiring more and more accounts, supervising more and more associates, and eventually, perhaps, owning her own firm. However, this chapter will encourage the novice practitioner to think of school psychology as a different type of profession – one that usually develops without a career ladder to climb. The authors will propose a model of career development for school psychologists that does not involve climbing ladders but rather emphasizes *career enrichment* through continuing professional development and professional association involvement.

The chapter begins with a discussion of general issues in professional and career development and of school psychology as a context for career development. Next, a review of the literature on job satisfaction will lead to a discussion of a limited number of traditional career ladder or "vertical" career advancement opportunities within school psychology. We will then review contemporary ideas about career enrichment and their relevance to career development within school psychology, and place these within the context of professional development stages. The chapter will conclude with recommendations for specific tasks in which practitioners typically will be, or should be, engaged at each stage of their professional development.

Professional and Career Development

Professional development typically refers to maintaining and enhancing skills necessary for a specific career and professional development – or lifelong learning – and is regarded as a professional responsibility (Armistead, 2008). Graduate training programs provide the "basics" of the profession but the completion of a graduate degree only marks the beginning of a school psychologist's professional development. The need for, and benefits of, continuing professional development (CPD) have

L.D. Armistead (✉)
Winthrop University, Rock Hill, SC 29733, USA
e-mail: armisteadl@winthrop.edu

T.M. Lionetti et al. (eds.), *A Practical Guide to Building Professional Competencies in School Psychology*, 245
DOI 10.1007/978-1-4419-6257-7_15, © Springer Science+Business Media, LLC 2011

been well documented (Armistead; Batsche, 1990; Brown, 2002; Fowler & Harrison, 1995). They include (a) meeting ethical and professional responsibilities, (b) becoming professionally competent, (c) continuing to be competent, (d) coping with changing roles and functions, (e) managing professional transitions, (f) developing specialties, (g) coping with technological change, and (h) maintaining credentials.

Career development generally refers to the manner in which people personally manage their careers within organizations, to the manner in which organizations facilitate the career progress of the people within those organizations, and to individuals managing their careers as they move between organizations. Traditionally, "careers" have been seen as a series of various positions and situations that compose a person's, especially a professional's, work life. Super's (1990) influential model of career choice and development originally comprised five sequenced stages with certain developmental tasks at each stage. The model reflected a traditional view of career choices being made early in life and careers proceeding in a predictable, linear fashion. Super later revised the model to reflect the contemporary reality of individuals frequently changing careers or respecializing within their careers. Such deviations from linear career paths may involve recycling through some of the following stages:

1. *Growth (childhood, adolescence).* The primary tasks are to develop a realistic self-concept, become aware of career possibilities, form likes and dislikes, and appraise one's interests and abilities. Although first experienced in one's youth, a person may recycle through this stage during periods of reexploration of career possibilities.
2. *Exploration (early 20s).* The primary task involves exploring career possibilities, examining various roles and occupations, and deciding on educational requirements to begin a career. During periods of reexploration of career choices, individuals would recycle through this stage and complete the same tasks.
3. *Establishment (25–45 years).* The primary developmental task is to get one's career started, get settled into it, and establish a stable lifestyle. During this stage, individuals develop professional reputations, and a great deal of career advancement typically occurs. This stage must, of course, recur after career changes.
4. *Maintenance (45–65 years).* During this stage, professionals traditionally were viewed as maintaining their positions and defending them against threats. A more contemporary view would include an emphasis on developing new skills, innovating, mentoring younger colleagues, and becoming a leader in one's profession.
5. *Disengagement (60 years and later).* The traditional view is that during this stage, professionals traditionally begin to slow down, work less, and become more selective about the tasks they undertake. Retirement planning usually becomes salient during this stage. Super (1990) suggests that individuals may experience some aspects of disengagement during periods of career transition.

Another way to view career development is through the familiar metaphor: "climbing the ladder." Traditionally, individuals were said to work their way up the career ladder with increasing responsibility, higher salary, and more prestige before reaching a "plateau," and then reducing their career involvement until retirement. Today, of course, it may be that individuals do not just climb ladders but frequently change to different ladders. Women may not follow the same pattern due to family responsibilities and other factors (Betz & Fitzgerald, 1987). Relatedly, there appears to be a contemporary trend toward women suspending or postponing careers during child rearing (Story, 2005). Despite these trends, this "vertical" career development model has been institutionalized to such an extent in the USA that military officers who are passed over for promotion twice are discharged or retired – a policy known as, "up or out" (Philpott, 2005). A similar career ladder within many colleges and universities is the tenure system in which faculty members have a certain number of years to achieve tenure. If not, they are dismissed from their positions. Brooks (1994) provides a final example: a prominent accounting firm dismisses accountants if they do not move up every 2 years or make partner in less than 7 years. However, Brooks points out, that some business hierarchies are becoming "flatter" and are providing fewer opportunities for vertical advancement. According to Brooks, Chevron has instituted a career enrichment program to increase employees' job satisfaction despite their not having further opportunities to advance within the corporate hierarchy.

Despite some trends toward career enrichment, it seems likely that the traditional view of a linear career path (with associated career ladder climbing) from youthful career exploration through retirement is embedded in the American psyche. The relationship of these models of career development to typical careers in school psychology has been little studied. Guest (2000), however, interviewed 25 school psychologists in the Pacific Northwest about their careers. They did not think of their careers as having progressed in stages. Rather, they discussed their careers changing over time in response to changes in client populations and changes in their expected roles. They saw changes in the profession (or in the legal regulation of it) influencing their career paths. Finally, they recalled career changes in terms of their own professional competence and belief systems. Guest reflected that the role of the school psychologist is so varied that the profession can be viewed as being a series of short-term "mini careers" rather than a single career with multiple stages. Nevertheless, traditional views of career development likely continue to influence many school psychologists' expectations about, and, possibly, satisfaction with their own careers.

A Context for Career Development

Sarason (1975) proclaimed that school psychology was born in the prison of the IQ test. Given their dissatisfaction with some aspects of their work, some school psychologists apparently still feel imprisoned by IQ tests (VanVoorhis & Levinson, 2006). School psychology's long-standing and close association with intellectual assessment and special education has been both beneficial and detrimental. School psychology has certainly benefited from special education's support for the employment of large numbers of practitioners in the schools. Charvatt (2005) estimated that there were about 38,000 practicing school psychologists in 2005. Despite continual growth, demand has always exceeded supply with shortages of school psychologists nearly every year since 1976 (Reschly, 2000). A side effect of this association with special education has been a continual struggle to define the field. Fagan (2000) suggests that the close association "appears to have stigmatized the field as essentially public school based, functionally connected to a limited psychometric technology, in a symbiotic relationship with the growth of special education" (p. 765). This "symbiotic" relationship with special education has complicated attempts to even define school psychology as a profession. The American Psychological Association (APA) contends that school psychology is a specialty of professional psychology, whereas others regard it as a separate profession – separate but related to professional psychology (Fagan & Wise, 2000).

Exploring this "separate profession" issue further is outside the scope of this chapter. However, with regard to career development, it might be useful to consider whether school psychology actually is a profession or is merely an occupation within (mostly) the public schools. Fagan (2000) writes that "the field of school psychology has achieved the major characteristics of professionalization: a body of knowledge that it shares with other specialties, a separate and identifiable literature, training programs with recognizable student and faculty groups, practitioner credentials, training and practice guidelines promoted through accreditation and credentialing, employment opportunities, professional associations, and codes of ethics" (p. 754). The field has also developed guidelines for, and requires of, its practitioners, a program of continuing professional development (Armistead, 2006). Avoiding issues of credentialing and professional association oversight, Fagan and Wise (2000) have proposed this definition, which may provide a basis for thinking about career development in school psychology:

> A school psychologist is a professional psychological practitioner whose general purpose is to bring a psychological perspective to bear on the problems of educators and the clients educators serve. This perspective is derived from a broad base of training in educational and psychological foundations as well as specialty preparation, resulting in the provision of comprehensive psychological services of a direct and indirect nature. (p. 4)

The dual knowledge base of school psychologists in both education and psychology has to be considered as part of the context for career development. Fagan and Wise (2000) have proposed the "guest in the school" metaphor to help school psychologists understand the nature of this relationship. They suggest that education could be compared to a house in which school psychologists may be perceived as, or feel like, outsiders or visitors. The "guest" metaphor is intended to sensitize new practitioners to the need to work to overcome being perceived by educators as having little in common with them.

Two trends may be relevant to this problem of school psychologists being "guests" in their schools. Traditionally, practitioners have served two or more schools on an itinerant basis. In recent years, however, an increasing number is assigned full time to single schools (Proctor & Steadman, 2003). For example, in what is known as a Student Services Specialist model of service delivery, the Charlotte-Mecklenburg Schools in North Carolina provide at least one school psychologist for each of 94 elementary schools. Proctor and Steadman report that school psychologists assigned to single schools reported higher rates of job satisfaction, greater perceptions of effectiveness, and lower rates of burnout. A second trend is the increasing numbers of women choosing school psychology as a career. Worrell, Skaggs, and Brown (2006) report that female school psychologists were more likely than men to have had teaching experience. They suggest that female teachers may be choosing school psychology to advance into higher paying, nonteaching jobs while remaining in education. It is possible that school psychologists with prior teaching experience will be better "guests" in education's house.

Regardless of possible motives, it is certainly apparent that more women are becoming school psychologists and this must be considered as part of the context for career development in the field. In the 1960s, only about 40% of practitioners were women (Reschly, 2000). Since then, the percentage has increased by about 10% per decade resulting in about 77% of practitioners and 74% of all school psychologists being women (Curtis, Lopez, Batsche, Minch, & Abshier, 2007). This survey of National Association of School Psychologists (NASP) members also showed, for the first time, that a majority (60%) of school psychology graduate program faculty members are women compared to about 18% in 1969–1970. It seems likely that this trend of feminization of the field will continue. In the most recent survey of graduate programs, Thomas (1998) reported that women comprise 80% of all graduate students and 78.5% of all doctoral students. There is little evidence that these changes in gender representation have influenced the nature of school psychological services. Apparently, female and male practitioners do not differ in the services they actually deliver or in their preferred roles (Curtis, Walker, Hunley, & Baker, 1999). In general, both would prefer to do less assessment and more consultation. One study, however, suggests that this tendency is less pronounced among women and that they may be slightly more satisfied than men with their current roles (Wilson & Rechsly, 1995).

School Psychologists' Job Satisfaction

School psychologists consistently report high levels of satisfaction with their jobs. In a meta-analysis of two national- and six state-level studies conducted between 1982 and 1999, VanVoorhis and Levinson (2006) report that about 85% of school psychologists were satisfied or very satisfied with their jobs. Aspects of their jobs with which they were most satisfied included positive relationships with colleagues, having an active work style, working independently, and being of service to children, schools, and families.

In 2004, Worrell et al. (2006) replicated the two national studies of NASP members which were included in the previously cited meta-analysis. They found that about 90% of school-based practitioners were satisfied or very satisfied with their jobs in 2004 compared with about 86% in 1992 and 1982. Aspects of their jobs that were most satisfying included job security, compensation, working conditions, and relationships with coworkers. Only two demographic variables were found to be significantly correlated with job satisfaction in the 2004 survey. Not surprisingly, school psychologists who intended to remain in their current position for 5 more years were more satisfied than those who intended to leave the profession. The second correlated variable was supervisor credentialing. About 67% of the school psychologists in this study had direct supervisors who were not credentialed school psychologists. They were less satisfied with their jobs than were the 33% who were supervised by school psychologists.

Areas of Job Dissatisfaction

Given the overall high level of satisfaction that school psychologists report about their jobs, it should not be surprising that they report relatively few areas of dissatisfaction. For example, in the VanVoorhis and Levinson (2006) meta-analysis, just three areas of dissatisfaction emerged. School psychologists reported being dissatisfied with compensation, school district policies and practices, and opportunities for advancement. Worrell et al. (2006) reported that two areas of dissatisfaction in the 1982, 1992, and 2004 national studies of NASP members emerged. School-based practitioners reported being least satisfied with school district policies and procedures and with opportunities for advancement but not dissatisfied with compensation.

Dissatisfaction with school district administrative policies, especially related to school psychologists' roles and functions, has been a long-standing concern within the profession (Bradley-Johnson & Dean, 2000). NASP's training standards (NASP, 2000d), credentialing standards (NASP, 2000c), and practice guidelines (NASP, 2000a) reflect an expectation that school psychologists should be trained to provide, and expect to provide, a broad range of psychological and educational services. School psychologists, in general, prefer to spend less time in traditional psycho-educational assessment and more time on direct services to children, problem-solving and organizational consultation, and applied research and program evaluation For example, school psychologists spend about 50% of their time in psycho-educational assessment activities compared with 20% of their time in direct intervention. As a group, they would prefer to reduce the time spent in assessment to 32% and increase time spent in direct intervention to 29% (Reschly, 2000). There are a number of reasons for the relative long-term stability of job roles despite calls for reform. School psychology's ties to special education is an important one. Through financial support for school psychology, special education strongly influences the number of school psychologists and the functions they serve. It remains to be seen whether recent changes in the Individuals with Disabilities Education Improvement Act (2004) especially with regard to response to intervention (RtI), will have large-scale effects on school psychologists' practices. Burns and Coolong-Chaffin (2006) provide data that suggest that school psychologists' daily activities can change in desired directions as a result of RtI.

School psychologists ranked satisfaction with opportunities for promotion and advancement 19th out of 20 different areas of satisfaction in the 1992 and 2004 national studies of job satisfaction (Worrell et al., 2006). There are several probable reasons for dissatisfaction with career advancement possibilities. One is the nature of school-based practitioners' positions. In commenting on this issue, Anderson, Hohenshil, and Brown (1984) wrote, "The position of school psychologist may be unique in that it is both an entry level and, often terminal position" (p. 229). Although some practitioners might aspire to supervisory positions in schools, there are relatively few such positions available to them, especially in supervision of psychological services departments. This can be inferred from the fact that just a third of school-based practitioners report being administratively supervised by someone trained in school psychology (Curtis et al., 2007). Furthermore, Worrell et al. point out that only 23% of practitioners are employed in districts with enough school psychologists to need a separate director of psychological services.

Administrative positions in schools such as director of special education or school principal sometimes require teaching experience and/or credentials for which some school psychologists may not be eligible. In any case, according to the 1992 and 2004 national surveys, few school psychologists are actually interested in administrative positions (Worrell et al., 2006). Reschly (2000) notes that a perception of few opportunities for advancement among school-based practitioners seems to be slightly lower among doctoral-level than specialist-level school psychologists. About 90% of all school psychologists are employed in public and private schools and the majority of practitioners (76%) are trained at nondoctoral levels (Curtis et al., 2007). Nondoctoral training results in limited options for practice outside the public schools in most states. It may be that school psychologists trained at the doctoral level perceive more opportunities for career advancement because of the greater possibility of credentialing and employment outside school systems.

Although school psychologists report dissatisfaction with opportunities for career advancement, it is not known how many of them actually wish to "move up the ladder" within education or psychology, or to change to a different career. In one of the few longitudinal studies of career changes among practitioners, Wilczenski (1997) reported that few of their participants left the field. Practitioners with 6–10 years of experience were the most likely to leave (8.5% did so). Those with 11–15 years were somewhat less likely. Practitioners with more than 16 years of experience maintained stable employment until retirement. Of the school psychologists in this study who did leave the profession, most left for further graduate education, went into private practice, or took positions in business. Some practitioners (3.4–15.4%, depending on cohort) did move into other positions in education.

Traditional Career Development Opportunities

Having discussed school psychologists' dissatisfaction with traditional opportunities for career advancement in the schools, we should consider what options actually do exist – for at least some school psychologists. As previously discussed, most school psychologists practice in the public schools and most of them wish to remain in the profession. Practitioners seeking career advancement through promotion to positions with greater responsibility, higher salary, and, perhaps, more perceived status will find a number of constraints on their choices. Within public education, a limited number of positions are available as directors of psychological services or as lead psychologists. The actual number of such positions is unknown. They are more likely to exist in larger, urban districts than in smaller districts, where school psychologists usually are responsible to the school superintendent or to a director of special education or of pupil services. For practitioners with a number of years of experience and a desire to supervise their colleagues either full or part time, such a promotion could be a very good career move.

Fagan and Wise (2000) report that the possibility of school psychologists advancing to other public school administrative positions has improved in recent years. The frequency of this actually happening, however, is unclear. This chapter's authors, however, are aware of some practitioners becoming principals, directors of special education, and, in one case, a school superintendent. In those cases, the practitioners had to complete graduate programs in educational administration. Some nontraditional positions, however, might not require additional administrative credentials. With the advent of state testing programs came new positions for directors of district assessment programs, and at least one school psychologist is employed in such a position. Most school psychologists certainly have the skills for such positions. In one large urban district, school psychologists have been employed in liaison positions with the department of social services, as facilitators of school reform initiatives, and as trainers in the staff development department.

Nontraditional settings are another option for school psychologists seeking an alternative practice setting and, possibly, a vertical career move. Gilman and Teague (2005) suggest five such settings: private practice, residential institutions, neuropsychological practices, pediatric settings, and early intervention or child guidance centers. Practicing school psychology in these nontraditional settings usually requires state board of psychology licensure, but most states require doctoral level training for such licensure, which limits the prospects of most school psychologists for employment in these settings. Fagan and Wise (2000) provide comprehensive information on practicing in these nontraditional settings.

Another vertical career development possibility is becoming a faculty member in a school psychology graduate training program. Approximately 50–60 positions have been available annually in recent years and positions often go unfilled (Nickerson & Gagnon, 2003). In addition to doctoral training, having at least 2 years of experience as a school psychology practitioner is a desirable qualification for school psychology faculty (Knoff, Curtis, & Batsche, 1997). These authors also suggest that in addition to professional knowledge, practitioners should have good supervision, consultation, interpersonal, and problem-solving skills, and should also be able to model ethical and professional practice of school psychology. With practitioner salaries averaging up to $70,600 for a 200-day contract (Curtis et al., 2007), it is possible that a vertical career move to an assistant professor position will not result in an increase in compensation. Both of this chapter's authors, however, have made that transition and can attest to benefits other than compensation that made the move worthwhile. Some school psychologists may become faculty members following retirement from a school system. This could make compensation less of an issue. A comprehensive treatment of this transition is beyond the scope of this chapter. The reader is referred to Nickerson and Gagnon for an introduction to the topic. NASP members can also access a 2.5 hour online CPD module on the topic at http://www.nasponline.org (Smallwood, Armistead, & Williams, 2007).

As previously discussed, most school psychologists are trained at the specialist level rather than the doctoral level, which is required for most practice settings outside the public schools (Curtis et al., 2007). This results in some school psychologists returning to graduate school in pursuit of a doctorate. To attend a traditional doctoral program on a full-time basis would be a very costly venture for a practitioner due to the loss of several years of salary before returning to full-time work. However, several nontraditional doctoral programs which are NASP or APA approved but offer courses in the evenings, on weekends, or during the summer are available now. They usually offer programs tailored to the needs of mid-career school psychologists interested in advanced training and, perhaps, in developing a specialty area.

Career Enrichment for School Psychologists

Most school psychologists will not be able to take advantage of the vertical career advancement opportunities discussed here. Some of these opportunities are only rarely available, especially in small school districts, and may require a doctorate or moving to a different location. Returning to graduate school to earn a doctorate will appeal to just a few practitioners. Therefore, as consistently shown in surveys over many years (VanVoorhis & Levinson, 2006), school psychologists may continue to be dissatisfied with their career advancement possibilities – unless, that is, they adopt a different perspective about career advancement. The authors propose that they adopt a perspective of *career enrichment*.

The paradigm for this career enrichment perspective is an individual professional starting a practice in a small community. She could be a physician, a lawyer, or perhaps, an accountant. Although quite skilled and professionally knowledgeable, she has a great deal to learn about developing a practice. She devotes much effort to doing so for a few years, but also keeps up with her CPD responsibilities and becomes active in her professional association. Over the years, she begins to specialize, develops a reputation in her area, and her advice is sought by her colleagues. She develops a presentation about her specialty, professional ethics, and occasionally delivers it at association meetings. A nearby university asks her to take on an intern one year, and the next year asks her to teach a course one night a week. She discovers that mentoring and part-time teaching actually enrich her practice – she gets more than she gives – and her clients benefit from her enhanced skills. As the years go by, she sometimes has an itch to join a bigger practice or take on partners or join the university faculty. (Her father's comments about her tiny office and "getting ahead" usually provoke these itches.) The itches subside, however, when she reflects on making a good living and valuing the quality of life in her community and the respect she has as a professional in that community. When she attends her 25th college reunion, she is pleased that some of her former classmates have been able to climb the ladder of success but realizes that path was not for her and is satisfied with the path she chose. She has a rich and satisfying career.

Could such a career enrichment paradigm apply to a career in school psychology – even one devoted primarily to practicing in the public schools? The authors contend that it can. They can point to colleagues who have been working in the same position in the same school for 25 or more years and have followed a career enrichment path similar to the paradigm presented above. From a traditional career advancement point of view, it would seem that they are still on the first rung of the career ladder. Yet, they are quite satisfied with their careers because, the authors believe, they have engaged in career enrichment. The fictional example presented above of a small-town practitioner's lifelong career enrichment includes examples of various professional activities that enriched her career.

Components of Career Enrichment

The Importance of CPD

Some career enrichment activities are familiar to school psychologists, especially CPD. The case for lifelong learning in school psychology is clearly made in the recently published *School Psychology: A Blueprint for Training and Practice III* (Ysseldyke et al., 2006). The *Blueprint's* authors contend that "the job of training programs is to ensure that students' skills are at a 'novice' level in all domains by the time they complete the coursework phase of their training, and are at a 'competent' level by the conclusion of internships, with the expectation that 'expert' practice will be achieved only after some postgraduate experience and likely only in some domains" (p. 11). They suggest that such expertise could take 5–10 years of practice to achieve and only with good professional development. Harvey and Struzziero (2000) point out that the level at which practitioners function is "context dependent." That is, they may be proficient in certain practice areas but complete novices in other areas. Nevertheless, they suggest that practitioners usually progress through these stages:

1. *Advanced students (or interns).* They professionally function at a basic level but wish to excel, tend to work cautiously and thoroughly, and often feel insecure.
2. *Novice professionals.* They become very engaged in their practices but may become disillusioned when they encounter situations for which they are not prepared and can become overwhelmed by multiple demands.
3. *Experienced professionals.* After a number of years of practice, they feel comfortable and confident in their work but risk burnout unless they can come to terms with the fact that there are no straightforward solutions to their clients' many problems. They tend to rely on their own experiences for new learning and often are not interested in CPD activities, which they regard as for novices.
4. *Senior professionals.* After 20 years or more, some are mentoring the next generation and are continuing to advance professionally but some become jaded with a sense that there is really nothing new in the field that they should learn.

Little is known about the proportion of school psychologists who stay in the profession for 20 years or more. We have previously discussed some of the issues related to leaving the profession. It is clear that some become dissatisfied and disillusioned and change careers. School psychologists who do stay in the field for 20 years or more may become "senior professionals" in terms of longevity, but they all will not be equally competent or content or have had as rich a career. One factor, apparently, is good CPD which leads to enhanced job satisfaction. Curtis, Hunley, and Grier (2002) found evidence that with more training and experience, practitioners seem to become more efficient at less preferred activities, especially those related to special education eligibility, allowing more time for preferred professional activities such as counseling. This increase in role diversity tends to enhance job satisfaction. In addition, there is some evidence that CPD along with supervision and peer support groups are effective in dealing with stress and burnout (Zins & Murphy, 1996). Finally, Kruger (1993) found that school psychologists with higher perceived effectiveness and sense of personal accomplishment experienced greater commitment to their profession and lower levels of burnout.

As previously noted, becoming professionally competent in all areas of one's practice is an immediate need for new practitioners. Benner (1984) contends that novice practitioners often "know about" practices that they do not yet "know how to" perform very well. Guest (2000), for example, interviewed school psychologists about their professional development experiences. They recalled that as beginners, they had "how to" difficulties in these five areas of their practice:

1. Organization, time management, and special education procedures (48%);
2. Feelings of inadequacy and uncertainty (40%);
3. Inadequate consultation skills (25%);
4. Inadequate preservice training for specific job requirements (24%);
5. Feeling overwhelmed with the needs of clients and the lack of resources to meet those needs (20%).

Asked about how they met these challenges, school psychologists reported receiving help from other psychologists, supervisors, former professors, and usually from informal rather than formal mentoring. Some of Guest's (2000) respondents described themselves as essentially on their own with little support from others. In addition to support from colleagues, CPD experiences were said to have been very helpful in overcoming these challenges. They cited professional workshops, conferences, and reading as having been important.

School psychologists also have to continue learning in order to *stay* competent. It has been suggested that half of a psychologist's knowledge base may be out of date in as little as 3–5 years (Hynd, Pielstick, & Schakel, 1981). Harvey and Struzziero (2000) suggest that experienced practitioners are especially prone to getting out of date because they feel competent in their work and, when making decisions, tend to rely on their past experiences rather than current research findings. They are also less likely than less-experienced practitioners to engage in CPD. Because of this, they may have difficulty coping with changing roles and functions as the field changes.

A comprehensive treatment of planning and implementing a lifelong learning/CPD program is not possible here. An in-depth source is Armistead (2008), which encourages school psychologists to assess their own competencies continually in relation to the demands of their work setting. They should then prioritize their needs for CPD taking into account, first, the needs of their clients; second, the needs of their employer; and third, their own personal interest areas. After assessing needs, school psychologists are encouraged to consider both traditional and nontraditional CPD activities. Traditional activities such as workshops and conference presentations are available through school psychology associations in almost every state. National professional associations such as NASP and APA also provide workshops and conferences. Both NASP and APA, however, have also developed nontraditional forms of CPD. Both offer on-line self-study modules and APA offers professional development credit for self-study of some of its publications.

Practitioners in most states are required to document professional development activities to renew their state license or certification to practice in the schools. Another type of credential, though, recognizes high quality training and practice but does not substitute for state department of education or state psychology board licensure. Nationally Certified School Psychologists (NCSPs) must complete 75 hour of continuing education activities every 3 years in order to renew their credential. The NCSP designation, therefore, serves as a recognition of practitioners who meet the profession's standard for lifelong learning.

Diplomate in School Psychology

Another recognition of quality training and practice is the Diplomate in School Psychology awarded by the American Board of Professional Psychology (ABPP). The diplomate is only available to doctoral practitioners licensed for independent practice. It is granted after an extensive review of a practitioner's credentials and practice, which includes an oral examination. Board-certified school psychologists holding the diplomate become members of the American Board of School Psychology (ABSP), which functions as a membership organization, promotes the board-certification process, and conducts examinations (Flanagan, 2000). The ABPP on-line directory currently lists about 150 diplomates in school psychology (http://www.abpp.org/abpp_public_directory.php).

Supervision, Mentoring, and Peer Support

Professional as well as administrative supervision is essential for career enrichment. Only about 12% of school psychologists, however, report receiving any professional supervision and only about 33% are administratively supervised by someone trained in school psychology (Curtis et al., 2007). Many practitioners think of supervision as being synonymous with a more experienced practitioner giving them advice in an hierarchical manner. An alternate way to think of supervision is a collaborative relationship between two practitioners. McIntosh and Phelps (2000) describe this as "an interpersonal interaction between two or more individuals for the purpose of sharing knowledge, assessing professional competencies, and providing objective feedback with the terminal goals of developing new competencies, facilitating effective delivery of psychological services, and maintaining professional competencies" (pp. 33–34). This sort of supervision can occur in mentoring and peer support groups. Both can be important sources of career enrichment. Often, novice school psychologists are assigned to a more experienced mentor by their school districts. If this does not occur, the authors encourage new practitioners to attempt to find a mentor on their own. In any case, we encourage all school psychologists to get involved in a peer consultation or support group. Often these develop naturally out of groups of school psychologists getting together socially. Zins and Murphy (1996) report that about 64% of the school psychologists they surveyed had participated in peer support groups. Most reported significant benefits including improved skills, expanded roles, increased professional enthusiasm, more professional association involvement, and a stronger professional knowledge base.

Developing a Specialty

One of the best ways for an experienced practitioner to enhance a practice is to develop a professional specialty. School psychologists tend to be generalists because they were trained to be generalists. Nevertheless, there is good reason to develop a specialty even while maintaining a general practice. The authors' experience includes colleagues who have specialized in pediatric and vocational school psychology, hearing impairments, autism spectrum disorders, Attention-Deficit/Hyperactivity Disorder, crisis prevention, early childhood, and the special needs of gifted and English language learners. Having multiple specialists within a psychological services department benefits everyone in the department and provides opportunities for enhanced opportunities for collegial supervision. Listserv discussion groups have been developed by school psychologists with specialty interests and can provide learning and support as well. NASP has about 20 special interest groups interested in such specialties as positive school psychology, rural school psychology, computer and technical applications, and crisis management. Many NASP special interest groups have their own listservs. Given that school psychologists describe talking with their colleagues as an important factor in their continuing professional development, their enthusiastic adoption of email listservs can be expected to continue (Kruger, Maital, Macklem, Weksel, & Caldwell, 2002).

Intern Supervision

Supervision of graduate training program practicum and internship students is recognized by the National School Psychology Certification System (NASP, 1996) as an approved professional development activity for school psychologists. It has been the authors' experience that school-based supervisors do report learning a great deal from their interns and experiencing satisfaction from contributing to the development of the next generation of school psychologists. Apparently, there have been few studies of the benefits of internship supervision from the supervisor's view point. However, Bloomquist (2006), in a dissertation study, replicated earlier studies of school psychologists' job satisfaction. She reported similar results for overall job satisfaction and areas of dissatisfaction. However, she also found that school psychologists who had supervised interns reported significantly higher levels of job satisfaction.

Although internship field site supervisors are often "senior" members of psychological services departments, many report having little training in supervision (Ross & Goh, 1993). Directors of psychological services might consider the advantages of providing such training. Novice practitioners would receive better supervision and, for experienced practitioners, such training would serve as career enrichment. Explicitly recognizing the status of experienced and senior school psychologists is also recommended. This could be accomplished by providing an appropriate title, assigning interns to them, providing perks such as travel allowances and asking them to mentor newly hired school psychologists.

Program Development and Evaluation

Despite a great deal of training in applied research and program evaluation, school psychologists usually do not do much of it. Reschly (2000) reports that on average, school psychologists devote about 2% of their time to this role, but would prefer devoting about 6% of their time to applied research and program evaluation. Doing so would enrich their practices, enhance job satisfaction, and provide a valuable contribution to their schools. Contemporary trends toward prevention of learning and behavior problems, developing social–emotional learning programs, developing crisis prevention programs, and multi-tiered service delivery systems provide an ideal milieu for school psychologists wishing to broaden their roles into this practice domain.

Presentation and Training

Experienced and senior school psychologists, especially those with a reputation in a specialty area or those who develop programs, are often asked to present professional development sessions for their colleagues at district, state, or national meetings. This is actually a learning, and career enrichment, experience which practitioners may use for NCSP renewal purposes. Reviewing Guskey's (2003) advice about effective training is suggested. There are various types of training sessions, including the large group lecture and discussion format, workshops, seminars, panels, and break-out sessions. Any of these training programs should have clear objectives about whether participants are expected to acquire awareness, knowledge, or skills, or all three. Not being clear about this is common in school district in-service programs. Workshops that merely convey awareness and knowledge seldom result in skill acquisition or changes in participants' practices. Guskey suggests that if skill acquisition is intended, effective training programs should include presentation of a knowledge base, modeling of skills, simulations and role playing, feedback, and then follow-up coaching in the practice setting.

Once a practitioner presents a training program at the district level, the next step is to take the program to a state or national school psychology association meeting. Almost every state has its own association in need of presenters, and ample opportunities exist to present at the national level. NASP's 2007 convention in New York featured 966 paper presentations, symposia and mini-skills sessions. There were also 67 half- and full-day professional growth workshops and over 400 poster presentations. It is apparent that a great many school psychologists find presentations to be a great opportunity to enhance their career and network with their colleagues.

Part-Time Private Practice and Consulting

Some school-based practitioners find that a part-time practice outside the public schools is another way to enrich and advance their careers. Worrell et al. (2006) suggest that a part-time practice may allow practitioners to utilize some of their preferred skills, such as counseling and parent consultation, to a greater extent than permitted in schools. Only about 4% of the NASP members surveyed (Curtis et al., 2007) reported full-time employment in private practice. However, about 8.6% reported a part-time practice secondary to other employment, mostly in the schools. In many states, of course, licensure for independent practice of school psychology is limited to practitioners trained at the doctoral level. Some states' licensure laws, however, provide for nondoctoral licensure with an alternative title. North Carolina's licensing board, for example, licenses nondoctoral psychologists, including school psychologists, as "Psychological Associates." South Carolina's Department of Labor, Licensing, and Regulation licenses nondoctoral school psychologists as "Psycho-Educational Specialists." Both credentials permit private practice of school psychology, the former under supervision of a doctoral practitioner and the latter independently. State school psychology associations and state licensing boards are sources of information for each state.

Part-Time Postsecondary Teaching

Previously we discussed the possibilities and difficulties associated with making a transition from practitioner to full-time faculty member in a school psychology graduate program. However, there are many opportunities for part-time employment. In fact, recent statistics indicate that about 44% of all postsecondary faculty in USA teach part time. The percentage varies from a low of 22% at public doctoral granting institutions to 67% at public associate degree institutions (Cataldi, Fahimi, & Bardburn, 2004). Unlike full-time positions which usually require a doctorate, part-time (or "adjunct" positions, as they are known) may not, especially at the undergraduate level. School psychologists trained at the specialist level with several years of experience could feel competent in teaching courses in introductory psychology, child development, statistics, tests and measurement, and other similar undergraduate courses in psychology.

Professional Association Membership and Involvement

The final, and perhaps most important, component of career enrichment in school psychology is joining and participating in local, state, and national professional associations. There are three important reasons for doing so. First, professional associations provide the context for many of the career enrichment activities previously discussed in this chapter. For example, it would seem most difficult to maintain an effective CPD program without utilizing the publications, conventions, and on-line resources that professional associations provide. Second, professional association membership is actually a hallmark of being a professional and identifying with the profession. By joining a professional association, a practitioner affiliates with his or her colleagues, and agrees to abide by the ethical and professional practice standards of the profession. Finally, professional associations provide an important opportunity for leadership development, and becoming a leader at some level – local, state, or national – is an important component of career enrichment and career development in school psychology.

Practical Strategies for Launching a Career in School Psychology

As noted in the previous sections, a career in school psychology begins in graduate school and continues through the stages of novice, experienced, and senior professional status. At each of these stages, there are tasks associated with both career development and continuing education, as well as multiple opportunities for enrichment of one's professional life. Table 15.1 summarizes examples of these tasks and opportunities, and suggests resources that might be helpful at various stages of development.

The foundation for a full and satisfying career in school psychology can be established during graduate education programs. This begins with activities that orient students to career options, and to the value of investing oneself in going beyond the minimum tasks required for successful completion of each course. Mentoring by university faculty in professional activities, such as publishing or

Table 15.1 Career enrichment: stages, tasks, and resources

Career enrichment in school psychology			
Career development stages	Professional development	Professional involvement	Available resources
Beginning student • Acquisition of basic knowledge in psychology and education • Exposure to roles and functions of school psychologists • Orientation to educational settings	• Exposure to local, state, and national conferences • Student memberships • Orientation to professional literature (journals, books, etc.)	• Exposure to local, state, and national conferences • Student memberships • Mentoring from advanced students, faculty	• University coursework • Association web sites and print materials
Advanced student • Mastery of skills and competencies needed for entry level practice • Field experiences (practica and internship) • Search for first school psychology position	• Attendance at state and/or national conferences • Student membership	• Student membership • Copresent at conferences with faculty • Coauthorship of publications with faculty • Possible student leader involvement	• University coursework • Mentoring by practicum and intern supervisors • Association web sites and print materials
Novice practitioner • Exploration of job market • Developing a professional identity • Planning and decision making re: future goals	• Development of personal CPD plan • Acquiring practice management and organizational skills • Further refinement of skills (mastery of more practice skills)	• Membership in professional association(s) • Active involvement in state associations • Self-study • Participation in peer support groups	• e-Communities • State/national conferences • Peer support • Mentoring by more experienced school psychologists • Supervision
Experienced practitioner • Career transitions to other positions (e.g., supervisor, trainer, etc.) • Role expansion • Coping with burnout and need for professional renewal	• Continuing education activities in accordance with personal CPD plan • Development of specialty area(s) • Maintenance of skills and acquisition of contemporary knowledge/skills • Providing CPD activities for district colleagues	• Association leadership at state/national level • Presenting at conferences • Adjunct teaching • Supervision of practicum students and/or interns • Mentoring of other staff or students • Advanced training and/or credentials (doctoral education, ABSP)	• State/national associations • Peer networks • Supervision
Senior professional • Career transitions to other positions • Planning for retirement	• Expansion of specialty area(s) • Maintenance of skills and acquisition of contemporary knowledge/skills	• Association leadership at state/national levels • Teaching (full time or part time) • Consulting • Mentoring	• State/national associations • Peer networks

presenting at state and national conferences, can introduce students to scholarly activity from the beginning of their preparation for the field of school psychology.

Membership and involvement in professional organizations add depth to the training of future school psychologists. Faculty members should model not only association membership, but also ways to utilize resources and networks provided by being a member of a state or national organization. Moreover, the importance of belonging to both a state and a national association should be communicated to students. Typically, membership in a state association enables students to develop a network of local contacts within the school psychology community. Resources from national organizations, such as the NASP or APA, provide extensive, up to-date information and practical strategies to assist school psychologists in their daily work. In addition, the advocacy efforts of both state and national organizations are essential in ensuring that public policy and legislation benefit children, families, and schools. Training programs can support students' participation in professional associations by requiring student membership in at least one school psychology organization or even paying for the first year of student membership.

In addition to maintaining membership in professional associations, school psychologists benefit from being actively involved as volunteer leaders for their state and national groups. Volunteers are particularly needed at the state association level, where limited resources typically require that activities be completed with a minimal budget. Students can get involved by volunteering to help with registration at a state conference (often in exchange for registration fees), or by assisting with various types of committee work. Most national leaders began their volunteer leadership through involvement with their state school psychology associations. At the national level, there are numerous opportunities for student volunteers at the annual NASP convention.

Novice school psychologists need to find and maintain a network of colleagues with whom they can receive and offer peer support. This network can begin by maintaining contact with fellow students following graduation, and can be extended through contacts made by attending local, state, or national school psychology conferences. As practitioners, school psychologists are often isolated at their work site from others who share a common knowledge base and "worldview" with regard to student learning and behavior. For this reason, having an informal peer support network is vital to surviving the first few years as a school psychologist.

With more years of experience, school psychologists can continue to benefit and grow from their collegial relationships, and professional associations are a vehicle for bringing members of the school psychology community together. Some state associations sponsor book club groups, which meet monthly to discuss new books relevant to our practice. Others may facilitate the formation of peer support groups, to assist their members in finding other school psychologists in specific geographic regions. E-communities and listservs offer on-line meeting places for school psychologists to discuss all of the various issues that confront us on a daily basis in our work with children and youth. Whether virtual or traditional, communities are a key component of career development in school psychology.

Summary

The authors contend that enduring and satisfying careers in school psychology do not just happen – they must be developed. Traditional career development up a vertical pathway through positions of more and more responsibility, status, and salary is available to only a few of us. Most of us, however, can be quite satisfied with a lifelong career path comprising career enrichment, professional development, and involvement in professional communities – our state and national professional associations.

Chapter Competency Checklist

DOMAIN 1 - Professional, Legal Ethical and Social Responsibility Domain

Foundational	Functional
Understand and explain the following:	Gain practice:
☐ Professional development	☐ Joining professional organization(s)
☐ Career development	☐ Volunteering in professional organizations
☐ Contextual factors impacting the profession of school psychology	☐ Forming a network of peer support with colleagues
☐ Job satisfaction	☐ Developing short-term professional goals
☐ Career enrichment	☐ Setting long-term professional goals
☐ Professional development	☐ Planning a job search
☐ Supervision, mentoring, and peer support	☐ Evaluating progress on professional goals
☐ Developing a specialty	
☐ Presenting and training	
☐ Part-time work	
☐ Professional memberships	

References

Anderson, W. T., Hohenshil, T. H., & Brown, D. T. (1984). Job satisfaction among practicing school psychologists: A national study. *School Psychology Review, 13*, 225–230.

Armistead, L. D. (2006). *NASP leaders guide to continuing professional development*. Bethesda, MD: National Association of School Psychologists.

Armistead, L. D. (2008). Best practices in continuing professional development for school psychologists. In A. Thomas & J. Grimes (Eds.), *Best practices in school psychology V* (pp. 1975–1989). Bethesda, MD: National Association of School Psychologists.

Batsche, G. (1990). Best practices in credentialing and continuing professional development. In A. Thomas & J. Grimes (Eds.), *Best practices in school psychology II* (pp. 887–898). Bethesda, MD: National Association of School Psychologists.

Benner, P. (1984). *From novice to expert: Excellence and power in clinical nursing practice*. Menlo Park, CA: Addison-Wesley.

Betz, N. E., & Fitzgerald, L. F. (1987). *The career psychology of women*. New York: Academic.

Bloomquist, A. J. (2006). *Intern supervision and job satisfaction among school psychologists*. Indiana, PA: Unpublished doctoral dissertation, Indiana University of Pennsylvania.

Bradley-Johnson, S., & Dean, V. J. (2000). Role change for school psychology: The challenge continues in the new millennium. *Psychology in the Schools, 37*(1), 1–5.

Brooks, S. S. (1994). Moving up is not the only option. *HR Magazine, 39*(3), 79–83.

Brown, M. (2002). Best practices in professional development. In A. Thomas & J. Grimes (Eds.), *Best practices in school psychology IV* (pp. 183–194). Bethesda, MD: National Association of School Psychologists.

Burns, M. K., & Coolong-Chaffin, M. (2006). Response to intervention: The role of and effect on school psychology. *School Psychology Forum: Research in Practice, 1*(4), 3–15.

Cataldi, E. F., Fahimi, M., & Bardburn, E. M. (2004). 2004 National Study of Postsecondary Faculty (NSOPF:04) report on faculty and instructional staff in fall 2003.

Charvatt, J. L. (2005). NASP study: How many school psychologists are there? *Communiqué, 33*(6), 12–14.

Curtis, M. J., Hunley, S. A., & Grier, J. E. C. (2002). Relationships among the professional practices and demographic characteristics of school psychologists. *School Psychology Review, 31*(1), 30–42.

Curtis, M. J., Lopez, A. D., Batsche, G., Minch, D., & Abshier, D. (2007). School psychology, 2004–2005: National and regional demographic characteristics, professional practices, employment conditions, and continuing professional development. *Paper presented at the annual meeting of the National Association of School Psychologists*, New York, March 26–31, 2007.

Curtis, M. J., Walker, K. J., Hunley, S. A., & Baker, A. C. (1999). Demographic characteristics and professional practices in school psychology. *School Psychology Review, 28*(1), 104–116.

Fagan, T. K. (2000). Practicing school psychology: A turn of the century perspective. *The American Psychologist, 55*(7), 754–757.

Fagan, T. K., & Wise, P. S. (2000). *School psychology: Past, present and future*. Bethesda, MD: National Association of School Psychologists.

Flanagan, R. (2000). The American Academy of school psychology: Promoting board certification for school psychologists. *Education, 2*, 212–219.

Fowler, E., & Harrison, P. L. (1995). Best practices in continuing professional development for school psychologists. In A. Thomas & J. Grimes (Eds.), *Best practices in school psychology III* (pp. 81–89). Bethesda, MD: National Association of School Psychologists.

Gilman, R., & Teague, T. L. (2005). School psychologists in nontraditional settings: Alternative roles and functions in psychological service delivery. In R. D. Morgan, T. L. Kuther, & C. J. Habben (Eds.), *Life after graduate school in psychology: Insider's advice from new psychologists* (pp. 167–180). New York: Psychology Press.

Guest, K. E. (2000). Career development of school psychologists. *Journal of School Psychology, 38*(3), 237–257.

Guskey, T. R. (2003). What makes professional development effective? *Phi Delta Kappan, 84*(10), 748–751.

Harvey, V. S., & Struzziero, J. A. (2000). *Effective supervision in school psychology*. Bethesda, MD: National Association of School Psychologists.

Hynd, G. W., Pielstick, N. L., & Schakel, J. A. (1981). Continuing professional development in school psychology: Current status. *School Psychology Review, 10*, 480–486.

Individuals with Disabilities Education Act. (2004). Pub. L. No. 108–446, 118 Stat. 2647.

Knoff, H. M., Curtis, M. J., & Batsche, G. M. (1997). The future of school psychology: Perspectives on effective training. *School Psychology Review, 26*(1), 93–104.

Kruger, L. J. (1993). Commitment to the profession of school psychology: An exploratory study. *Paper presented at the annual meeting of the National Association of School Psychologists*, Washington, DC, April 13–17, 1993.

Kruger, L. J., Maital, S., Macklem, G., Weksel, T., & Caldwell, R. (2002). The Internet and school psychology practice. *Journal of Applied School Psychology, 19*(1), 95–111.

McIntosh, D. E., & Phelps, L. (2000). Supervision in school psychology: Where will the future take us? *Psychology in the Schools, 37*(1), 33–38.

National Association of School Psychologists. (1996). *Continuing professional development program*. Bethesda, MD: National Association of School Psychologists.

National Association of School Psychologists. (2000a). *Guidelines for the provision of school psychological services*. Bethesda, MD: National Association of School Psychologists.

National Association of School Psychologists. (2000c). *Standards for the credentialing of school psychologists*. Bethesda, MD: National Association of School Psychologists.

National Association of School Psychologists. (2000d). *Standards for training and field placement programs in school psychology*. Bethesda, MD: National Association of School Psychologists.

Nickerson, A. B., & Gagnon, S. G. (2003). Preparing, applying and navigating through life as a junior professor. *The School Psychologist, 57*(2), 55–59.

Philpott, T. (2005). Defense seeks 'revolution' in managing officer careers. Retrieved 5/4/2007 from http://www.military.com.

Proctor, B. E., & Steadman, T. (2003). Job satisfaction, burnout, and perceived effectiveness of "in house" versus traditional school psychologists. *Psychology in the Schools, 40*(2), 237–243.

Reschly, D. J. (2000). The present and future status of school psychology in the United States. *School Psychology Review, 29*(4), 507–522.

Ross, R. P., & Goh, D. S. (1993). Participating in supervision in school psychology: A national survey of practices and training. *School Psychology Review, 22*(1), 63–81.

Sarason, S. B. (1975). The unfortunate fate of Alfred Binet and school psychology. *Teachers College Record, 77*, 579–592.

Smallwood, D., Armistead, L. D., & Williams, B. B. (2007). Professional transitions: Practitioner to trainer. On-line continuing professional development module available at http://www.nasponline.org.

Story, L. (2005). Many women at elite colleges set career path to motherhood. Retrieved 5/6/07 from http://www.nytimes.com.

Super, D. E. (1990). A life-span, life-space approach to career development. In D. E. Brown & L. Brooks (Eds.), *Career choice and development* (pp. 179–261). San Francisco, CA: Jossey-Bass.

Thomas, A. (1998). *Directory of school psychology graduate programs*. Bethesda, MD: National Association of School Psychologists.

VanVoorhis, R. W., & Levinson, E. M. (2006). Job satisfaction among school psychologists: A meta-analysis. *School Psychology Quarterly, 21*(1), 77–90.

Wilczenski, F. L. (1997). Marking the school psychology lifespan: Entry into and exit from the profession. *School Psychology Review, 26*(3), 502–514.

Wilson, M. S., & Rechsly, D. J. (1995). Gender and school psychology: Issues, questions, and answers. *School Psychology Review, 24*(1), 45–61.

Worrell, T. G., Skaggs, G. E., & Brown, M. (2006). School psychologists' job satisfaction: A 22-year perspective in the USA. *School Psychology International, 27*(2), 131–145.

Ysseldyke, J., Burns, M., Dawson, P., Kelley, B., Morrison, D., Ortiz, S., et al. (2006). *School psychology: A blueprint for training and practice III*. Bethesda, MD: National Association of School Psychologists.

Zins, J. E., & Murphy, J. J. (1996). Consultation with professional peers: A national survey of the practices of school psychologists. *Journal of Educational and Psychological Consultation, 7*(1), 61–70.

Chapter 16
Monitoring Professional Competence
in School Psychology

Edward P. Snyder, Timothy Lionetti, and Ray W. Christner

The aim of this book is to help school psychologists, new and seasoned, to develop the competencies needed to be a school psychologist. Throughout the text we conceptualize competence in school psychology similarly to the model published by NASP (2006) in *School Psychology: A Blueprint for Training and Practice III* (Blue Print III), as it serves as a guide for training and practice in school psychology and offers a developmental training model for school psychologists. The developmental model proposes that school psychologists do not enter the work force as experts but develop expertise as their careers progress. In keeping with this model, this book is intended to help school psychologists make progress on the continuum from novice to expert school psychologist. The eight overarching competency domains in school psychology articulated in Blue Print III are depicted in Fig. 16.1. As explicated in Blue Print III, for school psychologists to be effective, they must have a broad and deep understanding of the skills encompassed in each domain, as well as an ability to apply and integrate these skills fluently in everyday practice. This chapter offers a summation of the school psychology competencies described in each chapter. At the end of each chapter, a checklist is provided, which is to be used with the DECAF for the express purpose of assisting the novice and more seasoned school psychologist monitor and develop competence in school psychology by establishing professional goals.

Figure 16.1 also includes a depiction of a three-tiered intervention model that is being embraced by school psychology and education in general. For example, schools are beginning to create systems in which universal programs (i.e., Tier 1) are implemented to help prevent academic or emotional and social problems of students. At Tier 1, methods for schools to identify students who need more intensive services are in place. Tier 2 provides additional programming to meet the needs of these students in need of more intensive services. Students not responding to Tier 2 programs may then be provided with Tier 3 services which are the most intensive. A number of chapters have included a more detailed explanation of this model.

Competencies for School Psychologists

Recall from Chapter 1 that the domains of competence provide a vision of the skills and knowledge school psychologists develop on the path to competence. The Blue Print III domains fall under two broad categories, Foundational and Functional, and each in turn consists of an array of competencies (see Fig. 16.1). The Blue Print III domains of competence are conceptualized as an interconnected

E.P. Snyder (✉)
Department of Professional Studies, Edinboro University of Pennsylvania, Butterfield Hall 114,
Edinboro, PA 16444, USA
e-mail: esnyder@edinboro.edu

T.M. Lionetti et al. (eds.), *A Practical Guide to Building Professional Competencies in School Psychology*, 263
DOI 10.1007/978-1-4419-6257-7_16, © Springer Science+Business Media, LLC 2011

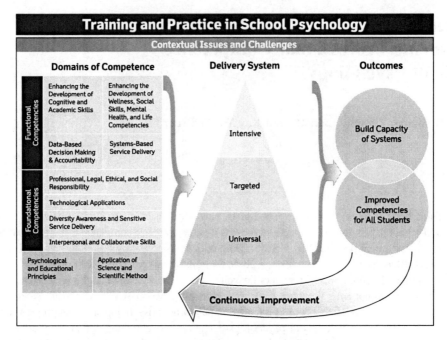

Fig. 16.1 Blue Print for training and practice model III. © 2006, National Association of School Psychologists, Bethesda, MD. Reprinted by permission of the publisher

Table 16.1 List of chapters addressing Blue Print III competency domains

Functional competencies

Domain – Enhancing the development of cognitive and academic skills
   Chapter 6: Assessing Student Skills Using Process-Oriented Approaches
   Chapter 7: Assessing Student Skills Using a Nontraditional Approach
   Chapter 8: Advocating for Effective Instruction: School Psychologists … Leaders
Domain – Enhancing the development of wellness, social skills, mental health, and life
   Chapter 9: Evaluating Children Emotional and Behavioral Concerns
   Chapter 11: Preventing and Intervening in Crisis Situations
Domain – Data-based decision making and accountability
   Chapter 12: Beyond Unproven Trends: Critically Evaluating … Programs
Domain – Systems-based service delivery domain
    Chapter 10: Facilitating Mental Health Services in Schools: Universal … Interventions

Foundational competence domains

Domain – Professional, legal ethical and social responsibility
   Chapter 2: Applying Law and Ethics in Professional Practice
   Chapter 3: Managing Your Professional Practice as a School Psychologist
   Chapter 13: Report Writing and Oral Communication of Results
   Chapter 14: Making A Career of School Psychology
Domain – Technological applications
   Chapter 15: Using Advancing Technologies in the Practice of School Psychology
Domain – Diversity awareness and sensitive service delivery
   Chapter 4: Competency in Cross-Cultural School Psychology
Domain – Interpersonal and collaborative skills
   Chapter 5: Consulting with Families, Schools, and Communities

set of skills resting on a foundation of psychology and education principals that apply the scientific method. As shown in Table 16.1, each chapter of this book is aligned with a Blue Print III Foundational or Functional domain of competence found in Fig. 16.1.

The remainder of this chapter summarizes each chapter along with brief descriptions of competencies related to each chapter. Chapters relating to Functional domains are described first, followed by chapters pertaining to Foundational domains of competence.

Functional Domains of Competence

As described in Blue Print III, functional competencies involve the ability to apply foundational knowledge in practice. New methods for the practice of school psychological services are being considered. Response to intervention (RtI) models is being implemented and methods for assessing children are expanding beyond the use of norm-referenced tests. Prevention-oriented mental health models offer the potential for helping to improve services for children. Accountability and empirically supported practices are being highlighted. The chapters of this text provide important points on how school psychologists develop competencies for practice in school psychology.

Enhancing the Development of Cognitive and Academic Skills Domain

In Chapter 6, Clements, Christner, McLaughlin, and Bolton provide an overview of an assessment that involves measuring mental processes of students. Clements et al. argue for the benefits of including an assessment method that focuses on understanding the attention, memory, language, and executive functions of students who encounter significant learning difficulties, and explain that cognitive assessments aimed at understanding the mental processes of students can accompany RtI methods. Limitations with assessing mental processes, such as when assessing intelligence, are also described in Chapter 6. These authors point out that intelligence explains only 50% of the variance associated with achievement, and intelligence is too often used as a tool for sorting and labeling of students.

Nedderiep, Poncy, and Skinner provide an excellent overview of the importance of nontraditional methods of assessment in Chapter 7. They point out the limitations with the traditional diagnostic model of assessment and suggest using a problem-solving process that is data-based and intervention driven. Nedderiep et al. explain that curriculum-based measurement (CBM) is a system of empirically validated indicators of proficiency of a variety of basic academic skills, and describe how CBM is useful for academic progress monitoring of students.

In Chapter 8, Poncy, McCallum, and Skinner describe the importance of school psychologists as instructional leaders in schools. It is important for school psychologists to understand how federal laws influence public schools (e.g., No Child Left Behind (NCLB) and Individuals with Disabilities Education Act (IDEA)). These laws emphasize accountability and the need for data-based decision making. The pressures of NCLB place school psychologists in a position to broaden their roles from that of an evaluator and a gate keeper of special education to assisting the school system leadership teams in meeting the achievement demands of NCLB. To develop competence as effective leaders of instruction, school psychologists need a fundamental understanding of instructional interventions, functional assessment, instructional hierarchies, program evaluation, and the nature of public school systems. Also, school psychologists need skills for applying a problem-solving model to school-wide instructional outcomes (i.e., problem identification, problem analysis, plan implementation, and plan evaluation).

Enhancing the Development of Wellness, Social Skills, Mental Health, and Life Competencies Domain

School psychology is no longer conceptualized as a service to individual students. Today, school psychologists must consider the context and system in which each student functions. Assessment and intervention must go beyond services to individual students needing special education and address all students functioning within a school system. Christner, Mennuti, Heim, Gipe, and Rubenstein explain the importance of prevention-oriented models for enhancing school-based mental health programs in Chapter 10. Schools must consider intervention programs based on the intensity of student problems. A tiered model of prevention and intervention is a hallmark signifying a comprehensive approach to mental health service delivery in schools. School psychologists may work in school systems with a three-tiered model providing universal, targeted, and intensive interventions for school-age students.

Over the past 15 years, the importance of crisis intervention for school psychology has become an unfortunate necessity. Reeves, Nickerson, and Brock point out in Chapter 11 that until recently, there have been few models of crisis intervention dedicated to school-based responses. Most recently, NASP developed the School Crisis Prevention and Intervention Training Curriculum (PREPaRE), one of the first training curricula specifically designed for school crisis preparedness and intervention. Further, Reeves, Nickerson, and Brock point out the importance of conceptualizing crisis prevention and intervention using the three-tier model of service delivery. At the base level are universal preventative services, followed by more intensive services, and then targeted services are the most intensive.

At the third tier of the mental health model are tertiary or targeted services for children with chronic mental health needs, such as students eligible for special education services as having emotional and behavior disorders. In Chapter 9, McCurdy, Lannie, and Jeffrey explain important competencies when providing assessment and intervention services for children needing intensive and targeted services. A key point for school psychologists to understand is how to determine if children with emotional and behavioral disorders are eligible for special education services. McCurdy et al. explain the ambiguous nature of how emotional disturbance is defined in IDEA 2004. McCurdy et al. point out that school psychologists need to develop multiple methods for assessing students. The usefulness of a three-tier service model is made clear in Chapter 9 by delineating the competencies needed at each tier.

Data-Based Decision Making and Accountability Domain

As mentioned throughout this text, much of what school psychologists do is related to data collection and accountability. In Chapter 7, Neddenriep et al. point out the benefits of using CBM data for designing and evaluating academic interventions for all children. Poncy et al. in Chapter 8 emphasize how school psychologists can be instructional leaders in schools by collecting and using instructional data within a problem-solving framework. Clements et al. in Chapter 6 describe how school psychologists may use methods of assessment aimed at measuring mental processes, such as memory, language, and intelligence. McCurdy et al. detail a variety of data collection methods in Chapter 9.

Miller and Sawka-Miller in Chapter 12 explain that schools are places in which empirically unproven or unsupported practices are frequently adopted and implemented. The importance of data-based decision making is clear as Miller and Sawka-Miller explain the importance for school psychologists to have skills in program evaluation. Although program evaluation in schools has not been a traditional role for school psychologists, they can assist with evaluating programs used by schools. To participate in program evaluation in schools, school psychologists should understand key program evaluation concepts: needs assessment, creating readiness, treatment integrity, social validity, impact, sustainability, and capacity building.

Systems-Based Service Delivery Domain

Blue Print III advocates for a service delivery system characterized by varying the intensity of interventions depending on the severity of student need. Chapters 9, 10, and 11 explain how a three-tier model of service delivery allows schools to better meet the mental health needs of students. Three-tiered systems provide services in ways that are proactive, and the intensity of services is based on student needs.

As schools move toward a system-based service delivery model, school psychologists may be in positions to help identify, implement, provide, and evaluate academic and mental health interventions for all students. By providing services to all students (not just students with intensive problems), school psychologists help build capacity in school systems to develop competencies of all students.

Foundational Domains of Competence

The foundational domains of competence elucidated in Blue Print III stand as important building blocks for competence in school psychology. It is important for school psychologists to have a firm understanding of how state and federal laws and regulations impact the practice of school psychology. School psychologists are legislated as part of special education services and this is why schools hire school psychologists. Under the umbrella of this domain are also the competencies of understanding professional ethics, becoming culturally sensitive, enhancing interpersonal and collaborative skills, and using advanced technologies. The following paragraphs explain how chapters of this book address foundational domains.

Professional, Legal, Ethical, and Social Responsibility Domain

Williams and Armistead in Chapter 2 provide an important overview of legal and ethical issues for school psychologists. The authors explain the federal structure of law in USA from which IDEA legislation emerges. Also, they describe important topics, such as RtI, discipline in schools for students with disabilities, medication and student rights in school, privacy rights of students, the NCLB, and the importance of the Schaffer v. Weast Supreme Court decision. Ethical guidelines from NASP and APA are explained along with a problem-solving model for handling ethical decisions as a practitioner. It is important to reemphasize that beyond knowledge of federal laws and professional ethics, school psychologists need to understand specific special education regulations required in the state where the school psychologist practices.

School psychologists assess individual students and provide reports to teachers and parents as a regular part of their traditional jobs. In Chapter 13, Lionetti and Perlis provide a unique and important chapter for developing competencies in this area. A primary task of many school psychologists is to assess students, meet with parents and teachers, and communicate and explain the results to an array of constituencies. Yet, there are few explicit guidelines for how to develop skills for providing oral and written reports. Lionetti and Perlis explain the legal and ethical importance of effective oral and written communication to all stakeholders in the school system. They explain how to develop cultural competence important for communicating with families. Furthermore, they provide specific suggestions for organizing and structuring psychological reports.

As with the previously mentioned competencies, the development of professional skills for school psychologists begins in graduate school and continues for the remainder of their careers. Fischetti provides an insight for furthering professional competencies for practicing school psychologists in Chapter 3. This chapter explains that school psychologists must plan for their individual professional development and the professional development of the system in which they are employed. School psychologists should concern themselves with managing a professional portfolio, keeping a school-based file of important events in school, and monitoring professional development. Fischetti emphasizes the importance of meaningful supervision for new school psychologists as they plan and implement professional development goals.

Similarly, in Chapter 14, Armistead and Smallwood explain the importance for school psychologists to think of developing their professional skills across their career. School psychologists begin their careers with the acquisition of foundational knowledge in psychology and education. Also, they begin to understand how to apply principles of scientific methodologies. Through training, school psychologists gain exposure to the variety of roles and functions of school psychologists and become oriented to different educational settings. Professional development for school psychologists begins with exposure to local, state, and national conferences; student memberships in professional organizations such as NASP; and becoming familiar with professional literature (e.g., journals and books).

Armistead and Smallwood (2009) help school psychologists understand expectations for their own professional development and provide practical suggestions for career enrichment. This chapter helps school psychologists establish realistic and meaningful professional goals for a career in school psychology. The authors emphasize the importance of professional supervision and support across the career of school psychologists.

Interpersonal and Collaborative Skills Domain

It is an obvious point to make, but school psychologists must have effective social skills to be able to work with people to address complex problems facing children in schools. The social nature of the work of school psychologists is emphasized throughout the previous chapters. With effective social skills in tow, the competencies for collaborating and consulting in schools can grow. In Chapter 5, Snyder and Quirk describe how collaborative school psychologists connect with parents and teachers, remain optimistic, and seek to empower team members. A key factor for developing foundational knowledge is for school psychologists to understand models and theories of consultation related to intervention design, special education consultation, and system level consultation.

Diversity Awareness and Sensitive Service Delivery Domain

In Chapter 4, Tomes describes how USA is becoming increasingly culturally diverse. The changes in cultural demographics of USA are seen in our public schools. Tomes describes the importance of being sensitive to cultural differences for the work of school psychologists and how it relates to all other aspects of the role of school psychologists. Specifically, Tomes provides information on developing cultural competence with assessment and report writing skills. To develop cultural competence, Tomes suggests that school psychologists develop an understanding of minority cultural groups by gaining exposure and experience working with people from different cultures. Of course, these experiences should occur with meaningful supervisory experiences. Similarly, self-understanding is important for school psychologists as they become increasingly sensitive to cultural differences.

Technological Applications Domain

The importance of advanced technologies (e.g., computers) in the profession of school psychology is no longer a debate. Armistead points out in Chapter 15 that advanced technology has made school psychologists more productive and efficient in all areas of the field, including assessment, consultation, and intervention.

Technology devices such as computerized scoring systems, word processors, spreadsheets, cell phones, personal data assistants, and assistive technologies for students are becoming commonplace in school psychology. While technology has assisted school psychologists to be more productive, Armistead describes the importance for school psychologists to become aware of ethical and legal issues involved with using technology. For example, school psychologists need to ensure the confidentiality of client information when communicating via cell phone or e-mail.

Monitoring Professional Competence in School Psychology

As previously described, the developmental model of school psychologist competence growth assumes that each school psychologist is a novice in the broad array of domains noted in Blue Print III. This assumption is based on graduate training where the budding school psychologist learns a broad knowledge-base in education, psychology, law, and ethics. Skills for psychological assessment, consultation, and intervention are also important parts of graduate training. While in a training program, competence is believed to be reflected in the grades earned, portfolios, practical experiences, and national certification tests such as PRAXIS. Once graduated and practicing, school psychologists do not have a specific way to monitor the acquisition of important competencies. To assist school psychologists in this vain, Chapter 1 introduced DECAF and at the end of each chapter a competency checklist was created. These tools were created to allow school psychologists to monitor a range of professional competencies across the eight competency domains articulated in Blue Print III. The DECAF and competency checklist at the end of each chapter are, the competency checklists at the end of each chapter list functional and foundational competencies from the Blue Print III domains that are addressed in that chapter. Its intended purpose is to aid school psychologists in the assessment and creation of areas to develop as they strive toward expertise in each of the foundational and/or functional domains. The reader is encouraged to use these tools to chart their progress and become experts.

Like Blue Print III and by using these tools, we envision two general outcomes for the service delivery of school psychologists: building the capacity of school systems and increasing the competence for all students. A model of service delivery for school psychologists that addresses universal, targeted, and intensive service for children is envisioned. School psychologists need to become competent with foundational and functional skills across a range of domains. Accomplishing competencies across Blue Print III domain successfully provides school psychologists with a broad base of knowledge and skills in education and psychology to function more effectively. It is an important part of professional development for school psychologists to feel empowered and effective in their work. This book is a tool to assist school psychologists to improve their competencies. School psychologists must be life-long learners and understand that competence in school psychology is a process of continual development.

A goal from the start of this book was to create a useful text for helping school psychologists develop professional competence. School psychology is a rewarding and challenging profession marked by continual professional development and discovery. Often times we find support and discover new ideas when we talk with other school psychologists about our practice. This book is like those conversations – insightful, candid, and practical. Along with all of the authors in this text, we have created a useful tool for helping school psychologists grow toward competence, and, therefore, helping the children they serve.

References

National Association of School Psychologists. (2006). *School psychology: A blueprint for training and practice III*. Bethesda, MD: National Association of School Psychologists.

Index

Lightning Source UK Ltd.
Milton Keynes UK
07 November 2010

162459UK00013B/3/P